DATE DUE

JAN 05 '94			
NOV 20 '94			
JUL 2 4 '98			

Immigration, Language, and Ethnicity
Canada and the United States

Barry R. Chiswick, Editor

The AEI Press

Publisher for the American Enterprise Institute
WASHINGTON, D. C.

1992

For Carmel, Abraham, and Benjamin

Distributed by arrangement with

University Press of America
4720 Boston Way
Lanham, Md. 20706

3 Henrietta Street
London WC2E 8LU England

Library of Congress Cataloging-in-Publication Data

Immigration, language, and, ethnicity : Canada and the United States /
Barry R. Chiswick, editor.
   p.   cm.
   ISBN 0-8447-3761-5
   1. Immigrants—United States.   2. Immigrants—Canada.
3. Linguistic minorities—United States.   4. Linguistic minorities—
Canada.   5. Language policy—United States.   6. Language policy—
Emmigration and immigration.   9. Ethnicity—United States.
10. Ethnicity—Canada.   I. Chiswick, Barry R.
E184.A1I443   1991
306.4'4971—dc20   92-12204
                                                              CIP

The AEI Press
Publisher for the American Enterprise Institute
1150 17th Street, N.W., Washington, D.C. 20036

Printed in the United States of America

Contents

LIST OF FIGURES

List of Tables

Acknowledgments

This project was made possible primarily by the enthusiastic support of two organizations. The William H. Donner Foundation's financial support and nonpecuniary encouragement were essential. Both James V. Capua, the president, and William T. Alpert, senior program officer, recognized the importance of the issues addressed in the project and made possible the Donner Foundation's backing.

The American Enterprise Institute for Public Policy Research (AEI) agreed to administer the project, host the conference, and publish the conference papers. They have done these splendidly. Christopher DeMuth, the president, Marvin Kosters, the director of economic policy research, and the AEI staff made it all a pleasurable experience.

I am also indebted to the Embassy of Canada, in Washington, D.C., for providing financial support for a Canadian Data Archive within the Social Science Data Archive at the University of Illinois at Chicago. The data archive made available to several of the authors public use samples, or microdata, from the 1980 U.S. Census of Population and the 1971 and 1981 Censuses of Canada.

The acknowledgments individual authors wish to make regarding supplemental financial support, research assistance, and commentary on their chapters are indicated in the chapters themselves.

This project involved two formal meetings at AEI. At a workshop attended by authors, commentators, and a few AEI staff scholars, drafts of each of the chapters were presented and discussed in considerable depth. The revised works were presented at the conference several months later, and then further revised in response to comments from the editor, the discussants, the large group in attendance at the conference, and various other sources. Three of the chapters on language skills (by Vaillancourt, Chiswick-Miller, and Bloom-Grenier) were also presented in a special session organized by William Alpert at the American Economics Association's annual meeting in December 1990, and I presented an overview of the project and the substantive findings at the Association for Canadian Studies in the United States Annual Meetings in November 1991.

An important choice for a binational project, whether explicit or implicit, is the language of communication. In deference to the language skills of the participants and the location of the conference, the language of discourse was English, and hence this volume is published in standard American English.

The cooperation of the chapter authors and commentators was vital for bringing both the conference and published volume to fruition. This public thank-you confirms my private individual acknowledgments.

BARRY R. CHISWICK

Contributors

WILLIAM T. ALPERT is senior program officer, William H. Donner Foundation, and associate professor of economics at the University of Connecticut. He has written articles on employee compensation, labor unions, and social insurance as well as a book, *The Minimum Wage in the Restaurant Industry*.

DAVID E. BLOOM is professor and chair of the economics department at Columbia University. He has done extensive research on labor markets and population economics.

MONICA BOYD is the first incumbent of the Social Science Chair in Public Policy at the University of Western Ontario and a former president of the Canadian Population Society. She is the author of many articles, books, or monographs in the areas of social stratification, gender, inequality, and international migration.

LINDA CHAVEZ is a senior fellow at the Manhattan Institute for Policy Research and the author of *Out of the Barrio: Toward a New Politics of Hispanic Assimilation*. She previously served as executive director of the U.S. Commission on Civil Rights.

BARRY R. CHISWICK is research professor and head of the economics department at the University of Illinois at Chicago. His research on immigration includes his books *Illegal Aliens: Their Employment and Employers*; *The Dilemma of American Immigration*, a multidisciplinary study written with coauthors; and his previous AEI volumes, *The Gateway: U.S. Immigration Issues and Policies* and *The Employment of Immigrants in the United States*.

HARRIET ORCUTT DULEEP is an economist at the U.S. Commission on Civil Rights. Her research field is labor market analyses, and she has participated in many of the commission reports on the economic status of minorities.

ROBERT S. GOLDFARB is professor of economics at George Washington University. His research has been conducted primarily in labor economics, especially wage determination and wage regulation. His recent research concerns economic methodology, focusing on the implications of implicit assumptions for economic models.

ALAN G. GREEN, an economics professor at Queen's University, Ontario, has done research on immigrants in Canada.

GILLES GRENIER is associate professor of economics at the University of Ottawa. He has published several articles in French and in English on the economic aspects of language and linguistic minorities in the United States and Canada.

WALTER S. McMANUS is a market analyst at the Delco Remy division of the General Motors Corporation. He has published several articles on the role of language in earnings determination, immigrant assimilation, and ethnic minorities.

PAUL W. MILLER, an associate professor of economics at the University of Western Australia, has done extensive research for Canada and Australia on labor market performance, particularly as it relates to educational attainment, gender, immigration, and ethnic and racial origin.

ALICE NAKAMURA is professor of business at the University of Alberta. Her research is in labor economics and economic statistics.

MASAO NAKAMURA, a professor of business at the University of Alberta, has focused his research on econometric analyses of the economic and financial behavior of firms and households.

MARK C. REGETS is an economist at the U.S. Commission on Civil Rights. His research concerns labor market analyses.

DAVID M. REIMERS, professor of history at New York University, has published many works dealing with immigration. His books include *Still the Golden Door: The Third World Comes to America* and *Ethnic Americans: A History of Immigration*.

CHRISTOPHER ROBINSON is professor of economics at the University of Western Ontario. He has done research in a variety of areas in labor economics, including wage determination, unionization, and migration.

xiv

PETER SKERRY is director of Washington programs for the UCLA Center for American Politics and Public Policy. He has just completed a book about the politics of Mexican Americans, entitled *The Ambivalent Minority.*

TERESA A. SULLIVAN is professor of sociology and law and chair of the sociology department at the University of Texas at Austin. She has written extensively on labor force demography and immigration issues and was a coauthor of the multidisciplinary study *The Dilemma of American Immigration.*

HAROLD TROPER is professor of history at the Ontario Institute for Studies in Education, University of Toronto. He is author or coauthor of ten books dealing with immigration and related issues.

FRANÇOIS VAILLANCOURT, professor of economics at the University of Montreal, is the author of numerous books, monographs, and articles published in French and in English on the economics of language and the economic status of linguistic groups in Canada, and in particular Quebec.

ARISTIDE R. ZOLBERG is University-in-Exile Professor in the political science department of the New School for Social Research. He is a coauthor of *Escape from Violence: Conflict and the Refugee Crisis in the Developing World* and is completing a comprehensive historical study of the regulation of international population movements.

Foreword

William T. Alpert

This excellent book, analyzing the immigration and language policies of Canada and the United States, is the first in a series of volumes resulting from a project called "Comparative Social Policies in Canada and the United States," sponsored by the William H. Donner Foundation of New York City. For more than twenty years the Trustees of the foundation have had a deep interest in America's northern neighbor. They recognized what scholars have only just begun to appreciate: that significant policy-related research often necessitates the examination of more than a single nation.

In 1988 the Trustees of the Donner Foundation set out to enhance the quantity and quality of research that focused on issues of joint and special concern to both Canada and the United States. They hoped that circulating their request for proposals would generate projects that would integrate realistic explication of social policy differences with the deeper common interests shared by the two nations.

This effort had two important objectives. The first was to generate research that would provide new insights and information regarding comparative social policy in Canada and the United States. Such information would be useful, for example, as the two nations grapple with their policies regarding immigrants and their concerns for linguistic minorities. The second objective was to stimulate binational teams of world-class scholars to produce first-rate thinking on Canadian and American social policy, with the expectation that this interest would persist long after the project ends.

The United States and Canada are natural laboratories for comparing the effects of differing social policies. The two countries share political, legal, cultural, and constitutional inheritances, as well as analogous federal structures, remarkably similar standards of living, and comparably pluralistic societies. Both are advanced industrial nations with important primary and manufacturing sectors and large, rapidly growing service sectors in their economies.

Yet it must be recognized that important differences exist—the melting pot verses the mosaic as metaphor for society; a universal health care system in one country with no true counterpart in the other; an enhanced federal role in the United States as opposed to a diminished federal role in Canada; a different emphasis in criteria for rationing immigration visas; different approaches to language policies and linguistic minorities; and numerous others.

The second social project authorized by the Trustees, entitled "Social Policy and the Labor Market: A Comparative Study of the United States and Canada," was coordinated by Richard Freeman of Harvard University and David Card of Princeton University. The third project supported by the Trustees, entitled "Economic Issues and Aging in Canada and the United States: Problems of Income Security," is coordinated by Theodore Marmor of Yale University. The fourth project supported by the Foundation, "Working Women and the Well-Being of Women and Children in the United States and Canada," is coordinated by Alice Nakamura of the University of Alberta. Two additional projects supported by other foundations are "Pressures for Harmonization and Comparative Tax Reform Experiences," coordinated by John Whalley, University of Western Ontario, and John Shoven, Stanford University; and "Income Maintenance from a U.S.–Canadian Perspective," under the direction of Walter Block of the Fraser Institute.

This volume brings together researchers in economics, demography, sociology, history, and political science who have special skills and knowledge relevant for the project. The book's significance is even greater because of the advent of the Canadian-U.S. free trade agreement, which lowers tariff and nontariff barriers to trade between the two countries; because of increased interest in reshaping immigration policy in the United States; and because of possibly major constitutional changes in the structure of the Canadian government. These three developments will affect the economic growth of the two nations as well as the relationship between the government and minorities, whether native-born or immigrant. The investigation this project has launched into the causes and consequences of immigration to Canada and the United States may greatly affect prospects for the eventual elimination of barriers to the free mobility of labor between the two countries.

Professor Barry R. Chiswick has admirably assembled a remarkable team of scholars from diverse disciplines to form a coherent discussion of immigration issues and language policies in Canada and the United States. Policy makers and policy analysts from both sides of the border will find invaluable material throughout this book.

The research emerging from the authors on the relative success and merits of Canadian immigration policy, which explicitly considers the skills of immigrants, and of American policy, which focuses less on immigrant quality and more on family ties, enriches the knowledge base. It suggests that in some areas similar outcomes are generated by differing Canadian and American immigration policies, but in other, perhaps more important areas the outcomes differ, with Canadian policies producing immigrants of higher caliber.

The volume also provocatively suggests that language policies have consequences beyond the simple preservation of a particular language and its attendant culture. These policies may involve the raising of incomes of speakers of the protected language or languages and the lowering of the incomes of speakers of other languages. Yet language maintenance programs that undermine the acquisition of dominant-language skills may have counterproductive effects. Important implications emerge regarding the causes and consequences of immigrants' and native-born linguistic minorities acquiring dominant language fluency.

On behalf of the William H. Donner Foundation I thank Professor Chiswick, the authors, and the commentators, who have done a splendid job. The Foundation is also grateful to AEI and to Dr. Marvin Kosters, AEI's director of economic policy studies, for his able assistance to the project. In addition to acting as host of the workshop and conference, administering the project, and publishing this volume, AEI provided considerable intellectual stimulation.

The rich deposit of knowledge presented in this book will motivate other scholars to explore additional facets of immigration and language issues, both in Canada and the United States. We also hope that this volume will help Canadian and American policy makers to better recognize the immigration and language concerns of their respective societies and to develop more appropriate policies to respond to them. And we trust that the end result of better understanding will be even closer ties between the Canadian and American peoples.

1
Introduction
Barry R. Chiswick

This volume is a comparative analysis of immigration and language issues, including experiences and policies, of the United States and Canada. The introduction first addresses the importance of immigration and language issues and their relevance for the two countries and then presents a summary of the studies.

The Rationale for the Project

Immigration and language issues are important because they help shape the size, characteristics, and cohesion of the population of a country. Immigration policy acts as a gatekeeper, determining both the number and characteristics of those permitted to enter and settle permanently by selecting from a pool of potential applicants. Immigration policy can also influence the cohesion of a population by the manner in which immigrants are selected. A population is likely to be more cohesive, that is, to have shared perceptions, practices, experiences, and expectations, if it draws its immigrants from the same small set of countries that supplied the original population rather than drawing its immigrants worldwide. Yet a cohesive immigration policy, by limiting the range of immigrants, reduces the size of the eligible pool and the diversity of potential immigrants, and thereby reduces many of the benefits of immigration.

Language policies exist in all countries, although they are more explicit in some than in others. Language is a means of communication that facilitates economic and noneconomic exchange. Without some common language a tower of Babel emerges, increasing transaction costs and decreasing economic welfare.[1] Yet the development of a dominant language—a lingua franca—can be costly, both in the political and social decisions required for "selecting" the language or languages and in their spread. The retention of the use of English in India and the rebirth of Hebrew as a language for everyday life in Israel are two examples of "neutral" lingua francas.

1

There is an important overlap, although it is not perfect, between immigration and language issues. Not all immigrants may know the dominant language spoken at their destination, but for some it may be the mother tongue or original language. Moreover, in many countries segments of the native population, neither immigrants nor descendants of recent immigrants, communicate in a language other than the dominant one and lack fluency in the dominant language.

One cannot fully address immigration issues without a discussion of language issues. To what extent is, or should, language be among the immigrant-selection criteria? To what extent does, or should, the nondominant speaker adjust to the dominant language, and vice versa? To what extent does dominant language fluency matter in terms of economic and noneconomic adjustments? Among immigrant-receiving countries, one also cannot fully address language issues without a discussion of immigration. What are the implications of adopting an official language, whatever that means in practice, for both linguistic minorities and nondominant language immigrants? An official-language policy need not imply a monolingual policy. A country can have two or more official languages, as Canada has. It can have different official languages in different political subdivisions, again, as Canada has.

Nor should languages be thought of in dichotomous terms—either perfect fluency or no fluency, an "official" language spoken either universally or not at all. To what degree do linguistic minorities maintain their nondominant language? How does this maintenance influence their dominant language fluency, economic behavior, and other outcomes?

Canada and the United States offer unique opportunities to study immigration and language issues. The two countries have much in common besides their long, shared border. Both are economically developed liberal democracies with institutions of essentially similar European origin, but modified according to the requirements of their particular circumstances. The bulk of the populations of both countries can trace their origins to Europe, but with increasing proportions from other continents. Both countries have large minorities that differ from the majority by race or ethnicity and, for some, by language.

The two countries differ, however, in sufficiently interesting ways to make a "compare and contrast" analysis fruitful. Canada has a large geographically concentrated native-born ethnic and linguistic minority, the French Canadians, who have lived there since 1608, before the English conquest in the mid-eighteenth century. They form a majority in one major political entity, Quebec, but they are also a significant minority in other political entities. No comparable situation exists for the United States.[2] The United States does have a large and growing Spanish-speaking population, concentrated in a few states; this population, however, is primarily a result of post-World War II migration, and Hispanics do not approach majority status in any state.

For French Canadians and for many Hispanic Americans, language is a key to ethnic identity. The two countries have responded to these concerns in different ways. Bilingualism is accepted in both countries, but the definitions differ sharply.

The importance and potential for cohesion or divisiveness as a result of "language politics" in both countries can be discerned merely by reading newspaper headlines. Although English and French are coequal official languages in Canada, language remains the key to the dissatisfaction of French Canadians with the current confederation. The issues of bilingualism in the United States, on the other hand, are mainly related to the extent of minority-language instruction in the schools, minority-language use in the workplace, and language usage by the government; they hardly infringe on the daily life of the majority population.

The two countries also differ in the extent to which language skills are relevant for obtaining an immigrant visa. English language skills play no direct role in obtaining a visa to enter the United States. Proposals to provide an explicit role for English language proficiency in the expanded skills-based visa categories in the 1990 Immigration Amendments were explicitly rejected in Congress. For Canada, on the other hand, the skills-based point system awards points for fluency in English or French when allocating visas to independent migrants—that is, those who are not the immediate relatives of Canadian citizens. In 1991, as part of a general increase in Quebec's autonomy for selecting immigrants who intend to settle in that province, the points awarded for fluency in French were increased and the points awarded for fluency in English were decreased for applicants to Quebec.

There are other compelling reasons for a joint study of Canada and the United States. Canadians and Americans know remarkably little about each other—Americans knowing especially little about Canada. Yet each country is the other's largest trading partner. The economic linkages will be further strengthened as the two economies adjust to the reduction in trade barriers brought about by the Free Trade Agreement. This melding of the two economies will have important impacts for both countries, although perhaps more for Canada than for the United States.[3]

Further improvements in the relationship between the United States and Canada may well depend on a deeper understanding of the

3

other country. Progress toward extending the free trade in goods and services to free migration of people across the U.S.-Canadian border, and the extent to which this enhances permanent migration, may depend crucially on the language and immigration policies of the two countries.[4]

Finally, it is often easier to see ourselves with greater clarity after examining another. Each country looks to the other as a laboratory for the testing of ideas, and in this regard the countries on either side of the border benefit from studies of the other side.

The Findings

The authors chosen for this project are all experienced scholars in their fields, nearly equally divided between Canadians and Americans. Many obtained coauthors from the other side of the border to enhance the range of expertise behind each chapter. Nearly all of the authors and coauthors reported to me that they learned much about the other country from this experience. By academic discipline, they are from economics, demography, history, sociology, and political science.

Except for the historical studies, nearly all of the chapters relied heavily on statistical analysis of the microdata file from the U.S. Census of Population and the Census of Canada. The analyses highlighted the comparative strengths of the public-use samples, or microdata files, from these two censuses. Explicitly or implicitly the authors make recommendations to the respective statistical agencies for further improvement in census data for the statistical and public policy analysis of immigration and language issues.

This volume is divided into four major sections—immigration history and policy, immigrants' demographic characteristics and earnings, the economics of language, and language, women, and minorities.

Two historical studies are included in Part One, concerning comparative immigration policies and refugee policies. David M. Reimers and Harold Troper provide a comparative analysis of the history of the immigration policies of the two countries in the postwar period. After several decades of tight restriction favoring northwestern Europe, both the United States and Canada liberalized immigration policies following the end of World War II. In so doing, they increased the numbers admitted as compared with the lean years of the 1930s and the war years. Starting in the 1960s they explicitly modified their policies to include third world, eastern hemispheric newcomers. Growing racial and ethnic toleration, economic forces, lobbying, and international factors all played roles in shaping the ways in which these two North American countries similarly developed greater openness in their immigration policies.

Yet differences between the two countries also played a key role in the outcomes. Economics was more important for shaping immigration policy in Canada than in the United States, and American policies were more closely tied to foreign policy questions than were Canadian. For America, faced with a 1,900-mile border with Mexico, the issues of undocumented immigration and temporary workers were especially important, but the same was not true for the United States's northern neighbor. Canadians also had to take into account their shared southern border with a very large, highly developed economy and their economic, cultural, and political ties to the evolving British Commonwealth.

Finally, the two countries had somewhat different traditions about immigration, and their historical experiences affected policy. Canada has a different governmental structure and a stronger tradition of immigrant recruitment than has the United States. For example, immigration has been dealt with in the same ministry as manpower or employment matters in Canada, whereas most immigration issues are handled by the Justice Department in the United States. Also, following national tradition, the immigration authorities are granted much more individual discretion in Canada than in the United States.

As a result, the two nations modified their immigration laws and policies in different ways in the postwar period. Yet in some important respects the outcomes are similar. Immigration to both countries, which had been primarily European in origin, now comes primarily from the third world countries of Asia, Latin America, and the Caribbean.

Administrative decisions and legislation enacted in 1990 will increase the volume of immigration to both countries, and immigration will remain more important relative to the population in Canada than in the United States. Some of the selection criteria converge, however, as the 1990 Immigration Amendments substantially increase the number and proportion of immigrants admitted to the United States on the basis of economic criteria (that is, skills and investments) and diminish somewhat the central role of family reunification.

One of the most difficult immigration issues confronting both North American countries has been refugee policy, the subject of Aristide Zolberg's chapter. In the United States and Canada, refugee policy has become a sphere of contention between "humanitarians" and "realists." The issues that divide them encompass domestic law enforcement, the conduct of foreign affairs, and an ultimate question—What are the obligations of a nation that is affluent, and even active on the international scene, toward those individuals seeking admission because of alleged persecution in their home country?

After World War II the United States and Canada took in hundreds of thousands of European refugees, as a consequence of the disruption of the war years, the persecution of minorities, and the westward expansion of the Iron Curtain. Concurrently, the international community moved toward a formal recognition of "refugee" as a distinct category of international migrant who warranted special consideration, including both protection and assistance, and priority in admission. Initially reluctant, the United States and Canada emerged as leading resettlement countries for "invited" refugees.

Today, however, the international refugee crisis consists increasingly of refugees from third world countries. Most of those seeking asylum are not victims of individual persecution, the criterion built into refugee policy, but rather individuals fleeing generalized violence and economic deprivation. Problems arise in distinguishing true refugees from economic migrants, and they are compounded by U.S. foreign policy considerations regarding Latin America and the Caribbean. These problems forced refugee issues into the political arenas of both the United States and Canada in the 1980s.

Quite unexpectedly, at the end of the 1980s a second crisis arose. Political liberalization in the Soviet Union and the other East European Socialist countries brought about a relaxation of barriers to emigration. The easing of departures posed a severe test to the admissions policies of the United States and Canada, more generous toward people fleeing Communist states than toward those fleeing other regimes. The very liberalization that led to the emigration also undermined to some extent these people's claim to refugee status. Ironically, with the very dawn of freedom the citizens of these countries could find themselves as immobile as they were before—no longer because they are not allowed to leave, but because, except for Jews going to Israel, they have no place to go.

Part Two of this volume focuses on the demographic characteristics and earnings of immigrants in Canada and the United States. It begins with Teresa Sullivan's analysis of the changing demographic characteristics of immigrants in Canada and the implications of these changes for the demography of the Canadian population. The implications are relevant also for the United States.

In low-fertility countries such as Canada and the United States immigration provides an important source of population growth, both through the admission of the immigrants themselves and through their offspring. Canada, a country with low and declining fertility rates, has historically received a great deal of its population growth through immigration. Changes in Canadian immigration policy in recent decades have altered the size, heterogeneity, and fertility patterns among immigrants to Canada.

Sullivan uses data from the United Nations and public use samples from the 1971 and 1981 Canadian censuses in her analysis. The heterogeneity of immigrants is examined by national origin, age and sex composition, language use, and birthplace, among other characteristics. The completed fertility profile of immigrant women is studied in both 1971 and 1981 using such variables as education, religion, recency of migration, continent of origin, and language use.

The results indicate that fertility is declining among immigrants and quickly reaches the low and declining norm among the native-born Canadian population. To some extent this trend is offset by the change of source countries for immigrants. Those migrating from the relatively new sending countries in Asia, Africa, the Caribbean, and Latin America have higher fertility rates than have the native-born Canadians and European immigrants. In general, however, the immigrants most likely to add to population growth by having above-average fertility, those from less developed countries, are also the immigrants who seem least similar to native-born Canadians and to other immigrants. Furthermore, at current and foreseeable, realistic immigration levels, immigration policy cannot reverse the gradual aging of the population in Canada. Because the ratio of annual immigration to the population is higher in Canada than in the United States, immigration would be even less successful in the United States as a policy to reverse the growing proportion of the aged in the population. Only a reversal of the low fertility rates of the native population and the acculturated immigrant population could achieve this objective.

Immigration policies have been more explicitly shaped by economic objectives in Canada than in the United States. In fact, beginning in 1967, independent applicants for immigration to Canada were systematically evaluated on a point system that reflected the applicant's skills and the economy's perceived needs. Points were awarded on the basis of job-related qualifications, such as English- or French-language proficiency, education, employment experience, and labor needs in Canada as a whole, as well as in the region where the would-be immigrant wished to settle. Alice Nakamura and Masao Nakamura test the hypothesis that the Canadian approach results in a higher "quality" of immigrant by a study of immigrant wages in the two countries.

7

The Nakamuras use data in the public use samples from the 1980 U.S. Census of Population and the 1981 Canadian Census to address this issue. They find that, on average, immigrant workers in Canada have higher hourly wage rates in relation to native workers than is the case in the United States. This finding is consistent with the fact that immigrant workers in Canada have more education, on average, relative to the native population than have immigrant workers in the United States.

In Canada as in the United States, additional years of schooling generate smaller percentage increases in earnings for immigrants than for native-born workers. But there is no difference in the pattern for immigrants in the two countries.

Initial conditions apparently do matter. The data show that higher unemployment rates during the early years in the labor market reduce the expected current wage rates for adult workers, with this effect being more severe for immigrant than for native workers. The Nakamuras find that the negative effects on current wage rates associated with a higher unemployment rate at the time of entry are about the same for American and Canadian immigrants.

The Nakamuras' analysis suggests that Canada can attract an immigrant population that, relative to the native-born, is more highly educated and has higher earnings than is the case for the United States. What could not be addressed, however, was whether potential international migrants differ in their preferences for the United States or Canada, and how these differences vary with demographic and economic characteristics.

In Part Three, this volume explicitly addresses economic dimensions of language issues. In his analysis of language policies in Canada and the United States, François Vaillancourt presents detailed comparative information on the evolution of these policies in Quebec, "English" Canada, and the United states. The pattern is particularly striking with regard to the major sectors of society—education, government, and business. He shows that the Canadian government's policy is to explicitly recognize and nurture the concept of a permanently bilingual English-French country. U.S. language policy, on the other hand, more implicit and diffuse, favors a monolingual country; bilingualism is tolerated on an individual basis, primarily for immigrants as a transitional mechanism to enhance English-language fluency.

In both countries the provincial or state governments restrict the rights of minority-language speakers—that is, those who do not speak English, or those in Quebec who do not speak French. At the national level in both countries, however, the government acts as a protector of minority languages. Thus, the less centralized structure of the Canadian government affords greater opportunity for the provinces to impose their language preferences on linguistic minorities. The allocation of responsibilities and power between the central government and political subdivisions is endogenous, however. The greater decentralization in Canada is a consequence of the bipolar linguistic nature of the population, with the two main language groups being the large minorities in different provinces.

Vaillancourt shows that in the past three decades Quebec's language policies have increased the role of French and diminished the role of English, rather than created a situation in which all individuals are bilingual. This evolution has been accomplished by mandating attendance in French-speaking schools for many in Quebec not of French ethnic origin and by mandating the use of French in certain workplace, government, and business situations. The demand for French speakers in Quebec has apparently grown faster than the supply as the economic return to fluency in French increased during the 1970s. A potentially more durable problem for the nearly 7 million people of Quebec is the increase in the transaction costs that a French-language enclave would experience in doing business with Quebec's most important trading partner—the 270 million people in English-speaking North America.

The study of language in the labor market, by Barry R. Chiswick and Paul W. Miller, explores the determinants of and labor market consequences for immigrants of proficiency in speaking the dominant language—English in the United States, English or French in Canada. The statistical analysis is for adult men using the self-reported data, including data on language skills, available in the 1980 and 1981 censuses of the United States and Canada, respectively.

Fluency in the dominant language in the two countries is shown to vary systematically with the immigrant's exposure to the language, efficiency in acquiring language skills, and economic incentives. That is, greater fluency is associated with greater pre-immigration exposure to the dominant language, a longer duration in the destination, a younger age at immigration, and a higher level of schooling. Immigrants are also more likely to be fluent if they immigrated unmarried, currently have children, and live in an area where few speak their native (non-dominant) language, among other variables. Those who can expect to receive greater economic rewards from a higher level of language proficiency are in fact more likely to make the investment and become more proficient. In other words, language fluency responds to economic incentives.

The Chiswick-Miller analysis of earnings is based on the human capital earnings function modified to incorporate immigrant assimilation. The determinants of earnings among immigrants are shown to be remarkably similar in the two countries—as if there were only one earnings determination process. Fluency in the dominant language has a large positive effect on earnings, independent of other personal characteristics and country of origin. Those who are fluent have earnings about 15 percent greater than those who lack dominant language fluency.

If immigrant economic success is a policy objective, the Chiswick-Miller study shows the importance of explicitly incorporating dominant language fluency, and the determinants of dominant language fluency, in the criteria for allocating immigrant visas. Canadian immigration policy has made more progress in this regard than U.S. policy. Although the U.S. 1990 Immigration Act is narrowing the gap in the proportion of visas issued on the basis of the applicants' skills, when these amendments were being debated in Congress the proposal to include English-language fluency in the selection criteria was defeated.

The final section of this volume, Part Four, offers studies of language skills and labor market outcomes for three groups of particular interest: female immigrants, linguistic ethnic minorities (French Canadians in Canada, Hispanics in the United States), and Asian-origin immigrants.

In her study of women, Monica Boyd compares Canada and the United States with respect to three topics: the presence of women in recent immigration flows, the linguistic composition of these flows, and the socioeconomic correlates of fluency in the dominant language. Females represent about half of all migrants to both Canada and the United States. Most enter as adults and on the basis of family ties. Like male immigrants, females increasingly come from third world regions. In both Canada and the United States, Asia became an important new source for female immigrants during the 1970s.

Using microdata from the 1980 and 1986 censuses of the United States and Canada, respectively, Boyd shows that female immigrants from third world countries and recent arrivals have a lower degree of fluency in the dominant language or languages. Immigrant women are almost twice as likely as men not to speak dominant languages. For immigrant women in both Canada and the United States, not knowing a dominant language is strongly correlated with low educational attainment and thus with functional illiteracy in the person's own native language.

Women who cannot speak the dominant language are employed primarily in the service and manufacturing sectors of the American and Canadian economies, and they receive lower earnings than do foreign-born women who can speak the host language. The earnings determination model indicates that in both countries education has a smaller effect on earnings for women who lack knowledge of a dominant language—that is, the economic benefits from dominant-language fluency increase with the level of education.

Neither Canada nor the United States has a comprehensive language training program targeted to all immigrants in need. Boyd reviews policy alternatives, actual policies, and the extent to which Canadian and U.S. policies include, or are targeted at, migrant women. She observes that even when language training is incorporated into government policy, eligibility criteria and program objectives may reduce the usefulness of these programs for immigrant women. Boyd concludes that the general stance toward immigrant adaptation and language training is similar in Canada and the United States, but she suggests that the development of language training policy in Canada is slightly more responsive to immigrant women.

Although French Canadians and Hispanic Americans have had sharply different historical experiences, they are alike in being Romance language minorities in countries where English is the dominant language. David E. Bloom and Gilles Grenier analyze the earnings of these two groups over time, relative to the English-speaking majority, using census data. Actual mother tongue is employed in the Canadian data, with separate analyses for Quebec and the rest of Canada. The absence of mother-tongue data over time for the United States forced them to use Spanish-origin as a proxy language variable. Separate analyses were performed for the high Hispanic concentration areas—southwestern states and metropolitan areas of New York and Florida—and other areas.

Using the microdata files from three Canadian censuses (from 1971 to 1986), Bloom and Grenier find that the relative earnings disadvantage of French speakers diminish over time. The decrease is greater in Quebec than in the rest of Canada. In Quebec, furthermore, English-French earnings differentials apparently no longer exist when other variables are the same. Even after correcting for the length of the interval, the decrease in earnings differentials is greater from 1971 to 1981 than from 1981 to 1986. For the United States, on the other hand, the Hispanic earnings differential is large in both 1970 and 1980 and shows little change, except for young adult Hispanics, for whom the differential widens in both the high-Spanish and low-Spanish areas.

Bloom and Grenier argue that political changes in Canada, especially in Quebec, increased the demand for French speakers or

PART ONE

Immigration History and Policy

2

Canadian and American Immigration Policy since 1945

David M. Reimers and Harold Troper

Canadians and Americans are currently reassessing their respective immigration policies. This dialogue is but the latest in a long series of immigration debates that have punctuated the postwar decades. Several times since 1945, both the United States and Canada have overhauled their immigration laws and regulations to admit new immigrants. These new flows reversed the restrictionist policies of the depression years and World War II. As table 2–1 indicates, the increases for Canada varied somewhat after 1945, but nonetheless showed substantial immigration.

In the case of the United States, the increases since 1945 have been steadily up, decade by decade and almost year by year. Table 2–2 indicates the American changes.

In the two countries public debate has focused on many of the same issues, and responses have been similar. Yet as we shall see, important differences in approach have also characterized the development of post-1945 immigration policies in the United States and Canada. Some of the key factors common to both in the postwar formulation of immigration policy include economic conditions, declining prejudice, foreign policy considerations, and the lobbying by various ethnic organizations. Yet these factors by no means carry the same weight in these two North American countries, and several other factors are quite different for the two as well.

Economic issues have been far more important to Canadians than to Americans. The former have consciously used immigration as a way to promote economic and population growth. In the United States some Americans use the positive argument for more immigration, but the advocates of increased immigration usually argue that immigrants do not hurt American workers and that the American economy can absorb additional newcomers. But for the most part, in the United States other issues dominate.

TABLE 2–1
IMMIGRATION INTO CANADA BY YEAR, 1945–1987

Year	Number	Year	Number
1945	22,722	1967	222,876
1946	71,719	1968	183,974
1947	64,127	1969	161,531
1948	125,414		
1949	95,217	1970	147,713
		1971	121,900
1950	73,912	1972	122,006
1951	194,391	1973	184,200
1952	164,498	1974	218,465
1953	168,868		
1954	154,227	1975	187,881
		1976	149,429
1955	109,946	1977	114,914
1956	164,857	1978	86,313
1957	282,164	1979	112,096
1958	124,851		
1959	106,928	1980	143,117
		1981	128,618
1960	104,111	1982	121,147
1961	71,689	1983	89,157
1962	74,586	1984	88,239
1963	93,151		
1964	112,606	1985	84,302
		1986	99,219
1965	146,758	1987	152,098
1966	194,743		
		Total	6,478,690

SOURCE: *Immigration Statistics 1987* (Ottawa: Employment and Immigration Canada, 1989).

Declining prejudice has also played a major role in shaping post-war policies. In 1945, bars against the admission of Asian immigrants and severe limits on immigration from Eastern and Southern Europe were still in effect in both Canada and the United States. The two countries also shared a sorry record of response to the crisis caused by Nazism and the Holocaust.[1] Yet after the war, growing racial and ethnic toleration made it possible to admit Southern and Eastern Europeans and, more recently, third world immigrants.

For the United States, as leader of the Western Alliance, consid-

TABLE 2–2

IMMIGRATION INTO THE UNITED STATES BY YEAR, 1945–1987

1945	38,119	1967	361,972
1946	108,721	1968	454,448
1947	147,292	1969	358,579
1948	170,570		
1949	188,371	1970	373,326
		1971	370,478
1950	249,187	1972	384,685
1951	205,717	1973	400,063
1952	265,520	1974	394,861
1953	170,434		
1954	208,171	1975	386,194
		1976	398,613
1955	237,790	1977	462,315
1956	321,625	1978	601,442
1957	326,867	1979	460,348
1958	253,265		
1959	260,686	1980	530,639
		1981	596,600
1960	365,398	1982	594,131
1961	271,344	1983	559,763
1962	283,763	1984	543,903
1963	306,260		
1964	292,248	1985	570,009
		1986	601,708
1965	296,697	1987	601,516
1966	323,040		
		Total	15,003,316

SOURCE: Annual reports of the United States Immigration and Naturalization Service.

erations of foreign policy played a large role in determining refugee policy. Canada also responded to the postwar refugee crisis, but with a difference. Canada was not a direct party to American adventures in Cuba, Chile, Vietnam, or El Salvador. Accordingly, Canada's reference point concerning admission of refugees was somewhat different from that of the United States.

Finally, ethnic group lobbying became a powerful factor in the determination of American immigration flows. This fact became apparent with the enactment of the Displaced Persons Act of 1948, and it has continued unabated since that time. For Canadians, lobbying has been less significant, but ethnic groups have become increasingly active.

While similarities of approach to these issues are numerous, in many respects the two countries are quite different. Not the least of the differences is the fact itself of the United States. Canadian immigration policy has always had to take the imposing American reality into account. Insofar as immigration policy has been factored into Canadian economic planning, that immigration policy has been influenced by the overarching American economic colossus. Whether Canadians like it or not, Canadian immigration is forever riding the roller coaster of American economic fluctuations, and the converse is not true for Americans.

In contrast, the southern neighbor of the United States is a poor, third world nation—Mexico. The long, relatively porous border between the two and the desire of so many Mexicans to migrate north has been of major concern to Americans. Moreover, many Central Americans have crossed Mexico and then illegally entered the United States. These population movements account for the debates over temporary workers and illegal immigration, problems less critical to Canada.

What is more, the United States has long been a magnet to the world, passively drawing immigrants to its shores. Not so Canada; just the reverse. For much of its history, Canada has been less a land of second chance than a land of second choice. During the post-1945 period, as doing most of the twentieth century, Canada actively intervened in the immigration process to solicit the immigrants it wanted. Canada did this on a basis that was both wholesale, attempting to induce large groups of immigrants to come to Canada, and retail, soliciting one by one. Often Canada's main competition was the United States or, rather, the dreams of America harbored by would-be immigrants. Oddly, these dreams of America could also work in Canada's favor. If the American front door was locked, many immigrants would come to Canada as their best chance to slip into the United States later, through the back door. Once in Canada, many stayed who had previously thought of the country as a doormat to America.

Canadian postwar immigration experience was also shaped by factors with no American counterpart. American states play little role in immigration policy, except perhaps to ask the federal government to provide funds for language, education, and other immigrant and refugee programs. Unlike American states, Canadian provinces share jurisdiction for immigration with the federal government. The degree to which any one province has chosen to exercise that jurisdiction has varied from province to province and period to period. Provincial concerns influence immigration policy, sometimes directly and always indirectly. This fact is particularly true for Quebec, a French-speaking island in a North American English-speaking sea. In recent years, Quebec has pressed its own social and economic priorities and has worked with the federal government to ensure that immigration to Quebec complement these priorities.

Furthermore, Canadian immigration law has traditionally left greater discretionary power in the hands of the minister responsible for immigration and his public servants than has U.S. law. In the United States, Congress and the president set immigration policy, leaving the Immigration and Naturalization Service little role in determining numbers, except in asylum cases. Perhaps this difference exists because in Canada, unlike the United States, the minister is directly responsible to Parliament, which passes immigration legislation. Thus the minister is given more leeway to act, although in theory his leash is shorter than his American counterpart's. Whether this direct accountability is a reason for the minister's wide discretionary power is hard to know. The fact of it is dramatic. In a majority government assured of the support of Parliament, the minister and his officials have had a generally free hand in setting and interpreting policy, even to the point of turning policy on its head without enacting new immigration legislation.

Evolution of Canadian Policy

Who in 1945 would have predicted massive increases in immigration, when fears of a 1930s-like depression dominated planning in both the United States and Canada? After a lumbering start, the post-World War II Canadian economy did not slide back into depression. With export markets leading the way, the Canadian economy surged ahead. Demand for Canadian raw materials and manufactured goods was strong in Britain and war-ravaged Europe. Demand became almost insatiable as the Marshall Plan poured additional billions into propping up the postwar economic infrastructure of non-Communist Europe. As long as the United States was intent upon beating back the threat of communism with U.S. dollars, ready buyers were available for Canadian raw materials, foodstuffs, and manufactured goods.

Nor was the export market the only area of Canadian economic strength. Many Canadians had done well during the war, although forced savings plans and shortages of consumer products kept a lid on spending. In the postwar period gratification no longer needed to

19

be delayed. An orgy of consumer spending on everything from new homes to university education, not available since the onset of the depression, stoked the fire of economic growth. The problem was a shortage of goods, not money.

Before long, Canadian officials confronted a problem the likes of which they had not known in almost thirty years—a shortage of workers. By late 1946, labor-intensive industries, especially in the core economic sectors of agriculture, mining, and lumbering, began to press the government for a relaxation of restrictive barriers against imported labor. Most Canadians remained cautious. Would the economic recovery stand the test of time? Many had their doubts. For their part, immigration officials dug in their heels against any wholesale importation of immigrants, especially of those in the Displaced Persons (DP) camps of Germany and Austria. The camps were filled with members of the Central and East European groups against which immigration barriers were imposed in the first place. Immigration officials, whose job it had long been to keep these same people out of Canada, proved unable or unwilling to think in any other terms.

The larger public was also uneasy. They might be sold on the economic benefits of renewed immigration, but they were certainly hesitant about allowing in those who stood first in line to get out of postwar Europe—Jews and Slavs.[2] In a public opinion poll taken in October 1946, almost half of those surveyed voiced disapproval of allowing Jews into Canada. This number was higher by far than the number opposed to any other immigrant group except the Japanese, who were recently defeated in the Pacific and against whom racist wartime propaganda had been vicious and effective.[3]

But unrelenting pressure from the business lobby, demanding to bring labor to capital, could not be denied. In the spring of 1947, Prime Minister Mackenzie King informed Parliament of his government's decision to reopen Canada's door to immigration. He cautioned that "it is of the utmost importance to relate immigration to absorptive capacity." In his mind, Canada's capacity to absorb immigrants was not tied to the number of immigrants as much as to their ethnic or racial origins. The prime minister was only reflecting the national mood when he observed that "the people of Canada do not wish to make a fundamental alteration in the character of their population through mass immigration."

Discrimination and ethnic selectivity in immigration would remain. "Canada is perfectly within her rights in selecting the persons who we regard as desirable future citizens. It is not a 'fundamental human right' of any alien to enter Canada. It is a privilege. It is a

20

matter of domestic policy."[4] There would be no lifting of restrictions against Asian immigration. Furthermore, care would be taken to ensure that immigration preference be given to applicants from groups that had proven in the past best able to assimilate into the existing Canadian society. In many ways, the government's reopening of the door to immigration in late 1947 was less a giant leap forward than it was a throwback to the policy, regulations, and racial priorities of an earlier era. To solve labor problems of today, Canada turned to yesterday.

Yet from this inauspicious beginning has come an almost revolutionary change in the Canadian community, a change brought on largely by immigration. In the forty years since the genie of renewed immigration was let out of the government's bottle, the character of Canada's population has been transformed. Canada's population doubled, from fewer than 13 million at the war's end to almost 26 million in 1990. Immigrants and their children account for much of that growth.

Equally crucial, the ethnic-cultural composition of Canada's population has been recast. The proportion of Canadians of non-British and non-French origin has increased dramatically, although the impact of change has been uneven across Canada. Change is more pronounced in Montreal and in the larger urban centers of Ontario and western Canada than in the Maritime Provinces. In Toronto, Canada's largest metropolitan area, for example, a postwar population of fewer than 700,000 has exploded to almost 2,500,000 in only forty years. In 1981, 40 percent of the heads of households in Toronto were foreign-born, the vast majority of them speaking neither English nor French as a mother tongue. Nor is this pluralism of origins restricted to European ethnics. Once a sleepy and conservative Anglo-Protestant backwash of British imperial hopes, Toronto today has significant populations of blacks, South Asians, Chinese, Hispanics, and Southeast Asians.

Had the larger postwar civic culture anticipated this long-term result of short-term immigration initiatives, it is doubtful they would so readily have consented to reopen Canada to immigration in 1947, even on a limited and ethnically selective scale. But no one could foresee the future and, more important, immediate problems of labor shortages had demanded solution. Immigrants afforded that solution. It was thus not with enthusiasm for renewed immigration but rather with determination to maximally utilize a new era of economic prosperity that Canada reopened its door to immigrant labor. Indeed, the link between renewed immigration and the labor market was so close in the postwar era that immigration selection and processing was, for the moment, jointly administered by personnel from the immigration and the labor departments.

First priority was given those immigrants believed to be most adaptable to the Canadian "way of life." To this end, British, American, and Northern European migrants were actively courted. Ontario was so concerned to get the type of immigrant it wanted that it flexed its jurisdictional muscles in immigration matters and inaugurated a highly publicized airlift of British settlers into the province. When British currency regulations threatened to choke off the flow of cash-starved prospective immigrants, the Canadian government negotiated special low air- and ships-passage rates to stimulate the flow.[5] Similar currency regulations hindered the ability of other desirable West European groups to emigrate, particularly the Dutch, and again the Canadian government intervened. In 1948 a three-year bilateral agreement was signed with the Netherlands to ensure the orderly transplant of approximately 15,000 Dutch farmers and farm workers to Canada.[6]

Labor-intensive industry was pleased by the government's renewed commitment to immigration. Business was far less pleased that so high a priority was being placed on the capacity of an immigrant to easily assimilate into Canadian society. If taken too strictly, this might preclude the importation of immigrants willing to fill low-wage and low-status laboring jobs rejected by preferred immigrants and native-born Canadians alike. To sustain the economic boom, business interests demanded that the government siphon off the best available labor from the DP camps of Europe. Largely as a result of this pressure, which was reinforced by the lobbying efforts of Jewish and East European communities in Canada, the federal government reluctantly began to process applicants in the DP camps while carefully monitoring the public mood for any negative reaction.

Some of the DPs also qualified for entry into Canada under the limited family-reunification provisions of the immigration regulations, but most of them were seen less as immigrants than as a cheap source of labor. Their arrival did not signal any liberalization in ethnic preferences, and humanitarian considerations did not stand high on the list of government priorities, either. There is little doubt that without labor shortages, few DPs would have been welcome to enter Canada. And even enlightened self-interest had its ethnic limits. To ensure that those entering Canada did not tilt the ethnic balance in a way the government and public did not want, initial care was taken to give preference to Northern Europeans, in this case refugees from the Baltic republics, rather than to Jews and Slavs.

Unfortunately for government planners, the demand for labor

was greater than could be met by those British or North European settlers ready to come to Canada. Nor was Canada the only destination game in town. As opportunities to migrate to the United States, Australia, or elsewhere in the West opened up for the "desirable" immigrants, Canadian officials found themselves fighting for their share of a shrinking pool. As a result, many of those previously regarded as undesirable or unacceptable became valued prospects for Canadian immigration. In the face of continuing demand for labor and with a grudging nod to ethnic-group lobbying, the door swung open to Jewish and Slavic immigrants, especially those with skills demanded by labor-starved Canadian industries or those willing to work in jobs that native Canadians were unwilling to fill. Furthermore, under pressure from Canadian ethnic communities and anxious to expand its DP labor recruitment programs, the government gradually streamlined family reunification procedures enabling Canadians to sponsor kin in DP camps.[7]

Not everyone was in favor of expanding family reunification procedures. Canadian citizens and immigrants of European origin had long been able to sponsor immediate family members who might otherwise not meet Canadian immigration criteria, although most nonwhites were generally barred access to the family reunification provisions of the immigration regulations before 1967. Even during the closed door era of the Great Depression, family reunification afforded the one small crack in an otherwise solid wall of restriction. Immigration authorities were generally able to control this flow by amending the list of eligible family members acceptable for sponsorship or by changing the terms of the guarantee demanded of the sponsor. When instructed to begin processing first-degree family in postwar Europe, cautious Canadian authorities again advised the government to go slowly. They were less concerned with the numbers of family members than with their race or ethnicity. Once inside Canada, officials warned, sponsored family members who might never have qualified for admission under the existing immigration regulations could turn around and sponsor others who might be equally unqualified or ethnically undesirable. This trend could eventually inflate the ranks of the unwanted racial or ethnic classes in Canada. To stop this end-run around the protective barrier afforded by the immigration regulations, immigration officials cautioned against setting aside the longstanding ethnic and racial controls on admission. But the government had made a commitment to increased immigration, albeit with ethnic and racial reservations. Family reunification for European ethnics was just part of the package.

It may have been moving with caution, but the government was moving. By the time the DP admission program ended, tens of thousands had entered Canada, and the routine processing of immigration from Europe was running smoothly. Immigration authorities, many of an earlier generation, who could not keep pace would have to go. In 1950 the old Immigration Branch of the Department of Mines and Resources, which had previously administered Canadian immigration policy, was revamped and a new staff introduced. The old guard was eased out. Reflecting the new priority being given to the active intake of immigrants, the status of immigration work was upgraded within a new Department of Citizenship and Immigration.

Before long, officials in the new department brought forward draft proposals for a new immigration act. The resulting Immigration Act of 1952 was designed to attract a continuing selective stream of immigrants under the general terms outlined by the prime minister in his 1947 policy statement. And in keeping with a longstanding practice of Canadian immigration legislation, the Act allowed the minister of immigration and his officials enormous discretionary powers to institute regulations that could open or close the door against virtually any group or individual. Although this "tap on, tap off" legislation was couched in the rhetoric of the liberalism demanded of a signatory to the United Nations Charter, it was far less yielding in matters of race and ethnicity than the advocates of a more progressive immigration policy might have hoped. At the discretion of the minister, individuals or groups might be rejected on account of nationality, geographic origin, peculiarity of custom, unsuitability of climate, or the omnibus provision that any individual or group demonstrated an inability "to become assimilated."[8]

Furthermore, in keeping with the cold war climate of the day, strict security checks were required of would-be immigrants. Security personnel, working under the umbrella of the Royal Canadian Mounted Police acted much like a separate estate, accountable only to themselves and virtually immune to criticism. A veil of secrecy was drawn over their activities and procedures. No credible mechanism for appeal was allowed to those who were barred on security grounds. It was rumored that these security provisions were secretly used to prop up racial and ethnic barriers that were slowly crumbling elsewhere. Certainly, security reviews were not applied evenhandedly to applicants of different ethnic origins. But ethnic and racial selectivity was, at most, a byproduct of the security review. Above all, the security service was preoccupied with the issues growing out of the cold war. In their zeal to guard against the left, security personnel were too often prepared to ignore if not abet the admission of some whose World War II records should have set off alarms in Ottawa, but did not. Whatever these Nazis or Nazi collaborators might have done in the past, in the eyes of Canadian security authorities they were free of communism, and many had proven records as anti-Communists.[9]

Through the 1950s, the racial assumptions on which Canadian immigration based its selectivity were being challenged, and immigration authorities slowly gave way. An important break with the past occurred in 1951, when Canada introduced small but symbolically important immigrant quotas for its nonwhite Asian Commonwealth partners, India, Pakistan, and Ceylon. This step was taken with an eye to the potential importance of newly independent third world countries, both as possible trading partners and at the United Nations, where Canada was playing a high-profile role. Even though the actual number of South Asian immigrants who entered Canada as a result of these changes was small, the fact of a government-approved program for the admission of visible-minority immigrants should not be minimized. In the main, however, the government's attitude on race and ethnicity remained cautious.[10]

A buoyant economy, a more enlightened spirit of racial tolerance, and a climate of cold war combativeness combined to erode many of the assumptions on which immigration policy of the day was based. Even the most optimistic officials had predicated their planning on the basis of steady or gradually diminishing Canadian labor needs and the continued inflow of desirable settlers from Northern Europe. Both of these assumptions proved wrong. As prosperity gradually returned to Northern and Western Europe in the late 1950s, the number of persons seeking to emigrate from Northern Europe declined. Canadian demand for labor, however, remained strong.

Labor-intensive industries clamored ever louder for more manpower and warned that continued Canadian prosperity was at stake. But where would immigrants come from? The DP camps were emptied of available labor, leaving only hard-core refugee cases in the care of international refugee officials. Soviet-dominated Eastern Europe closed its borders to emigration, and Western Europeans were coming in smaller numbers. As a result, business interests began to eye the pool of labor available in previously undesirable areas, Southern Europe and Italy in particular. After some initial resistance, the government responded.

At first hoping to restrict intake to the more "Germanic" northern Italians, the government opened immigration offices in Italy. While security personnel again warned against the strength of the Italian Communist party and the potential for infiltration by Communist subversives, a warning that security personnel attached to virtually any new government immigration initiative, the flow of Italian immi-

25

grant labor to urban Canada began. In short order, the number of southern Italians coming to Canada climbed to hundreds of thousands. By the mid-1960s, in the industrial heartland of southern Ontario and in urban Canada more generally, Italian labor became to the construction industry what an earlier generation of Jews had been to the needle trades and Ukrainians had been to the breaking of the prairie sod. Italians were soon followed by Greeks, Portuguese, and Yugoslavs.

In 1956 the government immigration program faced a new challenge, this time as a result of the Hungarian uprising. The Soviet suppression of the Hungarian uprising set off a rush of refugees westward into Austria. This first major European refugee crisis of the cold war came at a fortuitous moment for Canada. Its economy was buoyant and the country was generally aroused in sympathy for the Hungarian "freedom fighters." But Canadian authorities remained uneasy. Again security personnel advised caution. They warned that the Soviets might use this refugee movement to secrete subversives in unsuspecting Western countries. And the government, for its part, proved less concerned with spies than with the dollars-and-cents cost of generosity.

As the government dithered about expense, the media and the general public was swept up in sympathy for the Hungarian refugees. Voluntary agencies pledged to pick up much of the cost of refugee resettlement, and both the liberal and the conservative media hammered officials for their fumbling of the Hungarian refugee issue. The government finally moved. And like a freight train building up a head of steam, once the government moved, it swept every barrier out of its path. Setting aside the warnings of security personnel, the minister of immigration rushed off to Vienna. He was quickly followed by immigration teams mandated to skim the cream off the top of the refugee pool as quickly as possible.

The Hungarian refugee resettlement program was successful. It was not, however, a product of routine immigration procedures. Rather, it was approved by Ottawa as an exception to the Immigration Act. Normal procedures for immigrants, including their medical and security clearances, were set aside or deferred until after they arrived. But Canada did well by doing good. In short order almost 37,000 Hungarians were brought to Canada, most of them to urban areas, which by the mid-1950s were the new home to most immigrants.[11]

Evolution of U.S. Policy

Like Canada, the United States also moved cautiously in the admission of new immigrants after World War II. Conditions for immigration reform appeared bleak; many in Congress feared another depression after the war, and considerable racial and ethnic bigotry persisted. Yet the war raised troubling issues regarding American immigration, and reformers were quick to lobby for change. One group, the Citizens Committee to Repeal Chinese Exclusion, protested that while Chinese soldiers were fighting side by side with Americans, no Chinese were permitted to become immigrants. Acknowledging this embarrassing inconsistency, Congress repealed the Chinese Exclusion acts and in 1943 gave China a small quota. The legislators also permitted Chinese immigrants to become naturalized American citizens.[12]

In 1946 foreign policy considerations played a role in granting the Philippines and India small quotas and naturalization rights.[13] Few Americans wanted large numbers of these Asians to come to America, but the prevailing view held that some should be allowed. Clare Boothe Luce, congresswoman from Connecticut and prominent Republican, reflected the popular mood:

> We are utterly justified in controlling and keeping low Oriental immigration in terms of numbers, because of the fact that they in too great numbers may undermine our way of life, our living standards, our form of religion. . . . The proper reason for keeping Orientals out in great numbers is because of those economic facts, but it is certainly improper to keep them out altogether because they are Orientals.[14]

Chinese servicemen were also allowed to bring their spouses to the United States under the provisions of the War Brides Act, and several thousand did so. Moreover, Chinese-American citizens were able to bring their wives into the United States without regard to existing quotas.[15]

These minor modifications foreshadowed more major immigration liberalization. As the United States emerged as the major world power in 1945 and West European nations struggled to rebuild their economies, various political and religious leaders called upon the United States to open its door to the survivors of the Holocaust and the war, and to take action to relieve the refugee burdens carried by America's European allies in the emerging cold war. But the restrictive National Origins Quotas, which gave nations like Greece and Italy annual quotas of only a few hundred or thousand immigrants, stood in the way. Prodded by the American Jewish Committee and other groups, Congress enacted the Displaced Persons Act of 1948 and amended it in 1950. About 400,000 DPs were able to migrate to the United States through the device of mortgaging quotas for decades into the future.[16]

To the shock of Jewish lobby groups, the first Displaced Persons Act discriminated against Jews while favoring those from the Baltic republics and *Volksdeutsche,* persons of Germanic origin from outside Germany. While this act demonstrated the still potent force of anti-Semitism in the formation of immigration policy, it also, for the first time, permitted several hundred thousand persons to circumvent the National Origins Quotas.[17] President Dwight Eisenhower called for additional refugee legislation, and Congress passed the Refugee Relief Act of 1953, admitting another 200,000 refugees, including many Jews. As a sign of growing toleration, several thousand Asians were permitted to enter under this law.[18]

As important as these laws were, however, Americans, like their neighbors to the north, were reluctant to scrap their restrictive immigration system. When Congress passed the McCarran-Walter Immigration Act of 1952, the lawmakers retained the National Origins Quotas as the basic immigration law. Crude racial and ethnic slanders, so common in the 1920s, were generally absent from the committee hearings and congressional debates over the McCarran-Walter act. Instead, the committee reporting the bill noted that it would not dwell on issues of Nordic supremacy, but insisted that National Origins Quotas had served the nation well in the past and should remain the center of American immigration policy.[19]

President Harry Truman vetoed the McCarran-Walter act, insisting that it discriminated against nations that needed emigration most and that it was an insult to many of America's allies. As Truman said, "The basis of this quota system was false and unworthy in 1924. It is even worse now. At the present time, this quota system keeps out the very people we want to bring in. It is incredible to me that, in this year of 1952, we should again be enacting into law such a slur on the patriotism, the capacity, and the decency of a large part of our citizenry."[20] Congress viewed the situation differently, and it passed the bill over the president's veto.[21]

Although the 1952 law reaffirmed the National Origins Quotas, it also reformed policy concerning one area—Asia. The legislation created an Asia–Pacific Triangle, covering the Pacific, which permitted 2,000 immigrants from that region and gave Asian countries small annual allotments, usually of 100. It also permitted all Asian immigrants to become naturalized American citizens, a provision that affected about 80,000 Japanese immigrants living in the United States. The creation of the Asia–Pacific Triangle and the naturalization provision for Asians were largely the work of the Japanese-American Citizens League (JACL). The JACL effort succeeded because of the recognition by Congress of the loyalty of Japanese Americans during World War II, including the heroic exploits of the Japanese-American

442nd Regimental Combat Team fighting in Italy. One representative told Mike Masoaka of JACL, "I might say to you quite frankly, Mike, that I was one of those 'doubting Thomases,' and I was an unbeliever, and I was prejudiced, until I heard the people of your caliber speak to me, and I am for you."[22]

It quickly became apparent that the existing immigration law was an embarrassment in its discrimination against the admission of many American allies in the cold war. As noted, President Eisenhower only a year later called for special refugee legislation to bypass the small National Origins Quotas. Moreover, within the next ten years Congress enacted several other pieces of legislation to admit additional refugees from the Middle East, Europe, and China.[23]

An important development of the 1950s was President Eisenhower's use of the McCarran-Walter act's parole power for the admission of refugees. When Soviet troops crushed the Hungarian Revolution of 1956, the United States joined Canada in admitting refugees who fled across the border into Austria. The impediment for the United States was the small quota for Hungary; hence Eisenhower invoked the parole power to admit about 30,000 Hungarians.[24]

Some in Congress were not entirely happy with the president's decision. They justly observed that the parole power was intended for individual emergency cases, not large numbers of refugees, such as the Hungarians presented. Nevertheless, in 1958 the legislators enacted a law to permit these parolees to adjust their status to regular resident aliens—immigrants. The Eisenhower parole power initiative, which was grounded on foreign policy considerations, became an important precedent to which future presidents resorted again and again to admit substantial numbers of refugees, most of them fleeing communism. It was clear that when foreign policy touched upon immigration, the president would play a key role and Congress a lesser one.

Policy Reforms in the 1960s

By the 1960s both the United States and Canada were willing to make far-reaching changes in their immigration policies. In the United States, presidential action and special refugee admission legislation indicated that the McCarran-Walter act was not working as intended. By the 1960s President John Kennedy was calling for scrapping the National Origins Quotas and creating a new immigration policy. Although Kennedy was assassinated before his proposals could be considered by Congress, his successor, President Lyndon Johnson, also favored fundamental immigration reform.

The 1960s were ripe for a total overhaul of the immigration system. Not only did foreign policy considerations repeatedly run afoul of immigration policy, but other important influences also worked to reshape immigration in that decade. First, racial and ethnic tension was on the decline after World War II. The easing of immigration restrictions against Asians was but one sign of this shift in public opinion. In 1947, for example, California voters for the first time rejected a referendum placing limits on property ownership by Asian immigrants, and the next year the California Supreme Court declared all such restrictions unconstitutional.[25]

As for black Americans, the 1960s were a decade of civil rights protests and achievements. The Supreme Court, in *Brown v. Board of Education* (1954), had already declared segregation in schools to be unconstitutional before the massive sit-ins, demonstrations, and marches of the 1960s. The Supreme Court threw out other segregation laws, and Congress enacted some major civil rights legislation: the Civil Rights Act of 1964, covering public accommodations and employment, and the Voting Rights Act of 1965.[26]

Jews, Italians, and other Southern and Eastern Europeans also found prejudice on the decline after 1945. In the 1940s New York and other states enacted the first laws barring religious and racial discrimination in housing, education, and employment, and institutions began to change admission and hiring practices. This is not to argue that a meritocracy was achieved by the 1960s and that all anti-Semitism, anti-Catholicism, and hostility toward Southern and Eastern Europeans disappeared. Far from it. But undoubtedly a new era was dawning in American history.[27]

Second, the fears of a major postwar depression were not realized. After America's entrance into the war and throughout the postwar period, the American economy continued to expand. In the 1960s Americans witnessed another decade of substantial economic growth and low unemployment.

The priority given to economic growth, foreign policy considerations, and racial and ethnic harmony encouraged reformers to press their case for a new immigration policy. In the past, patriotic organizations like the Daughters of the American Revolution, the American Legion, and the United Order of Mechanics made common cause with trade unions concerned with the importation of cheap labor, to fight against any liberalization of immigration policy. But by the 1960s their voices fell mute while Protestant and Catholic churches and church organizations and Jewish groups joined ethnic groups like the JACL and the Sons of Italy to pressure Congress for a more open immigration policy.

While the climate for immigration reform may have become more favorable in the 1960s, it should be noted that the 1965 act was, nonetheless, a cautious reform. Its eventual impact was largely unforeseen by the legislators. For the Eastern Hemisphere, Congress replaced the National Origins system with a three-tiered preference system, based first on family unification (74 percent of the visas), then on economic needs of the United States (20 percent), and finally on refugee concerns (6 percent). The Eastern Hemisphere was allotted a total of 170,000 visas yearly, and each nation in that hemisphere was to be permitted an annual maximum of 20,000 (excluding immediate family members of U.S. citizens).[28]

When they chose to emphasize family unification, Congress believed that the patterns of immigration would not change significantly and that this emphasis would benefit primarily South and East European nations. Representative Emanuel Celler, a longtime advocate of reform and a key figure in determining immigration policy, was clear on this point:

> With the end of discrimination due to place of birth, there will be shifts in countries other than those of northern and western Europe. Immigrants from Asia and Africa will have to compete and qualify in order to get in, quantitatively and qualitatively, which itself will hold the numbers down. There will not be, comparatively, many Asians or Africans entering this country. . . . Since the people of Africa and Asia have very few relatives here, comparatively few could immigrate from those countries because they have no family ties in the United States.[29]

Moreover, the new law provided for tighter labor restrictions. The old system prohibited those who might adversely affect employment in the United States. But this employment restriction was not enforced, and it proved virtually meaningless. The new law called for the immigrants coming under the labor categories to obtain "the secretary of labor's clearance *prior* [italics author's] to the issuance of the visa," which was expected to be difficult to obtain.[30]

Finally, the 1965 act for the first time included a ceiling (120,000, excluding immediate family members of U.S. citizens) on the Western Hemisphere, including Canada. The limit was demanded by those in Congress who feared the growing immigration from this hemisphere. Neither Kennedy nor Johnson had originally favored a Western Hemisphere ceiling, but the latter accepted it as part of a compromise to win approval for scrapping the National Origins system.[31] In 1978 Congress merged the two hemispheres into a unified world system.

The Immigration Act of 1965 gave the United States a policy that envisioned 290,000 annual entrants, plus an estimated 50,000 entering as immediate family members of U.S. citizens. The numerical reality, however, turned out to be considerably different. Framers of the new law did not see that the numbers of those coming as quota-exempt immediate family members of U.S. citizens would continue to grow. Rather than the 50,000 family members of U.S. citizens who the supporters of the law thought might enter as quota-exempt immigrants, more than 200,000 have come in recent years.[32]

Refugee flows also pushed the totals higher. President Eisenhower had begun to admit Cuban refugees when Fidel Castro came to power in 1959.[33] Kennedy continued to favor Cubans who were "voting with their feet," and several hundred thousand were paroled into the United States before the Cuban missile crisis in October 1962 halted their immigration.[34] In early 1965 Castro indicated he might permit Cubans to leave again. When President Johnson signed the new immigration act at the foot of the Statue of Liberty in October 1965, he declared that the United States was willing to take all Cubans who wished to leave Castro's Communist state.[35]

Thus another airlift began between the United States and Cuba and continued until 1972, when it was terminated. About 360,000 more Cubans entered during these years, most of whom settled in the Miami area. While some lawmakers grumbled about the president's unilateral action, Congress nonetheless passed the 1966 Cuban Adjustment Act, which permitted these latest Caribbean refugees to become resident aliens and eventually citizens.[36]

In Canada, a downturn in the domestic economy in the early 1960s crippled the labor market. Canada curtailed active immigrant recruitment, and many in Europe without the resources necessary to finance a new beginning abroad deferred their plans to leave for Canada. Even as immigration work was scaled down and new arrivals dropped by 50 percent, one major policy shift was introduced paralleling changes to the south. In 1962, largely as a spillover from federal and provincial human rights initiatives and from the continually expanding Canadian presence on the international stage, racial and ethnic discrimination in the processing of independent immigrants was officially ended. Ethnic discrimination remained in cases of family reunification, largely for fear that any liberalization would open the door to rapid growth in the small Chinese and South Asian communities in Canada. But henceforth all independent applicants would be judged on the basis of individual skills or, more precisely, Canadian market needs.

This policy did not, of course, eliminate administrative discretion, which could easily be used or abused to enforce de facto discrimination. For example, the resources of the immigration bureaucracy were almost exclusively concentrated on areas of traditional immigrant preference—the United Kingdom, the United States, and Western Europe. By contrast, few on-site immigration services were available and little immigration promotion money spent in the third world. In 1960, for example, Canada mantained twenty-seven immigration offices outside North America. Twenty-four were in Europe and three in Asia (one of these being in Israel). None were in Africa or South America. Thus, a commitment to remove discrimination from immigration required more than a formal expunging of racism from the legislation and admission criteria. But the importance of officially striking overt racial discrimination from Canadian immigration regulations cannot be denied. And if these changes did not come fast enough or go far enough to satisfy many of the government's critics, at least the direction of policy change was clear. In 1963 a Canadian immigration office was opened in Egypt, in 1967 in Japan, in 1968 in Lebanon, in the Philippines, in the West Indies, and in Pakistan.[37] The racial composition of Canadian immigration was about to change. Table 2–3 indicates the shifting origins of immigrants entering Canada from 1957 to 1987.

In 1964, with the Canadian economy still in a slump and immigration numbers having leveled off, administrative responsibility for immigration was again transferred, this time to a newly established Department of Manpower and Immigration. The government's underlying intent in this reorganization was clear. While not overlooking the social impact of immigration on Canadian society, the government retained as its first priority of policy planning and administration the tailoring of immigration to fit short-term national employment needs.

One other problem, though minor in comparison with that of the United States, emerged for Canada in the 1960s: illegal immigrants. Among the illegals were aliens who remained after their tourist visas had expired, Asians who were smuggled into Canada, and extended family members of persons in Canada, who had misrepresented the closeness of their family relationship in order to gain entry. Processing these illegal immigrants strained the resources of immigration authorities and clogged the administrative process. Furthermore, the government proved unwilling to spend the money necessary to hire or train enough new staff to deal with the blizzard of paperwork created by the illegal immigrants. It was also reluctant to unleash the police in a wholesale crackdown on the illegals, many of whom were working as low-paid domestics or in other menial jobs. If decisive action were not forthcoming, some worried that the problem of illegals would just grow worse. In an effort to address the immediate problem while giving the bureaucracy a breathing space in which to

TABLE 2–3

Immigrants Entering Canada, by Region of Last Permanent Residence, 1957–1987
(percent)

Year	1957	1962	1967	1972	1977	1982	1987
United Kingdom	38.6	21.3	27.8	16.0	15.6	13.2	5.9
Continental Europe	52.8	50.7	43.9	27.0	20.0	24.8	20.4
Asia	1.4	4.0	9.4	18.8	26.9	34.7	44.0
Africa	.3	2.6	2.2	7.1	5.2	4.1	5.9
Caribbean	.3	2.6	3.4	6.5	10.4	7.4	7.2
South America	.7	1.3	1.3	3.6	6.9	5.8	7.2
United States	3.5	16.0	8.5	20.5	11.3	7.4	5.3
Other	2.7	1.5	3.5	.5	3.7	2.6	4.1
Total immigration	282,000	75,000	223,000	122,000	115,000	121,000	152,000

SOURCE: *Immigration Statistics 1973* (Ottawa: Manpower and Immigration, 1975); *Immigration Statistics 1987* (Ottawa: Employment and Immigration Canada, 1987).

reevaluate its regulations and procedures, authorities announced the first of several amnesties for illegals. But a long-term solution would not come that easily. Over the next twenty years, amnesties of various kinds were attempted in an effort to eliminate the problem of illegal immigrants by making them legal. Although these amnesties succeeded in regularizing the status of many illegal immigrants, they did not get to the root of the problem. Then, as now, the problem of illegal entry defied easy solution.

Partly in an effort to deal with questions of illegal entry, the government commissioned a general review of all aspects of immigration. A White Paper on immigration was released in 1966. The policy document, infused with the liberal spirit of the day, called for a complete and final overhaul of Canadian immigration regulations so as to exorcise any hint of discrimination on the basis of race or ethnicity. But it went further. Discrimination might be out but, again reflecting the mood of the 1960s, concern about population growth was definitely in. Although a far cry from the Malthusian warnings of an earlier day and insufficient to meet the demands of zero-population growth advocates, the White Paper questioned Canada's long-term ability to absorb large numbers of job-hungry immigrants at the prime of their fertility cycle.

But was there an optimum population size? And who should determine it? In the name of population control as much as national economic self-interest, the White Paper called for closer links between Canada's immediate labor needs and immigration. It urged a tightening of the family reunification regulations, long considered by many immigration officials to be the loose cannon on the immigration deck. The White Paper recommended restricting the right of landed immigrants to sponsor any but immediate dependents, and allowing Canadian citizens to sponsor only those relatives who met the educational and occupational standards already demanded of independent immigrants.

The White Paper was referred for discussion to a parliamentary committee on immigration. In an unprecedented show of lobbying muscle, ethnic communities organized to let their elected officials know their displeasure at any suggestion of narrowing the family and sponsorship categories. Warning that ethnic voters should not be taken for granted, church, labor, and ethnic leaders united to demand not a narrowing but a broadening of these categories. Members of Parliament, especially those from heavily immigrant or ethnic constituencies, withered in the political heat. They soon joined the chorus of those protesting against implementation of the White Paper recommendations to limit sponsorship. The proposed changes were set aside, at least in the form suggested in the White Paper. Equally important, the retreat from alienating a newly empowered immigrant and ethnic constituency signaled a new twist in Canadian political life. The political world was alive with talk of a "third force," a potent alliance of those of non-English and non-French heritage who felt they were too long denied access to the corridors of power.

Nowhere did the notion of a third force seem more real than in the heady days of the Royal Commission on Bilingualism and Bi-culturalism. The commission was set up in 1965 to examine the rocky relations between Canada's two charter groups, the English and the French. It was soon besieged by organized ethnic communities demanding that their ethnic-cultural heritages be accorded public recognition as equal partners in the nation-building process. This campaign, led largely by the dispossessed minorities from Eastern Europe, pretended to be a unity of ethnic political interest and of potential power for coordinated lobbying, a unity that was to prove illusionary. At the time, however, it looked very real indeed.

Confronted by the awareness that fully one third of Canadians were of neither British nor French origin, politicians suddenly took notice. The commission recommended that the "contribution of Canada's other ethnic communities" be acknowledged in government policy. In 1971 the federal government responded by declaring Canada to be a multicultural nation within a bilingual framework. Bi-culturalism was officially dead.[38]

Detractors have dismissed the multiculturalism policy, together with an accompanying nickel-and-dime program of grants in support of ethnic-cultural preservation and sharing, as little more than a government game of smoke-and-mirrors. Some attacked multi-culturalism as an unsuccessful federal effort to downplay the importance of French-Canadian nationalism by equating it with other forms of ethnic self-assertion then demanding to be heard. Others have argued that multiculturalism was a crude and equally unsuccessful attempt to buy ethnic voters with their own money. Still others regarded multiculturalism as a cynical manipulation of the powerless by a Canadian power elite. According to this interpretation, multi-culturalism was designed to keep "the ethnics" dancing in church basements instead of pressing for their legitimate place in the social, economic, and political governance of the nation.[39]

Even if one or all of these charges is true, the fact remains that these former-immigrant laborers and their children suddenly represented a political sleeping lion. The lion appeared to be friendly, but few politicians were so reckless as to stick their heads into its mouth to find out for sure. And at times, as during the White Paper debate on family reunification, politicians heard the lion roar and told one another, "It's a jungle out there."

Although the specific recommendations in the White Paper for family reunification were dropped, other White Paper recommendations were incorporated into immigration regulations. In 1967, paralleling American reforms of two years earlier, all vestiges of racial or ethnic discrimination were officially erased from the immigration regulations and procedures. Most particularly, racial discrimination was eliminated from the area of sponsored immigration. Although the definition of first-degree relatives was reined in somewhat, all citizens and landed immigrants in Canada, including those from the third world, were legally entitled to sponsor family members.[40]

On the contentious issue of family reunification, the government proceeded with caution. In the end, it took a little with one hand and gave a lot with the other. The list of those entitled to entry into Canada as first-degree relatives was narrowed. But at the same time a new class of immigrant, a nominated class, was announced. Nominated immigrants were primarily those nondependent relatives of Canadians who could demonstrate an ability to integrate with a minimum of difficulty. In effect they were expected to have the strengths of independent immigrants, but they were granted priority admission. Canadian sponsors also had less legal liability for nominated immigrants than for dependent family members. After 1978, virtually half of the immigrants admitted annually into Canada were in either the family or the assisted-relatives category.[41]

In almost the same breath as the government restructured family-reunification regulations and ended racial and ethnic preferences, it also overhauled the procedures by which independent applicants were admitted into Canada. Again, without enacting new legislation, the government undercut the free hand previously allowed immigration officials while linking immigration admissions still closer to domestic economic fluctuations. A point system, as it came to be known, was introduced. The desirability of each independent applicant would henceforth be calculated on a sliding scale measuring short- and long-term prospects for successful integration. In addition to education and employment experience, points were earned for personal character, for market demand for the individual's particular skills, for English- and French-language proficiency, for age, for proposed Canadian destination, and for prearranged employment. The point system could be adjusted on very short notice to reflect fluctuations in the Canadian economy. Although the immigration officer assessing each applicant retained some discretionary power in awarding points, in the main, the point system reduced the power of immigration officials arbitrarily to reject applicants. Henceforth all admissions were formally based on a universal system with objective selection criteria.

Immigration Policy in the 1970s and 1980s

Setting in motion new immigration policies that were less ethnically and racially restrictive did not end debate after 1970. One key issue for both Canada and the United States was refugees. The end of the Prague spring in 1968 sent a flood of Czechoslovakian refugees streaming westward in what seemed a repetition of the Hungarian exodus of a decade earlier. Driven by a mixture of humanitarianism, cold-war posturing, and economic self-interest, the Canadian government geared up for action. This time there was no waiting for voluntary associations to underwrite costs. With the Canadian economy on the mend and a crop of highly skilled labor ripe for the picking, immigration teams were quickly sent off. After the success of the Hungarian program, even the security service did not object. Again waiving many of its immigration regulations, Canada resettled approximately 12,000 Czechoslovakian refugees.[42]

While many Canadians applaud themselves for their magnanimity, there remains a less commendable side to Canada's refugee rescue programs. Liberal groups repeatedly charged the government with favoring the victims of Communist or other high-profile and unpopular regimes above refugees from right-wing tyranny, and evidence to support this charge is not difficult to find. The uneven treatment of refugees was clearly apparent in the care afforded Asian-Ugandan refugees, expelled by Idi Amin in 1972, and Chilean refugees, from the 1973 right-wing coup d'état against Salvador Allende's democratically elected left-wing government. In the case of the approximately 50,000 Asians carrying British passports who were expelled from Uganda, the British, fearing a domestic backlash against the increase of Asians in Britain, appealed to Canada for assistance. Building on the Czechoslovakian experience, Canada moved quickly to identify candidates for easy integration and eventually admitted about 5,600 Asian-Ugandans. For the first time, the issue of race played almost no part in the government's decision. If its response fell something short of a totally humanitarian gesture, the Canadian effort on behalf of Ugandan refugees was far from the kind of ethnically restrictive DP movement that previously proved the model for most Canadian postwar refugee initiatives.

The Chilean experience a year later was different. The Canadian government may have become color blind to race, but not so to ideology. And when it came to Chileans, immigration and security personnel saw red. The overthrow of Allende's Socialist government was engineered by the United States, Canada's closest ally; with corporate interests at stake, Canada was among the first to recognize the new Pinochet regime. It was not long before the problem of political refugees was front and center. A small group of Chileans entered the Canadian Embassy in Santiago seeking political asylum. Ironically, Chile respected the right to sanctuary in this case, yet Canada was not inclined to grant it.[43] As Canadian authorities scrambled to sort out this problem, the larger issue erupted concerning the acceptance of significant numbers of Chileans facing torture or imprisonment for their political views. Across Canada, a pro-refugee lobby coalesced under the wing of the Canadian Council of Churches and the academic community.[44]

Contrast with Asian-Ugandan refugees or with the earlier Czechoslovakian and Hungarian programs is unavoidable. Perhaps uneasy about taking in any large group of potentially left-leaning refugees or concerned about a negative U.S. reaction, the Canadian government proceeded with caution. Immigration authorities did not rush into Chile to process applications. Regulations were not waived—just the reverse. In spite of a storm of protest from liberal groups, immigration officials were slow to set up shop in Santiago and proved reluctant to forgo stringent immigration procedures, including security checks. Two years after the ousting of Allende and in the face of an international outcry at the continuing wholesale abuse of civil liberties by the Pinochet government, fewer than 2,000 Chilean refugees were granted safe haven in Canada. Once again, many of those who finally did get accepted were white-collar professionals with the kind of educational or work experience that might have won them entry into Canada as independent immigrants. This is not to argue that Chilean refugees were any more deserving of admission to Canada on humanitarian grounds than were Asian-Ugandans. No. But the story does illustrate that there was more to Canadian refugee policy than was apparent at first blush. If humanitarianism could take second place to economic self-interest, economic self-interest could take second place to political considerations.[45]

In 1976, as part of the immigration act passed that year, Canada hoped to clarify refugee policy. Significantly, the act recognized refugees as a class distinct from other immigrants and legally entitled them to Canadian sanctuary. Each year a percentage of the total immigration quota was to be set aside for refugees, the cost of their integration being covered by the government.

Chapter 3 in this volume, by Aristide Zolberg, covers post-1976 Canadian refugee policies in detail, but several points should be made here. The refugee provisions of the 1976 immigration act, which came into effect in 1978, were immediately put to the test during the Vietnamese "boat people" crisis. The strength of the pro-refugee lobby, stirred by media reports of the refugees' plight, took the government and the public alike by surprise. Even though many Canadians remained dubious as to the wisdom of Canada's accepting any boat people, the impassioned lobbying by many influential and articulate Canadians and the backing of the media prompted the government by the end of 1980 to admit more than 60,000 Vietnamese, Cambodians, Laotians, and ethnic Chinese from Southeast Asia, the highest per capita boat people resettlement program of any nation.[46]

But popular support for the admission of refugees was hard to sustain once the sense of crisis passed. What is more, the support eroded still further when individuals who might otherwise not be admissible to Canada began entering illegally or as tourists and claiming refugee status once in the country. As the number of refugee claimants within Canada grew, the refugee-determination-review system became clogged, and controversy raged over how to deal with these would-be refugees. This issue was dramatized when two ships illegally landed their respective cargoes of Sikh and Tamil refugee claimants on Canada's east coast. Over the objections of pro-refugee advocates, new legislation was passed in 1989 curtailing the right of refugees to seek asylum once in Canada and restricting other aspects of the refugee program. Many pro-refugee lobbyists believed Canada acted unconstitutionally and took a giant step backward from its recent commitment to refugee sanctuary. The courts agreed. A legal challenge to the new legislation was successful. Early in 1990 the Canadian Supreme Court tossed out the restrictive legislation as incompatible with the Canadian Charter of Rights and Freedoms. In the aftermath of the Court's ruling, the government's options remained unclear.[47]

Given the role of the United States in world affairs, the refugee problem might have been viewed from a different perspective. But many issues overlap the American-Canadian border. The Cubans were the first, but by no means the last, of the major refugee flows entering outside the provisions of the 1965 immigration act. In 1965 President Johnson not only signed the new immigration law but also escalated the American presence in Vietnam, which eventually led to the admission of about 900,000 Southeast Asian refugees. It was not the original intent of Washington to admit so many refugees. In 1973 Francis Kellogg of the State Department told a Congressional committee that the United States would aid refugees in Vietnam, but he did not "anticipate them coming to the United States. . . . It would be our opinion that they could be resettled in their own country."[48]

Events in Vietnam changed American policy. As the American-backed government collapsed dramatically in the spring of 1975, the Ford administration decided to admit more than 130,000 Vietnamese, about half by airlift in the waning hours of non-Communist control of Saigon. The 1965 act as modified in 1979 had set a quota of only 17,400 refugees annually. Clearly the administration disregarded the refugee limits of the law when it paroled these desperate people into the United States, for both humanitarian and foreign policy reasons.[49]

A few additional refugees entered in 1976 and 1977, but beginning in 1978 they were followed by the boat people. These included both Vietnamese and ethnic Chinese from Vietnam, who feared for their lives in the new Communist state. They were joined by Laotians and Cambodians, many of whom were fleeing almost certain death in Cambodia at the hands of the Khmer Rouge, which controlled Cambodia. Many of the Laotians, who like the Cambodians crossed into neighboring Thailand, had been American allies in the Vietnam War.[50]

By 1979 and 1980, 14,000 refugees were being admitted monthly by the Carter administration. Special legislation first sought by President Ford was enacted by Congress to admit and aid these latest refugees. The extra admissions indicated that the refugee provisions of the 1965 act were inadequate to satisfy what the State Department and the presidents thought to be proper refugee policies. As a result, Congress and President Carter joined to enact a new refugee law, which passed in the spring of 1980.[51]

The Refugee Act of 1980 streamlined refugee aid programs and set the "normal flow" of refugees at 50,000 annually. Reformers hoped this number would more realistically reflect refugee flows, and some in Congress now believed that with a new refugee program the president would no longer find it necessary to use (or abuse) the parole power.[52]

One other provision of the 1980 law deserves notice. Post-war refugee policy, beginning with the Refugee Relief Act of 1953, had defined refugees as those fleeing Communist governments or the Middle East. Practically no thought was given by the various administrations and the State Department to admitting refugees from right-wing governments that the United States supported.[53] The U.S. Senate had ratified the 1967 United National Protocol on the Status of Refugees, which theoretically committed the nation to accepting refugees who possessed a well-founded fear of persecution from governments, Communist or not. But what this meant in practice remained unclear. Only a few refugees from Chile's right-wing government (which the United States had helped to install), for example, found a welcome in the United States. The same was true for those escaping the repressive regimes of America's friends in Haiti, Francois and Jean-Claude Duvalier.[54]

Congressional critics, backed by support from many of the voluntary organizations (VOLAGs) that helped to settle immigrants, wanted Congress to incorporate the UN definition into American immigration law. Congress agreed, replacing the old anti-Communist definition with the UN one.

The 1980 Refugee Act, like so many other pieces of immigration law, was inadequate for future needs as conceived by policy makers; nor did it necessarily mark a major departure in the anti-Communist bias of refugee policy. The ink was scarcely dry on President Carter's signature when a new crisis loomed—the Mariel boat lift. Amid great confusion and shifting policies, the Carter administration permitted approximately 130,000 Cubans to enter Florida by boat from the Cuban port of Mariel in the late spring and early summer of 1980. Disregarding the new law, Carter created a new category, the "Cuban-Haitian entrants," for these people.[55] Several thousand Haitians were included with the Marielitos, at the insistence of congressional liberals, the Black Caucus, and the VOLAGs. These were Haitians who had been arriving illegally in Florida by boat, and many of them claimed refugee status. Their claims had mostly been rejected by the Immigration and Naturalization Service.

In addition to the Mariel crisis, conditions in Southeast Asia continued to prompt thousands to flee across the Thai border or by boat. Responding to these unfortunate refugees, some of whom were robbed, raped, and beaten by sea pirates, the Carter and Reagan administrations took in more than 50,000 annually until the late 1980s. These refugees, along with a few Cubans and persons from East European Communist nations and the Middle East, made the U.S. average refugee flow about 100,000 in the 1980s, not the "normal" flow of 50,000 projected by the 1980 Refugee Act.

By 1986 it appeared as if the crises in Asia and Cuba were over and the United States could admit fewer refugees. But world conditions abruptly changed to produce a potentially new refugee emergency. During the 1970s the Soviet Union permitted thousands of Jews (and a few Armenians and Pentecostals) to leave. At first, Soviet Jews headed for Israel, but by the late 1970s the majority were settling in the United States. Then in 1981 the Soviet government closed the door to virtually all emigration. Under the leadership of Mikhail

Gorbachev, however, Soviet authorities again began to grant exit visas. In 1987 the exodus was higher than it had been for the previous five years, and thousands more applied to leave in 1988, 1989, and 1990. With virtually all restrictions lifted and Jews free to leave if they wished, their status as refugees was suddenly cast into doubt. Thus, rather than celebrating the shift in Soviet policy, the United States found itself wrestling with a new concern: Did the designation of refugee still apply to large numbers of emigrating Soviet Jews? And could the issue of Soviet Jews bound for Israel become yet another stumbling block to peace in that region?

Numbers alone did not consume the attention of those interested in refugee policy. Although the 1980 Refugee Act dropped the anti-Communist definition of refugee, the Reagan administration demonstrated little interest in refugees escaping non-Communist regimes. The Reagan policy was most clearly illustrated in the cases of the Caribbean and of Central America, where it steadfastly refused to grant refugee status to Haitians and Salvadorans.

Aristide Zolberg in chapter 3 deals in detail with the question of refugee status and asylum for Central Americans and Haitians. We will point out here, however, that these issues prompted considerable debates in Congress and among refugee and religious groups, and they led to court fights by the advocates of the asylum seekers. While the Reagan and Bush administrations insisted that the vast majority of Central Americans coming into the United States illegally were driven by economic motives, these immigrants' supporters urged Congress to pass a law granting them temporary "safe haven" and suggested that the administration ease its asylum rulings. A few critics of the government, especially representatives of churches, opened their doors to give Central Americans sanctuary; but this movement had limited support. Moreover, the government prosecuted several sanctuary leaders for violating the immigration laws.[56] Advocates of asylum for Central Americans won a partial victory with passage of the Immigration Act of 1990, which permitted undocumented Salvadorans to remain in the United States for eighteen months.

As troublesome as refugee policy was to Americans, the most important immigration issue to emerge in the 1970s and 1980s for the United States was one that also concerned Canadians: namely, illegal or undocumented immigration. For Americans the issue was also related to that of temporary workers. The illegal immigration issue had appeared as early as the late 1940s. During World War II the United States and Mexico agreed to the Bracero Program, which provided for the admission of temporary workers from Mexico to work in American agriculture. Lasting until 1964, the program even-

43

tually saw some 5 million braceros working for short periods in the United States. Unintentionally, the program helped stimulate illegal immigration. Many Mexicans who were unable to sign on as braceros crossed the border and worked illegally in the agriculture of the Southwest, where they became a vital work force for the growers. Unions, church groups, and liberal political leaders claimed these "wetbacks," as Mexicans crossing the Rio Grande were called, depressed the standard of living of American agricultural workers.[57]

After several investigations by Congress and the administration, in 1954 President Eisenhower ordered the Immigration and Naturalization Service under Commissioner Joseph Swing to remove the undocumented workers. Using roadblocks, farm raids, and increased border enforcement, INS rounded up and deported over 1 million undocumented aliens in Operation Wetback.[58] INS proudly announced in 1955, "The so-called 'wetback' problem no longer exists. . . . The border has been secured."[59] Growers were persuaded to cooperate with the government on the promise of more braceros and in the next few years the number of braceros jumped from an average of 200,000 yearly to 400,000.[60]

Individuals and organizations opposed to undocumented immigration generally wanted the Bracero Program ended too. Most bought the key argument used against illegal immigrants—that braceros depressed the standard of living for American workers. The Kennedy and Johnson administrations accepted this argument, and Congress terminated the program in 1964.[61]

When Congress placed a ceiling on immigration from the Western Hemisphere and ended the Bracero Program, some predicted that illegal immigration would rise again. They were right. While precise figures about the extent of undocumented immigration are unavailable, there can be no doubt that in the 1970s and 1980s, the number of undocumented immigrants increased. By the late 1970s INS was apprehending over 1 million persons trying to enter the United States without proper documents. By 1986 the figure was over 1.6 million.

Most undocumented aliens crossing the border were Mexicans trying to escape desperate poverty or poor economic conditions at home. Yet as we have noted, in the 1980s a growing number of persons fled the violence of Central America. Added to these were persons who arrived in the United States as visitors or students and then found jobs and overstayed their visas. They included many Irish, Israelis, Afghans, Dominicans, and Filipinos. Indeed, few areas of the world were unrepresented. Unlike the earlier undocumented aliens, most of these immigrants found jobs in American cities.

In the 1970s, as the Border Patrol caught a growing number of people trying to enter the United States illegally from Mexico, Congress pondered the issue. The 1952 McCarran-Walter Immigration Act had made it a crime to smuggle illegal immigrants into the United States. But it had specifically exempted from criminality the hiring of illegals, in what was called the Texas Proviso, a clear victory for growers. INS leaders said the undocumented aliens were coming to work; if it were to become a crime to hire them, the flow would halt. The House of Representatives in 1972 and again in 1973 passed a law outlawing the hiring of illegal aliens, but the Senate took no action, and the issue festered for nearly a decade.[62]

With evidence mounting of a growing undocumented population in the early 1980s and with fears of an adverse impact upon American society, legislators again attempted to fashion a policy to halt or reduce the flow of illegal immigration.[63] The bills sponsored by Senator Alan Simpson and Representative Romano Mazzoli struck a compromise: they combined prohibitions on the hiring of undocumented aliens—employers' sanctions—with an amnesty for many of the illegal immigrants already living in the United States. The Senate passed the Simpson-Mazzoli bill in 1982 and again in 1983, but the House took no action. The two branches passed different versions late in the 1984 congressional session, the House by the close vote of 216 to 211. Attempts to compromise the two versions failed as Congress adjourned.[64]

In spite of the defeat of a bill coupling employers' sanctions with an amnesty, a consensus was emerging for a new immigration law. After long debate and a series of political compromises, Congress passed the Immigration Reform and Control Act (IRCA) in late 1986. The act made it illegal for most employers to hire undocumented workers and gave an amnesty to those who had entered illegally before January 1982 and who had resided here since that date. These included the Cuban-Haitian entrants. These two provisions were the heart of the compromise, but other provisions were vital for the IRCA's enactment. Growers won a victory with a special agricultural worker (SAW) program, granting an amnesty to those who had worked in American agriculture for ninety days between May 1985 and May 1986 and the promise of a future temporary farm-worker program. The measure also contained safeguards against discrimination involving the hiring of legal immigrants.[65]

A minor provision set aside 10,000 immigrant visas to be determined by lottery for those nations adversely affected by the 1965 immigration act. This inclusion was largely the work of Representative Brian Donnelly of Massachusetts and was aimed to aid Ireland especially. As expected, hundreds of thousands of Irish applications swamped INS for these "Donnelly visas," and prospective Irish migrants won 40 percent of the slots. In 1988 Congress added another 20,000 such visas allocated by lottery.[66]

The inclusion of the Donnelly visas, was typical of the way in which immigration policy catered to lobbying by various religious, ethnic, racial, and economic groups. IRCA would not have been passed without compromises. The amnesty was necessary to offset employers' sanctions. Hispanics and liberals worried about discrimination in the labor market, and special provisions covering this issue were designed to ease their fears. The SAW and temporary-farmworker sections appeased growers and their allies, and without this support the bill might have gone down in defeat. Funds were promised for additional immigration enforcement, and this promise helped win votes for those who believed American immigration was out of control and American borders too porous. Liberals wanted safe haven for Central Americans, but the Senate deleted that provision. Liberals had to be content with provisions to check discrimination and with an amnesty.

Enactment of IRCA marked a major departure for postwar immigration policy. After this time the federal government was committed to employers' sanctions to halt undocumented immigration. How this commitment would be implemented was left to future funding and to the ability of INS to carry out its mission. Several states had already enacted employers' sanctions, but these were rarely enforced—not encouraging news for those who feared that illegal immigration had a major impact, socially and economically, on American society. Initial reports on IRCA's enforcement were mixed.[67]

Recent Issues

What of recent immigration debates and issues in the United States and Canada? In the United States the basic 1965 law that made family preferences the core of American policy came under scrutiny in the late 1980s. As we have discussed, the family unification system, like much of immigration policy, was a compromise—in this case to end National Origins Quotas without changing the historic pattern of primarily European immigration. Directly after enactment of the 1965 bill, as was expected, Italy, Greece, and other formerly restricted European nations increased their emigration to the United States. Economic conditions improved in Europe, however, while the United States experienced a slump in 1973 and 1974 and high inflation. European emigration began to fall.

The unforeseen consequence of the 1965 act was the dramatic increase in third world immigration to the United States. By using family networks, selected professional migration, refugee admissions, and the provisions exempting immediate family members of U.S. citizens, Asians, Mexicans, and peoples from the Caribbean were able to increase their immigration to the United States. By the 1970s they accounted for the bulk of the newcomers. Table 2–4 indicates the shifting pattern of the origin of immigrants to the United States from 1955 to 1988.

In the 1980s some politicians expressed alarm at this migration. They worried that so many non-European immigrants might be unable to assimilate into American society. Senator Alan Simpson, a major figure in shaping immigration policy, wrote in a 1981 letter to the *Washington Post*, "a substantial proportion of these new persons and their descendants do not assimilate satisfactorily into our society." He suggested that they "may well create in America some of the same social, political, and economic problems that exist in the countries from which they have chosen to depart. Furthermore, if language and cultural separation rise above a certain level, the unity and political stability of our nation will—in time—be seriously eroded."[68]

Few spokesmen suggested outright cuts in third world immigration. Most people's attention was drawn to the assimilation issue and, most particularly, to English-language usage. A movement begun in 1983 by Senator S. I. Hayakawa of California demanded that English be made the official language of the United States. Although so-called U.S. English advocates have not succeeded in amending the Constitution as they had hoped to do, they have managed to pass bills in more than a dozen states, including California, making English the official state language. Exactly what these laws, aimed primarily at Hispanics, accomplish is not clear. They may very well be meaningless when it comes to enforcement.[69] In February 1990 a federal judge in Phoenix, Arizona, declared the state's constitutional amendment making English the language "of all government functions and actions" to be a violation of federally protected free speech.[70] But in the mid-1980s signs of a new nativism were growing, with increasingly frequent incidents of violence directed against Asians.[71]

Other critics of the 1965 law argued that American immigration policy did not sufficiently select the skilled and educated workers needed in the United States. Only 20 percent of the preference slots were awarded to those with desired skills, and family members of those coming under these preferences were counted toward the 20 percent—which meant that only about 5 percent of immigrants were being admitted in response to the economic needs of the United

TABLE 2–4

IMMIGRANTS ADMITTED TO THE UNITED STATES
BY REGION AND PERIOD, FISCAL YEARS 1955–1988

(percent)

Region	1955–1964	1965–1974	1975–1984	1985	1986	1987	1988
All regions	100.0	100.0	100.0	100.0	100.0	100.0	100.0
Europe	50.2	29.8	13.4	11.1	10.4	10.2	10.1
North and West	28.6	11.0	5.2	5.0	5.0	5.2	5.1
South and East	21.6	18.7	8.1	6.0	5.4	5.0	5.0
Asia	7.7	22.4	43.3	46.4	44.6	42.8	41.1
Africa	.7	1.5	2.4	3.0	2.9	2.9	2.9
Oceania	.4	.7	.8	.7	.6	.7	.6
North America	36.0	39.6	33.6	31.9	34.5	36.0	38.9
Caribbean	7.1	18.0	15.1	14.6	16.9	17.1	17.5
Central America	2.5	2.6	3.7	4.6	4.7	4.9	4.8
Other N. America	26.4	19.0	14.8	12.7	12.9	14.0	16.6
South America	5.1	6.0	6.6	6.9	7.0	7.4	6.4

SOURCE: Annual reports of the Immigration and Naturalization Service.

States. Critics suggested fewer should be admitted as family members and more should be admitted to address American economic considerations, and that perhaps a system like Canada's should be adopted. After hearings and debates in Congress, the Senate in 1988 and again in 1989 passed a bill modifying the preference categories.[72]

The changes were not radical, for Senate leaders were aware of the importance of family unification to ethnic groups, notably Asian and Italian; too substantial a shift would doom their proposals. Moreover, they did not want to appear to be cutting Hispanic or Asian immigration dramatically, for fear of being called bigoted. Indeed, proposals to make it more difficult to admit brothers and sisters of American citizens came under attack by Asian organizations.[73] Under various drafts of the legislation, 55,000 additional ("independent") immigrants who could best contribute to the economic interests of the United States would be admitted. Early proposals included tightening family preference rules and giving preference to those with English-language skills, capital, education, occupational training, and work experience. Senator Edward Kennedy admitted that these provisions would aid Europeans, and some noted that Ireland in particular, which had been a source of illegal immigration to the United States since 1982, would be a prime beneficiary.[74] Some even tagged the new proposal "the Irish bill."[75]

Representative Peter Rodino, responsible for immigration legislation in the House, indicated little enthusiasm for such changes, and the House Judiciary Committee took no action in 1988. Rodino retired in 1988, however, and Bruce Morrison took charge of the House committee that explored immigration changes. After several years of debate and extensive hearings, the House and Senate finally agreed in late October 1990 to a new, far-reaching immigration bill.

In the end Congress decided not to antagonize the Asian and Latin American nations that used the family unification system to send emigrants to the United States; indeed, the legislators increased the number of places available for families of permanent resident aliens. At the same time, Congress substantially increased immigration for those coming with skills needed in the United States, and it developed a method not unlike Canada's for determining these places. Congress also added visas for those countries that had been disadvantaged by the 1965 changes. Ireland was supposed to increase migration to the United States under these changes, but so were Eastern Europe and Africa.

All of these changes increased potential immigration to the United States to approximately 700,000 annually for three years and then 675,000. These figures did not include refugees, of whom nearly

100,000 were expected yearly. The amnesty enacted in 1986 took effect in the late 1980s and early 1990s, giving some 3 million persons the right to become resident aliens: it appeared as if the decade of the 1990s would be the highest in American history for immigration. INS reported over 1 million immigrants in 1989 and projections for some 10 million in the 1990s, not counting undocumented aliens.

The Immigration Act of 1990 was the result of compromise, but it had the potential to lead to substantial increases in immigration. Other issues still remained, however. If IRCA did not work efficiently, what of those undocumented immigrants who had entered after 1982? And what, too, of future refugees? Thousands of Southeast Asians were still fleeing their land, and thousands more waited in refugee camps. Moreover, conditions in Eastern Europe were unstable, with a potential for a refugee exodus. A decade ahead lay the Chinese occupation of Hong Kong and the potential there for a new refugee exodus. Thus it was safe to predict that Congress and the president would soon confront the task of drafting new immigration policy; indeed, the new law provided for future governmental reviews.

In Canada the immigration act in effect in the 1970s had originally been passed into law in 1952. It had been amended a number of times, and the immigration regulations that directed the day-to-day–operations immigration work were under constant review. But among public servants there was growing sentiment in favor of a major reformulation of Canadian policy and law. Indeed, the Canada that the 1952 act was designed to serve was no more; the social and economic assumptions that the legislation had been designed to complement were no longer relevant. In the twenty years since passage of the 1952 legislation, Canada had grown in population and international stature. The racial and ethnic priorities of those who wrote the legislation seemed embarrassingly out of step in a liberal democracy. Nor were Canadian immigration priorities still dominated by the need for unskilled agricultural labor. Canada was now among the most urban and industrial of Western states, and immigrants streamed into Canada's major cities. To compete in an ever more technological and service-oriented world marketplace, Canada required skilled and capital-productive immigration. New thinking on immigration was required.

In September 1973, the minister of manpower and immigration announced a high profile and comprehensive public review of Canadian immigration policy. But the effort hardly seemed justified by the final product. After almost a year and a half of public hearings, reviews of expert briefs, and wide discussion of immigration procedures and statistics, the review commission issued its four-volume Report of the Canadian Immigration and Population Study.[76] Offered more as a discussion paper than as a blueprint for the future, the Green Paper on Immigration, as the report was commonly known, did not recommend nearly so radical a departure from existing immigration philosophy or procedures as many had hoped. It reaffirmed the need for a hand-in-glove relationship between immigration and labor supply. "One touchstone . . . for judging the success of immigration policy," the Green Paper held, "is how well it responds to the needs, present and future, of Canada's labor market." But unlike the earlier White Paper, the 1973 document was bullish on the need for population increase through immigration. Pointing to the declining national fertility rate and an already low mortality rate, the Green Paper foreshadowed a time in which the resources of those generating wealth would be far outstripped by those requiring support. Whatever the short-term benefit of short-term immigration pump priming, the long-term necessity of immigration as a balance to offset an aging Canadian population would become paramount. The Green Paper posited that "the number of immigrants Canada admits may progressively become, not only the main determinant of eventual population size, but also the chief factor responsible for the pace at which growth occurs."[77]

The timing of the public debate on the Green Paper was unfortunate. It took place in the shadow of yet another economic recession. With unemployment rising, any increase in immigration numbers was a hard sell. The discussion of long-term Canadian demographic needs was drowned out by a heated debate over immediate employment problems and charges that immigrants took away jobs from "real" Canadians. The debate also encouraged racists, hovering at the margins of respectable social discourse, to vent their hostility against the growing proportion of third world immigrants entering Canada. Indeed, following the removal of racial criteria from immigration selection and the opening of immigration offices in areas of nontraditional Canadian immigration, the admission of persons of color, visible minorities from the third world, increased quickly. In 1967, shortly after Canadian immigration operations were upgraded in Asia and the Caribbean, fewer than 15 percent of immigrants to Canada were black or Asian. By 1975, as the Green Paper debate raged, the percentage of visible minorities among Canadian immigrants had more than doubled. By 1985, the arrival of non-Europeans topped 60 percent.[78] To its credit, the larger Canadian civic culture rejected appeals to racism. Undeniably, of course, anxiety about the changing ethnographic face of Canada, especially urban Canada, exists. Canada also has a long way to go before systemic racism is eliminated. But there is virtually no credible support for turning back the immigrant clock to an earlier era of racial and ethnic selectivity.

In 1976, however, even as echoes of the Green Paper discussion could still be heard, the government pushed its own immigration agenda, which included an updating of immigration law. The resulting Immigration Act of 1976 represented an important step in the history of Canadian immigration. Never before had an immigration act specifically delineated national responsibility for the immigrant as well as for the receiving society. The preamble to the new act pledged the government's continuing commitment to family reunification and, for the first time, affirmed Canada's international obligations to ease the distress of refugees, the displaced, and the persecuted.

Also for the first time, the act implemented a modified form of quota system. Each year the federal government, in consultation with the provinces, was to set a target for the number of immigrants Canada would accept the coming year. The number was to be more of a guide than an exact promise of what was to be. Depending on prevailing conditions at home and abroad, the final number might be above or below the target. It was hoped, however, that a target figure, including that for refugees, would allow federal and provincial authorities to allocate their respective resources in a rational way. In 1980, at the height of the "boat people" crisis, slightly more than 28 percent of all immigrants admitted to Canada were refugees. During the next ten years, the percentage hovered between 14 and 20 percent.[79]

In spite of the progressive tone in the preamble to the new immigration legislation and the important breakthrough in the area of refugees, the act promised more of the same when it came to family reunification and economic issues. Certainly, much of the underlying policy was familiar. Those family members eligible for reunification with kin in Canada, aside from spouses or dependent children under ten, still had to assure government personnel that their education, employment records, or skills were an immediate asset to Canada. A new class of immigrant was created: the entrepreneurial class. Individuals who proved to have sufficient capital to invest in an enterprise that would generate new employment and wealth were welcome to apply for Canadian immigration. Since the new legislation came into effect, entrepreneurial or business immigrants jumped from fewer than one percent to greater than six percent of immigrants entering Canada.[80] Of these, the most prominent group of entrepreneurial class immigrants to Canada have come from Hong Kong. With the impending Chinese takeover of Hong Kong in 1997, many Hong

Kong businessmen began hedging their bets on the future by placing capital in more secure investments abroad. Canada became a favorite destination for capital in flight. But for some, the chance to transfer both capital and citizenship was also a priority. As a result, the late 1980s witnessed a significant influx of well-off Hong Kong Chinese into Canada, particularly into Vancouver and Toronto.[81]

For independent immigrants not blessed with a minimum of $250,000 to invest in Canada, the going got rough. Under immigration regulations, those with more modest resources and no family or sponsors were increasingly out of luck unless they had jobs waiting for them. This requirement is not easy. Before offering employment to a would-be immigrant, a prospective employer must satisfy immigration officials that there is no satisfactory candidate in Canada able to take the job.

In the 1990s public attention has remained fixed on the high-profile issues of refugees, the concentration of visible minority immigrants in Canadian cities, and the social and economic impact of entrepreneurial immigrants, accused by some of buying their way into Canada. Obviously, each of these issues has racial overtones. Although some visible minority group members might disagree, public discussion has not yet turned into a referendum on white Canada's tolerance of nonwhites. While many Canadians may have concerns for the future of their country, to date the civility of the Canadian polity remains intact. One cannot deny, however, that the profile of race and race-dominated issues has risen on the public agenda.

As the government monitors the public mood, some policy planners are focusing on the future. Mindful of the racially pregnant issues that hold the public eye, they look elsewhere. In so doing they are turning more and more to an examination of the demographic and economic issues raised by a falling national birthrate and the need for immigrants to meet Canada's expected population shortfall. How these issues will be resolved, if they can be resolved, remains to be seen. It is safe to assume, however, that immigration and its social and economic fallout will not soon recede from government priority or public consciousness.[82]

In sum, after several decades of tight restriction, both the United States and Canada liberalized immigration policies following the end of World War II. In so doing, they increased the numbers they admitted, as compared with the lean years of the 1930s and the war; in recent years they have modified their policies to include third world newcomers. Growing racial and ethnic toleration, economic forces, lobbying, and international factors all played roles in shaping the ways in which these two North American countries developed policies. Issues of race, domestic affairs, economic shifts, and foreign policy are likely to influence the development of both American and Canadian immigration policy in years to come.

Yet differences between the two also play a key role in policy outcomes. Immediate economic self-interest proved more important in determining Canadian policy than it did for U.S. policy. On the other hand, foreign policy issues were more closely tied to immigration policy in America than in Canada. For Americans, faced with a 1900-mile border with Mexico, the issues of undocumented immigration and temporary workers were especially important. Canadians were more concerned with their larger neighbor to the south and with the aspirations of French-speaking Quebec.

Finally, the differing immigration traditions of the two countries created differing impacts on policy. Canada has a different governmental structure from America's and a stronger tradition of immigrant recruitment. As a result the two nations have modified their post-1945 immigration laws and policies in distinct ways.

What of the future of immigration to these two North American countries? Obviously it is difficult, if not impossible, to predict the outcome of the current immigration debates. With immigration one can only expect the unexpected. In the past, public officials developed a system that did not follow predictions. Pressures to emigrate to these two nations have shifted since 1945. Finally, the uncertainty of world events makes any predictions risky and even foolhardy. But regardless of the outcome of discussions about immigration, many of the factors that influenced policies in the United States and Canada between 1945 and 1990 will continue to do so in the near future.

3

Response to Crisis—
Refugee Policy in
the United States and Canada

Aristide R. Zolberg
With the Assistance of Ursula Levelt

Throughout the West, refugee policy has become a subject of contention between "humanitarians" and "realists." The issues that divide
them encompass domestic law enforcement, the organization of economic life, and the conduct of foreign affairs; ultimately they reach
into the very basic question of what obligations the members of
affluent national communities have toward strangers in dire need
abroad, or knocking at their door. This contention is a recent development, resulting from a growing discrepancy between the mechanisms
established for dealing with refugees in the wake of World War II and
elaborated in the era of the cold war, and the challenges of a changing
world situation.

    After World War II, in the light of the tragic consequences of their
failure to provide havens for victims of persecution in preceding
years, the Western democracies moved toward formal recognition of
"refugees" as a distinct category of international migrants to whom
they owed special obligations. Under conditions of universally restricted immigration, refugee status entails precious privileges and
entitlements—a claim to protection and assistance from international
organizations, a temporary haven in some other country, and sometimes permanent resettlement. In the formation of an international
regimen, refugees were limited to victims of "persecution," a process
deeply rooted in Western political experience. The designation was to
be based on objective qualifications, to distinguish refugees from
ordinary migrants. Albeit reluctant to adhere to international com-
pacts that limited their freedom of action in the sphere of immigration,
the United States and Canada developed refugee policies of their
own, and emerged as the leading resettlement countries for Euro-

peans uprooted by World War II, as well as subsequently for those who fled Communist regimes.

Both countries still take in large numbers of people for resettlement. In recent years, however, many questions have been raised about the appropriateness of the criteria they use for selecting those invited to move to the head of the lengthening line of applicants for admission as refugees. In addition, in the past decade and a half the United States and Canada, as well as the other Western democracies, have been confronted with a massive influx of uninvited asylum seekers, mostly from poor, developing countries; some come as legal visitors, others as illegals. This influx precipitated a reappraisal of the adequacy of established mechanisms for determining the validity of asylum claims; but the considerations raised broadened into a more fundamental debate over the appropriate balance between a democracy's obligation on the one hand to protect its borders against intruders and its obligations on the other hand toward unfortunate foreigners. Quite unexpectedly, in the late 1980s a third major challenge arose from the collapse of European Communist regimes and the consequent liberalization of their emigration policies. The new situation has the makings of a proverbial catch-22: So long as the citizens of the Communist countries could not leave, they were generously admitted by the United States and Canada as refugees; now that they can leave, they must take their place at the very end of a lengthening queue. What is to be done?

The Development of Refugee Policy, 1945–1980

The European Refugee Crisis and the U.S. Response. By virtue of its newly achieved hegemonic position, at the end of World War II the United States was faced with a major responsibility for the relief and resettlement of European refugees who could not or would not return to their countries of origin.[1] Its response involved on the one hand the construction of an international refugee regime, culminating in the creation of the United Nations High Commissioner for Refugees (UNHCR), and on the other hand a substantial loosening of immigration restrictions. The statute and convention governing the UNHCR initially pertained only to European victims of events that occurred before 1951. In contrast with prewar efforts that focused on particular groups, however, the regime contained elements of a more universalistic approach, in that the organization's mandate extended to any individual who had experienced "persecution," as determined by a specialized staff of "eligibility officers." Yet throughout the 1950s, the United States itself shunned the convention and was generally unsupportive of the international refugee organizations it helped create.[2] The principal reason was the opposition of congressional states-rights advocates to any treaty that might constitute a source of federal authority to interfere with segregation. The increase in admissions occurred partly as a response to constituency pressures from "new" immigrants, but mostly at the initiative of the executive branch, as a weapon in the cold war.[3]

The main problem was to find ways of getting around the prescribed annual maximum of 150,000 and the National Origins Quota system, designed to minimize the new immigration, including that of the Central and Eastern Europeans who constituted a large percentage of postwar refugees. The first breach in the wall was made in December 1945 when, under pressure from the Jewish community, President Truman ordered unused quotas to be opened up for persons under the jurisdiction of the U.S.-sponsored United Nations Relief and Rehabilitation Agency, with some preference for Jewish survivors. Meanwhile, the occupation authorities urged resettlement for the millions of additional displaced persons who flooded into the American occupation zone and constituted an obstacle to reconstruction. Later, in the face of another huge outpouring in anticipation of a closing of the gates in Eastern Europe, even restrictionists urged resettlement as an "ideological weapon in our ideological war against the forces of darkness, the forces of Communist tyranny."[4] The outcome was the Displaced Persons Act of 1948, signed the very month the Berlin blockade began.

Conscious of the tragic consequences of interwar restrictionism, throughout the postwar period immigration reformers sought to establish a guaranteed number of entries to which refugees would have first claim. Proposals to this effect hovered at around 20 percent of an annual immigration quota that might be enlarged to 300,000 worldwide—amounting to some 60,000 refugee entries a year. Their proposals remained blocked in Congress, however, along with proposals for immigration reform more generally, by virtue of the prevailing seniority system that ensured conservative control of the appropriate committees, regardless of which party controlled the Congress. Since the restrictionist Immigration and Naturalization Act of 1952 (INA) made no provision for refugees as a general category, refugee policy continued to be carried out by way of ad hoc measures, justified on foreign policy grounds. The Refugee Relief Act of 1953, which provided for the admission over the next three years of 209,000 persons who could not be accommodated under the low quotas for their respective countries, was bluntly identified in a National Security Council memorandum as a device to "encourage defection of all USSR nations and 'key' personnel from the satellite countries" in order to "inflict a psychological blow on communism" and, "though less important, . . . material loss to the Soviet Union," as the emigration entailed a brain drain of professionals.[5]

In 1956 the United States seized upon Khrushchev's hint of greater freedom for the satellites, and it encouraged an uprising in Hungary. The Soviet tanks rolled in on November 4, however, triggering the exodus of a few thousand freedom-fighters as well as many others who took advantage of the temporarily open border. Some 200,000 altogether managed to get out. Resettlement was rapidly organized by the International Committee on European Migrations and the UNHCR, with the United States and Canada each taking about 20 percent of the total, and nearly every one of the Western nations receiving a share of the remainder. As too few visas were available under the existing refugee act, the Eisenhower administration resorted to an obscure provision of the INA that gave the attorney general discretionary authority to parole any alien into the United States for reasons of emergency or if it were "deemed strictly in the public interest." Albeit intended to deal with medical emergencies or judicial proceedings, parole came to be used repeatedly from then on to admit persons from Communist countries. This development shifted control of refugee policy from the Congress toward the president, in keeping with the postwar trend respecting external affairs more generally.

Upon expiration of the 1953 law, the Refugee-Escapee Act of 1957 made additional room for existing applicants from the same groups, but also included a more general provision for admitting as refugees in the future "persons fleeing persecution in Communist countries or countries in the Middle East." In 1960, the United States adopted a "Fair Share Act," whereby it undertook to admit, under the attorney general's parole authority, refugees remaining in European camps in the proportion of one for every four resettled by other nations; by the nature of things, this policy again exclusively involved people originating in Communist countries.

The dominance of foreign policy considerations in the admission of refugees evoked little concern at the time, not only because of the cold war consensus, but because it was congruent with the dictates of a "humanitarian" perspective. Given the elimination of right-wing dictatorships from all of Europe excepting Spain and Portugal, severe political oppression was encountered almost exclusively in the Soviet Union and its satellites. The immigration impact of the policy was limited, because tight restrictions on exit made for few defectors except for Germans (before the Berlin Wall), most of whom were absorbed by the Federal Republic. Similarly, defectors from the People's Republic of China went mostly to Hong Kong.

At the time of the collapse of the Batista regime, Washington opened the door to Cubans by way of a "passive admissions policy," rendered possible by the absence of numerical limitations on Western Hemisphere immigration. Some 200,000 landed between January 1959 and the end of 1962, when the missile crisis prompted Cuba to close its border. The Cubans were initially regarded as temporary exiles who would return when the Castro regime fell or was overthrown, an objective on whose behalf they enlisted into the Bay of Pigs operation. In retrospect the Cuban case can be seen as a major turning point—for the first time the policy of encouraging defection entailed providing first asylum for non-Europeans in the United States itself. The case illustrates not only the prominence of foreign policy considerations in the making of refugee policy, but also the key role of refugee policy in the formation of refugee flows: "If Castro's policies created the potential for mass exodus, U.S. policies made the exodus possible."[6] After the Bay of Pigs the United States envisaged the exiles' permanent settlement, and in 1962 it devised a Migration and Refugee Assistance Act that alleviated the costs incurred by localities.

The Dawn of Reform. In 1965, the reformers finally succeeded in changing the immigration system. Under the "Kennedy-Johnson" amendments to the INA, part of the annual quota for the Eastern Hemisphere (Europe, Asia-Pacific, and Africa) was reserved for refugees as a statutory category (seventh preference). They were granted a mere 6 percent of entries, however, amounting to 10,200 annually. The preference system was not applicable to the Western Hemisphere (Canada, Latin America, and the Caribbean), which was also subject for the first time to an annual limit on admissions. Now that a quota had been set aside, parole authority was to be used only for urgent individual cases as provided for under the INA. Despite the efforts of liberal internationalists who sought to adopt the UN definition, refugees were still defined exclusively as people fleeing Communist countries or originating in the Middle East.

Even as the new law was being completed, the United States harnessed its refugee policy to the pursuit of economic warfare against Cuba. The boycott and sanctions that isolated Cuba from 1962 on fostered severe economic difficulties, and these in turn brought about a rapid deterioration in the material and political positions of the middle strata of Cuban society. At the end of September 1965, President Fidel Castro declared that all who wished to leave Cuba were free to do so. The change of policy may have been prompted by a desire to rid Cuba of the discontented and to redistribute the emigrants' housing. A few days later, on the occasion of signing the newly enacted immigration law at the foot of the Statue of Liberty, President Johnson responded that "those who seek refuge here will find it." In flagrant violation of the legislative intent of the new act, he indicated that he would use his authority to parole massively those seeking family reunion and others languishing in Cuban prisons.

Following a short-lived boatlift, Cuba and the United States negotiated a program of orderly departures by way of "freedom flights." Over the next seven years the program brought an estimated 270,000 Cubans to the United States, excluding draft-age men and political prisoners, but including many professionals and skilled workers, characterized by an expert congressional witness as "consumer refugees."[7] Although the operation was a great success from a foreign policy perspective, opposition began to surface in Congress around 1970, on the grounds that the influx was adding to U.S. welfare rolls. In any case, in April 1973 Cuba once again closed its borders, possibly because the program fostered a costly brain drain.

Although in 1967 the United States finally adhered to the United Nations Convention and Protocol, its admission policy remained grounded in foreign policy and constituency considerations. Most notoriously, during this period the Nixon administration adamantly refused to cooperate wth the UNHCR in resettling Chileans persecuted by the Pinochet regime it helped bring to power in 1973. A few hundred were belatedly paroled into the country by President Ford's attorney general, and an additional number by the Carter administration. Altogether, however, out of some 20,000 Chileans resettled by the International Committee on Migration, only 1,100 were taken in by the United States.

Meanwhile, persons originating in Communist countries continued to receive a generous welcome. The Soviet Union still adhered to its highly restrictive exit policy, although in the 1960s voices arose within the Kremlin to rid the country of the politically disaffected and of the Jews. But there was lingering concern that this might occasion a brain drain, that letting out Jews would invite pressure from Germans and Armenians for exit visas as well, and that a liberal emigration policy for minorities more generally would anger ordinary Russians.[8] The situation of Soviet Jews was somewhat paradoxical. As a group they had successfully availed themselves of occupational opportunities to achieve well above average standing in the occupational structure. But in addition to the harsh conditions faced by Soviet citizens generally, Jews were subjected to discrimination, and their cultural life was severely restricted. In the latter part of the decade, they initiated a public campaign for exit visas, which evoked considerable external support in the United States and in Western Europe, including from Communist parties. Eager to conclude Salt II and to broaden trade, in the spring of 1971 the Soviet Union responded by granting thousands of exit visas, and it expanded the program at the end of the year. This was rationalized on the basis of Soviet nationality policy, whereby each group is identified with a homeland; as the territory-less oddity, Jews were allowed to leave for their designated "homeland" abroad, Israel. In fact, most Soviet Jews aspired to go to the United States; but it was understood by all concerned that the homeland fiction must be maintained. The Soviets probably welcomed the choice, because a large flow to Israel would evoke objections from their Arab allies. From the outset the Nixon administration extended parole to all who wanted to come to the United States and provided the administrative wherewithal to facilitate their movement.

In 1972, however, the Soviets began requiring highly educated emigrants to pay a considerable sum to compensate the state for the costs of their training; this ruling was obviously directed against the Jews. The measure prompted legislative action in Congress to make trade concessions conditional on the liberalization of emigration policy. Despite their reluctance to allow human rights issues to intrude on détente, President Nixon and Secretary of State Kissinger bowed to congressional pressure. The Soviet Union reacted by temporarily suspending the collection of the education tax and allowing emigration to rise to unprecedented levels; but its policy changed again in the wake of the Yom Kippur War. The American linkage between human rights and trade concessions was then formalized by enactment of the Jackson-Vanek Amendment to the Trade Act of 1974, whereby most-favored nation treatment may not be granted to any "nonmarket economy country" that limits the rights of its nationals to emigrate. For most of the remainder of the decade, Jewish emigration fluctuated widely as a function of the general state of relations between the superpowers and the short-term economic interests of the Soviet Union; after peaking in 1979, when about 50,000 Soviet Jews were admitted to the United States, emigration ground to a halt. A similar pattern prevailed with respect to Soviet citizens of German descent, whose exit was linked to trade negotiations with the Federal Republic of Germany.

The next major wave originated in Vietnam. In the face of the impending Communist victory in early 1975, the United States undertook to relocate its political and military associates as well as their families. Over 200,000 left within the first year, of whom some 123,000 were admitted to the United States for permanent resettlement. Since they were fleeing from communism, they were eligible for conditional entry under the seventh preference; because the numbers vastly exceeded entries provided for, however, most were admitted instead under the president's parole authority. Concurrently, the United States provided support for first asylum countries in the region as well. By 1977 the outflow subsided considerably and became more manageable.

In this period Congress was taking advantage of Watergate and its sequels to reassert congressional authority over the making of foreign policy. Concurrently, after a decade of passive resistance on the part of the traditional restrictionists, the coming to power of an administration sensitive to human rights and the assumption by Senator Edward Kennedy of the chairmanship of the Judiciary Committee opened the possibility of a comprehensive recasting of the statutory apparatus of immigration and refugee affairs, still governed by the framework devised in 1952. To this effect, in late 1978 Congress created a select commission, scheduled to present recommendations in 1980. With regard to refugees, the major goals were to provide for a more realistic number of admissions, to allocate them in accordance with international norms, and to reduce executive discretion in the use of parole.[9]

Just as SCIRP got underway, however, a refugee flood of unprecedented proportions was generated in Southeast Asia. Many were ethnic Chinese who, as in most of Southeast Asia, constituted a wide-flung trading diaspora whose activities were deemed incompatible with the imperatives of a command economy. As was reported by a special refugee advisory panel to the secretary of state, many "fled primarily because of the economic or social conditions prevailing in their country of origin" rather than because of persecution.[10] The crisis was exacerbated by allegations that the Vietnamese authorities were conniving to secure profit by shipping people out, in collusion with capitalist entrepreneurs from neighboring countries; and especially, in late 1978, by the refusal of the first asylum countries in Southeast Asia to allow further entries. The crisis was dramatized by the plight of the "boat people." The administration responded once again by stepping up admissions under the attorney general's parole authority. Arrivals from Southeast Asia increased from 7,000 in fiscal year 1977 to 20,574 in 1978, 76,521 in 1979, and an all-time yearly high of 163,797 in 1980. Concurrently, the United States played a major role in the Geneva Conference (1979), which sought to alleviate the crisis of first asylum by organizing resettlement on a multilateral basis.

The crisis prompted the enactment of a new refugee law without awaiting completion of the select commission's work. The Refugee Act of 1980 established a normal baseline of 50,000 entries a year, approximately three times the previous level.[11] Parole authority was henceforth to be used only for individual cases, but the president was given authority to admit a higher number in a given year if justified on the basis of humanitarian concerns or the national interest. The level and allocation among various groups was to be determined in consultation with Congress. Thus, to accommodate the second Vietnamese wave, in May 1980 President Carter obtained congressional agreement for 234,000 admissions. In keeping with the longstanding aspirations of the reformers, the law incorporated the UNHCR Convention definition of refugees—namely, people outside their country and deprived of its protection, "who have been persecuted or have a well-founded fear of persecution based on race, religion, nationality, social class, or political opinion," and who are not firmly resettled elsewhere. Although the Senate version included also persons displaced by military or civil disturbance, the provision was eliminated in conference. This episode was subsequently invoked as evidence that Congress did not intend to include those fleeing civil war.

Still in effect today, the law provides for two types of procedures for the determination of refugee status. The first is the overseas admission process, whereby aliens apply and are processed outside the United States, at specially designated locations. With estimates of eligible people worldwide then around 8 million, the bulk of whom were in first-asylum countries awaiting resettlement, and many wishing to come to the United States, some mechanism was needed for selecting those to be invited. The criterion proposed by the administration was whether the refugees were of "special concern" to the United States. As set forth by the new coordinator for refugee affairs in his testimony, this referred to people with cultural, historical, or family ties with the United States; persons whose lives were in danger, who had no other place to go; and others toward whom the United States had a "special responsibility" as a consequence of previous involvement, as in the case of Southeast Asians. Worried that "of special concern" might entail a step back to the discriminatory National Origins Quotas system, organizations such as the American Civil Liberties Union and Amnesty International urged the adoption of a more universalistic criterion. In response to this pressure, the House changed the language to "of special *humanitarian* concern to the United States" (italics mine), as to indicate "that the plight of the refugees themselves as opposed to national origins or political considerations should be paramount." This wording prevailed, and the legislative intent it represented was further emphasized by a reference to the criterion of "urgent need" in the "purposes" section of the final act.[12]

In practice, however, the criteria for overseas admission remained essentially unchanged. In the period encompassing fiscal years 1981 to 1984, the United States admitted 374,495 refugees from overseas, an average of over 90,000 a year rather than the 50,000 anticipated; and as in the past, over 90 percent of them originated in Communist countries.[13] This proportion resulted not for lack of candidates for resettlement or asylum from non-Communist countries, including several on America's own doorstep.

The 1980 law also established for the first time, in keeping with international law and the established practices of other liberal states, a statutory process whereby any alien physically present in the country—irrespective of immigration status—could claim asylum on the grounds of meeting the criteria used to define refugees.[14] This provision was considered but a minor matter; there had been so few asylum applicants that the INS did not develop formal operating procedures until 1972; and as recently as 1979, asylum seekers amounted only to about 3,000, originating mostly in Warsaw Pact countries. Successful claims were to be charged against the annual refugee quota; although no upper limit was established, the lawmakers anticipated that asylum seekers would take up no more than 5,000 of the 50,000. Asylum subsequently emerged, however, as one of the most perplexing and controversial aspects of refugee policy.

Beyond this, the lawmakers altogether omitted from consideration aliens already in the United States who did not clearly meet the Convention definition, but who would have reason to fear returning to their countries. These cases were dealt with by way of Extended Voluntary Departure (EVD).[15] Developed by the INS in the 1960s, EVD is a discretionary device controlled by the executive branch, subject neither to judicial review nor to consultation with Congress. It may be put into effect when the State Department determines that conditions in a given country make it dangerous for its nationals in the United States to return. At various times it has been granted on a group basis to Afghans, Cubans, Czechoslovakians, Chileans, Ethiopians, Hungarians, Iranians, Nicaraguans, Poles, Romanians, and Ugandans; on an individual basis it has been granted to Lebanese.

Finally, the law also sought to regularize the allocation of federal aid to public (state and local) and private agencies involved in resettlement. The initial proposal was for two years, a slight reduction from the period provided for under the latest ad hoc measure on behalf of refugees from Southeast Asia. In the final version, however, it was raised to three years.

The Canadian Variant. By and large, postwar developments in Canada paralleled those in the United States, as is indicated by the titles or subtitles of leading works on the development of its refugee policy: "None Is Too Many," referring to the answer of an immigration official to the question of how many Jewish survivors might be admitted; "Indifference or Opportunism?"; and "Double Standard," referring to the importance of security concerns and the generosity accorded Communist "defectors" as against victims of right-wing regimes.[16] By 1951 Canada received over 120,000 European displaced persons, with priority given to agricultural workers who met its immigration preferences, and lingering discrimination against Jewish survivors; Hungarians were welcomed in 1956, as were Czechoslovakians in 1968, but Chinese were not. Despite the favorable disposition of the Department of External Affairs, the immigration bureaucracy (housed within the Ministry of Employment rather than Justice) objected to the UN-HCR Convention because agreement to an international instrument would restrict the government's right to deport putative refugees on security grounds; hence Canada signed the agreement only in 1969, after the coming to power of the reformist Trudeau government. As related by Troper and Reimers in chapter 2, this government also undertook a major reform of the immigration system: racial and ethnic discrimination was largely eliminated, and more attention was given to manpower planning. In the Canadian as opposed to contemporaneous U.S. reforms, however, no admissions were reserved for refugees. Refugee policy continued to be formulated on an ad hoc basis, largely at the federal cabinet's discretion.

This policy pertained almost entirely to overseas admissions; like the United States, Canada occasionally granted permanent residence on humanitarian grounds to persons already in the country, but it lacked a proper asylum policy. The 1967 reforms (Section 34 of the Immigration Regulations), however, permitted visitors to apply for permanent residence ("landed immigrant status") from within Canada and gave anyone who had been ordered deported the right to appeal to a newly created Immigration Appeals Board (IAB), which might grant them permanent residence on compassionate or humanitarian grounds.

Generally speaking, the Trudeau government welcomed opportunities for "helpful, international action, dear to the hearts of many if not all Canadian liberals."[17] This disposition, however, was modulated by considerations of foreign policy and was exercised selectively with regard to the social characteristics of the refugees. Following the Soviet invasion of Czechoslovakia in August 1968, the government considered applications for immigration visas under the relaxed standards traditionally offered to refugees from Warsaw Pact countries, and it actively recruited the most qualified, to whom it offered generous assistance. Eventually some 11,000 were accepted for resettlement.

In August 1972, the British government requested help in relocating Asian Ugandans expelled by Idi Amin. Despite significant unemployment and the possibility of adverse public reactions to the admission of a large number of Asians, the government took the opportunity to confirm Canada's rejection of racial discrimination, and for the first time it provided a haven for non-European refugees. A total of 7,069 were admitted, once again generally well-educated and highly skilled, or having some working capital. To deal with the influx the government organized mixed ad hoc assistance committees in the major cities, composed of officials and volunteers. This innovation was subsequently institutionalized as a significant element of refugee policy.

The Chilean crisis a year later evoked a more diffident reaction. At the time of the coup, some fifty persons took refuge in the Canadian embassy in Santiago, mainly professionals and academics with their families. Although the Canadian government was urged by UNHCR and a variety of internal groups to open its doors immediately, the government was nervous about admitting a critical mass of left-wing intellectuals and possibly antagonizing the United States. Hence they proceeded cautiously and ordered full security screening, which delayed the process. Nevertheless, Canada ultimately admitted 6,990 Chileans, approximately five times the U.S. number.

From 1968 on Canada also became a haven for American war-resisters and deserters. This decision was in keeping with the Trudeau government's critical stance toward U.S. policy in Vietnam. The issue of granting political asylum to U.S. citizens, which would have created serious diplomatic tensions, was avoided because most of them arrived legally as tourists, exempt from visa requirements, and subsequently could obtain permanent residence by way of section 34. In 1970, 45,000 visitors availed themselves of this opportunity, among them a significant number of American self-exiles.

More generally, section 34 was coming to be appreciated far and wide as a loophole for getting around Canada's selective immigration policy.[18] In 1970 the number who obtained permanent residence in this manner amounted to an extra 20 percent of immigration. Applications rose rapidly, reaching 8,700 in October 1972—a rate of over 100,000 a year—and creating a huge backlog. In the face of this circumstance, the government revoked section 34 and required all visitors staying for more than three months to register and obtain employment visas if they wished to work. But ever more suspected "non-bona fide visitors" showed up at the airports, and appeals against deportation orders piled up at the rate of almost 1,000 a month, while the IAB could handle only about 100. Hence in the fall of 1973 the government undertook to recast its immigration and refugee policy. Meanwhile the authorities established a sixty-day period during which de facto residents could regularize their status. Of the 25,593 people who did so, the two largest groups originated in the United States and Hong Kong. Another 26,000 were regularized under other programs.

Despite Canada's uninvolvement in the war, after the fall of Saigon in 1975 the government announced that Vietnamese and Cambodian students or visitors could apply for permanent residence and could sponsor relatives still at home or in refugee camps, under relaxed criteria. Later it committed itself to admitting 3,000 refugees without relatives in Canada. Additional numbers were brought in subsequently, including "boat people," for a total of 14,060 as of June 1979. Between 1976 and 1979 Canada also relaxed immigration requirements for 11,010 Lebanese.

A new immigration law was enacted in 1976. Together with regulations issued in 1978, it provided recognition for the first time of refugees as a separate admissible class, selected according to distinctive criteria.[19] The Canadian system differs from the current American one in that refugees are located within the immigration framework, as was the case in the United States from 1965 to 1980; but like its American counterpart, it distinguishes between the admission of refugees from abroad and the attribution of asylum to people already in the country. Those eligible abroad include not only "Convention" refugees, but also "designated class" persons, those who do not qualify under the Convention but who are deemed worthy of special consideration. The minister must prepare an annual refugee plan covering all Convention and designated-class refugees whose resettlement costs are underwritten by the federal government, in consultation with the voluntary sector. The initial level for 1979 was established at 10,000, including 5,000 Southeast Asians, 2,300 Eastern Europeans, 500 Latin Americans, 200 Convention refugees from other parts of the world, and a contingency reserve of 2,000. A distinctive feature is the provision for the admission of some additional thousands on the basis of private sponsorship by any group that undertakes to assist the refugees for a period of one year. The groups must consist of a minimum of five citizens or permanent residents, including relatives, voluntary associations, and even corporations.

Persons already in the country who meet the Convention criteria are granted asylum by way of "inland refugee determination." Beyond this, however, the 1976 act also provided for the possibility of a "special-measures landing program" for persons who do not meet the Convention definition, but who are unwilling to return to their country of origin due to war or severe political instability. Eligibility is based on a "B-1 list" of countries established by the federal government. Temporary safe haven is thus a matter of executive discretion, as in the American EVD.[20]

Much of the debate in the course of enactment focused on asylum: the immigration bureaucracy objected that too liberal a procedure would impede effective administration of immigration policy, whereas the refugee-advocacy network generally criticized the proposed provisions for being overly legalistic and narrow, and leaving applicants to be judged for suitability by the criteria applied to regular immigrants.[21] They insisted that applicants should be accorded the benefit of the doubt when uncertainty existed about the evidence of persecution, and given the right to appear in person at the relevant hearings; but immigration officials asserted that this procedure would lead to inordinate backlogs and would encourage baseless claims.

The second Southeast Asian refugee crisis erupted even as the system came into effect. As empowered under the new law, in December 1978 the government established an "Indochinese Designated Class" and subsequently attended the July 1979 Geneva conference with a commitment to admit 42,000 refugees above the 8,000 already provided for in the 1980 plan, on the basis of a matching formula of one federally-assisted refugee for every refugee sponsored by the voluntary sector. This approach evoked such an enthusiastic response that the numbers initially allotted to the private sector were quickly oversubscribed and the government subsequently increased admissions by another 10,000. Altogether, some 60,000 Southeast Asians were settled over a period of eighteen months, of whom 26,000 were government-assisted and 34,000 privately sponsored.[22]

Root Causes of the Asylum Crisis of the 1980s

In the 1970s Canada and the United States converged toward similar refugee policies.[23] Both were founded on the implicit assumption that the major task was to select from within a fairly stable pool of refugees a limited number for resettlement in North America, on the basis of somewhat different combinations of interest and obligation. Developments in the world at large quickly negated the several components of this assumption, however, and undermined the policies that rested on it. These developments precipitated in both countries efforts to recast refugee policy in keeping with the changes. The impact of the developments in question was very different in the two cases, and the responses were shaped also by distinct features of the general political situation in each of the two countries. Hence, by the end of the 1980s the accent was on divergence rather than convergence.

The challenges arise from two somewhat distinct problems, which have combined to produce a worldwide crisis: on the one hand an escalation in the production of refugees in the developing countries, and on the other hand a sharp increase in immigration pressure on the world's affluent states.

From the mid-1970s onward, massive new flows of refugees were generated in various regions of Asia, Africa, Latin America, and the Caribbean. The number of people outside their country of origin and not resettled increased at this time from a previous range of between 5 and 10 million to a higher one of between 10 and 15, and the same upheavals also produced an even larger mass of internally displaced.[24] These refugees arose mostly as a byproduct of two major historical processes: the formation of new states in ethnically heterogeneous territories, where cultural differences are compounded by economic and political inequality; and confrontations over the social order in countries where grave inequalities persist and are maintained by authoritarian regimes. These two processes combined often to generate complex and violent conflicts—separatism and communal confrontations, revolutionary challenges and preemptive counter-revolutions. In contrast with the European experience earlier in the century, relatively few people in the developing world have been uprooted by international wars. But refugee-generating domestic conflicts are often exacerbated by the direct or indirect intervention of outside parties, a process that contributes to the extension of conflicts in time and space and thereby to an escalation of the violence. In large part these interventions are related to the interactions of the superpowers which, after achieving a precarious equilibrium in the early 1960s by way of mutually assured destruction, subsequently engaged in confrontations throughout the periphery.[25]

As was the case with their European predecessors in the wake of the two world wars, most of today's refugees are victims of generalized violence rather than of persecution properly speaking. Conflicts of any kind are more violent today than ever before because both governments and their opponents have access to extensive firepower in all its forms. Violence is more likely to generate refugees because even very poor peasants are today much better able to move in the face of violence than were their forebears. How many of them are driven out of their country and where they go are largely a function of location in relation to international borders, of existing migratory networks, and of the disposition of relevant neighbors or receivers further afield.

The political upheavals that occasioned the crisis concurred with economic hard times in many of the regions affected. Mutual causal connections link the two phenomena: stagnant or shrinking economies, or growing ones that are very unevenly distributed in relation to regions and social strata, contribute to social and political conflicts; and the outbreak of violence in poor agricultural countries usually occasions catastrophic economic consequences. In effect most refugees from the developing world today are driven by an inextricable mixture of economic and political factors.

Although during the postwar period there were considerable refugee movements in Asia and the Middle East, these movements were essentially contained within their regions of origin and dealt with by receivers with little or no assistance from the international community. The major exception was the exodus of Palestinians, which prompted the creation of the United Nations Work and Relief Agency. But the new waves imposed unprecedented burdens on the international community. Most landed in neighboring countries, themselves badly hit by the global economic downturn, where they appeared destined to linger on indefinitely in ragtag camps, unable to return to their country of origin or to find a permanent haven. With little opportunity to fend for themselves, the refugees constituted a mounting burden for the UNHCR, which itself depended on handouts from a limited number of governments and voluntary agencies, and especially for the hosts or potential hosts. Albeit initially isolated, by and by the refugee flows interpenetrated with the global migration system, and the crisis was thereby brought to the doorstep of the more developed countries.

The central dynamic of the migration system can be stated briefly: The dramatic inequality of economic and political conditions of a world more integrated than ever before steadily increases the disposition of ever larger masses of people to migrate from the less developed to the more developed countries. Every corner of the globe has been restructured by market forces, which have uprooted the last remnants of subsistence economies; concurrently, information about variation in the opportunities available in different locations is more widely available than ever before, and the relative cost of transporta-

70

tion is at its historical lowest. Consequently, a growing share of the world's growing population is propelled in search of work. Most move within their own country; but once the first step has been taken, many respond as a matter of course to the possibility of working abroad. Opportunities of one sort or another are available because of the perennial profitability of foreign labor.

Actual international migrations, however, fall far short of their potential because the countries to which people would like to go exercise a considerable degree of control over inward movement. In effect, it is the potential receivers that determine the size and characteristics of international migrations. Generally speaking, affluent countries with democratic political regimes seek to protect their internal labor market and to minimize culturally heterogeneous flows. They normally admit small numbers of immigrants in relation to existing population, selected on the basis of family ties or ethnic affinity and of specific objectives of labor procurement. It was against the background of prevailing restriction that exceptional arrangements arose to admit refugees; but the emphasis on persecution was explicitly designed to limit those who might qualify.

A period of unusual openness during the postwar boom decades contributed to fostering the aspirations of potential migrants in the world at large. In the face of the subsequent hard times of the early 1970s, most of the receivers reduced or eliminated labor-oriented immigration, leaving family reunion and refugee status as the major grounds for entry. Since all components of the global migration system are interconnected, the closing of some of the gates increased the pressure at the others. As we have seen, around the same time, under the prodding of concerned domestic groups, the United States and Canada responded to the incipient refugee crisis by reforming their admission and asylum procedures in accord with the UNHCR Convention and increasing their normal intake. Quickly broadcast among those awaiting resettlement, these developments precipitated the formation of long queues for inclusion in the annual quotas; under the prevailing definition, however, the claims of many of the developing world's refugees were often ambiguous.

Taking matters into their own hands, a number of the waiting refugees managed to get to one or the other receiving country, and pressed their claims at the gate or after entry. Concurrently, with fewer opportunities to be admitted as workers, more people from the developing world entered the rich countries illegally or overstayed their temporary workers' or visitors' visas. When faced with the threat of deportation, these people also sought to obtain special consideration as refugees. The combined effects of the narrowing of immigration opportunities and of the refugee crisis thus fostered what has been termed the "asylum strategy of immigration," producing a huge increase in applications for refugee status throughout Western Europe and North America, with a significant proportion of them questionable even under a broad interpretation.[26]

The processes in question are usually regionalized, determined not only by geographical proximity but also by political and economic linkages between countries of origin and of destination.[27] Accordingly, migratory pressures on Western Europe originate mainly in Asia and Africa, both north and south of the Sahara; those directed at the United States stem mainly from the Caribbean and Central America. But unlike any situation encountered in Europe, the United States received a massive flow of people from its adjoining region, mostly undocumented. This flow was driven by the violence and economic hardship characteristic of land-based dictatorships, and it was compounded by American activities in the region of origin. Canada is somewhat buffered by its greater remoteness from the developing world, as well as by its avoidance of involvement in international conflicts. Nevertheless, in the 1980s it too began to experience the consequences of efforts by both Europe and the United States to tighten their gates.

The Dilemma of Mass Asylum for the United States

The Mariel Turning Point. An unanticipated consequence of cold war refugee policy, the Mariel crisis prompted a fundamental reassessment of the American stance toward the unquestioned provisions of asylum and resettlement for citizens of Communist countries.[28] When President Fidel Castro interrupted the freedom flights in 1973, over 100,000 approved emigrants were left stranded; their expectations of departure soared in 1978, when for the first time the exiles were allowed to visit their home country. Early in 1980 the CIA predicted that Cuba might resort to large-scale emigration to reduce the discontent occasioned by deteriorating economic conditions, and Castro himself threatened to unleash a torrent of people; yet no preparations were undertaken for this eventuality.

Bogged down by the hostage crisis and a difficult electoral campaign, the Carter administration was taken by surprise when at the beginning of April some 10,000 Cubans invaded the Peruvian embassy and asked for political asylum. After some hesitation, Castro allowed an airlift, but shortly reversed himself. Then on April 19 he announced that everyone could leave, he opened up Mariel harbor, and he invited the exiles to retrieve their relatives. Taking matters into their own hands, the Cuban-Americans launched a massive boatlift.

Despite entreaties from the Carter administration, concerned that a large wave of arrivals would increase unemployment, the Cubans refused to stop. After presidential candidate Ronald Reagan seized upon the boatlift as a campaign issue, President Carter himself began to vacillate and was pressured by fellow Democrats to respond positively. Senator Edward Kennedy argued that the president should act under the terms of the new law, according to which his emergency powers were limited to the granting of temporary safe haven: but the White House leaned toward outright resettlement.

Accordingly, the INS began distributing to the new arrivals applications for asylum. But the State Department lacked the capacity for processing such a large number. As the exodus continued to soar, bringing in its wake some thousands released from prisons and mental institutions, the administration began having second thoughts. The problem was compounded by a concurrent expansion of asylum claims by Haitians. While the administration insisted these were undocumented immigrants, the black community charged that the differential treatment was motivated by racial discrimination. The White House task force managed to dodge the various issues involved by awarding to all the arrivals the status of "entrant," a newly created ad hoc category that enabled beneficiaries to remain in the United States while their status was being resolved, but it did not allow them to apply for permanent residence. In 1984, however, the Justice Department concluded that by virtue of a 1966 law, Cubans could become permanent residents and citizens, while Haitians could not. In time, most of the Cubans were resettled in established communities, leaving only a few thousand criminals and mentally ill under detention, awaiting the outcome of negotiations for their repatriation. Most of the Haitians subsequently qualified for amnesty under IRCA.

The Mariel experience provoked a transformation of the basic doctrine governing American refugee policy:

> More threatening . . . to our refugee policy than the boatlift itself would be the responses it aroused, both in government and in the American public. Thereafter, American refugee policy would be . . . shadowed by fears of another Mariel, another mass migration. Not the Refugee Act, but the Mariel boatlift would become the benchmark against which all refugee policies were measured; xenophobia and fear would, once again, influence United States refugee policy and direct our practices.[29]

Cubans were no longer welcome defectors, but "bullets aimed at Miami." Whereas throughout the cold war years refugees had constituted an American weapon, they had now become a weapon for the other side. Within a few years the Reagan administration would invoke the threat of an invasion of "feet people" to mobilize support for its interventionist policies in Central America.

Haitian Interdiction. The Haitian case highlights three issues simultaneously: the inherent ambiguity of the categoric distinction between migrants and refugees, on which both American policy and the international refugee regime more generally are based; the reluctance of the United States to provide asylum to citizens of a country whose regime it supports; and the development of deterrence as a response to the prospect of massive first asylum, with ominous consequences.

Burdened with a long history of political instability, Haiti is the only country in the Western Hemisphere that falls within the World Bank's bottommost category of "low income economies." Its links with the United States were reinforced during the lengthy period of military occupation, from 1915 to 1934; even afterward, Haiti remained a de facto U.S. protectorate. In the absence of economic development, many of the country's rural poor were driven to seek work abroad, in the sugar-cane fields of the Dominican Republic as well as of Puerto Rico. The three decade-long "kleptocracy" launched by François Duvalier in 1957 was an especially brutal regime whose prime instrument was the notorious militia, known as "Tonton Macoutes"; but it was treated benevolently by the United States, which viewed it as a reliable ally in the cold war against Castrist Cuba. In the late 1950s Duvalier set out to destroy the political opposition, composed largely of professionals from the mulatto upper class. Many fled to the United States; albeit not recognized as refugees, their entry was relatively unproblematic because the law then in force imposed no numerical restrictions on immigration from independent countries of the Western Hemisphere, and educated professionals usually met the "qualitative" requirements. In their wake, however, came a larger stream from more modest strata, driven by deteriorating political and economic conditions. These movements fostered the emergence of well-rooted Haitian communities in Miami, New York City, and Montreal.

In the 1970s poor Haitians from the rural areas also began making their way to the United States in unreliable fishing vessels, landing surreptitiously along the east coast of Florida. Those apprehended were generally detained; as the result of court rulings, however, in 1978 the INS began releasing Haitians on recognizance and allowing them to work.[30] More of them also filed for asylum; by June 1978, the Miami office had a backlog of nearly 7,000 cases. The rise in applications may have been induced to some extent by the comportment of the immigration judges who, frustrated at having claims to refugee status voiced at the end of lengthy deportation proceedings, began asking the Haitians at the very outset whether they were planning to request asylum. To cure the problem, the INS instructed the judges to accelerate proceedings, leaving the Haitians less time than usual for preparation of their case and for translation during the hearings. Not a single one of more than 4,000 applicants processed in this manner obtained asylum. This fact led a federal judge to conclude that the program was "offensive to every notion of constitutional due process and equal protection," and to order that Haitians whose claims had been rejected not be deported until they had a fair chance to present their case (*Haitian Refugee Center v. Civiletti*, 1980).

At the beginning of 1981, some 35,000 Haitians were living in south Florida, where hostilities burst out betwen them and the Cubans. Initially denied the favorable treatment accorded to the *marielitos*, for the reasons indicated the Carter administration subsequently declared newly arriving Haitians to be entrants also. But the incoming Reagan administration singled them out as an especially threatening group. Beginning in May 1981, Haitian boat people apprehended on the mainland were for the most part incarcerated in the Krome detention center, on the edge of the Florida Everglades. After the state of Florida brought an action against the federal government because of overcrowded conditions, Krome was limited to 1,000 inmates, with the surplus scattered among other facilities throughout the country. But this procedure in turn meant that most of the Haitians were deprived of access to Creole-language legal assistance. As the result of further court challenges, eventually most were released. Together with Cubans, in 1986 they became eligible for permanent residence under a special provision of IRCA.

In the intervening period the Reagan administration undertook to resolve the Haitian problem by preventive measures. In September 1981 the Haitian government agreed to assist the United States in stopping the clandestine migration of its residents to the United States, in exchange for U.S. assistance in enforcing its emigration laws: at that time Haiti required an exit visa of all its citizens. Hence, by its collusion with the Haitian authorities, the United States was aiding and abetting Haiti's brutal exactions and contradicting the policy it was pursuing vis-à-vis the Warsaw Pact countries, from which it demanded unconditional freedom of exit. President Reagan then proclaimed an unprecedented policy of interdiction on the high seas. The U.S. Coast Guard was authorized to stop and board unflagged vessels outside the territorial waters of the United States and to determine whether their passengers were undocumented aliens bound for the United States; if so, they would return them to Haiti. Still in effect, most of the interdiction activity is carried on by Coast Guard cutters in the Windward Passage, between Haiti and Cuba, on the basis of helicopter surveillance.

The agreement specified that the United States would not return any person qualifying for refugee status and that it would inform the Haitian government of those it did return. The Haitian government in turn gave assurances that it would not prosecute "interdictees" for having illegally departed. INS instructions provide for compliance with U.S. statutory obligations regarding refugees, but observers have charged that the process of interdiction is inherently incompatible with asylum determination procedures. Thus, in carrying out this process the United States is led to violate its own statutes as well as international law.[31] Virtually all Haitians are returned directly to their country. Of the 21,461 interdicted from the program's inception through December 1989, only six were brought to the United States to pursue their asylum applications. Of these six, two lived in the United States before and three were teachers able to articulate their claims. According to the Lawyers' Committee on Human Rights, information derived from asylum requests filed in the immigration court in Miami indicates "that if appropriate inquiry were made on the cutter, many of those intercepted would very likely have been able to assert compelling asylum claims." They concluded, therefore, that "at least hundreds of refugees have been wrongfully returned to Haiti over the course of the program and denied protection in violation of refugee law."[32] Legal challenges have not proven very effective, however, in defending Haitian boat people, because interdiction takes place in international waters, outside the jurisdiction of U.S. courts (*Haitian Refugee Center v. Garcey*, 1985). Moreover, the Coast Guard's activities and its consequences of interdiction are not visible to the American public.

In keeping with the original agreement, the Coast Guard informs the Haitian authorities of the returnees' identity. Although U.S. embassy personnel are instructed to ascertain whether or not they experience punishment afterward, the Americans lack the facilities to carry out the task effectively. Follow-up interviews were discontinued after the overthrow of Jean-Claude Duvalier in February 1986, on the grounds that fear of persecution was removed and because of financial constraints. Yet subsequently Haiti has been in effect under military rule and has suffered endemic violence, at the hands of ill-paid soldiers and policemen and of former Tonton Macoutes who have kept their weapons.

The interdiction program appeared quite effective through the mid-1980s, in that very few Haitians were apprehended in Florida. But in 1988 the number of people turned back on the high seas increased by 33 percent as compared with the previous year; in FY 1989 it reached 4,489, the highest annual level to date. The INS attributed this increase to rumors that the Bush administration would allow everyone who arrived within a ninety-day period to stay in the United States—possibly an echo of legal developments regarding South Texas. But in a significant departure from previous statements on the subject, the Miami district director of INS acknowledged that the increase may have had something to do with the deteriorating political situation in Haiti as well. The Coast Guard responded by assigning a second cutter, as well as by flying two surveillance planes off the Florida coast.

The renewed exodus was reflected also in increased apprehensions. Krome was again overcrowded, and by May 1989 it was in "lockdown," under the control of a seventy-member riot squad. Telephone access was shut down and the INS began transferring inmates to other, more remote facilities, including Port Isabel in Texas. The Haitian Refugee Center in Miami then successfully sued the INS on charges that these transfers deprived the Haitians of their rights to legal counsel, and the INS was required to return the inmates to Miami.

The Central American Exodus. Vastly exceeding the Cuban and Haitian waves, the influx from Nicaragua, Guatamala, and El Salvador, estimated at possibly one million altogether, brought the dilemma of mass first-asylum to a head. But the contention this fostered was fueled further by the contributions of U.S. actions to the exodus and by the Reagan administration's determination to harness refugee policy to controversial foreign policy objectives.

The revolutionary and counterrevolutionary conflicts that engulfed the Central American region in the 1970s and 1980s were rooted in the persistence of an explosive social configuration. It centered on an extremely unequal distribution of landed property, maintained by brutally authoritarian governments with links of dependency to the United States. The same conditions drove many people northward in search of material survival, either legally, under the successive arrangements governing movement from the Western Hemisphere, or illegally, in response to opportunities provided by American employers. The presence of established Central American communities in the United States in turn facilitated a rapid expansion of the northward movement when violence broke out.[33]

Salvadorans began attracting official attention in 1980, when apprehensions rose by about 40 percent. Rather than "voluntarily depart" as they had typically done in the past, thousands applied for asylum. In subsequent years, apprehensions included an increasing proportion of women and children, a development consonant with uprooting occasioned by generalized violence. In the late 1980s estimates of Salvadorans in the United States hovered at about half a million; there were also about 100,000–200,000 Nicaraguans and an equal number of Guatemalans.

From the outset, U.S. authorities steadfastly refused to award asylum or grant Extended Voluntary Departure status to Salvadorans and Guatemalans—a policy based on mutually reinforcing domestic and foreign policy considerations. On the domestic side, the foremost reason was to foreclose the evolution of the United States into a mass first-asylum country for groups that might never leave. Concomitantly, the United States sought to foster adequate safe havens in Central America itself, and it accordingly provided substantial support for refugee programs administered by the UNHCR in the region. The availability of these alternatives was used in turn to dissuade Congress from passing safe haven legislation. Guatemalan asylum applicants were usually turned down on the grounds that they failed to take advantage of the safe haven provided by Mexico.

On the foreign policy side, U.S. support for the Salvadoran government and concomitant announcements of its progress in controlling the insurrection precluded the recognition of Salvadoran nationals as having a reasonable fear of persecution or facing life-threatening danger. In April 1986, President Duarte requested safe haven for his citizens because he feared that the impending enactment of IRCA would occasion a massive wave of returns that would further destabilize the situation in his country. Although some State Department officials urged a change of policy, Secretary Shultz remained adamantly opposed, as did the INS.

Most of these considerations applied to Guatemala as well, but they worked somewhat differently for Nicaragua. During the transitional period between the Somoza and Sandinista regimes (July 1979 to December 1980), Nicaraguans already in the United States were granted EVD, in keeping with the traditional policy toward "victims of communism." But as the exodus grew, EVD was denied to the newcomers, and their asylum applications were generally turned down as well. The administration pointed to the influx as a consequence of the coming to power of leftist regimes, and it used this claim to harness support for its interventionist policy. But in 1986 and 1987 the policy was reversed once more, as will be discussed below.

In contrast, the refugee advocacy community insisted that asylum seekers, regardless of numbers, must be duly processed in accordance with U.S. law and treaty obligations and must be granted the benefit of the doubt, in keeping with international refugee law. If they did not qualify as Convention refugees, they should be granted temporary safe haven from the violence that engulfed their region. Furthermore, some critics of the administration's policy pointed out that the floods of "feet people" were attributable to the activities of oppressive oligarchic governments supported by the United States in the cases of El Salvador and Guatemala, and to the deteriorating situation in Nicaragua occasioned by U.S. sponsorship of the contras and relentless U.S. economic warfare in the case of Nicaragua. These critics reasoned that by virtue of its nefarious role, the United States contracted special obligations toward the victims of violence. Congressional action as well as litigation have obliged Justice Department officials to clarify and defend their policy and, to some extent, to modify their practices.

The asylum impasse. The current controversies arise from the problem of growing numbers, from the nature of the root causes determining massive flight to the United States, and from the structure of the adjudication process. The last issue arises from the fact that a single agency is in charge of two essentially incompatible tasks: protection of the vital interests of a particularly vulnerable category of persons, in accordance with U.S. and international law; and the policing of immigration. Concerned essentially with preventing unauthorized entry, the INS views an application for asylum as merely taking a shortcut to jump to the head of the immigration queue or to avoid deportation. Central Americans and Haitians face in effect a "presumption of ineligibility" for asylum, which is translated into procedures and practices that make it next to impossible for even the most deserving asylum seekers to wend their way successfully through the process.[34]

Any alien present in the United States or at its borders, regardless of legal status, may undertake "affirmative action" by applying for asylum to an INS district director. The applicant is then interviewed under oath by a special INS examiner in a nonadversarial manner, but with right to counsel and to supportive witnesses. The district directors refer to the State Department's annual "Country Reports on Human Rights Practices" as a principal source of information, thus ensuring a paramount place for foreign policy considerations in the adjudication process. The report of the interviewer and the district director's assessment of the case's merits are then forwarded to the State Department's Bureau of Human Rights and Humanitarian Affairs (BHRHA) for an advisory opinion.

These opinions constitute a critical aspect of the entire system. A GAO study of 1,450 asylum applications filed in 1984 has shown that far from being advisory, they are overwhelmingly decisive. Yet the size of the special asylum staff at the BHRHA is insufficient to process the enormous number of requests. Staff members are specialized by geographic region, and they usually write their opinions on the basis of the same Country Reports. Although they may ask for corroborating information from the country desk officer or even from the U.S. embassy staff, they seldom do; nor do they consult other widely available sources of information. Critics have charged that as a consequence, the bureau's opinions are both perfunctory and unduly biased toward U.S. foreign policy.[35]

If, after being denied asylum, the alien is placed under deportation or exclusion proceedings, a new application may be filed with the immigration judge by way of "defensive action." This action is also treated as a request for temporary withholding of deportation or exclusion if the alien can establish that his or her life or freedom would be threatened upon return. The proceedings are similar to those in the affirmative action case, except for their adversarial character. The judge's decision may be appealed by either party to the Board of Immigration Appeals (BIA), located within the Department of Justice. Determination is based on a review of the existing file only, and may result in a return of the matter to the immigration court for proper proceedings. The BIA's decision itself may be appealed to either a federal district court (if the alien has been ordered excluded) or a U.S. circuit court (if ordered deported), and further to the U.S. Supreme Court.

In the first years of operation, the vast majority of applicants did not take their claim beyond the first negative decision. In response to criticism about the apparent lack of independence of the review and appeals agencies, at the beginning of 1983 the Department of Justice organized immigration judges and the BIA into the Executive Office for Immigration Review (EOIR), a unit separate from the INS. Although most judges began as trial attorneys for the INS, they were reportedly more sensitive to asylum matters. A BIA decision of 1987 (*Matter of Pula*) liberalized the standard for granting asylum, thereby significantly improving the appellant's chances of success.

To meet the criteria for mandatory withholding of deportation, the INS required the alien to demonstrate a "clear probability"—that is, a better than fifty-fifty chance—that persecution would occur. The agent of persecution is normally the government, but it may also take the form of death squads and the like. To establish eligibility for asylum, the alien must provide objective evidence of actual persecution or of grounds for a "well-founded fear" of persecution, such as detention, denial of rights, torture, and so forth. The Supreme Court's decision in *INS v. Cardoza-Fonseca* (March 1987) liberalized the eligibility standard by taking into consideration the subjective element of fear, as provided for under UNHCR guidelines. Accordingly, the BIA changed its standard of proof of well-founded fear from clear probability to what a "reasonable person" might infer under the circumstances in question.

Subsequently the BIA ruled that aliens fleeing generalized violence and upheaval did not qualify for asylum (*Matter of Mogharrabi*, 1988). This ruling was based on its interpretation of the legislative history of the 1980 act. In particular, the board denied asylum to Salvadorans on the grounds that violence is a normal byproduct of civil wars or revolutions, and that individuals harmed by such violence are not being persecuted on the statutory grounds (*Matter of Maldonado-Cruz*, 1988). The paradoxical consequence was that "the higher the general level of violence, terror, and persecution in a country, the more burden there is upon the applicant to show individual targeting."[36] In an earlier case (*Bolanos-Hernandez v. INS*, 1984), the Ninth Circuit Court of Appeals (West Coast) characterized this line of reasoning as "a clear error of law," demonstrating "the Board's ability to turn logic on its head" and concluding that far from disqualifying an individual's claim, widespread violence may make the threat "more serious and credible." Yet the BIA refused to apply the ruling outside the Ninth Circuit—and so the absurdity persists. The BIA further narrowed the grounds for asylum by differentiating between persecution on grounds of "immutable characteristics"—nationality, race, and religion—and persecution on grounds of "membership in a particular social group" and "political opinion." This distinction means that an activist on behalf of human rights or democracy has less claim to protection than a more passive target.

Even if the claimant does manage to prove a well-founded fear, asylum can be denied on a variety of other grounds. One is the use of fraudulent papers to enter the United States or to circumvent overseas refugee admission procedures (BIA, *Matter of Pula*, 1987). This policy constitutes a serious handicap, because flight often precludes possession of appropriate documents. Thus, although under the law undocumented persons are formally allowed to apply for asylum, in practice the person's immigration status figures prominently in the determination process, and "consistently outweighs factors relating to refugee status."[37] Asylum can also be denied if, before entering the United States, the alien was in a safe country that offered the possibility of asylum. This factor is especially important in the case of Central Americans, who usually arrive by way of Mexico. Mexico, however, is not a signatory to the UNHCR Convention and Protocol, and it does not accept as refugees persons deported from the United States.[38]

In August 1987 the INS published a plan to tighten procedures further by removing jurisdiction over asylum cases from the district directors and by vesting it exclusively with line officers. In the face of a storm of protest from the refugee advocacy community, however, the agency withdrew the plan. Issuance of new regulations was delayed, reportedly because of internal disagreement within the agency.[39]

The GAO study mentioned earlier found that few applicants who had been denied asylum were deported, mostly because of the practical difficulties in locating them in order to carry out the order. The incidence was significantly higher, however, for Salvadorans. This higher incidence has persisted as a deliberate policy. In 1986, the Miami district director of INS decided to halt Nicaraguan deportations. This decision was probably made with sanction from his superiors, as a trial balloon. Two months after the Reagan administration rejected a direct appeal from President Duarte, Attorney General Edwin Meese announced that Nicaraguans would not be deported, instituted an expedited process for granting them authorizations, and encouraged those whose asylum claims had been denied to reapply. This new policy was tantamount to granting them EVD. Accordingly, in FY 1988 the INS deported 3,691 Salvadorans but only 200 Nicaraguans.[40]

The harsh policy toward Salvadorans was dealt a severe blow in April 1988 when U.S. District Court Judge David Kenyon determined the practices of the INS to be "inherently coercive and often deliberately intimidating"; such practices included locating facilities in inaccessible places and denying telephones and writing materials (Orantes-Hernandez v. Meese). He also observed that "this conduct is not the result of isolated transgressions by a few overzealous officers, but . . . a widespread and pervasive practice akin to a policy."[41] The judge issued a permanent injunction against the INS to stop employing threats, misrepresentation, subterfuge, or other forms of coercion to induce Salvadorans to abandon their asylum claims and accept "voluntary departure" to El Salvador, and he ordered them to provide lists of agencies providing free or low-cost legal aid. The decision also included factual findings about the human rights situation in that country. Judge Kenyon stated that "a substantial number of Salvadorans who flee . . . possess a well-founded fear of persecution pursuant to United States asylum laws. . . . People from a wide cross section of Salvadoran society suffer human rights abuses. Trade unionists, members of farmwork unions and cooperatives, religious workers, human rights activists" and many others, together with family members and associates, "have been particularly subject to abuses." But there remained many obstacles to the implementation of this order, and the U.S. government has appealed.

The safe haven controversy. The issue of safe haven first appeared on the congressional agenda in 1981, when Congress passed a resolution urging the Reagan administration to grant EVD to Salvadorans. From the outset the effort was characterized by the administration as simply an attack on its foreign policy rather than an effort motivated by humanitarian concerns. In response to the administration's adamant refusal, various initiatives were subsequently launched in Congress, in the courts, and even in the country at large. The most dramatic challenge has come from the "sanctuary movement," an effort to provide a privatized version of safe haven, which won wide support from major religious denominations. Sanctuaries have also been established by local government bodies. This form of civil disobedience is of necessity limited, however, and does not solve the predicament of the masses of people in need of protection. In 1986 an attempt was made to attach a safe haven provision for Central Americans to IRCA, but it failed at the last minute. Yet passage of the new immigration law itself rendered the need for temporary protection more urgent than ever, because IRCA was expected to reduce the possibility of employment for unauthorized workers. In the late 1980s the focus shifted from the issue of Salvadorans or even Central Americans to the more general problem of first asylum and control over the determination of refugee policy.[42]

In early 1987, two Democrats, Representative Joe Moakley of Massachusetts and Senator Dennis DeConcini of Arizona, sponsored a bill that would suspend deportation of Salvadorans and Nicaraguans for two years following enactment, pending a study by the GAO on whether these groups would face persecution if they returned. The bill passed in the House in July, but it failed to reach the Senate floor before the end of the session because of the adamant opposition of the ranking minority member of the immigration subcommittee, Senator Alan Simpson.

In the intervening period, Representative Roman Mazzoli, chairman of the House Judiciary Committee, who had opposed the

Moakley proposal, introduced a "generic temporary safe haven" (TSH) bill that specified three general criteria for granting EVD: (1) physical danger due to armed conflict; (2) environmental disaster; (3) U.S. national interest. The proposal was supported by the State Department, on condition that it be amended to ensure "that temporary safe haven remain temporary." The department's proposals to that effect involved strict controls on TSH declarations (a short initial period, consultation with Congress before any extension, and a limit on the total period for any country); and on individual recipients (registration within a limited period, annual re-registration, time-limited work permits, and no possibility of adjusting status to permanent residency). Generally supportive of broadened asylum, refugee advocates sought to reduce executive discretion by making TSH declarations mandatory under specified conditions, and to make the measure less restrictive with respect to conditions imposed on recipients.

But the INS insisted that current EVD procedures were adequate, and that giving them the force of law would create a "magnet effect." This position was echoed by FAIR, whose spokeman declared, "There is nothing so permanent as a temporary resident." Revised along the lines advocated by the State Department, the Mazzoli bill obtained support from some concerned Republicans seeking to block the Moakley-DeConcini measure, and it passed the House in October 1988. But this success had no effect, because there was no companion bill in the Senate.

Both bills were reintroduced in the 101st Congress, Mazzoli's as a bipartisan measure. At the initiative of its new chair, Representative Bruce Morrison, the immigration subcommittee amended the Moakley bill to avoid a magnet effect; but it remained limited to Central Americans. In May 1989, the subcommittee reported the bill without recommendation to the full committee.

While further action was pending, a new case of safe haven arose following the Chinese government's brutal response to the democracy movement. In keeping with a directive from President Bush, Attorney General Dick Thornburgh ordered the INS to take all steps necessary to "defer enforcing the departure" (DED) of all PRC nationals who were in the United States on June 6, 1989.[43] The proclamation created a catch-22 situation, however. Holders of student visas were not allowed to work off-campus, but beneficiaries of DED would be. As nearly all Chinese students had to work to survive, they would be inclined to give up their student visas in exchange for DED status; but by doing so they would become deportable when this status expired, a decision to be taken at the discretion of U.S. authorities. Although the INS devised a short-term solution, the situation aroused considerable concern among the Chinese in the United States, among refugee advocates, and in Congress, where over a dozen bills were introduced on the subject. On July 11, the Senate unanimously passed an amendment to the pending Simpson-Kennedy immigration bill, allowing PRC nationals to remain in the United States until June 5, 1993, unless the president certified to Congress that it was safe for them to return. Shortly afterwards the House immigration subcommittee reported without dissent both a bill introduced by Representative Nancy Pelosi, a California Democrat, to waive the two-year home-country residence requirement for PRC exchange visitors, and Chairman Morrison's own proposal for including the Chinese in the Moakley bill.

On June 21, the Senate immigration subcommittee finally held a hearing on the DeConcini bill. Although Senator Kennedy urged the same spirit of generosity toward Salvadorans and Nicaraguans as toward nationals of the PRC, Senator Simpson remained strongly opposed. He emphasized that EVD in the past was granted only to people from countries outside the Western Hemisphere who could easily reach the United States, and that in contrast with the majority of Salvadorans and Nicaraguans, the Chinese were in the United States legally. The State Department objected specifically to the inclusion of El Salvador, arguing that the level of violence had dropped considerably since the early 1980s.

In late July, the House Judiciary Committee combined into a single bill (H.R. 45) Moakley's safe haven for Nicaraguans and Salvadorans, Morrison's proposal for broader protection for the Chinese, and Mazzoli's framework to create "temporary protected status" (TPS) as a new *legal* category to replace the administrative EVD. This bill would allow nationals of all or part of a country to remain in the United States for specified periods if the attorney general found certain conditions to exist, such as an ongoing armed conflict, an environmental disaster, or some other "extraordinary and temporary conditions." TPS holders would be allowed to work, but would not be eligible for public benefits; and they would have to register, so as to be identifiable and thereby returnable once the danger disappeared. Protection would extend for three years, with six-month extensions possible after that. The Congressional Budget Office estimated that about 60 percent of the estimated 500,000–1,000,000 Salvadorans and Nicaraguans would apply as well as 40,000 PRC nationals. Albeit generally ineligible for federal public benefits, they could receive state and local assistance at a cost of some $150 million a year. Passage of the consolidated measure was virtually certain in the House, since the Democratic majority had approved prior versions of its several components by large margins. Support from the Nicaraguan exile community, heretofore at best lukewarm, was expected to reverse earlier opposition from key conservatives. Indeed, the bill won broad House approval on October 25, with twenty-one additional favorable votes over the previous year.

The DeConcini proposal, still covering only Central Americans, was finally approved by the Senate Judiciary Committee on November 2, but with restrictive amendments initiated by Senator Simpson. They included a registration fee; a reduction of the registration period from 180 days to 90 days after enactment; and the specification that applicants would be ineligible for benefits if present in their country of origin on or after January 1, 1989, unless permission was granted in advance by the attorney general. This restriction was designed to disqualify Nicaraguans and Salvadorans who visited their home countries, where they claimed to face danger.[44] But prospects for speedy consideration on the Senate floor were dashed when Simpson insisted that by virtue of its broader scope, H.R. 45 should not be considered a companion bill, but should be referred for hearings to the subcommittee. In mid-1990 the measure was still pending, but since the simultaneous progress of TSH was attributable in some measure to support from conservatives concerned over Nicaraguans, the electoral defeat of the Sandinistas in February 1990 cast the measure's future in doubt.

Despite the inclusion of PRC nationals in H.R. 45, both houses also enacted separate bills on their behalf. After the differences were reconciled, the measure was approved unanimously in the House and by a voice vote in the Senate. Yet despite this overwhelming support, the administration opposed it on the grounds that its DED program made the law redundant, and that the Chinese government might retaliate by ending student exchanges altogether. President Bush vetoed the measure on November 30, 1989, explaining that the administration objected to "Congressional micro-management of foreign policy. Such legislation puts America in a straightjacket and can render us incapable of responding to changing circumstances." The key issue was thus not Chinese reactions, but rather presidential authority in the realm of foreign affairs, in keeping with confrontations over other elements of refugee policy.

At the same time the president insisted he would "always adhere to the principle that no one will be returned forcibly to a country where he or she faces persecution," and he said he had directed the attorney general and the secretary of state to arrange "effectively the same protection" for the students as they would have received under the vetoed law. He ordered an "irrevocable waiver" of the two-year home-country residence requirement for J-1 (student) visa holders, and he said the students could apply for clemency until January 1, 1994. But despite these assurances, many members of Congress were appalled, and on November 30 the Democratic leadership announced that overriding the president's veto would be the first item of business on the agenda in the next session. The subsequent visits of National Security Adviser Brent Scowcroft and Deputy Secretary of State Lawrence S. Eagleburger to China as special envoys, along with the revelation that they had gone there secretly immediately after the June massacre, further fueled congressional anger on both sides of the aisle, making an override even more likely. Nevertheless, the president campaigned vigorously to garner support for his position. The congressional furor notwithstanding, polls indicated the American public was about evenly divided on the question whether to condemn China or to soft-pedal criticism in order to maintain good relations.

As expected, on January 24, 1990, the House voted 390–25 to override, with 145 Republicans joining 245 Democrats against the president. The ranking Republican member of the House Foreign Affairs Committee characterized the vote as "a referendum on human rights that will be heard around the world." But the White House pulled out all the stops, and on the next day the Senate sustained the veto by a narrow margin of four votes. The president said this constituted an endorsement of his China policies, and he promised to protect from forced deportation all Chinese in America. After a time he upgraded his directive to an executive order, as the critics demanded.

Strengthening border controls. Albeit not generally considered as an element of U.S. refugee policy, the Immigration Reform and Control Act of 1986, which purported to deter undocumented border-crossers and overstayers by denying them access to the U.S. labor market, was designed to provide a major weapon in the escalating preventive war against self-propelled asylum seekers. Despite employer sanctions, however, Central Americans continued to pour in; hence the INS was driven to explore other possibilities. After Attorney General Meese's departure from office in 1988, agency officials sought to reverse his Nicaraguan asylum policy, which they believed fostered a stream of new arrivals. They urged the State Department to secure the assistance of Mexico and Central American countries in slowing down the flow.

Mexico's interests in the matter differed from those of the United States, however. The region's upheavals turned it into a massive first asylum country. Guatemalans, who began arriving in 1981, were initially turned back; but subsequently Mexico allowed the UNHCR to establish camps on its side of the border. After these were attacked by Guatemalan forces, most of the refugees were moved further inland. Although Guatemala stopped generating refugees after the 1985 change of government, it served as a transit country for northbound Nicaraguans and Salvadorans. In order to maintain good relations with its neighbor, Mexico exercised little surveillance over its 600-mile southern border. As of March 1987, Mexico hosted some 40,000 Guatemalan and 5,000 Salvadoran refugees under UNHCR protection, as well as an estimated 120,000 unrecognized others. The situation remains quite manageable, so long as most Central Americans go on to the United States; hence there is no reason to expect Mexico to cooperate in bottling up its guests.[45]

Consequently, deterrence could be effected only at the U.S. border. A key element of the new INS strategy was to process asylum requests at the point of entry, so as to maximize control over the applicants, to foreclose their dispersion inland, and to contain settlement within established communities. Accordingly, in December 1988 the INS announced that the asylum claims of newly arriving Central Americans would be processed at Harlingen, Texas, the major point of entry. Misperceiving this as an opportunity to obtain asylum, thousands of people waiting in Mexico rushed across the border; subsequently, however, the newcomers were immobilized in south Texas while awaiting disposition of their applications, without employment or place to live.[46] Crowding at the INS office in downtown Harlingen became so bad that city officials evicted the agency for violating health and fire codes. In the face of the growing local problem, in early January the U.S. District Court issued a temporary restraining order that allowed many of the applicants to move onward to other destinations, where their applications would be adjudicated.

Within forty-eight hours, several hundred Nicaraguans arrived in Miami. The influx precipitated a conflict between the city of Miami, with a Cuban-born mayor and a high percentage of Hispanic residents, which welcomed the Nicaraguans and sought to assist them, and Dade County, which charged that the city was thereby encouraging more Nicaraguans to come. But city and county officials were united in pressing the federal government for financial assistance. In the wake of this influx came the shooting of an unarmed young black man by a Hispanic police officer, which sparked rioting in Miami's black neighborhoods. The incident was attributed by some to the black community's resentment of the generous treatment accorded the newcomers by the city government, as well as by the federal authorities, in contrast with the treatment of Haitian blacks.

On February 20, 1989, INS Commissioner Alan Nelson announced a new procedure for the detention and deportation of undocumented aliens arriving in south Texas, as well as for the speedy processing of asylum claims in situ. Accordingly, the temporary restraining order was lifted. But a subsequent survey indicated that whereas on paper the adjudication process appeared both quick and thorough, "[t]he reality . . . does not extend far beyond the appearance because almost no one in south Texas is voluntarily applying for asylum."[47] Affirmative applications had to be filed at the Port Isabel processing center, about twenty-five miles outside of Harlingen; this center was a large detention facility, where most of the processing in fact pertained to apprehended aliens. A total of 886 applications were submitted from the inception of the program through July 1989, about two-thirds of them by Nicaraguans, whose rate of approval was 18.6 percent. In keeping with the established pattern, the rate was much lower for Salvadorans (3.6 percent), Hondurans (1.4 percent), and Guatemalans (0 percent).

Regarding defensive applications, observers suggest that the INS was continuing to implement the policy of intimidation prohibited by the Orantes injunction, particularly against apprehended aliens traveling singly. This policy resulted in a high rate of deportation and voluntary departure. Families were given a fair hearing, however. On April 28, 1989, the U.S. district judge determined that the INS had violated his previous order, as indicated by the fact that none of the sixty-seven Salvadorans deported from Port Isabel in the previous month were represented by counsel. He then issued another injunction, requiring the INS to arrange for legal rights presentations to be given immediately to all detainees at Port Isabel and prohibiting deportations in the intervening period.

The problems persisted. Toward the end of 1989 the violence in El Salvador escalated, and the following January it was reported that increasing numbers were being detained by Mexican authorities in collaboration with INS personnel stationed in Mexico. They were also detained entering the United States, where the Rio Grande Valley detention centers were again filled to capacity.[48] But the newly appointed INS commissioner, Gene McNary, said that to ease the agency's budget problems, no more than about 670 people would be held at the Harlingen center.[49] The INS released dozens of Salvadorans daily on recognizance bonds, allowing them to continue to other parts of the country whle awaiting adjudication. But early in February, the commissioner reversed himself sharply and announced renewed plans to detain all Central Americans who entered the United States illegally; he also committed the INS to one-day asylum determination and to the systematic deportation of all who failed to qualify for refugee status. Tents were erected to increase the Harlingen center's holding capacity to 2,500, with plans to raise it further to 10,000. Extra Border Patrol agents were dispatched as well.

After years of dogged effort, in the latter part of 1990 advocates of a more generous refugee policy achieved a number of successes, which together amounted to a major change in U.S. policy.[50] In Congress the supporters of safe haven secured the incorporation of measures to that effect as amendments to the comprehensive Immigration Act of 1990, signed by President Bush on November 29.[51] One provision allows the attorney general to grant temporary protected status (TPS) to aliens who, if they returned to their country, would be in danger for reasons such as violent conflict or natural disaster. An affirmative vote of three-fifths of the senators is required for legislation adjusting the status of such persons to be considered by the Senate. Beneficiaries will be authorized to work but not eligible for most public assistance. The law also incorporates the substance of the Moakley-DeConcini proposal. El Salvador is specifically designated as a country whose nationals are eligible for TPS, effective on the date of enactment, and for an eighteen-month period beginning January 1, 1991. To be eligible Salvadorans must have been in the United States since September 19, 1990, and must register during the first six months of 1991; registration and the work authorization must be renewed every six months.

Based on his authority under the new law, in February 1991 the attorney general granted TPS to aliens currently in the United States who were unable to return to Lebanon, Kuwait, and Liberia by virtue of political upheavals in those countries. Officials estimated some 51,000 persons to be eligible. Surprisingly, as the period for Salvadoran registration neared its close in mid-1991, few had applied. It was suggested that for many of the eligible, the benefits of a period of legal residence and work authorization were overshadowed by the risks of reporting their whereabouts to the government. But advocates charged also that Salvadorans were deterred by very high fees, resulting from a legislative glitch. Although with regard to the general TPS provision the 1990 law specified an application fee of $50, for Central Americans it merely authorized the INS to charge a "reasonable" amount to cover program costs. In fact the INS charged them $405, prompting a suit by the San Francisco-based Lawyers' Committee for Urban Affairs on behalf of poor Salvadorans in California, where at least half of the estimated one million eligible under the law are believed to live. Bowing to pressure from Congress and from immigrant rights groups, in May the INS adopted new regulations reducing the fee to $255 and provided some waivers for people falling below the federal poverty level. On June 3 a federal judge ordered the agency to issue waivers to all who could not afford the fees and to reconsider all applications for waivers denied since registration began the previous January. The registration period was subsequently extended.

In July 1990 the INS finally issued its long delayed final version of asylum regulations under the 1980 refugee law. In keeping with the longstanding demands of advocacy groups, the agency planned to establish a corps of about ninety specially trained asylum officers who would interview each applicant and solicit comments from the State Department, but who will be encouraged to make independent decisions, and who may draw on information about political conditions in various countries from a new documentation center. The new rule will grant applicants the benefit of the doubt: individuals will no longer be required to show that they have been or would be singled out for persecution if there is a "pattern or practice" of persecuting similar people. They may qualify for asylum on the basis of their own testimony, without corroboration, if the testimony is credible in light of general conditions in the home country. Although asylum advocates generally took a wait-and-see stance, Arthur Helton, director of the Refugee Project of the Lawyers' Committee for Human Rights, acknowledged that the new rules constituted "a constructive step," and the *New York Times* commented editorially that refugees "will have more assurance that their claims will receive fair consideration."[52]

Finally, in preliminary settlement of a five-year old ACLU-initiated law suit charging that Salvadoran and Guatemalan applicants were denied proper asylum procedures, on December 19, 1990, the government agreed to stop detaining and deporting most illegal aliens from those countries; to allow unsuccessful candidates as well as those who never filed to apply anew; and to allocate $200,000 to voluntary agencies for locating and advising persons affected by the settlement, estimated at some 500,000. In the final settlement, approved in San Francisco federal district court on January 31, 1991, the government acknowledges that neither foreign policy nor "the government's opinion of political or ideological beliefs of the applicant" constitutes a proper consideration in asylum cases.

Asylum Pressures—The Canadian Response

Because of Canada's low-profile foreign policy and its generally internationalist and humanitarian orientation, foreign policy considerations have not dominated refugee policy to the same extent as in the

United States. Concomitantly, refugee policy in the 1980s did not generate the same degree of heat. The involvement of voluntary agencies in the reception and resettlement of the second Southeast Asian wave, however, and the formalization of their role in the refugee process by way of the 1978 law and regulations contributed to the institutionalization of a well-grounded humanitarian network. This network henceforth acted as a critic of governmental actions and proposals, and it initiated proposals of its own. As in the United States, the organizations in question resorted to the courts to challenge laws and regulations considered contrary to the interests of the refugees or in violation of human rights. Moreover, they began to coordinate their actions with their U.S. counterparts. A first "Canada-United States Church Consultation on Refugee Protection and Safe Haven" met in Washington, D.C., in April 1985, and a second in Niagara Falls, Ontario, in June 1989.

In the 1980s, annual refugee admissions ranged between 15,000 and 25,000, with the privately sponsored proportion steadily rising; the plan for 1988 provided for 13,000 admissions financed by government and 9,000 privately. Three designated classes were in effect: (1) Southeast Asians; (2) political prisoners and other targeted persons still in their country, but who would meet the Convention criteria if they were outside; this designation applied mostly to Chileans, Guatemalans, and Salvadorans; (3) self-exiles from authoritarian regimes—mostly Eastern Europeans and Russians. Critics pointed out that over half of the federally assisted refugees originated in Eastern Europe or Southeast Asia, and that many of them appeared to be moving primarily for economic reasons. The nongovernmental organizations also complained that for financial reasons the government processes privately sponsored refugees first, and they ended up filling a larger part of the annual quota than anticipated.

As in the United States, however, it was asylum that emerged as the most controversial policy issue. A key feature in the process of obtaining asylum is the possibility of gaining access to a country where the request can be made. With most of Europe rapidly closing down and the United States maintaining strict visa requirements, Canada emerged as a residual haven. At the beginning of the decade, some eighty countries benefited from visitor visa exemptions; concurrently, with the elimination of section 34, acquisition of refugee status emerged as a major device for obtaining permanent residence. During the waiting period, asylum seekers were allowed to work and received various social and medical benefits. The number of claims increased from 500 in 1977 to 6,792 in 1983–1984, and then 8,374 in

1985; they jumped to 18,282 in 1986, including would-be immigrants from countries such as Portugal, Turkey, and Jamaica.

Visitors from "B–1 list" countries could also obtain permanent residence under the "special measures program," used mainly as a device to clear the IAB's caseload of people who probably would have been granted refugee status anyway. In the first half of the 1980s this program accounted for about 20 percent of total refugee admissions. The list included Chile, Iran, Lebanon, and Sri Lanka. In 1981–82 the government was prevailed upon to send a fact-finding team to Central America, Mexico, and the United States to assess the situation regarding Central Americans; but whereas other such missions had resulted in a liberalization of requirements for the appropriate group, in this case the team reported that no apparent need existed for a resettlement scheme outside the region. Critics charged that the rejection of Central Americans was "attributable to political, administrative, and ideological considerations," in keeping with an established pattern of policy.[53] Advocates did not disarm, insisting that the flight of Central Americans to Canada "is in every sense a genuine refugee movement, since the U.S. government will deport them to their country of origin if they are apprehended—and in many cases that means certain death."[54] El Salvador and Guatemala were subsequently included on the B–1 list. In most cases, the special measures program was implemented in conjunction with the imposition of a comprehensive visa requirement on the country in question, designed to stop the flow of claimants. It has been suggested that this "good cop / bad cop" approach was designed to reduce opposition to the new visa policy.[55]

Concern over the rising number of refugee claimants was exacerbated by increasing alarm over illegal immigration, which in Canada arose almost exclusively by way of legal visitors who overstayed.[56] To meet the problem, the Immigration Advisory Council recommended the requirement of visas from all countries except the United States, as well as stricter enforcement of existing employer sanctions and a more reliable social security card. Accordingly, in early 1984 the government removed a number of countries from the visa-exempt category—initially Guyana, Jamaica, Peru, and Guatemala; later Sri Lanka, Bangladesh, India, and Portugal. But foreign and domestic policy considerations came into play as well; Turkey was allowed to retain its exemption because it was "a good friend of NATO," and Israel was granted one de novo.[57] At the same time Canada declared another regularization period, extended ultimately to July 1985.

From the perspective of refugee advocates, the main problems with existing asylum procedures were the lack of guarantee of a personal hearing for each applicant and the Immigration Appeals Board's want of autonomy. In 1984 the Concerned Delegation of Church, Legal, and Humanitarian Organizations therefore proposed reconstitution of the Refugee Status Advisory Committee as a more autonomous Refugee Review Board, with final decision-making authority, subject only to judicial review in the federal court. The minister then called upon Rabbi W. Gunther Plaut to produce at least two models from which the government could choose.[58]

The other problem was in effect resolved in 1985, when as the result of a challenge by church groups, the Supreme Court established that the IAB must grant an oral hearing in all cases (*Harbhajan Singh et al. v. The Minister of Employment and Immigration*). But this ruling had the effect of further delaying asylum determination. By the time their cases were reviewed, many of the claimants had married Canadians, held long-term jobs, or otherwise demonstrated that they were so much a part of Canadian life they should be permanently admitted on humanitarian grounds, even if not qualified for refugee status.[59] In 1986 an administrative review cleared a backlog of 22,000 asylum cases; many immigrants who had been working in Canada illegally but usefully were given permission to stay. But the review encouraged others to come; and with processing taking as long as three years, by March 1987 the backlog reached 23,000 and was increasing at the rate of nearly 4,000 a month.[60]

Asylum is often associated with illegal immigration in the popular mind. In August 1986, 155 Tamils were discovered in two small boats off the coast of Newfoundland, and a Gallup poll conducted in September indicated that 72 percent of Canadians thought the country was doing more than enough to help refugees, and 58 percent wanted cuts in the admission levels. In keeping with this, at the end of October the government introduced new legislation to streamline the immigration process. Just as consideration got under way, the enactment of IRCA in the United States precipitated the exodus to Canada of several thousand Salvadorans and Guatemalans, who feared being deprived of their jobs. The number of new asylum claims rose swiftly in the early months of 1987, half of them from Central Americans. Immigration Minister Benoit Bouchard responded with a series of stopgap measures. In February he abolished the B–1 list, so that claimants had to get on the long asylum-determination queue, and without any assistance while waiting. Visa procedures were generally tightened, and airlines were made to enforce them by denying passage to persons lacking valid travel documents. Official estimates suggested the proposed new rules would reduce the number of asylum claimants from the current 2,000 a month to 800. After the orders went into effect, Central Americans without proper documentation were stopped at the border and told they must apply from the United States. Camps were improvised in Plattsburgh and Buffalo. In response to critics, Canadian authorities insisted they had an agreement with the United States that no one awaiting determination would be deported; but the INS did not acknowledge any such commitment.[61]

In May the government introduced its long-awaited plan for amending the refugee provisions of the 1976 law. The measure (Bill C–55) was in keeping with the Supreme Court's 1985 decision, but it fell considerably short of the recommendations of the refugee network. It replaced the Immigration and Refugee Advisory Board with a new independent body, the Immigration and Refugee Board (IRB), comprising separate sections for immigration and refugee matters. The IRB provided for a two-stage process, with an initial screening to establish the claimant's "eligibility" and "credibility" and a second full hearing before the Refugee Determination Board to decide on refugee status itself.[62] The screening for eligibility was designed mostly to eliminate applicants who had already been awarded refugee status in another country, or who arrived from a "safe third country" where they had a reasonable opportunity to claim protection, as determined by the federal government. A positive decision by one member of the screening panel would be sufficient to move to the second stage; but if rejected, the claimant might be immediately deported to the third country in question. A government report issued in March 1988 noted that 35 percent of all arrivals from West European countries and 80 percent from the United States might be disposed of in this manner.

While the bill was under consideration, in July the authorities caught 174 Sikhs who had been illegally landed in Nova Scotia from a freighter; upon their arrest, they asked for refugee status. The incident occurred at a time when a Gallup Poll showed a record-low level of support for the Mulroney government's overall performance. In the wake of a public outcry, the government called an emergency session of Parliament to consider Bill C–55, as well as another bill, C–84, which drastically increased penalties for organizing or assisting efforts to smuggle foreigners into Canada.[63] In the same vein as the U.S. policy of Haitian interdiction, it also allowed the authorities to board ships on the high seas and to turn them back without entertaining any refugee claims. Aliens landed from such vessels could be detained without a hearing for twenty-eight days (instead of seven) and deported, subject to court approval, if they were found to be security risks.

Critics charged that Bill C–55 shifted the burden of proof onto the claimants, and denied them the ability to work or attend school while awaiting adjudication. They also pointed out that since designated-class refugees were not affected, the existing double standard would be further accentuated.[64] The screening for eligibility was widely interpreted as aimed against Central and Latin Americans. Since it was unlikely the United States would be declared unsafe, the prospect loomed of Salvadorans and Guatemalans being sent back to the United States, which would in turn deport them to their country of origin. As one critic saw it, "In short, Canada may use the United States as a means of subverting the UN Convention."[65] In October 1988 the Canadian section of Amnesty International submitted a report to the chairman of the IRBC that cited cases of Central American refugees at risk who had been returned by the United States, as well as other aspects of the U.S. situation. The report concluded that Canadian government assertions that it would not return genuine refugees "are meaningless if the definition of safe third country is questionable."[66]

Refugee advocates persuaded the Senate to liberalize both bills, and the government in turn yielded some ground in order to secure passage; but the House of Commons retained a tough enforcement stance throughout. The Senate proposed that the list of safe third countries be drawn up by the chairman of the IRB rather than by the Cabinet, but this proposal did not survive in the final bill; the measure does, however, impose as an explicit standard of reference the country's record in protecting refugees against *refoulement*. On the whole, although the changes introduced by the Senate "failed to dismantle the strong enforcement orientation of the bills, they did attenuate the extent of the protectionist victory."[67]

Meanwhile, at the end of 1987 the backlog of asylum applications climbed to about 85,000; some 40,000 more were added the following year. With the more restrictive procedures scheduled to come into effect on January 1, 1989, sharp increases in applications were reported in the final months of 1988. Estimates of the backlog reached as high as 120,000, including dependents. As the law went into operation, the government also announced it would clear the backlog within two years by appointing more personnel; meanwhile, the applicants would be allowed to work. An internal government study reportedly concluded that about 28,000 of the 85,000 would be deported, but critics suggested the number might be as high as 60,000.[68] There were speculations that, as in the past, Canada would couple the inauguration of a tougher stance with an amnesty; but the minister of immigration laid this to rest. She sweetened the pill, however, by announcing an increase in the immigration quota for 1989 from 120,000 to 160,000.

In accordance with the two-stage plan, asylum seekers must now first pass an eligibility and credibility hurdle before their claims are formally heard.[69] This test takes place almost immediately upon entry before a two-person panel consisting of an immigration department adjudicator and a member of the independent Immigration and Refugee Board. Benefit of the doubt is ensured to some extent by the fact that the unanimous decision of the panel is required to reject a claim, whereas the positive decision of a single panel member moves the claimant to the second stage. Aliens not deemed credible or eligible are to be deported. The right of appeal at this stage is very restricted, and those who avail themselves of it are to be removed from Canada pending a court decision on whether it will hear the appeal. Applicants who clear the hurdle are permitted to work while awaiting the second hearing, which takes place before a panel of two members of the IRB's refugee division. Again, a positive decision by only one member of the panel is sufficient, and the right of appeal is limited to questions of law and "capricious" findings of fact.

Persons applying at U.S. border crossings—mostly Central Americans—are to be interviewed on the American side, so that those rejected will not have actually entered Canada. Although unsuccessful applicants may file an appeal, there is no guarantee that they will be able to stay in the United States while awaiting the outcome. There is reportedly an informal agreement, however, whereby applicants are allowed to wait in the United States on condition of signing a voluntary departure notice, which has the effect of foreclosing the possibility of a future asylum application in the United States and of facilitating their deportation if Canada turns them down. The INS may also choose to detain them during the waiting period. Furthermore, asylum applicants who are admitted to Canada for a second hearing and are then denied asylum will not be accepted by the United States. They must therefore be deported from Canada to their homeland or some other country willing to take them.[70]

It is premature to evaluate the system's actual operations, since it has been in effect for only a short time. As of mid-1990, the government had not yet issued the "safe third country" list, probably to avoid dealing with the delicate matter of the United States. R.L.E. Fairweather, chairman of the IRB, reported in November 1989 that the new system was more efficient than the old, and that in most cases final determination is reached within three to four months as against the previous two to five years. He also pointed out that there has been a notable reduction in claimants from countries that are not generally recognized as refugee-producing, particularly Trinidad, Jamaica, and Portugal. Although he attributed this to the immediacy of the hearings, it should be remembered that Canada concurrently adopted more stringent visa requirements. As a result of the elimination of several low-approval groups, there has been an increase in the rate of positive decisions.

From January 1 to November 30, 1989, of the 11,948 claims that came before the IRB, 5,672 (47 percent) were fully disposed of.[71] The largest countries of origin were Lebanon (1,808), Somalia (1,793), Sri Lanka (1,727), and El Salvador (889). Nearly 95 percent of claimants cleared the first hurdle, and approximately 90 percent the second. Considering both initial and full hearings, 74.4 percent of the initial applicants were granted status, 18.8 percent were rejected, and another 6.8 percent withdrew or abandoned their claims. Of the 4,217 claimants who were confirmed as refugees, the largest groups originated in Sri Lanka (931), Somalia (830), Lebanon (666), Iran (405), El Salvador (318), China (112), and Czechoslovakia (109). Among those rejected at the first stage, the largest groups were from Jamaica (42), Poland (29), Lebanon (29), and the United States (23). At the full hearing level they included Lebanon (90), El Salvador (56), Sri Lanka (40), Czechoslovakia (37), China (36), and Poland (31).

This generous record is undoubtedly attributable to the Immigration and Refugee Board's autonomy, which is bolstered by the establishment of a Documentation Centre that enables it to secure information from nongovernmental sources as well as international organizations. A sample of its Country Profiles, which form the basis for hearings, suggests they are based on wide documentation from a variety of scholarly and periodical sources, and are unusually even-handed. For example, the one on El Salvador (August 1989) discusses the controversial matter of the "treatment of returnees." It points out that "organizations monitoring human rights in El Salvador support the view that returning refugees are often subject to abuses," with citations to Amnesty International and the Interchurch Committee on Human Rights in Latin America; but it also reports that the State Department and the Salvadoran government dispute these findings. It is noteworthy that a number of Salvadorans who were denied asylum in the United States obtained it in Canada.

Chairman Fairweather concluded his speech by suggesting that "restoring credibility internationally was very important; restoring the faith of Canadians in the process was even more critical." He cited recent Gallup Poll data as evidence that Canadians' faith in the immigration process has increased, and that there is growing support for higher immigration levels, even though numbers have doubled over the past few years.[72] But the Canadian Council of Churches has challenged some of the law's provisions as unconstitutional and life-threatening. A federal court ruled that there was cause for action, and arguments were heard in January 1990. Critics have also pointed out that given a rejection rate of only 5 percent, the initial "credibility" hearing is unnecessary and wasteful.

The Dilemma of Glasnost—From Refugees to Emigrés

Until the sweeping changes occurred in the formerly Warsaw Pact countries, all of their citizens who were able to get out, with or without permission, were admitted to the United States as "invited" refugees, or were assured of favorable adjudication of their asylum requests. The same policy prevailed in Canada as well. As indicated earlier, this policy was tacitly predicated on restricted exit, and hence it entailed a small number of actual admissions, except in emergency situations such as those in Hungary and Czechoslovakia. After Mariel, however, the United States took care not to encourage any massive exodus of which it might be the major recipient. This policy was made clear at the time of the 1981 coup in Poland. Although Polish visitors were granted EVD, the Reagan administration indicated it would not engage in massive resettlement; this announcement in turn prompted Austria to keep its border closed, in effect keeping the Poles bottled in. This orientation persisted into the late 1980s.[73]

The progress of political liberalization in the Warsaw Pact world, however, drastically altered the situation: the lowering of barriers to exit vastly expanded the pool of candidates for emigration, but it simultaneously reduced their qualification as refugees. Initially, the United States attempted to meet the demand by increasing admissions within the existing system. But as the exit gates opened yet wider, this attempt became totally inadequate. As anticipated by some analysts, considering the immigration policies that keep admissions well below the continuing level of demand, an ironic paradox arose: with minor exceptions, the populations of those countries would remain as immobilized as they were before. This situation would occur no longer because they were not allowed to leave, but because they had no place to go.[74] In the United States this prospect has called into question the established distinction between refugee and immigration policy, and it has precipitated a reconsideration of both.

With the dawn of glasnost, the Soviet Union again began letting out more Germans and Jews, along with some others. Jews left with Israeli visas, issued in Moscow by the Dutch embassy, which has represented Israeli interests since the break in diplomatic relations; and Pentecostals were allowed to leave on Israeli visas as well. Initially the United States maintained its established policy. The emigrants traveled to a reception center in Vienna, and after a short stay went to await completion of the process in Rome, where those wishing to go to the United States rather than Israel were issued refugee visas by the INS. On the eve of the radical changes, about 70 percent of Soviet Jews chose to go to America; the annual quota was some 10,000 (for FY 1986, 9,500), with applications running slightly above 20,000. In keeping with the general practice regarding citizens of Communist countries, determination of "persecution" was perfunctory; for those processed, the approval rate approached 80 percent.[75] Objections were voiced by the Israeli government, who deplored the deflection of the principal stream of potential immigration.[76]

The first problem was occasioned by the outbreak of violence in Azerbaijan in late 1987, which prompted a rapid increase in Armenian applications for exit visas and concomitantly for admission to the United States as refugees. The State Department responded with a plan to reallocate as many as 15,000 of the refugee slots scheduled for Southeast Asia to Soviet citizens. But this triggered vociferous objections in Congress, because at the time Thailand was pushing boat people out to sea on the grounds that it could provide no more first asylum because of the slow pace of resettlement. The president then expanded the quota by 15,000 to 83,500, but without requesting additional funds.

As applications poured in, at the beginning of July 1988 the U.S. consulate in Moscow abruptly suspended all scheduled departure interviews until October 1. The suspension did not affect Jews, who continued to leave with Israeli visas, but occasioned severe hardship for Armenians, many of whom had quit their jobs and vacated their homes to come to Moscow in the expectation of speedy departure. The two explicit reasons given were, first, that the quota for the first half of the fiscal year was already filled, and second, budgetary constraints; the move also reflected a determination by State Department lawyers, however, that Armenians were being accepted as refugees without any finding of persecution, in violation of the 1980 law.[77] The move was bitterly ironic because it came on the heels of President Reagan's visit, in the course of which he urged Secretary Gorbachev to lift remaining restrictions on emigration.

In the face of a new outcry at home and abroad, the embarrassed State Department appealed for private support from relatives and religious groups, and later in the month it resumed processing of the 3,000 applications filed before July 1. But a more demanding standard of documentation was established, leading to the rejection of some 100 Armenians, and no new applications were accepted for the rest of the year. In mid-September, the INS office handling Jews in Rome also began enforcing the more demanding standard, so that by December there were 175 rejected applicants awaiting further disposition. The rate of turndown of both Armenians and Jews rose considerably after the INS began taking in new applications at the beginning of 1989.

In the fall of 1988 the president proposed an additional 9,500 refugee admissions for Warsaw Pact countries, bringing the total to 24,500, of which 16,000 were designated for the Soviet Union. But this increase was clearly insufficient, and at the beginning of December the outgoing administration announced that it would deal with the increasingly embarrassing situation on an interim basis by admitting up to 2,000 Soviet Armenians and Jews a month under the attorney general's parole authority. These admissions would include all who did not qualify as refugees in Moscow or Rome. Applicants would first have to produce an affidavit of financial responsibility, however, from some individual or organization, as required of ordinary immigrants. Albeit admitted to the United States, the parolees would not be eligible for permanent resident status nor for citizenship, except indirectly for example by marrying a U.S. citizen. Soviet Jews in Rome could of course go to Israel instead. In January 1989 the president reallocated another 9,000 visas to the Soviet Union.

As a long-term solution, however, Washington contemplated creating a new category of admission altogether, similar to Canada's "designated classes." In April 1989, the incoming Bush administration submitted to Congress a proposal for 30,000 additional immigrants in each of the next five years, "whose admission would be in the foreign policy interest of the United States." Requirements would be less rigorous than for refugees or ordinary immigrants; but the beneficiaries would not be given any assistance. Most of the 30,000 places would be allocated to Soviet citizens, and some to Vietnamese. The proposal was sponsored in the House by Representative Lamar Smith, a Texas Republican, but it found no takers in the Senate. It received a lukewarm reception from most of the organizations assisting Soviet Jews, which insisted refugee status must be preserved. In keeping with this, Representative Morrison sponsored a measure that would temporarily designate Soviet Jews and Evangelical Christians, as well as Southeast Asians, as categoric refugee groups. This designation would make it unnecessary to demonstrate individual qualification. An initial version was vetoed by President Bush, who objected that the bill impinged on his authority to conduct foreign relations. The measure was then quickly redrafted, approved by both Houses, and signed by the president on November 21, 1989. In effect until October 1, 1990, the measure was subsequently renewed for another year.

In the intervening period, the Soviet Union further relaxed its travel and emigration regulations. Accordingly, the U.S. consulate in Moscow braced itself for an explosive increase in visa applications. The consul declared that "U.S. policy is that all citizens of the Soviet Union who want to go to the United States will be offered the opportunity to go under one of our immigration programs," but he failed to specificy how this might be done. The number of departures for August 1989 was the highest in twenty years, and in September the number of Soviet Jews waiting in the processing center outside of Rome climbed to 14,000. The denial rate reached 54 percent in Moscow and 20 percent in Rome. Few of those rejected in Rome availed themselves of parole.[78]

There were indications of growing disagreements among the various agencies concerning how best to handle the situation. In mid-September the administration unveiled a new plan to become effective at the end of the month, together with proposed refugee admissions for FY 1990. The stations in Rome and Vienna were to be closed, and so Soviet Jews would have to apply for U.S. visas in Moscow. There it would be easier to turn down those who did not qualify as refugees, since they would obtain instead Israeli visas from the Dutch. The plan also provided for the establishment of direct charter flights from Moscow to Israel. The new policy was also applicable to Pentecostals. President Bush asked for a small increase in admissions, from 116,500 (including midyear additions) to 125,000. They were to be allocated mostly to the Soviet Union, whose quota rose to 50,000; but he requested funds for only 84,000, with the balance of the refugees to be assisted by voluntary organizations, as in Canada.[79]

The plan evoked harsh criticism from both sides of the congressional aisle, on both procedural and substantive grounds, and it prompted firmer support for the Morrison bill. But response among concerned groups in the country at large were more mixed. Albeit enthusiastically welcomed by Israeli officials, the plan occasioned considerable soul-searching among American Jewish organizations; they were torn between their commitment to freedom of choice and to receiving Soviet Jews in the United States on the one hand, and their commitment to Israel on the other. The *New York Times* argued in a September 15 editiorial that the administration was properly trying to deal with the evolving situation by escaping "the emotional grip of the word 'refugee,' with all its legal obligations." The newspaper pointed out that if the administration's proposal for 30,000 "special human-itarian visas" were approved, then as many as 100,000 Soviet citizens might be admitted in FY 1990 (50,000 as refugees, 30,000 under the new visas, and up to the 20,000 per-country-limit as ordinary immi-grants, under the various family reunification and skill preferences). The *New Republic* (October 2) also endorsed the new policy, and it editorialized that although Russians Jews preferred to come to the United States, entries were severely limited, and so "decency requires reserving precious spaces for those who have no place to go."

Washington originally planned to close the Rome-Vienna route only after processing the immigration requests of all Soviet Jews with exit visas dated before October 1; but on November 2, consular of-ficials announced that those who qualified must also obtain an Israeli visa from the Dutch embassy by November 5, and that the centers would be closed as soon as those applications were disposed of, leaving only Moscow. In December, Aeroflot and El Al signed a commercial agreement providing for direct flights from Moscow to Tel Aviv; but the Soviet authorities withheld approval in the face of Arab objections to the growing immigration, exacerbated by Prime Minister Shamir's suggestions that the newcomers might be settled in the occupied territories.

Under pressure by the Bush administration, President Gorbachev finally relented in late September 1990; in the intervening period alternative routes were opened through neighboring countries.[80] In October President Bush authorized 131,000 refugee admissions for the 1991 fiscal year, an increase of 6,000 above the previous level; 50,000 of these are allocated to Soviet nationals, all of whom will receive federal assistance—as against only 40,000 in 1990.

In February 1990 the House subcommittee held hearings on the administration's H.R. 2646. But the bill was unlikely to progress, because Chairman Morrison appeared intent on resolving the prob-lem through his own immigration reform bill. This proposed bill would allow up to 750,000 immigrants to enter each year—120,000 above the level proposed by the pending Kennedy-Simpson bill.

The outcome of the congressional give-and-take was the Immi-gration Act of 1990, which somewhat meets Morrison's objectives. For fiscal years 1992–1994, the law establishes an annual maximum number of admissions for all categories of immigrants, excluding refugees, set at 714,000. Imposed for the first time ever, in response to demands for more limited immigration, this "hard cap" is neverthe-less well above the level of current nonrefugee admissions (approxi-mately 600,000). Some of the additional visas are allocated to close relatives, while others are set aside for professionals and highly skilled workers, raising the total numbers in the occupational prefer-ence categories from 54,000 a year to 140,000. It is likely that these categories will be filled in part by immigrants from the ex-Warsaw Pact countries, who hitherto were admitted as refugees but no longer qualify as such. Beginning in fiscal year 1995 the cap will no longer be so hard, and the annual maximum will be allowed to rise if needed to accommodate family reunion. The new law also provides that Hong Kong is to be considered a separate foreign state for the purpose of its per-country ceiling, so that its annual maximum will gradually rise from the present 5,000 to the worldwide 20,000 limit. It further allo-cates 1,000 visas to displaced Tibetans. Finally, effective in fiscal year 1991, the number of persons granted asylum who can adjust annually to permanent resident status will double from 5,000 to 10,000.

Conclusion

Refugee policy in Canada and the United States has been shaped by commitments to disparate objectives, and by contradictory dynamics at home and abroad. The record can be looked at from very different perspectives. Over the past forty-five years, both countries have ad-mitted for permanent resettlement large numbers of people from a wide variety of sources, ranging from groups with established com-munities in the host country to entirely new groups that are culturally very different from previous immigrants. The United States has incor-porated more refugees than any other country in the world; but Canada has taken in a much larger mass in proportion to population size, in keeping with its relatively greater general immigration. In the 1970s, both countries reformed their admission system to institu-tionalize a distinct gate for refugees as defined under international law. But they continued to select them mostly on the basis of their putative contributions to domestic and foreign policy objectives.

In the 1980s, the challenges arising from the combined effects of the proliferation of refugees in the developing world and of rising immigration pressures on the more developed countries occasioned an unexpected asylum crisis, which vastly exceeded the capacity of the established adjudication systems. The impact of these processes was much more severe in the United States. By virtue of its proximity to the Caribbean and Central American region, of the accessibility of its coast and land border, and of its role in the economic and political life of the countries in question, the United States was faced with a massive influx of undocumented economic migrants and asylum-seekers. The predicament of many of them was such as to foreclose a neat categorization.

Matters were exacerbated by the Reagan administration's intervention in Central American conflicts. A paradoxical situation arose with respect to El Salvador, whereby large numbers of people fled to the United States to escape the life-threatening activities of a government that Washington supported. Consequently, the issue of mass first asylum, which under the best of circumstances would pose severe ethical and material problems to the receiving countries, became especially contentious. The strange result was that although the United States refused to grant de jure protection to victims of violence in Central America and the Caribbean, it provided a de facto haven to very large numbers. If this vast limbo is included, the United States ranks among the leading first asylum countries in the world, and it is the only one of the affluent democracies to fall within that category.

Canada, by contrast, is relatively insulated from migration pressure by its geographical situation. The impact of the worldwide crisis has been limited to an increase in overstayers who arrived by air as legal visitors—largely a spillover from streams directed toward Western Europe, including Britain. Once the government determined to bring the situation under control, it easily did so by implementing a more demanding visa policy—which the United States possessed all along. As a minor actor in world affairs, Canada maintains a low-profile foreign and security policy. This policy precludes partisan involvement in conflicts within the developing world, and in recent decades it has focused on development assistance. Hence refugee policy is much less dominated by foreign policy considerations, and by the same token it is much less controversial. The combination of these factors facilitated the actions of the refugee advocacy community, which in the late 1980s achieved a measure of success in institutionalizing an asylum determination process that affords claimants the benefit of the doubt.

In particular, Canada has devised an adjudication system that separates the functions of border control and asylum determination; this separation has been accomplished by diversifiying the personnel of the appropriate boards, and by providing them with a measure of autonomy regarding information. A similar separation of functions within the U.S. Justice Department is adumbrated in the final regulations adopted in 1990. Although the apparent effectiveness of Canada's system is predicated on a degree of border control that the United States cannot expect to achieve, the costs to the United States of granting asylum seekers the benefit of the doubt will be more than offset by the added protection it will afford to people in genuine need.

How many are likely to come knocking at the door in the future? And how might they be received? It is evident that Canada and the

United States constitute interactive components of a single regional system of international migrations, and this is likely to be reinforced by the further progress of economic integration. Although this is usually invoked to argue on behalf of a coordination of policing activities, it also provides an opportunity for cooperation in fulfilling humanitarian obligations incumbent upon the two countries.

In this as in other spheres of international affairs, we face a more fluid situation than at any other time since the end of World War II. Yet a few things are fairly clear. The emerging nonconfrontational relationship between the superpowers will eliminate a major factor that exacerbated the developing world's refugee crisis. Indeed, several of the conflicts that contributed to an escalation of the number of refugees worldwide in the 1970s and 1980s have already begun to wind down, and in some cases have been fully settled.[81] On this basis there are grounds also for cautious optimism regarding the incidence of region-wide refugee-generating upheavals, where international and domestic conflicts are intertwined. Yet while some of the refugees confined in camps scattered throughout the third world will be going home, many will linger because of the devastation wrought by the violence that originally drove them out. Moreover, the structural conditions that exacerbate the tensions of state-formation among the new states of Asia (including the Middle East) and Africa, and which fuel social explosions in land-based authoritarian systems in Latin America and elsewhere, are unlikely to change very profoundly in the foreseeable future. We should therefore expect some of the old refugee-producing conflicts to revive and new ones to emerge occasionally as well. Moreover, the dissolution of Communist regimes has begun to loosen ethnoregional configurations that were frozen in place for many decades, and whose dynamics will undoubtedly generate forced population displacements—some of which will spill beyond these countries' borders.

As in the past, most refugees will remain in first asylum countries within their region of origin, by choice as well as by necessity, because others will be unwilling to provide opportunities for resettlement. Countries that face severe problems of their own will thereby be heavily taxed. There is a call for "fair sharing" of the burden by the international community—a sharing that involves not only providing funds, but devising imaginative ways of transforming great misfortune into constructive energy, channeled toward developmental undertakings that themselves contribute to the reintegration of the human beings involved. Although the United States is a mainstay of the international organizations charged with protection of refugees, including both the UNHCR and UNRWA (for Palestinians), Canada's relative contribution to development assistance is far superior. Although discussion of the potential "peace dividend" for the United States has been limited to the domestic sphere, it should be extended to encompass assistance to the developing world, particularly to regions to whose plight the United States has contributed. The evolving relationship between the superpowers also provides an opportunity for cooperation on the reconstruction of lands devastated by their confrontations.

Although most of the world's refugees yearn to return home, a significant residue of people will need permanent resettlement; hence there will be a perennial pressure to gain admission to the United States, Canada, and the other affluent Western democracies. Moreover, the experience of being uprooted inevitably fosters a greater awareness of alternatives. Not surprisingly, many aspire to relocate in a safer country that also provides better economic opportunities; and these apirations arise also among some who are left behind. But these processes in turn contribute to the creation of ambiguity: are these "true" refugees, or mere economic migrants? The ambiguity is not the result of misrepresentation, but inherent in the situation itself. Under conditions of egregious inequality of conditions between countries, these pressures will persist; and it stands to reason that they will be directed toward countries with which links have been established.

Economic studies of both Canada and the United States have established that immigration at the present level or even well above it is a good thing. Hence, the total costs of a generous refugee admission policy are unlikely to be very high. Their higher incidence on particular localities and social groups must be taken into account, however, and compensated for in appropriate fashion.

Both countries will continue to be faced with asylum-seekers who do not qualify as Convention refugees because they are victims of violence rather than of clear-cut persecution. Although there is growing recognition that this feature is characteristic of the contemporary situation, it is most unlikely that the international community will revise the statutory definition of refugee in such an expansive direction.[82] One approach, suggested by international humanitarian law, involves extending the principle of nonrefoulement to persons displaced by warfare. The Geneva Conventions of 1949 prohibit the repatriation of civilians into internal armed conflicts where breaches of the Geneva Conventions are occurring. The UNHCR executive committee's 1985 Note on International Protection also states that the principle of nonrefoulement extends beyond "Convention" refugees to victims of violence. Since no country can be expected to provide havens for all those in need throughout the world, this approach might be combined with the principle that they owe special obligations to their neighbors, and the more so if they bear some responsibility for their predicament. More applicable to the United States than to Canada, this approach argues in favor of temporary safe haven according to criteria specified by law, and with guarantees that the haven be indeed temporary, so as not to disadvantage others in the immigration queue.

Most of the potential migrants originating in former Warsaw Pact countries will no longer qualify for admission to the United States and Canada as refugees.[83] On some grounds, however, it can be argued that they should be afforded special consideration for admission, at least for a time. Having insisted all along that the states in question must grant their citizens freedom of exit, as those states are now willing to do, the Western democracies collectively share an obligation to provide places where some of their citizens can go. Some can avail themselves of special arrangements pertaining to homelands—Jews, ethnic Germans; others qualify as immigrants to the United States, Canada, and other immigration countries under various skill preferences. As a consequence of the interruption in the chain of migration during the no-exit years, however, few of them qualify by virtue of ties of kinship; this is especially problematic in the American case, where family reunion accounts for the bulk of entries. But in devising means for overcoming this handicap, care should be given to minimize burdens on others—including the countries of origin that are in transition toward democracy and economic restructuring. Special admission programs should be added to the existing annual levels. The criteria for selecting the special immigrants should not occasion a brain drain, and they must apply also to other regions of the world that have been disadvantaged under the prevailing immigration system.

APPENDIX 3–A1
Ceilings on Refugee Admissions and Actual Admissions to the United States, Fiscal Years 1981–1991

	1981	1982	1983	1984	1985
Ceilings	217,000	140,000	90,000	72,000	70,000
Applicants	193,230	94,769	104,190	107,437	93,415
Approvals	155,291	61,527	73,645	77,932	59,436
Approval rate, %	91	80	78	82	76
Actual admissions	159,252	97,355	61,681	71,113	68,045

	1986	1987	1988	1989	1990	1991
Ceilings	67,000	70,000	87,500	114,500	125,000[a]	110,000
Applicants	81,017	101,718	n/a	n/a	n.a.	
Approvals	52,081	61,529	70,874	95,505[b]	n.a.	
Approval rate, %	84	81	87	74	n.a.	
Actual admissions	62,440	64,828	76,487	107,230	n.a.	

Note: n.a. = not available.

a. Includes 111,000 federally funded and 14,000 for private sector initiative, including 10,000 Soviets and 4,000 for any region.

b. 87,881 cases pending.

Sources: 1981–1988: Helsinki Watch, *Detained, Denied, Deported: Asylum Seekers in the United States* (New York: Helsinki Watch Committee, June 1989); 1989–1990: *Refugee Reports*, December 29, 1989; 1991: *Refugee Reports*, May 18, 1990 (from INS and Department of State data).

APPENDIX 3–A2
CEILINGS AND APPROVAL RATES ON REFUGEE ADMISSIONS TO THE UNITED STATES BY REGION, FISCAL YEARS 1984–1991

	1984	1985	1986	1987	1988	1989	1990	1991
Africa								
Ceiling	2,750	3,000	3,500	3,500	3,000	2,000	3,000	3,000
Approval rate, %	59	55	60	69	65	n.a.	n.a.	n.a.
Asia								
Ceiling	52,000	50,000	45,500	40,500	47,000	50,000	51,500	52,000
Approval rate, %	89	77	86	81	89			
Eastern Europe, Soviet Union								
Ceiling	11,000	10,000	9,500	10,000	30,000	50,000	46,500	45,000
Approval rate, %	73	77	89	84	82.5			
Latin America								
Ceiling	1,000	3,000	3,000	4,000	3,500	3,500	3,500	3,500
Approval rate, %	54	92	87	66	84			

n.a. = not available.
SOURCE: See appendix 3–A1.

APPENDIX 3–A3
U.S. Asylum Cases Filed with INS District Directors, 1981–1989

	Number of Applications	Granted	Denied	% Approved
1981	61,568	1,175	3,346	25
1982	33,296	3,909	7,255	35
1983	26,091	7,215	16,811	30
1984	24,295	8,278	32,344	20
1985	16,622	4,585	14,172	24
1986	18,889	3,359	7,882	30
1987	26,107	4,062	3,454[a]	54
1988	60,736	5,531	8,582	39
1989	n.a.	6,942	31,547	18

n.a. = not available.
a. This figure does not reflect substantial numbers of drafted denials that were not completed prior to the end of F.Y. 1987, due to clerical shortage.
SOURCE: Helsinki Watch, *Detained, Denied, Deported,* p. 80; *Refugee Reports,* December 29, 1989, p. 14; see appendix 3–A1.

APPENDIX 3–A4
U.S. Asylum Cases, Approval Rate, by Selected Nationalities, 1984–1989
(percent)

	1984	1985	1986	1987	1988	1989
Afghanistan	40	23	63	26	39.5	29.5
Cuba	3	9	2	38	31.9	29.0
El Salvador	2	3	4.5	3.6	3	2.3
Ethiopia	23	32	46	47	77	65.8
Guatemala	0.3	1	2	3.8	5	1.9
Haiti	6	0.6	0.3	0	31.5[a]	3.0
Hungary	27	42	47	20	28.9	28.4
Iran	60	53	58	67	75	57.4
Nicaragua	12	8.5	27	84	53	25.6
Poland	32	37	50	47	53.7	29.2

a. Actual numbers were six approved, thirteen denied.
SOURCE: Helsinki Watch, *Detained, Denied, Deported,* p. 80; see appendix 3–A1.

APPENDIX 3–A5
Canada, Humanitarian Landings, 1984–1988

	1984	1985	1986	1987	1988
Convention refugees	5,681	6,126	6,557	7,566	8,637
Designated classes[a]	9,783	10,738	12,764	14,185	17,938
Administrative review[b]	0	0	6,596	17,139	855
Other humanitarian[c]	9,043	8,725	6,251	5,709	4,222
Total humanitarian	24,507	25,589	32,168	44,599	31,652
% of total immigration	28	30	32	29	20

a. Major source countries are Kampuchea, Laos, Vietnam, Chile, El Salvador, Guatemala, Poland, Yugoslavia, and the Soviet Union.
b. Includes equivalent of U.S. "amnesty."
c. Includes "special measures" program; major source countries are El Salvador, Guatemala, Iran, Lebanon, and Sri Lanka.
SOURCE: Anthony H. Richmond, "Recent Developments in Canadian Immigration" (Toronto: York University, November 1989).

Commentary on Part One

Alan G. Green

Chapters 2 and 3 present us with an excellent description of the slow and painful evolution of postwar immigration policy in Canada and the United States. For both countries the immediate postwar years presented a particular dilemma. How were governments to restructure their respective economies after facing a decade of depression and war?—hardly normal conditions on which to project the future. Furthermore, how were these two Western countries to deal with the millions of homeless European refugees created by the dislocations of the Second World War?

According to the authors, the two countries found similar solutions but arrived at them from very different roads. The common solution was to reopen the doors to a flood of new immigrants, especially the European displaced persons, and as the postwar years progressed to slowly break down the social barriers that had marked the prewar core of immigration policy in both countries. Probably not unsurprisingly, this shift toward a less biased policy position came about two decades after the end of hostilities—that is, first in 1962 and then with the point system in 1967 for Canada, and, in 1965 for the United States.

The process by which these changes came about, however, was very different. In the U.S. case, foreign policy concerns dominated the changes in immigration policy—especially the overriding concern with the potential rise of communism. For Canada, the main concern was with the economy. How were the labor force needs of a small open economy to be met? Canada, like the United States, had experienced a sharp fall in birth rates during the 1930s. The cohort of young women and men that should have been entering the work force in the 1950s didn't exist. Furthermore, Canada was in the midst of a great investment boom. The solution was to reopen the door to immigrants. As the economy shifted toward a more sophisticated manufacturing base, this general demand for labor became focused on importing skilled workers. This shift, coupled with the decline of large-scale European emigration, forced the government in the 1960s to continue the process that had begun in the 1950s—to widen the search for talent to nontraditional sources, that is, Southern and Eastern Europe, and then Asia.

The treatment of refugees followed the same basic process. In the 1950s and 1960s, both Canada and the United States responded to the Hungarian crisis, in the 1970s they responded to the Southeast Asian refugee movement. The basic difference was in Cuban emigration. Canada was clearly not involved in this mass movement to the same extent as was the United States, nor did it face the problems of Mexican emigration northward.

Again, as in the case of general immigration policy, the nature of the response to refugee problems was different in the two countries. Canada and the United States both adopted refugee policies on humanitarian and social considerations, and we should not lose sight of this generosity. For the United States, however, foreign policy factors clearly determined which refugee groups would be admitted; Canada, less involved in these foreign policy matters, was more concerned about which groups would most easily mesh with the needs of the economy. In Canada refugee movements were considered part of the general immigration policy. The selection of who was to be admitted reflected the perceived need for skilled immigrants. The United States did not attempt such screening, basing admissions rather on humanitarian and social considerations.

Unfortunately the authors did not fully exploit the implications of these differences in policy formation. Beginning with the establishment of the Per Centum Act in 1924, U.S. immigration was exogenously determined. To understand changes in U.S. immigration policy the place to start is with the response of Congress to external shocks. The handling of the postwar refugee problem is one example of this type of response. In Canada, however, policy changes are apparently determined endogenously, that is, as a response to changing domestic concerns. The best example is the concern about short-term labor market conditions. This concern has led to the tap-on, tap-off approach to establishing how many and who will be admitted yearly. On a longer-term note, the shift toward more highly trained immigrants was a response to the sharp increase in needs for skills as the economy shifted toward a more sophisticated level of technology in the 1960s.

In addition to more clearly articulating these basic differences in the determinants of postwar policy formation, the authors might have explored the economic consequences of the two different approaches. In the case of the United States, the exclusive focus on humanitarian and social factors has potential implications on the development of the domestic labor force. Recent studies have suggested that the level of training of recent admittees may be lower than it is for the native population—possibly a factor in the slowdown of U.S. economic performance. These are perhaps only short-run effects, but they are a matter of concern. In the Canadian case, the greater attention to economic factors in determining the immigration flow may modify this consequence, but it is not without some difficulties. Such a policy can run into bureaucratic rigidities over which skills are needed. A case in point is the admission of professional engineers. Currently they receive a zero-weighting on occupational demand. The engineering profession, however, is forecasting a serious shortage of trained and experienced engineers before the end of the decade. This inconsistency in perceived needs shows the problem of allowing rules to override market factors in determining the solution to economic problems.

The other major difference between Canadian and U.S. policy formation that was not sufficiently explored in these chapters was the important role played by the provinces in Canada. In the United States, one gathers, immigration policy is determined exclusively by the federal government. The basic nature of the Canadian Constitution permits provinces to share with Ottawa in the formation of immigration policy. The interesting feature about this policy is that in the early decades of the century, when Canada was expanding westward, its immigration policy was also largely determined by the federal government. The provinces turned these decisions over to Ottawa. This condition lasted well into the 1950s. It was only beginning with the Quiet Revolution in Quebec in the early 1960s that change occurred. Quebec, seeking to offset its declining birthrate and fearful of what this decline would mean for the preservation of the French language, sought to formulate its own immigration policy. This proactive approach was adopted and expanded in 1975 to provide provinces an explicit mechanism to consult on these matters. Now all provinces are consulted annually about what they see as their local labor needs and how these might be accommodated through changes in immigration policy. In the last several months Quebec has sought to gain even more influence over immigration regulations. These concerns were an important part of the Meech Lake agreement. It is worth stressing that greater control over immigration was the first item for the new round of negotiations between Quebec and the federal government after Meech failed.

The increased decentralization of decision making on immigration policy in Canada is worth noting. This trend does not appear to be occurring in the United States, although with the states witnessing vastly different rates of immigration (higher in Florida and California, for example), local concerns will clearly make themselves heard in Washington. How both countries formulate new immigration policies in the midst of growing regional pressures is clearly an area that needs more work.

Finally, one would have liked to see some comparative statistics on the level, timing, and composition of immigration to Canada and to the United States over the postwar period. The actual effects of immigration policy in general and refugee movements in particular may well prove to be interesting in terms of linking the rhetoric of policy with the reality of arrivals. These are minor matters, however. One must compliment the authors for providing us with an important start on the process of analyzing the patterns of immigration movement to North America; they have set an agenda for future research in this key policy area.

PART TWO

Immigrants' Demographic Characteristics and Earnings

4
The Changing Demographic Characteristics and Impact of Immigrants in Canada

Teresa A. Sullivan

That the population explosion did not become an immigration explosion is a result solely of immigration restrictions in the host countries.[1] The combination of high postwar fertility and declining mortality has produced in the developing countries very large cohorts of young people at the prime ages for immigrating. Given that there are many more potential immigrants than the host countries have been willing to admit, admissions-rationing has become the dominant function of the immigration policy of host countries.[2]

In Canada, the famous 1947 speech by Prime Minister Mackenzie King reversed the previous exclusionary policies and stated that Canadian policy would be to accept immigrants up to its "absorptive capacity."[3] Although absorptive capacity has never been measured, in the Immigration Act of 1976 the federal government of Canada recognized that immigration to Canada has economic, social, and demographic impacts. Some have claimed that the demographic impact of immigration is second only to labor market demand as an important immigration issue for Canadians.[4] During the past few years, Canadian policy makers have indicated growing concern about the prospect of national population decline if fertility remains at low levels.[5] As one recent government document explained, age structure data "make explicit the long-term consequences of a level of fertility below replacement level with positive net migration. . . . Canada's population tends toward a constant size, a size that depends solely on the level of immigration."[6] Nevertheless, Canada does not yet have a population policy, and immigration policy has remained loosely linked to broader population concerns.

Even if Canada's absorptive capacity were taken to be the criterion for immigration policy, "absorption" is difficult to conceptualize

119

in demographic terms. Just as the economic impact of immigrants depends in part on the changing conditions of the receiving economy, so the demographic impact of immigrants depends in part on changing demographic conditions. Demographic absorption implies that the changes in the host population are relatively minor, and it can be analyzed in either the short term or the long term. Short-term absorption implies that the immigrants would not greatly change the existing social and demographic characteristics of the country. Over the long term, absorption implies that immigrants contribute minimally to population growth. Because Canada's rates of natural increase have fallen rapidly, the potential impact of immigration has increased, so that the long-term issue of differential population growth becomes more important.

This chapter seeks to explore three dimensions of demographic absorption: magnitude, heterogeneity, and vital rates. Magnitude and heterogeneity are helpful in understanding the short-term impacts of immigration. Magnitude refers to the numbers of immigrants admitted and their size relative to the existing population. In a population that is growing through natural increase, as in the United States, even an increase in the number of immigrants admitted might not change the crude net migration rate: that is, the number of immigrants per 1000 population estimated at midyear. But as rates of natural increase slow or even turn into natural decrease, future population growth depends on the entry of immigrants and their levels of fertility. The numbers of immigrants admitted is a function of public policy and enforcement mechanisms against unauthorized entry.

Heterogeneity refers to the diversity introduced into a population by immigration. Relevant forms of heterogeneity are age and sex composition, national origin, racial or ethnic composition, and linguistic or religious diversity. Age and sex composition are important because of their relationship to the general division of labor and to potential population growth. Racial, ethnic, linguistic, and religious diversity are important because they may exacerbate existing social tensions—for example, between French- and English-speaking linguistic groups—or because they may introduce new tensions into the society. The amount of diversity introduced by immigration is potentially a function of public policy, although stated policies often have unforeseen consequences.

Finally, vital rates—fertility and mortality rates—represent the continued impact of immigration on the next generation of Canadians. Fertility rates are the most important aspect of the long-term demographic absorption of immigrants. In this chapter I will consider differential fertility rates, but other relevant measures include rates of morbidity and mortality, nuptiality rates, and internal migration, remigration, or emigration. Government policy can influence vital rates, especially through the quality and availability of health care. But government-influenced changes in vital rates are difficult to accomplish and are frequently seen as illegitimate areas for public policy in Western-style democracies.

While I will analyze these dimensions separately, they do of course interact. Heterogeneity that is tolerable when the immigration levels and rates are low may become intolerable when net migration rates are higher. By the same token, little resentment may be aroused even by high rates of immigration if the newcomers are quite similar to the existing population. High fertility rates among a small immigrant group, or among a group of relatively homogeneous immigrants, will have less visibility than high rates among a large or heterogeneous group. In the final section of this chapter, I will examine the relationship of indicators of heterogeneity to the number of children ever born. Before that, however, I will examine census data on the size and heterogeneity of the Canadian immigrant population.

Size

The numbers of immigrants admitted to Canada each year varies according to administrative criteria that take into account economic conditions, refugee situations, and a number of other considerations.[7] In 1988, Canada expected to admit about 130,000 immigrants.[8] Although such magnitudes might seem small in comparison, say, with the 450,000 admitted to the United States, the relative numbers are large. In 1981, when the total population of Canada stood at 24.1 million, there were 3.9 million foreign-born, or about 16.1 percent of the total.[9] By comparison, although the United States had over four times as many foreign-born residents (14.1 million), they amounted to only 6.2 percent of its enumerated population in 1980. These figures mark both Canada and the United States as unusual among independent states, for in the 1980 round of censuses the median proportion of foreign-born was only 2.7 percent and the upper quartile was 6.6 percent.[10] Among some other large receiving countries, the proportions of foreign-born were 6.8 percent in Argentina, 14.8 percent in New Zealand, and 20.6 percent in Australia.

Table 4–1 presents data on the crude rates of net migration for four major receiving countries: Canada, Australia, New Zealand, and the United States. The crude rate of net migration is the residual when natural increase is subtracted from annual rates of growth. Most demographers would expect that the lower the crude rate of net

121

TABLE 4–1
CRUDE RATES OF NET MIGRATION IN FOUR RECEIVING COUNTRIES,
1950–1987
(average annual net migration per 1,000 population)

Country	1950–1960	1960–1970	1970–1974	1986–1987
Canada	6.9	3.6	4.4	1.8
United States	1.8[a]	2.0[a]	1.7[a]	3.2
Australia	9.0	7.7	4.6	6.2
New Zealand	4.8	1.7	5.6	−1.5

a. Official estimates.
SOURCE: (1950–1974) United Nations 1979, table 143, p.254; (1986–1987) calculated from United Nations 1989a, table 3, p. 173 and table 4, p. 184. Except as noted, net migration was calculated as the difference between total population change and natural increase.

migration, the less problematic the absorption of the immigrants. Table 4–1 shows that since the 1950s there has been a substantial change in both the rates of these receiving countries and in their relative ranking.

Table 4–1 indicates that in 1950–1960, the Canadian population was adding nearly 7 immigrants per 1000 persons every year. By 1986–1987, this figure had dropped to fewer than 2 per 1000 per year. The Canadian rates were well below Australian rates for every time period, although they exceeded U.S. rates until the 1986–1987 period. Canadian rates exceeded New Zealand rates in every period except 1970–1974. One source, in fact, indicates that indeed New Zealand may show no measurable net migration for the 1985–1990 period.[11]

Taken in conjunction, these data suggest that although the rates of net migration for Canada may be stabilizing, Canada will still rank among the leading host countries in the world. Moreover, Canada has a large foreign-born population both in absolute numbers and relative to its population size. Nevertheless, unless there is a large increase in the numbers of immigrants admitted each year, issues of heterogeneity and rate of change will be more important demographically than will size alone.

Heterogeneity

In common with the other host countries, Canada was settled principally by immigrants from other parts of the world, often with little or no official recognition. Since the advent of national immigration policies, however, the host countries have experimented with restrictions based on ascribed and achieved characteristics of immigrants. This section examines ascribed characteristics such as national origin, age, and sex, over which the immigrant has no choice. It also examines religions and language use. Although these characteristics are ascribed at birth, the individual can alter them, perhaps in accordance with preferences within a written policy. Canada has no religious preference, but its policy encourages speakers of English or French.

Nationality. As happened in the United States following the 1965 amendments to the Immigration and Nationality Act, changes in Canadian immigration legislation led to major shifts in the sending countries of immigrants. Table 4–2 indicates that in 1971, 28 percent of all immigrants and almost one-fifth of immigrants since 1966 had come from the United Kingdom. The second largest group was "other Europe," a residual code that would include the Iberian peninsula and much of Eastern Europe. Italy and the United States ranked third and fourth, with the United States accounting for a slightly larger percentage of recent immigrants and Italy accounting for a slightly larger percentage of all immigrants. Together, these four groupings accounted for more than 55 percent of recent immigrants and 53.1 percent of all immigrants.

The most dramatic shift by 1981 was the increase in the proportion of Asian immigrants.[12] Unfortunately, the 1981 Canadian census did not provide more detailed codes for countries of origin, an absence that is especially unfortunate given this shift. By 1981, more than 40 percent of recent immigrants were Asians, and Asians had risen from constituting 5.3 percent of all immigrants in 1971 to 14 percent of all immigrants in 1981.

The 1986 census provided more detail on Asian working-age immigrants, who by then made up 16.8 percent of the foreign-born.[13] East Asia was the birthplace of 6 percent of all immigrants, and Southeast Asia accounted for another 5 percent. South Asia was the birthplace of 4 percent, and West Asia of 1.8 percent of all immigrants. In other words, by 1986 there were as many Asian immigrants as there were U.S. and Italian immigrants combined.

Nearly as impressive was the rise in the proportions of immigrants from Latin America and the Caribbean to 13.6 percent of the new immigrant stream and more than 7 percent of the total foreign-born population.[14] By 1986, 8.5 percent of all working-age immigrants came from this area, 5 percent came from the Caribbean, and 3.5 percent came from Central or South America. Comparable propor-

TABLE 4–2

PERCENTAGE OF FOREIGN-BORN RESIDENTS AND RECENT IMMIGRANTS, BY NATIONALITY, CANADA, 1971 AND 1981

	All Foreign-born Persons				Recent Immigrants			
Nationality	1971	1981	Change in proportion	% change in number	1971	1981	Change in proportion	% change in number
Total, all nationalities, %	100.0	100.0	0.0		100.0	100.0	0.0	
Total, all nationalities, in thousands	3,299.8	3,874.2		17.4	579.2	424.35		−26.7
Proportion born in								
U.S.	9.5	8.2	−1.3	1.3	11.2	8.1	−3.1	−47.0
Belgium & Luxembourg	0.8	0.6	−0.2	−11.9	0.4	0.4	0.0	−26.7
France	1.7	1.4	−0.3	−3.3	2.6	1.3	−1.3	−63.4
Germany	6.5	5.1	−1.4	−7.9	3.9	1.4	−2.5	−73.7
Netherlands	4.0	3.6	−0.4	5.7	1.5	1.4	−0.1	−31.6

Republic of Ireland	1.1	0.4	−0.7	−57.3	0.9	0.3	−0.6	−75.6
United Kingdom	28.1	22.9	−5.2	−4.3	19.5	13.7	−5.8	−48.5
Greece	2.4	2.3	−0.1	12.5	3.9	0.7	−3.2	−86.8
Italy	11.7	10.0	−1.7	0.3	9.5	1.7	−7.8	−86.9
Poland	4.9	3.8	−1.1	−8.9	1.0	1.2	−0.2	−12.1
USSR	4.7	3.3	−1.4	−17.6	0.3	1.4	0.9	241.9
Other Europe	13.3	13.1	−0.2	15.6	15.0	8.1	−6.9	−60.4
Asia	5.3	14.0	8.7	210.1	13.4	40.5	27.1	121.4
Africa	1.4	2.7	1.3	126.4	3.4	4.9	1.5	5.6
Latin America & Caribbean	3.1	7.3	4.2	176.5	9.6	13.3	3.7	1.5
All Other	1.3	1.0	−0.3	−9.7	3.8	1.6	−2.2	−69.2

NOTE: Recent immigrants refer to immigrants who entered Canada no more than five years before the date of the census.
SOURCE: Statistics Canada, Census of Canada, 1971 and 1981 Public Use Sample tapes. The 1971 data are inflated from a one-in-one hundred sample. The 1981 data are inflated from a one-in-fifty sample.

tions from the traditional European source countries included Germany (5.2 percent) and the Netherlands (3.4 percent).

Immigration from Africa also showed dramatic relative shifts, although the absolute numbers were smaller. By 1986, 2.8 percent of all working-age immigrants came from African countries, a proportion roughly equivalent to that of immigrants from what is now the Soviet Union—2.9 percent.

The broadened Canadian immigration policies brought in newcomers from the three continents of developing countries—Asia, Africa, and Latin America. These are also the countries of highest fertility, and they might contribute to higher-than-average population growth. Because Canadian immigration policies favor speakers of the two national languages, however, diversity in national origin need not imply diversity in language. And the assimilation implied in language use might also characterize fertility rates.

Sex and Age Composition. The international migration of women is relevant to the future growth of the foreign-stock population, but it is also closely related to the reasons for immigration and to immigration policy. A simple expectation among most demographers, for example, is that economically motivated migrations and relatively recent migrations will be male-dominant. By contrast, female-dominant sex ratios should characterize established migration streams and refugee streams. Admission policies that favor family reunification should lead to higher proportions of women. Because both Canada and the United States have family reunification policies, one might expect similar sex ratios. But the U.S. policy is more heavily oriented toward family reunification; its sex ratio should be lower. In 1980 the sex ratio among U.S. immigrants was 88 males per one hundred females, while the Canadian ratio in 1981 was 98. By contrast, Australia and New Zealand both had male-dominant immigrant populations, with sex ratios of 107 and 104 respectively.

The immigrant stream appears to be quite similar to Canada in sex composition. The nationwide Canadian sex ratio has been dropping, from 98.8 in 1981[15] to 97.4 in 1986.[16] The sex ratio of the foreign-born has also been dropping, from 101.4 in 1971 to 97.7 in 1981. Tabulations for the working-age foreign-born population in 1986 showed a sex ratio of 95. As one might further expect, the recent Canadian immigrants have a much lower sex ratio (93) than the entire foreign-born population, suggesting a recent feminization of the immigrant stream.

Because reasons for immigrating are closely linked to nationality, one would expect a great deal of variation in the sex ratio by nationality. For example, in the United States the sex ratio for Cubans, a refugee population, is considerably lower than the sex ratio for Mexicans, an economic migration. Moreover, there is often a time lag between the arrival of the "leading edge" of immigrants and the arrival of their families. So we might expect that the nationalities most recently arrived in Canada would have the most unbalanced and male-dominant sex ratios, while older groups, for reasons of differential mortality if no other, would have unbalanced female-dominant-sex ratios.

Table 4–3 provides at least some evidence for these hypotheses. As expected, the Asian immigrant stream is male-dominated, but as more Asians entered, the sex ratio moved toward greater balance. The 1971 sex ratio was 115.7, consistent with an economic migration, and the 1981 ratio was 102.4, consistent with continued economic migration and the effects of family reunification. Among recent immigrants, the sex ratio had dropped to a slightly female-dominated figure of 96.4. Other evidence that suggests greater female representation among the older sending countries includes the very low sex ratios for the United States, the United Kingdom, Germany, and Poland, and the dropping sex ratios among recent immigrants from Belgium and Luxembourg, France, Ireland, Greece, and Italy.

There is also countervailing evidence to the expected pattern. Among Africans, for example, the sex ratio has become more male-dominated. Immigration from the Netherlands, including recent immigration, remains strongly male-dominant. And one of the lowest sex ratios is found for Latin American and Caribbean immigrants. This ratio is low and stays low, suggesting perhaps an economic migration of women seeking work in Canada. Similar patterns are seen in the United States among Caribbean immigrants,[17] and studies in Latin America often show that migrations of relatively short distances are female dominant. The short airplane trips from Caribbean capitals to Canada may make this international migration more similar to traditional internal migration patterns. Thus, a regional effect might explain an otherwise anomalous finding.

Economic immigrants are usually relatively young—often persons in their mid- to late-twenties. The selection system for Assisted Relatives and other independent immigrants reinforces this tendency by awarding ten units for persons twenty-one to forty-four. Two units are deducted for each year under twenty-one or over forty-four.[18] Refugees, by contrast, who are not usually self-selected, are likely to be of any age. Although Canada receives refugees, the bulk of its immigration is undertaken for economic reasons, and so we would expect a relatively young immigrant group. The data on the age

TABLE 4–3: MALE-FEMALE SEX RATIOS OF FOREIGN-BORN RESIDENTS AND RECENT IMMIGRANTS, BY NATIONALITY, CANADA, 1971 AND 1981

Nationality	All Foreign-born Persons				Recent Immigrants			
	1971	(Number)	1981	(Number)	1971	(Number)	1981	(Number)
Total, all nationalities	101.4	(3,299,800)	97.7	(3,873,700)	103.5	(579,200)	92.9	(424,350)
Proportion born in								
U.S.	84.4	(315,100)	81.9	(315,850)	102.2	(65,300)	71.0	(34,550)
Belg./Lux.	100.8	(25,500)	107.3	(24,050)	50.0	(2,100)	93.8	(1,550)
France	116.2	(56,200)	111.1	(55,000)	121.7	(15,300)	94.6	(5,450)
Germany	100.8	(212,900)	97.3	(198,200)	92.2	(22,300)	73.9	(6,000)
Netherlands	118.1	(133,500)	108.6	(137,700)	140.1	(8,900)	141.7	(5,800)
Republic of Ireland	99.5	(38,800)	111.3	(16,800)	82.8	(5,300)	91.7	(1,150)
United Kingdom	86.1	(927,700)	86.9	(888,450)	97.0	(112,900)	95.1	(58,250)
Greece	118.7	(78,300)	108.9	(89,400)	135.8	(22,400)	93.8	(3,100)
Italy	120.0	(385,700)	112.2	(388,850)	121.3	(55,100)	98.6	(7,250)
Poland	115.9	(160,400)	95.8	(147,750)	100.0	(5,600)	80.0	(4,950)
USSR	104.6	(156,100)	103.0	(127,000)	100.0	(2,000)	98.3	(5,950)
Other Europe	121.6	(445,100)	111.4	(510,750)	96.2	(86,700)	98.8	(34,400)
Asia	115.7	(173,000)	102.4	(543,200)	118.3	(77,500)	96.4	(171,850)
Africa	100.9	(45,600)	105.3	(106,350)	102.0	(19,800)	106.5	(20,650)
Latin Am./Carib.	84.5	(102,600)	85.3	(284,650)	91.1	(55,800)	84.2	(56,650)
All Other	93.0	(44,200)	109.9	(40,200)	91.2	(22,200)	106.1	(6,800)

NOTE: Recent immigrants refer to immigrants who entered Canada no more than five years before the date of the census.
SOURCE: Statistics Canada, Census of Canada, 1971 and 1981 Public Use Sample tapes. The 1971 data are inflated from a one-in-one hundred sample. The 1981 data are inflated from a one-in-fifty sample.

TABLE 4–4

AGE STRUCTURE OF ALL FOREIGN-BORN RESIDENTS, 1971, 1981, AND
1986, AND RECENT IMMIGRANTS, CANADA, 1971 AND 1981

	All Foreign-born			Recent Immigrants	
	1971	1981	1986	1971	1981
Total, all ages	3,299,800	3,874,200	n.a.	579,200	424,350
0–4	51,800	33,300	n.a.	50,400	28,350
5–9	108,800	86,600	n.a.	57,100	37,850
10–14	119,800	153,350	n.a.	36,500	35,800
15–19	150,100	207,550	112,900	36,900	38,700
20–24	253,300	221,750	175,150	88,600	59,400
25–29	290,300	305,950	200,350	117,100	66,050
30–34	277,700	415,950	257,550	70,500	45,850
35–39	275,800	374,400	342,850	40,800	27,350
40–44	278,300	325,800	310,950	25,400	15,400
45–49	276,000	298,800	278,850	14,200	11,850
50–54	194,300	302,050	263,000	11,400	12,700
55–59	172,700	294,550	258,600	8,400	11,300
60–64	212,000	199,750	262,900	8,700	11,900
65–69	210,800	173,150	176,600	6,400	10,250
70–74	168,200	186,250	139,050	3,400	5,700
75–79	124,800	155,600	125,400	1,600	3,450
80–84	81,100	88,350	89,200	1,200	1,450
85 +	41,100	51,200	49,850	400	1,000
Median age	42	42	n.a.	25	25

n.a. = data are not available. The 1986 data are limited to ages fifteen and over.
SOURCE: Statistics Canada, Census of Canada, 1971, 1981, and 1986 Public Use
Sample tapes. The 1971 data are inflated from a one-in-one hundred sample.
The 1981 and 1986 data are inflated from a one-in-fifty sample.

composition of the foreign-born and of the immigrants in particular
bear out this expectation.

Table 4–4 presents the age composition of the foreign-born and
the recent immigrant population of Canada. The median age for the
foreign-born population in both 1971 and 1981 was forty-two, indicating the substantial replenishment of the foreign-born that was already
noted. The age of the new immigrants has hardly changed; both in
1971 and in 1981, the immigrants who had entered during the past
five years had a median age of twenty-five years. In this respect the
newest immigrants were most similar to the native-born Canadians,
whose median age was slightly over twenty-six years.[19]

Figures 4–1 through 4–4 present modified age-sex pyramids for

FIGURE 4–1
AGE DISTRIBUTION OF FOREIGN-BORN RESIDENTS, 1981

Proportion of Group

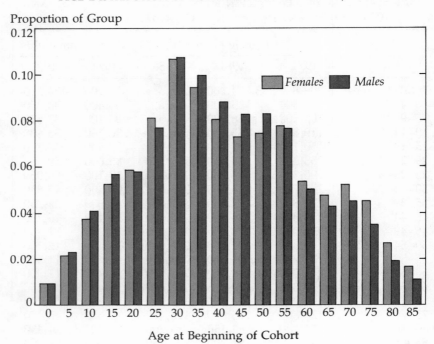

Age at Beginning of Cohort

SOURCE: Author.

immigrants in 1981 and 1971 and for the recent immigrants in 1981 and 1971. The age-sex pyramids combine information on age composition and sex ratios. This information is presented in a different form in table 4–5. It shows striking patterns of diversity, far from what one might call a normal pattern of age-sex dispersion:

• *A female-dominant sex ratio among young children.* Normally, this ratio exceeds 100 in a developed country, because the sex ratio at birth is about 105 and infant mortality is low.

• *Higher than expected sex ratios in the school-attending years (five to nineteen).* While some male dominance usually continues for the reasons outlined above, these ratios exceed the expected ratios. In 1981 these sex ratios are higher than the sex ratios at birth, indicating differential migration of young males.

• *Higher than expected sex ratios among those aged thirty to forty-nine in 1971 and thirty-five to fifty-four in 1981.* Again, this trend is almost surely due to male-selective migration.

130

FIGURE 4–2
AGE DISTRIBUTION OF FOREIGN-BORN RESIDENTS, 1971

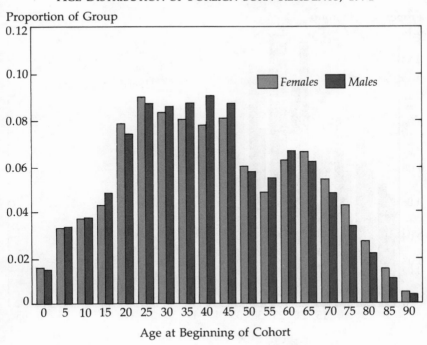

Proportion of Group

Age at Beginning of Cohort

SOURCE: Author.

• *An anomalously high sex ratio at ages fifty-five to sixty-four in 1971.* This ratio is probably attributable to high, male-dominant post-World War II migration.

The sex ratios at the older ages are consistent with usual patterns of mortality. A more detailed study of mortality was not possible because the only census-based technique available, census-survival ratios, was unusable. The survival ratios exceeded 2 at every age below sixty in 1971, and they exceeded 1 at every age below seventy-four in 1971. The peak survival ratio was 5.92 for children aged zero to four in 1971 (data are not shown). These ratios are impossible, of course, and their calculation from the data indicates only the continued flow of immigrants between 1971 and 1981, a fact that has already been demonstrated.

Figure 4–5 provides comparative data on the foreign-born from the 1986 census. Although this figure is limited to the population

131

FIGURE 4–3
AGE DISTRIBUTION OF RECENT IMMIGRANTS, 1981

Proportion of Group

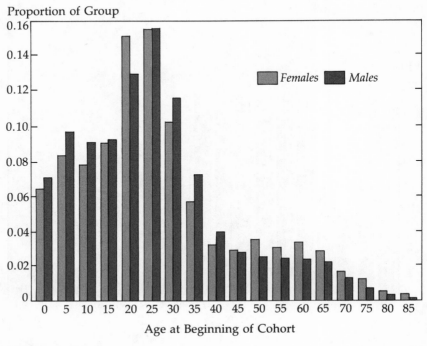

Age at Beginning of Cohort

SOURCE: Author.

aged fifteen years and older, many of the preceding trends can still be discerned in it.

Language Use. Language use has already been demonstrated to affect the earnings of the immigrants in Canada.[20] Tables 4–6 and 4–7 show the relationship between language use and the birthplace of immigrants, for 1971 and 1981. By 1986, Canada awarded a maximum of fifteen points for knowledge of official languages.[21] Even these earlier data, however, reveal that only a small proportion of immigrants use neither English nor French. In 1971, this proportion reached a high of less than 25 percent among Italians; by 1981, Italians were still the group with the highest proportion, but the proportion had dropped to 15 percent. The proportion of Asians using some other language dropped from 15.9 percent to 13.8 percent, despite the great increase

132

FIGURE 4-4
AGE DISTRIBUTION OF RECENT IMMIGRANTS, 1971

Proportion of Group

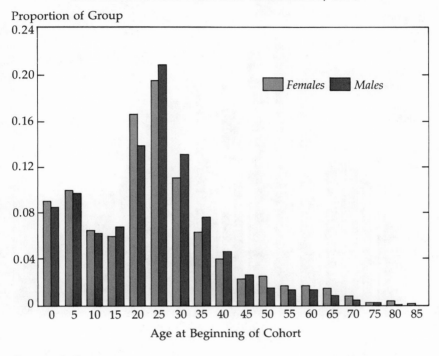

Age at Beginning of Cohort

SOURCE: Author.

in their numbers, and the proportion of Latin Americans began at less than 3 percent in 1971 and dropped to less than 1 percent in 1981.

The middle columns of tables 4–6 and 4–7, however, indicate the presence of a great deal of language diversity in the homes of the immigrants, even though they may speak English or French elsewhere. In 1981, the proportion speaking another language at home exceeded 50 percent for Greeks, Italians, Soviets, and Asians. Poles were nearly as high, with almost 45 percent speaking another language at home.

The language diversity in the homes of working-age immigrants in 1986 was similar, but greater national-origin detail was available in the 1986 enumeration. The highest proportions using an official language at work and another language at home were found among immigrants from Greece (70.9 percent), Southeast Asia (69.8 percent),

133

FIGURE 4–5
AGE DISTRIBUTION OF FOREIGN-BORN RESIDENTS, AGED 15 +, 1986

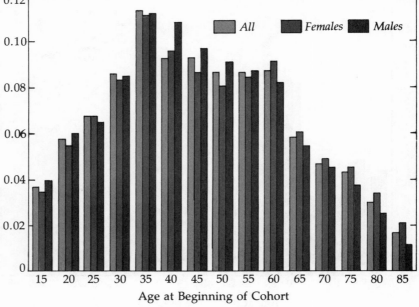

SOURCE: Author.

East Asia (63.9 percent), Yugoslavia (62.7 percent), Italy (60.9 percent), West Asia (60.4 percent), the Soviet Union (59.5 percent), Portugal (58.8 percent), and South Asia (57.7 percent).

Because linguistic diversity is an important issue in the absorption of immigrants into a population, this strikingly high use of the official languages is a useful indicator. Canada has explicitly incorporated linguistic ability into its selection criteria for assisted relatives and other independent immigrants. Knowledge of one of the official languages is worth a maximum of fifteen points in the 100-point schedule. The "pass work" is seventy points.[22]

Ethnic Congruity. A final indicator, called congruity, might help us to understand who immigrates to Canada. This indicator cross-classifies country of birth, reported ancestry, and home language to look for congruity or incongruity—similarity or failure to match. In constructing this measure, country of birthplace was the anchor variable. If

TABLE 4–5: MALE-FEMALE SEX RATIOS OF ALL FOREIGN-BORN
RESIDENTS AND RECENT IMMIGRANTS, BY AGE, CANADA,
1971 AND 1981

Age	All Foreign-born Persons		Recent Immigrants	
	1971	1981	1971	1981
Total, all ages	101.4	97.7	103.5	92.9
0–4	96.2	98.8	97.6	103.2
5–9	102.6	105.7	101.8	107.4
10–14	102.4	105.7	101.5	106.9
15–19	112.9	105.9	117.1	94.5
20–24	96.2	96.0	86.5	78.9
25–29	98.0	92.7	110.6	93.1
30–34	103.6	98.7	123.1	105.1
35–39	109.9	103.0	126.7	118.8
40–44	116.1	106.8	119.0	113.9
45–49	108.3	111.8	121.9	86.6
50–54	98.9	109.1	60.6	64.9
55–59	112.2	95.7	83.0	73.8
60–64	107.6	91.1	85.1	66.4
65–69	96.1	91.7	56.1	72.3
70–74	89.4	86.0	61.9	67.6
75–79	79.6	77.9	100.0	50.0
80–84	79.8	68.1	20.0	52.6
85–89[a]	71.3	64.4	0.0	25.0
90–over	69.7	n.a.	n.a.	n.a.

n.a. = data are not available.
NOTE: Recent immigrants refer to immigrants who entered Canada no more
than five years before the date of the census.
a. Category includes all those age 85 and above in 1981.
SOURCE: Statistics Canada, Census of Canada, 1971 and 1981 Public Use
Sample tapes.

either the reported ancestry or the language used at home was inconsistent with the birthplace, the case was identified as incongruous.
Two groups of immigrants are likely to be incongruous using this
measure. One group consists of persons who are members of minority groups in their home countries. They may feel fewer obstacles to
immigration than those who are members of majority groups.[23]
Countries such as Canada and the United States, which have drawn
their residents from all over the world, may claim that "everyone
belongs to a minority," so that members of minority groups elsewhere
may feel more comfortable.

TABLE 4-6
LANGUAGE USAGE OF FOREIGN-BORN POPULATION, CANADA, 1971
(percent)

Birthplace	Use French or English at Home and Officially	Use French or English Officially, Another Lang. at Home	Use Lang. Other than French or English at Home and Officially
All nationalities	67.8	25.7	6.6
U.S.	98.1	1.7	0.3
Belgium & Luxembourg	82.7	17.3	—
France	94.1	5.5	0.4
Germany	63.4	34.4	2.2
Netherlands	80.2	19.0	0.7
Ireland	99.7	0.3	—
U.K.	99.0	0.9	0.1
Greece	14.9	65.0	20.1
Italy	19.4	56.1	24.4
Poland	46.4	48.1	5.5
USSR	38.8	54.1	7.1
Other European	46.9	42.6	10.6
Asia	40.1	44.0	15.9
Africa	76.3	22.8	0.9
Latin America	86.5	10.8	2.7
All other	71.0	24.7	4.3

SOURCE: Statistics Canada, Census of Canada, 1971 Public Use Sample tapes.

A second incongruous group consists of the descendants of immigrants, who may themselves consider immigration more readily than would those whose ancestors have long resided in the same place. For a family that has already migrated internationally, the next move may not look like such a discontinuity with the past, and longstanding allegiances are not threatened.

Congruity among Canadian immigrants declined between 1971 and 1981. In 1971 the rate of congruity was about 69 percent, and by 1981 it had declined to about 63 percent. Higher than average congruity was found in 1971 among the immigrants from Ireland (96 percent), the United Kingdom (95 percent), the United States (88 percent), Greece (84 percent), and Italy (79 percent). Much lower levels of congruity were found among immigrants from the new

TABLE 4–7

LANGUAGE USAGE OF FOREIGN-BORN POPULATION, CANADA, 1981
(percent)

Birthplace	Use French or English at Home and Officially	Use French or English Officially, Another Lang. at Home	Use Lang. Other than French or English at Home and Officially
All nationalities	67.4	27.1	5.5
U.S.	98.3	1.6	0.1
Belgium & Luxembourg	88.8	11.0	0.2
France	94.5	5.3	0.3
Germany	76.1	23.1	0.8
Netherlands	85.0	14.5	0.5
Ireland	99.1	0.9	—
U.K.	99.3	0.7	—
Greece	26.1	62.1	11.9
Italy	30.0	55.0	15.0
Poland	50.9	44.9	4.2
USSR	40.4	53.9	5.8
Other European	49.9	41.6	8.6
Asia	35.5	50.7	13.8
Africa	73.9	24.5	1.6
Latin America	82.5	15.0	2.5
All other	87.6	11.7	0.7

SOURCE: Statistics Canada, Census of Canada, 1981 Public Use Sample tapes.

areas, Benelux countries and Eastern Europe. The congruity levels for Latin America and the Caribbean were 5 percent; Belgium and Luxembourg, 9 percent; the Netherlands, 19 percent; Poland, 28 percent; the Soviet Union, 46 percent; Africa, 47 percent; and Asia, 55 percent. By 1981, the areas of greatest incongruity had changed little: the Netherlands remained under 1 percent, Latin America and the Caribbean were 12 percent, Germany was 21 percent, Belgium and Luxembourg were 22 percent, the Soviet Union was 48 percent, and Africa was 57 percent. The highly congruous sending areas changed little in 1981, although Greece and Italy dropped by more than 10 percent in the proportion congruous.

What is the consequence of incongruity for assimilation or absorption? On the one hand, the incongruous immigrant might have

TABLE 4–8

CHILDREN EVER BORN, BY AGE, CANADIAN TOTAL POPULATION, 1941–1981, AND CANADIAN FOREIGN-BORN POPULATION, 1971–1981

Age	Canadian Total Population				Canadian Foreign-born Population	
	1941	1961	1971	1981	1971	1981
15–19 years	529	735	634	429	600	443
20–24 years	1,003	1,327	910	687	828	774
25–29 years	1,640	2,178	1,706	1,285	1,483	1,286
30–34 years	2,425	2,775	2,621	1,880	2,200	1,824
35–39 years	3,206	3,102	3,158	2,330	2,621	2,242
40–44 years	3,795	3,231	3,348	2,842	2,698	2,537
45–54 years	4,167	3,130	3,257	3,333	2,641	2,819
55–64 years	4,398	3,506	3,049	3,330	2,684	2,856
65 years +	4,818	4,038	3,565	3,248	3,208	2,855

NOTE: Children ever born indicates per 1000 ever-married women.
SOURCE: Statistics Canada, 1981 Census of Canada, Population, Nuptiality and Fertility Catalogue, V. 1-national series (August 1985), table 1, pp. 92–906; Statistics Canada, Census of Canada, 1971 and 1981 Public Use Sample tapes.

greater incentive to assimilate to the norms of the host country. On the other hand, incongruous immigrants might see the new host country as an environment for preserving the differences that distinguish their group or their family. As the following section will indicate, there is at least some indication that the latter effect might be more important.

The Fertility Change

Canada, in common with most of the developed world, has experienced sharply dropping fertility rates. Canada's fertility was once quite high, especially in Francophone (and Catholic) areas. In 1971, Canadian total fertility rate (TFR) was 2,135.8 children per thousand women,[24] a rate that if continued for a long time with existing mortality rates would replace the population but would lead to no population growth. By the time of the 1981 census, Canadian TFR had declined to 1,670 children per thousand women,[25] and by 1988 the rate had rebounded only slightly to 1,690. The projected TFR for the year 2000 is 1,700,[26] a rate that is far below replacement. The United States

TABLE 4–9
MEDIAN, MEAN, AND STANDARD DEVIATIONS FOR CHILDREN EVER
BORN, BY BIRTHPLACE, CANADA, 1971 AND 1981

	1971			1981		
	Median	Mean	Standard deviation	Median	Mean	Standard deviation
U.S.	3.0	3.44	2.82	3.0	3.07	2.18
Belgium &						
Luxembourg	2.0	2.65	2.51	3.0	2.90	2.02
France	2.0	2.48	2.06	2.0	2.24	1.81
Germany	2.0	2.60	2.21	2.0	2.28	1.65
Netherlands	4.0	4.06	2.35	3.0	3.76	2.26
Ireland	2.0	2.63	2.08	3.0	3.07	2.02
U.K.	2.0	2.56	1.99	2.0	2.50	1.77
Greece	3.0	2.57	1.53	2.0	2.59	1.53
Italy	3.0	3.34	2.19	3.0	3.04	1.77
Poland	2.0	2.71	2.09	2.0	2.61	1.84
USSR	2.0	3.07	2.64	2.0	2.64	2.07
Other European	2.0	2.82	2.41	2.0	2.53	1.91
Asia	3.0	3.19	2.24	3.0	3.58	2.25
Africa	2.0	2.53	1.98	3.0	3.04	2.01
Latin America,						
Caribbean	3.0	3.04	2.35	3.0	3.46	2.47
All other	2.0	2.20	1.71	2.0	2.54	2.48

SOURCE: Statistics Canada, Census of Canada, 1971 and 1981 Public Use
Sample tapes.

is only slightly higher, with an estimated 1988 TFR of 1850, projected
to rise to 1,860 by the year 2000.

For at least twenty years, then, with a projected continuation for
thirty years, Canada has been at or below replacement level fertility.
Over the long run, Canadian population will decline unless pre-
vented by two factors: continued positive net migration and the
change in birth rates achieved if the immigrants have higher fertility
than the native-born. As we have seen, Canada continues to have
substantial positive net migration, and the new immigrants come
disproportionately from the high-fertility parts of the developing
world, especially Asia.[27]

Canadian immigrants are like the Canadian native-born in that
their fertility has declined. Table 4–8 uses children ever born (CEB) to
trace the number and pacing of children both for the total Canadian

TABLE 4–10: COMPLETED FERTILITY FOR EVER-MARRIED FOREIGN-
BORN WOMEN, AGED FORTY AND OLDER, CANADA, 1971
(grand mean = 2.89)

	N	Gross Unadjusted		Net Adjusted for Independents	
		Deviation	Eta	Deviation	Beta
Education					
8 yrs. and less	3,689	.40		.34	
9–11 yrs.	1,754	− .25		− .20	
12–13 yrs.	1,519	− .54		− .47	
Some univ.	253	− .54		− .50	
Univ. degree +	152	− .45		− .43	
			.18		.16
Recent migrant					
No	7,040	− .01		− .01	
Yes	327	.17		.13	
			.02		.01
Religion					
Catholic	2,015	.47		.36	
Anglican	1,576	− .36		− .26	
United Church	1,102	− .14		− .08	
Menn./Hutterite	87	1.68		1.54	
All other	2,587	− .14		− .14	
			.16		.13
Origin					
Asia	256	.30		.19	
Africa	49	− .36		− .21	
Latin Am./Carib.	74	.15		.10	
All other	6,988	− .01		− .01	
			.03		.02
Congruity					
Yes	5,614	− .09		− .04	
No	1,753	.29		.14	
			.07		.03
Language usage					
Eng./Fr. only	5,397	− .10		.04	
Eng./Fr. offic.	1,324	.03		− .28	
No Eng./Fr.	646	.73		.23	
			.10		.06
Multiple R squared					.053
Multiple R					.231

NOTE: Gross-unadjusted and net-adjusted-for-independents columns show
deviations from the grand mean.
SOURCE: Statistics Canada, Census of Canada, 1971 Public Use Sample tapes.

TABLE 4–11: Completed Fertility for Ever-married Foreign-
born Women, Aged Forty and Older, Canada, 1981
(grand mean = 2.82)

	N	Gross Unadjusted	Net Adjusted for Independents
		Deviation Eta	Deviation Beta
Education			
8 yrs. and less	7,613	.37	.31
9–11 yrs.	4,234	−.07	−.02
12–13 yrs.	4,806	−.34	−.28
Some univ.	1,373	−.45	−.46
Univ. degree +	331	−.78	−.77
		.17	.15
Recent migrant			
No	17,495	−.05	−.04
Yes	862	1.07	.76
		.12	.09
Religion			
Catholic	6,018	.21	.16
Anglican	2,833	−.32	−.17
United Church	1,996	−.20	−.09
Menn./Hutterite	166	1.49	1.35
All other	7,344	−.03	−.08
		.12	.09
Origin			
Asia	2,598	.37	.22
Africa	327	.22	.29
Latin Am./Carib.	683	.64	.56
All other	14,749	−.10	−.07
		.10	.08
Congruity			
Yes	12,512	−.06	−.03
No	5,845	.12	.06
		.04	.02
Language Usage			
Eng./Fr. only	12,362	−.11	.01
Eng./Fr. offic.	4,281	−.04	−.22
No Eng./Fr.	1,714	.92	.47
		.15	.09
Multiple R squared			.065
Multiple R			.255

Note: Gross-unadjusted and net-adjusted-for-independents columns show deviations from the grand mean.
Source: Statistics Canada, Census of Canada, 1981 Public Use Sample tapes.

141

population and for the foreign-born population. The first four columns of the table show four decennial enumerations, from 1941 through 1981, and the pattern of fertility decline is very clear. Not only do the total numbers of children decline, but there is also some delay in childbearing. In 1981, one thousand women aged thirty to thirty-four have produced only 1,880 babies.

But among the foreign-born women, the numbers and the pace of childbearing are at least as low as those of the total population, and many times even lower. In 1971, when all Canadian women aged thirty to thirty-four reported 2.6 children on average, the foreign-born women reported only 2.2 children. By 1981, both the total population and the foreign-born were reporting about 1.8 children per woman.

The number of children ever born varied by a number of factors. In 1981, four national-origin groups had mean CEB's higher than 3: immigrants from the Netherlands, the United States, Italy, and Asia. What is interesting about this statistic is that the first three countries have quite low fertility; the annual rate of natural increase in both the Netherlands and Italy is zero, and in the United States it is about 0.6 percent. Therefore, immigrants from these countries have high fertility relative not only to Canada, but also to their home countries. Asia, of course, is a residual category, although it is generally true that most of Asia is far higher than replacement level fertility. A more detailed discussion of these data is reported in Table 4–9.

Tables 4–10 and 4–11 present a multiple classification analysis of completed fertility for immigrant women in 1971 and 1981. Completed fertility is assessed at age forty and over, because in Canada as in most other countries there is negligible fertility beyond that age. The covariates are education, recency of migration, religion, national origin, congruity, and language use. Education has long been negatively associated with fertility. The recency variable is used because more recent migrants might differ in their fertility behavior, especially if they are part of a family reunification program. Religion is included because of the historically high fertility of Canadian Catholics and Hutterites; both religious groups continue to receive immigrants. Congruity and language use are included as possible indicators of assimilation.

In 1971, education and religion are the most important variables, although the relationship between education and fertility is not monotonic. Recent migrants, Asian and Latin American migrants, incongruous migrants, and migrants who retain a language other than the official languages have higher fertility. The explanatory power of the model is weak, however, almost surely because the traditional determinants of fertility—age at first marriage, husband's occupation, and income—have not been included in the model.

The model for 1981 is better behaved in that education becomes monotonic. The effect of religion weakens, although Catholics and especially Mennonites and Hutterites have higher fertility. Recency of migration becomes much more important, with recent migrants having on average one child more than earlier migrants. Continent of origin becomes a stronger predictor, with higher coefficients for Asia, Africa, and especially Latin America. Incongruity remains associated with higher fertility, and the relationship with language intensifies.

The data on children ever born are not conclusive on the relationship of immigration to Canada's population growth. For example, the immigrants' children might not have accompanied them to Canada, or their children might reimmigrate to another country. Nevertheless, to the extent that Canada continues with family reunification as a priority, these children have at least a plausible claim on the attention of the policy maker.

If increased population growth were specifically enunciated as an objective of Canada's immigration policy, then there would be a clear tension between the goals of growth and absorption. Both long-term and short-term absorption, as I have called them, imply admitting immigrants who are similar in many respects to other Canadians. But these data suggest that greater population growth means admitting more people who are different from other Canadians in terms of their continent of origin and their use of nonofficial languages. Population growth also implies admitting women with lower levels of education than is common in Canada, and seeking immigrants of incongruous ethnic background. And because fertility norms seem to converge quickly, to achieve continued growth Canadian immigration policy makers would have to seek ever more diverse immigrant groups to continue the growth. The alternative is to assume that immigrant fertility will quickly converge to Canadian norms, and to raise the levels of adult admissions.

Conclusion

Immigration policy in Canada seeks to achieve many objectives, including enhanced economic development,[28] family reunification, and humanitarian concern for refugees.[29] An additional demographic objective is nearly always listed last, but sounds a consistent note. Immigration "will help to forestall a projected decrease in the Canadian population."[30] About one-fifth of Canada's annual population growth may now be attributed to immigration.

Potentially, immigration fuels population growth in two ways: first, by the addition of the immigrants themselves; second, by the addition of their children. The data in this paper suggest that most immigrants have rather low fertility, and that this finding is robust over several censuses. If the demographic objective gains a high priority, then increasing the number of immigrants appears to be a more successful strategy than relying on their subsequent fertility. The alternative—seeking high-fertility populations to immigrate—is unlikely to succeed because of the rapid convergence of fertility norms among the native-born and the foreign-born.

However the demographic objective is achieved, Canada's already multicultural society seems destined to encompass even greater diversity.

5
Wage Rates of Immigrant and Native Men in Canada and the United States

Alice Nakamura and Masao Nakamura

Many would argue that national and regional economic objectives have shaped Canadian immigration policies more explicitly than U.S. policies. Policy history in the two countries is dealt with in other chapters in this volume. Here we simply draw attention to a recent manifestation of the Canadian economic emphasis that has attracted interest in the United States.

Beginning in 1967, independent applicants for immigration to Canada were systematically evaluated on a point system that reflected perceived needs for labor. Points were awarded on the basis of job-related qualifications such as English or French language proficiency, education, employment experience, and job skills, and the match between an applicant's qualifications and labor needs in Canada—both in the nation as a whole and in the region where the would-be immigrant wished to settle.

American employers have sometimes recruited abroad to meet labor needs. In the United States as in Canada, the perceived potential for fitting into society and finding work is a factor considered in ruling on the applications of independent immigrants. But U.S. immigration policies have not required a would-be immigrant's economic qualifications to be judged as explicitly as Canadian policies have. Also, in relative terms, the United States has admitted larger numbers of immigrants as refugees or for family reunification.

These differences in emphasis between Canadian and U.S. immigration policies are frequently cited in immigration policy discussions in the two countries. In the United States, recent indications of decline in the "quality" of immigrants and concern about productivity have led to suggestions that U.S. immigration policies be revamped along Canadian lines. Despite interest in the differences between the immigration policies of the two countries, however, we know of no comparative studies that quantitatively examine the differences in the outcomes of these policies. Public interest in intercountry policy differences clearly stems from expectations of differing outcomes. The purpose of this study is to begin to fill the gap in the understanding needed to examine the relative strengths of U.S. and Canadian immigration policies.

Our research approach is outlined in the following section. In the subsequent sections we discuss data sources and variable definitions, empirical results, and finally, findings and conclusions.

Research Strategy

Does evidence suggest that, on average, immigrants to Canada are better suited to contribute to the economy than are immigrants to the United States? In appraising the economic effectiveness of Canadian versus U.S. immigration policies, this question is central.

Immigrants can contribute to the economy of the receiving country in two basic ways. First, they may have more human capital than native workers. Second, the job specializations of immigrants may meet specific occupational or regional labor needs. In other words, immigrants can serve to raise the general skill level of the work force, or they can help to relieve labor bottlenecks.

A comparison between aspects of the human capital endowments of Canadian immigrant workers and those of U.S. immigrant workers is relatively straightforward. But how can the match between immigrant workers and labor needs be judged?

One approach pursued in this study is to compare the average wage rates for immigrant versus native workers. This comparison is made for workers in all occupations, and then for selected occupational groups. The motivation for making these average wage comparisons is that immigration policies that result in better matches between the qualifications of those admitted and labor needs should make it easier for immigrants to find jobs that pay well and have good future earnings prospects.

Of course, simple averages of immigrant and native wage rates take no account of differences in worker characteristics, such as years of schooling or years of work experience, although both the average levels and the distributions of these characteristics may differ greatly between immigrant and native workers. Our approach to this problem is to compare the Canadian and U.S. coefficient estimates for such variables as years of schooling in multiple regression equations for the (natural logarithm of the) hourly wage rate. The coefficient of each variable in a multiple regression can be interpreted as the expected change in the dependent variable due to a unit change in the associated explanatory variable—controlling for the effects of all other explanatory variables included in the regression equation.

Evidence that immigrants to Canada are economically more successful than immigrants to the United States would suggest—but not conclusively prove—that Canadian immigration policies are more effective in an economic sense. Both selection and retention issues complicate the interpretation of empirical findings.

The actual composition of immigrant flows into a country depends not only on the criteria for approving immigrants, but also on the types of people who apply to enter. The United States is thought to be the country of first choice for many international migrants, and Canada a common second choice when approval of immigration to the United States is denied or deemed unlikely. Hence it is possible that Canadian immigration policies can be effective in promoting the selection of immigrants who can contribute to the economy, and yet that immigrants to Canada are less desirable from this perspective than the immigrants to the United States.[1]

Furthermore, immigrants do not necessarily remain in the countries to which they are admitted as residents. Possibly, Canadian immigration policies have resulted in an influx of immigrants who are truly better qualified from an economic perspective than are the immigrants admitted to the United States. But successful immigrants who came to Canada may tend to emigrate elsewhere, such as to the United States.

Data Sources and Variable Definitions

Our empirical analyses are based on census of population data. In particular, we use microdata for immigrant and native working men twenty-five to fifty-five years of age, from the 2 percent 1981 Canadian Census Public Use Sample Individual File and from the 0.1 percent 1980 U.S. Census Public Use Microdata Sample A.

The variables used in this study are listed in table 5–1, together with their definitions. Most of the variables have been used in other single-country studies of immigrant wage rates or earnings. We will briefly review the definitions of the commonly used variables, and introduce two labor market variables that have not been used in other studies.

The variable that is the focus of much of this study, and the dependent variable (in logarithm form) for our multiple regression equations, is the Hourly Wage Rate. Values for this variable were

147

TABLE 5–1

DEFINITIONS OF THE VARIABLES USED IN THIS CHAPTER

Variable Name	Definition
Hourly Wage Rate	Hourly wage rates are computed as reported earnings for the previous calendar year, divided by weeks of work in that year times a measure of hours of work per week
Years of Schooling	Number of grades completed
Potential Experience	Age minus Years of Schooling minus 6
Potential Experience Squared	Squared values of the Potential Experience variable
Disability Dummy	A dummy variable equal to 1 if a person has a disability limiting work, and equal to 0 otherwise[a]
Marriage Dummy	A dummy variable equal to 1 if a person is legally married with spouse present, and equal to 0 otherwise
Language Problems Dummy	A dummy variable equal to 1 if an immigrant to the U.S. indicates difficulty with English, or for residents of Canada with a primary language other than the main language for the province of residence[b]
Entry Unemployment Rate	The national unemployment rate at the expected time of entry into the Canadian or U.S. labor force, or the average national unemployment rate for the period of entry
Average Local Wage	Computed using Hourly Wage Rate figures for all male workers 25–55 years of age, grouped by state and urban status[c] for the U.S., and by province and place of residence[d] for Canada

a. Included only for the United States.
b. French for Quebec, English otherwise.
c. Central SMSA areas; other, for U.S.
d. Census Metropolitan Area; other, for Canada.
SOURCE: Author.

calculated as reported earnings for the previous calendar year divided by the product of weeks of work for that year and a measure of hours worked per week. Qualitatively similar results to those reported in this chapter were also obtained using weekly earnings or annual earnings as the indicator of economic success. The remaining variables listed in table 5–1 are the explanatory variables included in our multiple regression equations.

Neither immigration officials nor economists can directly measure the accumulated job related human capital of individuals. They must instead use as proxies measures of time spent in activities believed to produce human capital. The proxy measures for human capital used in this study are Years of Schooling, Potential Experience, and Potential Experience Squared.

For Canadian immigrant and native workers, our Years of Schooling variable was assigned values based on two Public Use Sample variables: first, "Highest Grade of Elementary or Secondary," and second, "Years of University." The first of these variables provides information on the highest grade of elementary or secondary school attended (less than grade 5; grades 5–8; grades 9, 10, 11, 12, 13). A value of 2.5 was assigned for individuals who reported having attended less than grade 5, and a value of 6.5 was assigned for those with reported years of schooling falling in the category of grades 5–8. The "Years of University" variable gives the total number of completed years of education at degree-granting educational institutions (none; less than one year; one year; and so on, up to six years or more). For each Canadian worker, the value for this variable was added to the value already determined for elementary and secondary education, with 0.5 and 6 used, respectively, for individuals with values of less than one year or six years or more for the Years of University variable.

For U.S. immigrant and native workers, the assigned values for our Years of Schooling variable are based on the person-record variable, "Highest Year of School Attended." The "Highest Year of School Attended" is coded 03 through 14 for the first through the twelfth grades, and 15 through 22 for the first through the "eighth year or more" of college. The values assigned to our Years of Schooling variable are these public-use microdata code values minus two.

Our data sources contain no information about years of work experience. Most men enter the work force right after finishing their formal schooling, however, and they continue to work year after year from that time until retirement. Hence labor economists often construct a Potential Experience variable. As is common in labor economics studies, our Potential Experience variable is defined as a worker's reported age minus Years of Schooling minus six, to account for the pre-grade 1 years. It is expected that wage rates rise throughout the earlier years of most workers' lives, but that beyond some point reduced energy levels and health problems associated with advancing age cause wage rates to plateau and finally to decline with further increases in Potential Experience. In order to allow for this expected nonlinear response, Potential Experience Squared is also included in our regression equations.

Three dummy variables have been included in our regression equations to control for attributes found to be important in other studies of immigrant earnings. (A dummy variable takes the value of 1 when some stated condition holds, and the value of 0 otherwise.) The first of these is a Disability Dummy, which equals 1 for individuals with a disability limiting work; this is available for the United States only. The second is a Marriage Dummy, which equals 1 for individuals reported to be currently married. The third is a Language Problems Dummy. The Language Problems Dummy equals 1 for immigrants to the United States reporting difficulty with English, and also for immigrants and for native workers in Canada whose primary home language is not the main language for the province where they claim to live (French for Quebec, English for the other provinces).

In much of the literature on the economic success of immigrants, the focus is on the individual qualifications, motivations, and choices of the immigrants themselves versus native-born workers.[2] Of course, this personal characteristics orientation is also prevalent in much of the rest of the empirical literature on individual work behavior and earnings.[3] One reason for this is that the microdata sets on which these studies are based contain little information about employer and labor market attributes. No employer or labor market attributes are given in the microdata sources on which this study is based, either. But we have added two labor market variables to the microdata records.

The first of these variables is the Entry Unemployment Rate, which is the national unemployment rate for the expected year of entry into the Canadian or U.S. labor market. Values for this variable were assigned as follows. For each immigrant and each native worker, we first determined the age of expected entrance into the labor force as the person's current age minus years of potential experience. The age of expected labor market entrance was used to determine the year of expected labor market entrance. For native workers, the Entry Unemployment Rate is the national unemployment rate in the year of expected labor market entrance.

In the Canadian Public Use Sample data, the following years of periods of arrival for immigrants are distinguished: before 1946, 1946–1955, 1956–1960, 1961–1965, 1966, 1967–1970, and single years of arrival for 1971–1981. In the U.S. Public Use Microdata Sample, the arrival times that are distinguished are: before 1950, 1950–1959, 1960–1964, 1965–1969, 1970–1974, and 1975–1980.

For each immigrant whose arrival year or period is prior to the year of expected labor market entrance, the value of the Entry Unemployment Rate variable was assigned in the same way as for native workers. Immigrants whose time of arrival is prior to the expected year of entrance into the labor market probably have had a period of acculturation, and may even have attended school in their new country, prior to looking for a first job. Kossoudji calls these immigrants "child migrants," and finds that their job and earnings experiences differ in important ways from the experiences of immigrants who entered the work force prior to or at the time of arrival in the United States.[4] We refer to the other immigrants as adult-at-entry immigrants. For each adult-at-entry immigrant, the value for the Entry Unemployment Rate variable is the national unemployment rate for the year of arrival—or the average of the national unemployment rates over the reported period of arrival. The national unemployment rate figures used in assigning values to the Entry Unemployment Rate variable are shown in table 5–2.

The second labor market variable included in this study is the (natural logarithm of the) average hourly wage rates for all male workers in each province (for Canada) or state (for the United States) and place of residence.[5] Studies of where immigrants live reveal that the geographical distribution for immigrants is quite different than that for native workers.[6] Wage levels differ from place to place. Some of this variation may reflect differences in the local cost of living. The types of jobs available in different localities are undoubtedly another factor reflected in regional wage differences.

In this study, we are interested in investigating the match between immigrant job skills and labor needs. From this perspective, it seems desirable to examine immigrant versus native wage rates, controlling for wage levels in the places where these individuals live. For example, an immigrant doctor or lawyer or businessman might play an important role in the economic life of a small urban center and be well paid in this context; yet this immigrant might earn less than an immigrant in the same line of work in a high-priced, major urban center. In the major urban center the earnings of immigrants in the given line of work may be fairly low in comparison with native workers because of an oversupply of workers of this sort. In this example, the immigrant filling a needed professional role in the small

151

TABLE 5–2

UNEMPLOYMENT RATES FOR THE UNITED STATES AND CANADA,
1945–1980

	U.S.	Canada		U.S.	Canada
1945	1.9	3.4	1965	4.5	3.9
1946	3.9	3.4	1966	3.8	3.6
1947	3.9	2.3	1967	3.8	4.1
1948	3.8	2.3	1968	3.6	4.8
1949	5.9	2.8	1969	3.5	4.7
1950	5.3	3.6	1970	4.9	5.9
1951	3.3	2.4	1971	5.9	6.4
1952	3.0	2.9	1972	5.6	6.3
1953	2.9	3.0	1973	4.9	5.6
1954	5.5	4.6	1974	5.6	5.4
1955	4.4	4.4	1975	8.5	6.9
1956	4.1	3.4	1976	7.7	7.1
1957	4.3	4.6	1977	7.0	8.1
1958	6.8	7.0	1978	6.0	8.4
1959	5.5	6.0	1979	5.8	7.4
1960	5.5	7.0	1980	—	7.5
1961	6.7	7.1			
1962	5.5	5.9			
1963	5.7	5.5			
1964	5.2	4.7			

SOURCE: Figures for 1945–1970 for the U.S. are from *Long-Term Economic Growth, 1860–1970*, series B2; figures for 1971–1979 for the U.S. are from table B–29 of the Economic Report of the President, 1980; and figures for Canada are from various issues of the *Canada Year Book*.

urban center would be viewed as better matched to the labor needs of the economy, and this would be evident from his wage rate relative to (or controlling for) the average wage level in his place of residence.

Empirical Analysis

The coefficient estimates for two of the explanatory variables included in our multiple regressions will be examined for evidence concerning the closeness of the match between immigrant qualifications and labor needs. These two variables are the Years of Schooling and the Entry Unemployment Rate variable.

The coefficients for the Years of Schooling variable included in our regression equations can be viewed as estimates of the rate of return to years of schooling. These estimates provide the basis for comparisons of the rates of return on schooling for immigrant versus native workers in the two countries. Immigrants who are better matched to labor needs should have an easier time than native workers in finding jobs that provide favorable returns on years of schooling.

The Entry Unemployment Rate variable is treated as an indicator of labor market conditions at the time when an immigrant or native worker first entered the labor market in the designated country.

Other studies offer evidence that the career opportunities and lifetime earnings profiles of native workers are affected by labor market conditions at the time of initial entry into the labor force.[7] We would expect effects of this sort to be even more severe for immigrants. Immigrant workers are less likely to have the information and contacts that become more important for finding good jobs as jobs become more scarce. Also, employers may be uncertain about the value of education and job experience obtained in other countries. Hence they may prefer native workers, even those with somewhat poor formal qualifcations, so long as native workers are available.

Human Capital of Immigrant versus Native Workers. The Kossoudji study finds important differences in the economic experience of child versus adult-at-entry immigrants.[8] Thus we show separate results throughout for all immigrants and for the adult-at-entry immigrants. In this particular study, we find no important differences in the results for all immigrants versus the adult-at-entry subgroup. This similarity could not have been foretold, however, without examining the empirical results. Separate results are also presented for workers in seven occupations, which are listed alphabetically in table 5–3. Sample sizes are given in table 5–3 for the different immigration-status and occupational-specific data samples for which results are shown in the remaining tables in this chapter.

Average values are shown in table 5–4 for our Age and Potential Experience variables. Columns 3 and 6 of the top panel of table 5–4 show that the average age for native male workers is somewhat younger in Canada than in the United States. But from columns 1 versus 4 and columns 2 versus 5 we find that the immigrant workers in Canada are older on average than the immigrant workers in the United States.

Average values for Years of Schooling are shown in the bottom panel of table 5–5. From columns 1, 2, and 3 versus 4, 5, and 6 of the bottom panel of this table, we see that both immigrant and native workers in Canada have less schooling on average than their U.S. counterparts. The Average Potential Experience values shown in the bottom panel of table 5–4 reflect the average age and schooling patterns, as would be expected given how Potential Experience is defined. Native workers have slightly more and immigrant workers considerably more years of Potential Experience in Canada than in the United States.

From the evidence discussed so far, it is unclear whether immigrant workers in Canada have more job-related human capital than immigrant workers in the United States. On average, the immigrant workers in Canada are less educated but are older and probably have worked more years than the immigrant workers in the United States. Some additional observations, however, can be made based on the figures in table 5–5, and these figures may be relevant in appraising Canadian immigration policies. In particular, for all occupations and for each of the specific occupations listed except health, immigrant workers in Canada have higher average levels of education in comparison with native workers than is the case for immigrant workers in the United States. In fact, immigrant workers in Canada actually have more years of schooling on average than native workers for all but one of the separate occupations; for the United States, this is true only for the health and teaching occupations. This pattern could be evidence of the success of immigration policies in Canada in fulfilling their purpose of ensuring an influx of immigrants who will enhance the productive capacity of the Canadian economy. Or it could mean that, as the preferred destination second to the United States of many international migrants, Canada is selecting its immigrants from an applicant pool that on average has somewhat less formal education than the applicant pool for the United States—although it is well educated in comparison with the native Canadian work force. If this is the case, immigrant-native patterns for average years of schooling might still be similar to those evident in table 5–5, even if exactly the same policies for selecting immigrants had been applied in both the United States and Canada.

Looking now at the multiple regression coefficient estimates for the Years of Schooling variable shown in the top panel of table 5–5, we find as expected that the estimated rates of return on education are lower, as expected, for immigrant than for native workers. We do not find, however, that the rates of return for Canadian immigrants are higher than for U.S. immigrants, either in absolute terms or relative to native workers in each country, as might be expected if the Canadian aims of matching immigrant qualification to labor needs have been successfully met.

TABLE 5–3
Numbers Used in Samples in This Chapter

	Canada			United States		
	Adult-at-entry immigrants	All immigrants	Native workers	Adult-at-entry immigrants	All immigrants	Native workers
All	11,961	16,652	19,680[a]	1,944	2,628	34,221
Clerical	664	955	4,066	121	173	2,344
Health	191	281	849	51	85	526
Managerial	1,078	1,821	7,422	183	288	4,853
Operative	2,685	3,261	7,787	289	334	3,169
Sales	801	1,296	6,085	92	142	2,829
Service	1,195	1,529	4,591	235	286	2,382
Teaching	383	745	2,587	30	57	1,136

a. The 1981 Canadian Census Public Use Sample Individual File used in this study contains 59,039 records, with information for all of our variables, for working men 25–55 years of age. All the records falling into the designated occupational groups (clerical, health, and so forth) were utilized in our analyses. For "all" occupations, however, we used a random one-third sample of the available 59,039 usable records.

SOURCE: See the text.

TABLE 5–4: Average Age and Potential Experience, Working Men 25–55 Years of Age, in Years

	Canada[a]			United States[b]		
	Adult-at-entry immigrants	All immigrants	Native workers	Adult-at-entry immigrants	All immigrants	Native workers
Age						
All	41.5 (8.3)	39.6 (8.5)	37.1 (8.7)	39.3 (8.7)	37.7 (8.6)	37.7 (9.0)
Teaching	43.2 (6.8)	40.0 (7.6)	36.7 (7.2)	39.0 (7.5)	37.8 (7.9)	37.3 (8.3)
Managerial	42.8 (7.7)	40.3 (8.1)	38.7 (8.3)	41.8 (7.9)	39.3 (8.1)	39.1 (8.8)
Service	41.3 (8.0)	39.8 (8.9)	37.6 (8.9)	38.6 (8.8)	37.1 (8.8)	37.7 (9.3)
Sales	41.3 (8.0)	38.9 (8.3)	37.3 (8.8)	37.7 (8.2)	36.7 (7.9)	37.9 (9.0)
Operative	40.8 (8.5)	39.5 (8.6)	36.7 (8.7)	38.7 (8.6)	37.7 (8.7)	36.7 (8.8)
Clerical	40.7 (8.9)	38.3 (9.0)	36.6 (9.1)	38.7 (8.9)	36.5 (8.8)	37.9 (9.1)
Health	40.6 (7.6)	39.0 (8.0)	35.5 (8.3)	38.7 (7.2)	37.1 (7.4)	36.2 (8.4)

Potential Experience[c]

All	24.3 (9.8)	21.7 (10.2)	19.5 (10.2)	21.9 (9.8)	19.4 (10.1)	18.5 (10.0)
Service	25.8 (10.1)	23.7 (10.5)	20.8 (10.4)	22.5 (10.1)	20.4 (10.5)	13.4 (10.6)
Operative	24.5 (9.7)	23.1 (9.8)	20.6 (10.0)	23.3 (9.6)	22.0 (9.9)	19.3 (9.8)
Sales	23.0 (9.2)	20.3 (9.4)	19.4 (9.9)	19.0 (9.3)	17.0 (8.9)	18.1 (9.8)
Managerial	23.0 (8.9)	20.0 (9.2)	19.0 (9.4)	21.3 (9.0)	18.4 (9.0)	18.2 (9.4)
Clerical	22.6 (10.2)	19.9 (10.3)	18.9 (10.3)	19.5 (9.1)	16.9 (9.2)	18.5 (10.0)
Teaching	19.9 (7.3)	16.5 (8.0)	13.9 (7.7)	15.1 (7.6)	13.4 (7.9)	13.8 (8.3)
Health	19.6 (9.0)	17.3 (9.3)	15.2 (9.5)	13.9 (7.9)	12.1 (7.8)	12.6 (8.9)

NOTE: Standard deviations are given in parentheses.
a. 1981 census.   b. 1980 census.
c. Potential Experience is defined as a worker's reported age minus years of schooling minus six.
SOURCE: See Data Sources and Variable Definitions section of text.

TABLE 5–5: COEFFICIENT ESTIMATES AND MEAN VALUES FOR YEARS OF SCHOOLING, WORKING MEN 25–55 YEARS OF AGE

	Canada[a]			United States[b]		
	Adult-at-entry immigrants	All immigrants	Native workers	Adult-at-entry immigrants	All immigrants	Native workers
	Coefficient estimates					
All	.032c (.002)	.038c (.002)	.048c (.002)	.035c (.005)	.042c (.004)	.058c (.001)
Health	.044d (.018)	.031d (.014)	.034c (.010)	.143c (.026)	.131c (.023)	.104c (.017)
Teaching	.035c (.013)	.053c (.011)	.046c (.005)	.129c (.048)	.093d (.045)	.058c (.009)
Managerial	.028c (.007)	.043c (.005)	.056c (.002)	.056c (.019)	.044c (.015)	.066c (.004)
Clerical	.016e (.009)	.015d (.008)	.027c (.005)	.005 (.018)	.015 (.017)	.045c (.006)
Sales	.015e (.009)	.018d (.007)	.045c (.004)	.054e (.033)	.070e (.029)	.066c (.006)
Service	.015d (.007)	.021c (.007)	.043c (.005)	.021 (.018)	.019 (.018)	.041c (.006)
Operative	.013c (.005)	.014c (.005)	.027c (.005)	.003 (.015)	.009 (.014)	.057c (.007)

Mean values

All	11.2 (4.2)	11.9 (4.1)	11.6 (3.5)	11.2 (5.0)	12.2 (4.9)	13.2 (3.1)
Health	15.1 (3.9)	15.7 (3.7)	14.2 (3.8)	18.8 (2.1)	19.0 (1.8)	17.6 (2.8)
Teaching	17.3 (2.5)	17.5 (2.1)	16.7 (2.3)	17.9 (2.0)	18.4 (1.9)	17.5 (2.1)
Managerial	13.7 (3.4)	14.3 (3.3)	13.7 (3.2)	14.4 (3.8)	14.9 (3.4)	14.9 (2.6)
Clerical	12.1 (3.5)	12.4 (3.3)	11.6 (2.6)	13.1 (4.0)	13.5 (3.6)	13.4 (2.5)
Sales	12.3 (3.3)	12.7 (3.2)	11.9 (2.7)	12.7 (3.7)	13.6 (3.4)	13.9 (2.5)
Service	9.5 (3.6)	10.1 (3.6)	10.8 (3.6)	9.8 (4.5)	10.5 (4.5)	12.3 (2.8)
Operative	10.2 (3.3)	10.4 (3.2)	10.1 (2.4)	9.0 (4.3)	9.4 (4.3)	11.4 (2.4)

NOTE: Standard deviations are given in parentheses. For the coefficient estimates shown in the top panel, the standard deviations are heteroskedasticity-corrected. Coefficient estimates that are significant with 99, 95, and 80 percent levels of confidence using a two-tailed t-test are denoted, respectively, with the superscripts c, d, and e.
a. 1981 census.   b. 1980 census.
SOURCE: See Data Sources and Variable Definitions section of text.

Hourly Wage Rates. Admitting immigrants who are well educated in comparison with the native-born population does not necessarily mean that these immigrants will enhance the economic growth of the receiving country. The skills these immigrants have may not be in demand. Also, observable proxy indicators for accumulated human capital, such as years of schooling, may overstate the qualifications of immigrant versus native workers because of systematic differences in unmeasured factors such as the quality of education. A more direct indicator of the economic contribution of immigrants to the receiving country is the relationship between the incomes of immigrant workers and native workers.

Average hourly wage rates for immigrant and native workers are shown in the top panel of table 5–6. The Canadian figures are in Canadian dollars and the U.S. figures are in U.S. dollars; hence the figures in table 5–6 are not an appropriate basis for making direct intercountry wage comparisons. These figures can be used, however, for making Canadian-U.S. comparisons between the relationships of immigrant to native wage rates. Ratios of the average wage rates of immigrant versus native workers are shown in the bottom panel of table 5–6. The pattern of values is interesting.

Looking at the top line in the bottom panel of table 5–6, for all occupations it can be seen that immigrant workers in Canada have a slightly higher average wage than the native workers, while immigrant workers in the United States have an average wage that is 5 percent to 9 percent lower than for native workers. This suggests that the relatively high levels of schooling of immigrant versus native workers in Canada is of value and is being actively utilized in the Canadian economy.

The occupations for which figures are shown in table 5–6 are arranged in that table according to the average wage rates, from highest to lowest, for adult-at-entry immigrants to Canada. The ordering of these occupations would be the same if it were based on all immigrants or on native workers in Canada, but it would be considerably different if it were based on U.S. average wage figures. Nevertheless, for the United States as for Canada, the teaching, managerial, health, and sales occupations have higher average wage rates, for immigrant and native workers alike, than have the operative, clerical, and service occupations.

From the bottom panel of table 5–6, we see that in the better paid occupations in both Canada and the United States immigrant workers have higher average wage rates than natives have. In fact, for the United States the ratios shown in the bottom panel are generally greater than those for the better paid teaching, managerial, health, and sales occupations, and they are generally less than those for the more poorly paid operative, clerical, and service occupations.

Entry Unemployment Rate. Finally, coefficient estimates and mean values are shown in table 5–7 for the Entry Unemployment Rate variable. For Canada, the immigrant versus the native worker coefficient values display the pattern that was expected: the immigrant coefficient estimates are more negative, except for the managerial group. This expected pattern is less evident for the United States, perhaps due both to smaller sample sizes and to the fact that the available information about the year of arrival is much less precise for the U.S. than for the Canadian immigrants.

Recall that for the United States, only six intervals for time of arrival are distinguished: before 1950, 1950–1959, 1960–1964, 1965–1969, 1970–1974, and 1975–1980. For Canada, on the other hand, seventeen time-of-arrival periods or years are distinguished: before 1946, 1946–1955, 1956–1960, 1961–1965, 1966, 1967–1970, and single years of arrival for 1971–1981. Perhaps this is also why no clear patterns of Canadian-U.S. differences emerge from table 5–7. Our expectation had been that the coefficient estimates for the Entry Unemployment Rate variable would be less negative for Canada than for the United States, because of immigration policies in Canada that are intended to admit immigrants with good job prospects. Instead, we find that the all-occupations figures in the top row of table 5–7 are remarkably similar for the United States and for Canada.

Findings and Conclusions

We have found that, on average, the hourly wage rates of immigrant workers as compared with native workers in Canada are higher than is the case in the United States. This is consistent with our finding that, compared with the native populations, immigrant workers in Canada have more education on average than is true for immigrant workers in the United States.

In Canada, as in the United States, immigrant workers earn lower rates of return on their years of schooling than native workers earn. We find no evidence, however, that this rate-of-return disadvantage is less severe for Canada than for the United States. Nor are the estimated levels for the rates of return on Years of Schooling higher for Canadian than for U.S. working immigrants.

Finally, we find that higher Entry Unemployment Rate values do

TABLE 5–6: AVERAGE HOURLY WAGE RATES AND IMMIGRANT-TO-NATIVE RATIOS OF THESE AVERAGES, WORKING MEN 25–55 YEARS OF AGE

	Canada[a]			United States[b]		
	Adult-at-entry immigrants	All immigrants	Native workers	Adult-at-entry immigrants	All immigrants	Native workers
	Average hourly wage[c]					
All	11.35 (15.46)	11.51 (15.34)	11.02 (10.50)	8.50 (8.96)	8.86 (8.98)	9.34 (12.97)
Teaching	16.51 (12.25)	15.78 (14.90)	15.69 (40.25)	11.58 (9.12)	11.72 (8.97)	9.97 (8.10)
Managerial	14.66 (10.70)	14.74 (12.77)	14.32 (9.11)	11.91 (9.89)	11.59 (9.18)	11.87 (17.84)
Health	12.73 (9.22)	12.14 (9.36)	11.22 (11.32)	15.14 (10.30)	14.79 (10.10)	13.09 (27.27)
Sales	11.65 (27.07)	11.16 (21.76)	10.78 (11.22)	11.69 (20.93)	11.13 (17.29)	9.58 (7.84)

Operative	10.28 (14.07)	10.42 (15.90)	10.19 (16.98)	6.74 (5.81)	6.87 (6.04)	8.28 (12.16)
Clerical	9.26 (7.73)	9.23 (6.90)	9.25 (5.14)	7.96 (6.07)	8.65 (8.90)	8.54 (6.84)
Service	7.84 (7.88)	8.04 (7.94)	9.41 (7.40)	5.51 (6.90)	6.09 (7.93)	7.72 (15.96)
Ratios of the immigrant to the native figures						
All	1.03	1.04		.91	.95	
Teaching	1.05	1.01		1.16	1.18	
Managerial	1.02	1.03		1.00	.98	
Health	1.13	1.08		1.16	1.13	
Sales	1.08	1.04		1.22	1.16	
Operative	1.01	1.02		.81	.83	
Clerical	1.00	1.00		.93	1.01	
Service	.83	.85		.71	.79	

NOTE: Standard deviations are given in parentheses.

a. 1981 census.   b. 1980 census.

c. In Canadian dollars for Canada and U.S. dollars for United States.

SOURCE: See Data Sources and Variable Definitions section of text.

TABLE 5–7: COEFFICIENT ESTIMATES AND MEAN VALUES FOR ENTRY-UNEMPLOYMENT-RATE VARIABLE, WORKING MEN 25–55 YEARS OF AGE

	Canada[a]			United States[b]		
	Adult-at-entry immigrants	All immigrants	Native workers	Adult-at-entry immigrants	All immigrants	Native workers
	Coefficient estimates					
All	−.047[c] (.005)	−.044[c] (.004)	−.011[d] (.004)	−.055[c] (.016)	−.043[c] (.013)	−.010[c] (.003)
Health	−.076[e] (.051)	−.061[e] (.044)	−.037[e] (.025)	−.181[d] (.088)	−.077[e] (.059)	−.017 (.027)
Clerical	−.072[c] (.021)	−.069[c] (.017)	−.006 (.008)	−.107[d] (.050)	−.061[e] (.041)	.011 (.012)
Teaching	−.063[d] (.028)	−.032[e] (.020)	−.025[d] (.011)	−.012 (.105)	−.122[e] (.073)	−.013 (.014)
Operative	−.046[c] (.011)	−.047[c] (.010)	−.017[d] (.007)	−.062[e] (.046)	−.037 (.040)	−.009 (.011)
Service	−.029[c] (.017)	−.032[c] (.015)	−.016[d] (.009)	.002 (.050)	−.033 (.040)	−.027[d] (.014)
Sales	−.050[d] (.023)	−.040[d] (.017)	−.008 (.008)	−.023 (.073)	.035 (.051)	.002 (.012)
Managerial	.000 (.016)	−.017[e] (.011)	−.020[c] (.006)	.062 (.054)	−.002 (.038)	−.006 (.008)

Mean values

All	5.39 (1.41)	5.41 (1.41)	4.85 (1.72)	5.47 (1.17)	5.37 (1.18)	4.77 (1.17)
Health	5.78 (1.23)	5.84 (1.28)	5.47 (1.65)	5.53 (1.23)	5.47 (1.19)	5.27 (1.38)
Clerical	5.51 (1.48)	5.56 (1.45)	4.88 (1.70)	5.65 (1.20)	5.51 (1.26)	4.75 (1.15)
Teaching	5.46 (1.13)	5.56 (1.24)	5.61 (1.45)	5.56 (1.25)	5.51 (1.22)	5.15 (1.32)
Operative	5.44 (1.42)	5.41 (1.40)	4.66 (1.66)	5.51 (1.15)	5.42 (1.16)	4.71 (1.07)
Service	5.44 (1.43)	5.40 (1.45)	4.64 (1.74)	5.60 (1.20)	5.51 (1.24)	4.72 (1.15)
Sales	5.39 (1.44)	5.36 (1.45)	4.88 (1.69)	5.48 (1.17)	5.36 (1.21)	4.82 (1.20)
Managerial	5.29 (1.39)	5.32 (1.40)	5.00 (1.65)	5.39 (1.11)	5.27 (1.17)	4.82 (1.22)

NOTE: Standard deviations are given in parentheses. For the coefficient estimates shown in the top panel, the standard deviations are heteroskedasticity-corrected. Coefficient estimates that are significant with 99, 95, and 80 percent levels of confidence using a two-tailed t-test are denoted, respectively, with the superscripts c, d, and e.
a. 1981 census.
b. 1980 census.
SOURCE: See Data Sources and Variable Definitions section of text.

reduce the expected current wage rates for workers, with this effect being more severe for immigrant than for native workers. No Canada-U.S. patterns have been detected in the coefficient estimates for the Entry Unemployment Rate variable, however. In particular, we are not able to show that the negative effects on current wage rates associated with the Entry Unemployment Rate variable are more severe for U.S. than for Canadian immigrants.

We do not have clear-cut evidence that Canadian immigration policies have been more effective than U.S. policies from an economic perspective. But we hope that our methodology and results will be helpful to other researchers in pursuing the understanding needed for informed policy making in this area. The difficulty of obtaining evidence of the superior performance of the Canadian policies suggests, in the meantime, that there may not be a compelling immediate need to increase the emphasis on economic factors in U.S. immigration policies.

Commentary on Part Two

Robert S. Goldfarb

Both the Sullivan and the Nakamura chapters are extensive empirical studies. Each one implicitly challenges the reader to decide how interesting and useful are its empirical findings. Since each chapter's topic potentially has considerable policy content, part of the challenge is to determine how the empirical findings might address or inform policy concerns. My discussion focuses on the nature of each study's findings and the relevance of these findings to policy choice.[1]

Sullivan Chapter

Teresa Sullivan's chapter provides an informative, descriptive analysis for Canada of the links between immigration flows and population levels and growth. More specifically, it analyzes how the size of immigrant flows and selected characteristics of the immigrants included in these flows are likely to affect two results: first, the attainment of particular population growth rates, and second, the ease of absorption of immigrants. Sullivan's description of features of migrant flows includes interesting ways of characterizing the heterogeneity of immigrants.

Descriptive information is sometimes interesting and sometimes not. The descriptive information in this study is interesting precisely because it might be used to inform the policy choice process or to point out the perhaps unrecognized implications of actual policy choices.[2] So Sullivan's chapter suggests a two-part question about the nature of immigration policy choice: first, how can one characterize the objectives of actual immigration policy choice, and second, quite apart from the actual choice process, what should the objectives of immigration policy choice be? This question is relevant to the Sullivan study because the usefulness of the information she provides and the way in which it can be used to inform the policy process depend on the objectives of policy. Especially critical is whether population levels or population rates of change actually are or should be central objectives of immigration policy.

This line of reasoning leads to alternative ways to characterize immigration policy. The alternatives can be a basis for analyzing how the descriptive information in the Sullivan study might shed light on policy choices. I make no claims that this list is definitive. I suspect it is biased in two ways: it reflects an economist's way of looking at things, and it was formulated with more knowledge of U.S. than Canadian experience.

My list contains four alternative characterizations of immigration policy. Each alternative has a positive and a normative interpretation, corresponding to the distinction between how immigration policy is actually formulated and how it should be formulated. Different alternatives provide different slants on how a Sullivan-type analysis might inform policy choice.

Alternative I—An Optimum Population

One possibility would be that immigration policy focus on explicit economic goals, and these goals could be captured in the form of an optimal population target. That is, given a country's natural endowments of land and raw materials and its stock of manmade capital equipment, there exists a population level that will result in the most favorable level of economic welfare for the nation.

Suppose such a population level could actually be calculated, and the calculation indicated that current population was considerably below the optimum. This information could be used to generate immigration goals: immigration targets would be set to bring population levels closer to the optimum. Of course, if the calculation indicated a current population above the optimum, the goal would be to minimize immigration.

The information that Sullivan provides would certainly help inform an immigration policy based on optimal population goals. But in order for the information to be used in this way, we would first need an acceptable calculation of what Canada's optimal population level actually is. Such a calculation does not seem to be readily available, much less widely accepted. More generally, one needs to ask whether it is reasonable to suppose that actual Canadian policy is based on an optimal population idea, and whether it would be normatively attractive to base immigration policy on an optimal population target.

It seems clear that actual Canadian immigration policy is not based in any direct and obvious way on optimal population targets. There is no evidence of a widely accepted calculation of an optimal population level for Canada, and Sullivan herself indicates that "Canada does not yet have a population policy." Moreover, discussion of this issue at the conference by those knowledgeable about Canadian policy brought out the fact that 1978 legislation included the concept of demographic goals and required a yearly plan to be produced at the ministerial level. The reported response has been to produce a ministerial annual report with virtually no content in terms of concrete demographic goals. In addition, in 1986 the minister of national health and welfare announced the creation of a Demographic Review Secretariat "to study possible changes in the size structure and distribution of the population of Canada to 2025, and to report on how these changes might affect Canada's social and economic life." The review secretariat issued a report, *Charting Canada's Future*, in 1989. The report is descriptive rather than prescriptive, but it does contain the following statement strongly suggesting that optimal population views are not in political ascendancy in Canada: "The consensus among those economists who have considered the question is that, within broad limits, population growth or sheer numbers of people is not a major factor in economic growth or economic well-being in modern economies that play an active role in world trade. Canada is such an economy."[3]

Even if an optimal population view does not drive actual immigration policy, is it normatively attractive? That is, could one argue that it ought to strongly influence actual policy? At least two quite different considerations come into play here. First, as the discussion below about other possible ways of characterizing immigration policy indicates, some normative concerns about immigration are not well captured by an optimal population concept. The reader needs to weigh the normative merits of these different concerns.[4] Second, an important practical question concerns our ability to produce the concrete and believable numbers needed to apply this kind of approach.[5]

Alternative II—Other Economic Goals

A second possibility would be that immigration policy focus on explicit economic goals or constraints, but that these goals or constraints not be based on an optimal population concept. The focus here would be on economic aspects of population other than general population levels.

This alternative has at least two important subcategories. The rate-of-change variant focuses on rates of change of population, rather than levels. The distributional variant focuses on distributional issues or particular kinds of immigrants.

The rate-of-change variant starts from the plausible proposition that economic costs are associated with changes in population size per se, quite independent of any notion of a desirable level of population.[6] Moreover, these costs become more significant the more rapid the rate of change in population. Even if one rejects the concept of a

169

desirable (optimal) general population level, the notion that rapid change in population involves economic costs can still have considerable appeal. Rapid population loss in Jamaica or East Germany and very large and rapid influxes of Soviet Jews to Israel or of Vietnamese boat people to other Asian economies can impose severe adjustment and crowding costs on these economies. These costs can largely be avoided by stretching out such movements, without necessarily reducing their size.

Geographical concentration of population change within a country can also result in large adjustment and crowding costs. A given number of Cuban migrants to the United States might represent minimal adjustment costs if these migrants were geographically dispersed, but significant local adjustment and crowding costs if they all ended up in Miami. The mysterious notion of absorptive capacity makes the most sense when interpreted as the economy's ability to take in immigrants without incurring severe adjustment and crowding costs.

Not all rate-of-change conceptions view population change as a bad thing. The opposing view sees positive levels of immigration as having beneficial effects, because immigrant inflows are believed to help energize and revitalize the host country.[7]

One element of Sullivan's chapter seems to fit under this rate-of-change category of population goals. In a departure from its otherwise descriptive character, her chapter at times implies that Canadians are or ought to be concerned by the possibility of declining population in Canada, and that immigration policy might assume the goal of offsetting this decline.

The distributional variant of immigration goals focuses on distributional issues, or particular kinds of immigrants. Falling population may be viewed as disadvantageous by older population cohorts, worried about adequate financing of old age benefits or fearing a decline in the value of their life savings held as housing assets. Moreover, particular subsets of the native labor force can suffer distributional losses because of labor market competition from immigrant labor. Conversely, however, particular kinds of immigrant labor can be used to advance the nation's economic goals. For example, domestic skill shortages might be ameliorated by selectively and temporarily opening the immigration "spigot."[8]

Do Canadians implicitly view changes—especially declines in population—as a bad thing, quite apart from views about a desirable level of population? Some experts claim that despite a diversity of opinion in Canada about what the optimal level of population might be, there exists a deeply held subterranean fear of population decline.

Consistent with this claim is the observation in *Charting Canada's Future* that "without immigration, continuation of Canada's below-replacement fertility rates would eventually lead to Canada's disappearance."[9] A second claim relates the fear of population decline to the issue of financing income support programs. A third claim holds that in Quebec there is concern over population decline because of an underlying fear about the survival of a Francophone society. Such a fear goes considerably beyond the purely economic factors to which this Alternative II category is limited.

Suppose that a Canadian fear of population decline does in fact exist. Given these possible sources for the fear, would it be appropriate to use immigration policy to counteract the decline? The answer depends on the motivation for the fear. If it concerns the very disappearance of Canada as an entity, immigration can assuage this fear. If it concerns the ability to finance transfer programs, an immigration policy targeted away from older cohorts may be usable to ameliorate the problem. If instead the fear concerns the dying out of Francophone culture and society, immigration will not provide a solution unless Francophone immigrants happen to be available. Sullivan's descriptive stress on the heterogeneity of immigrants illuminates the ability or inability to use immigration to preserve a culture or society.

Alternative III—Noneconomic Goals

A third possibility would be an immigration policy with well-specified goals that are primarily noneconomic, though they may be subject to economic cost constraints. That noneconomic considerations are of major importance in the immigration policies of many nations seems incontrovertible. As Barry Chiswick has written,

> Political factors often unrelated to, or contrary to, apparent economic self-interest have determined immigration and emigration policies. The virtual prohibition for nearly a century of immigration into the United States of persons of Asian origin and Israel's policy of encouraging the immigration of Jews, no matter how poor, aged, or unskilled, are but two examples of immigration policies motivated by noneconomic considerations.[10]

Recent U.S. immigration policies on refugees and family reunification seem primarily noneconomic in motivation.

Aristide Zolberg suggests that it may be useful to think of immigration policy as having a primarily negative function—the policing function of keeping people out. Such an exclusionary goal may be motivated by many underlying ones, such as avoidance of the re-distribution of labor earnings and preservation of the ethnic identity of constituent groups. This focus on the assumed negative primary goal of immigration policy starkly highlights a contrast between Alternative III and Alternatives I and II. Under the earlier alternatives, immigration is at least sometimes viewed as a good thing: a positive level of immigration is considered a device whose careful application could help attain fundamental goals. Under the third, policing view, immigration is a negative, frightening phenomenon. A positive level of immigration is considered a failure to achieve perfect exclusionary policing.[11]

Is Canada's actual policy describable as motivated primarily by noneconomic goals? If so, does the exclusionary policing function comprise these goals, or are they more positive? The policy usefulness of the Sullivan analysis under Alternative III seems to depend on the existence of some more positive noneconomic goals. For if the underlying goal actually is perfect, exclusionary policing, the tradeoffs described in Sullivan's analysis between immigration levels and population growth would, if indulged in, represent a policy failure.[12]

Alternative IV—No Consistent Goals

The fourth and final possibility is that the regulation of immigration cannot be characterized as having consistent goals. It is better de-scribed as a complex interaction emerging from the interplay of many competing interest groups. Many of these groups press for some particular, sometimes narrow policy goal, with vague ideas about how their favored policy might affect the general national welfare results of immigration. In this view, the amorphous policy blob slith-ers along, probably relatively aimlessly, until some politically power-ful group's interest in immigration policy is awakened or revitalized. This awakening might take place because particular interests the group holds dear are suddenly seen as threatened, or because the group suddenly recognizes advantages to moving immigration policy in certain directions. The group then enters the political arena to press for its favored subset of immigration policy changes. In this world, a descriptive essay like Sullivan's provides information for individual interest groups that can help inform their understanding of the implications of alternative policy proposals. The usefulness of the descriptive information can vary widely, depending on a particular group's goals and concerns.

This consideration of a list of alternative ways of characterizing immigration policy seems to support the initial contention—that the usefulness of the information Sullivan provides and the way it can be used to inform the policy process depend crucially on the nature of policy objectives. The list also highlights the diversity of possible relationships between immigration policy and population policy.

Nakamura and Nakamura Chapter

The Nakamuras have information on both Canada and the United States, with both descriptive and policy aspects. Descriptively, the Nakamuras propose to explain the economic progress of immigrants in the United States as compared with Canada. In terms of policy, they investigate the effects of U.S.-Canadian differences in rules for admitting immigrants. In order to analyze the economic progress of immigrants, the Nakamuras employ an earnings-function methodology widely used in labor economics. Their particular innovation within this methodology is the set of statistical control variables they include.

The Nakamura chapter can be read in different ways. One interpretation views the chapter as suggesting and applying a methodology for investigating the progress of immigrants in terms of their earnings. The earnings-function methodology used has been applied elsewhere to measuring the progress of immigrants. The availability of several replications of this basic methodology suggests that results across studies can be compared.

What might we learn from such a comparison? Different studies applying the same general methodology often include different sets of explanatory variables. Indeed, often a particular study's methodological innovation will be the incorporation of explanatory variables not used in previous studies. The use of different explanatory variables from study to study raises two issues. First, suppose that one study makes a good theoretical case for incorporation of a particular variable, and the variable seems to work well empirically. This would argue for the use of that empirical variable in other, and especially future, studies. The Nakamura and Nakamura study contains some innovative variables that other studies lack; but it also omits innovative variables that are included in other studies.

A second and more important issue involves the results obtained by studies that include different sets of explanatory variables. Do these studies yield similar results for those variables common to all the studies, or do results for shared variables significantly diverge? If consistent results are obtained even with different sets of explanatory variables, we can have more faith in the robustness of the shared results. If results are inconsistent, more statistical work will be needed to try to sort out which additional variables seem to be causing the divergence in results.

I find useful, interesting, and provocative the Nakamuras' addition of an unemployment and an average wage rate variable.[13] But how do their results for shared variables compare with those of other studies that include different sets of variables? While I cannot claim to have done an in-depth comparison across many studies, some less comprehensive comparative evidence suggests that results for shared variables are consistent across several studies.[14]

A second way to read this chapter is as an empirical comparison of Canadian versus U.S. experience. The Nakamuras have samples for each country, and the reader might well be interested in whether the experiences in each country were similar or distinctively different. If the essay is to be read in this way, it is useful to ask some questions before carefully scrutinizing the empirical results. First, are there critical differences between Canada and the United States that would lead one to expect differences in patterns of immigrant earnings? If the answer is yes, then can these differences in principle be statistically controlled in the Nakamura study, and are they? Now suppose there are some critical differences that cannot be or are not controlled. These uncontrolled differences may lead one to have very strong expectations about whether statistical earnings equations for Canadian immigrants ought to look very different from those for U.S. immigrants.

Nakamura and Nakamura actually follow a strategy like the one I have suggested. They believe that a crucial difference between the two countries may lie in the rules for allowing immigrants to enter the country. Since the effects of these differences in rules cannot be completely controlled statistically, the Nakamuras expect regression results to differ in a systematic way for the two countries. Their expectations are only partly borne out by their statistical results.

My own attempt to apply this investigative strategy to a Canadian-U.S. comparison leaves me with a daunting list of reasons why the two countries' immigrant earnings functions might diverge. While the list leads me to expect a divergence between the two countries' earnings functions, the complexities of the list do not permit me to come up with a concrete expectation about exactly how the equations might be predicted to differ.[15]

So how do the two compare? The Nakamuras find some differences between U.S. and Canadian immigrants in the levels of variables; for example, average education levels of immigrants seem to differ. But when they look for differences in the earnings-function relationship—that is, how the level of a variable such as education affects earnings—the differences they expected often do not appear. For example, they "do not find that the rates of return [that is, to schooling] for Canadian immigrants are higher than for U.S. immigrants . . . as might be expected if the Canadian aims of matching immigrant qualification to labor needs have been successfully met." Another example is the entry-unemployment-rate variable. The Nakamuras expected to find a less negative unemployment rate effect for Canada than for the United States; instead they find "remarkably similar" numbers.

This remarkable similarity in the immigrant-earnings functions for the two countries deserves to be taken quite seriously, since it reappears in the Chiswick and Miller study. As Chiswick and Miller describe their results, the "determinants of earnings among immigrants are remarkably similar in the United States and Canada; it is as if there is one earnings-determination process for the two countries." Given my expectation that the earnings functions would not be identical, I found this surprising.

A third way to read the essay does not stress its methodology, nor does it focus on a Canadian-U.S. comparison. Instead it sees the study as an empirical investigation of a statistical data set dealing with immigrants, and therefore looks for interesting empirical results.

The chapter has some interesting empirical results in addition to those already cited about the similarity of U.S. and Canadian immigrant-earnings functions. Most interesting is the finding that the earnings of immigrants relative to natives is higher in Canada than it is in the United States. I suspect the authors also find this to be among their most interesting findings, since they list it first in their conclusions. The different U.S. and Canadian patterns of immigrant-to-native earnings by occupation group are also quite interesting. It is also reassuring that labor market conditions when the immigrants enter the labor market seem to matter for their subsequent earnings. This focus on the effects of labor market conditions at date of labor market entry is one of the worthwhile innovations in the Nakamura study.[16]

A fourth way to read this essay is for the light it sheds on immigration policy debates. In their introduction, the authors refer to differences in the degree to which economic objectives have shaped Canadian versus U.S. immigration policies. The Nakamuras see these differences as provoking policy debates. For example, some people argue that U.S. criteria for admitting immigrants should be redesigned along Canadian lines. The authors say that "a prime objective of this study is to provide Canadian-U.S. empirical evidence relevant to this debate."

The Nakamuras conclude that their evidence "is mixed concerning the effectiveness of Canadian versus U.S. immigration policies as an instrument for enhancing the growth of the Canadian economy." Even if their empirical results had been more consistent with their a priori expectations, however, the gap between these empirical findings and the design of actual or optimal policies would still be immense. I do not think that this kind of empirical approach can be persuasive primarily for its direct implications for debates about policy design. Nor do I think it needs to be, since the three alternative ways to read the Nakamuras' study are of substantial interest.

Bibliography

Chiswick, Barry. "The Impact of Immigration on the Level and Distribution of Economic Well-Being." In *The Gateway: U.S. Immigration Issues and Policies*. Edited by Barry Chiswick. Washington, D.C.: The American Enterprise Institute, 1982, pp. 289–313.

Goldfarb, Robert. "Occupational Preferences in the U.S. Immigration Law: An Economic Analysis." In *The Gateway: U.S. Immigration Issues and Policies*. Edited by Barry Chiswick. Washington, D.C.: American Enterprise Institute, 1982, pp. 412–48.

Ministry of Health and Welfare, Canada. *Charting Canada's Future*. Ottawa, Canada: Minister of Supply and Services, 1989.

Sauvy, Alfred. *The General Theory of Population*. Translated by C. Campos. New York: Basic Books, 1969 (originally published in French, 1966).

PART THREE

The Economics of Language

6

An Economic Perspective on Language and Public Policy in Canada and the United States

François Vaillancourt

This chapter has four purposes. The first is to describe in a comparative and synthetic way the language policies of Canada—Quebec and the rest of the country—and of the United States in the 1980s, with reference to their emergence and evolution in the 1960s and 1970s. The second is to analyze their expected efficiency and equity impacts, using the framework of the economics of language and language planning. The third is to examine the empirical evidence available on the impact, both direct (micro) and global (macro), of these policies. The fourth is to put forward a few thoughts on appropriate language policies from an economic perspective. The choice of these purposes reflects both the need to ensure an adequate knowledge of the policies under discussion and the author's familiarity with the economics—as opposed to the politics or sociolinguistics—of language. The chapter is divided into four sections, corresponding to the four topics described above.

The Language Policies in Canada and the United States

This section provides both a brief chronology of language policies since 1965 and a description of the language policies in place in the late 1980s in Canada and the United States. The description for Canada distinguishes between Quebec and the remainder of Canada (English Canada), given the important differences in language policies between these two entities.

The Chronology of Language Policies, 1965–1990. Table 6–1 presents the main legislative and administrative dates that have shaped language policies in Canada and the United States since 1965. This

TABLE 6–1
A Chronology of Language Events, 1965–1990

| Year | Canada | | United States |
	Quebec	English Canada	
1965			Voting Rights Act is adopted.
1968			Bilingual Education Act (BEA) is enacted at federal level.
1969	Bill 63, promoting the French language, is adopted.	Official Language Act is adopted at federal level. New Brunswick Official Language Act is adopted. Ontario authorizes French public school.	English is mandated the official language of Illinois.
1970		Federal grants for minority and second language education are introduced.	HEW issues a memorandum on education of limited English-speaking ability (LESA).
1971			
1972			
1973			
1974	Bill 22, Official Language Act, is adopted.		Supreme Court makes Lau decision, based on Civil Rights Act. Equal Education Opportunity Act (EEOA) is passed. BEA is reauthorized.

TABLE 6–1 (continued)

| Year | Canada | | United States |
	Quebec	English Canada	
1975		French language use in courts starts in Ontario.	HEW Office of Civil Rights issues Lau guideline remedies.
1976			
1977	Bill 101, Charter of French Language, is adopted.		Executive Order 12 044, the Plain English Law (PEL), is issued. English and Hawaiian are ruled official languages of Hawaii.
1978			New York State enacts PEL. BEA is reauthorized and expands the target population of its program to limited English proficiency (LEP) students.
1979		Federal Criminal Code is amended to allow for trials in language (English or French) of the accused, if the province agrees.	PEL is enacted in Maine.
1980			EEOC issues guidelines on language requirements for employment.

(Table continues)

TABLE 6–1 (continued)

| Year | Canada | | United States |
	Quebec	English Canada	
			PEL is enacted in Connecticut and Hawaii. Lau regulations are put forward.
1981		New Brunswick enhances Bill 88 on French language rights.	Lau remedies of 1974, having not been published in the Federal Register, lacked the legal basis of regulations; the Lau regulations are withdrawn.
1982		Federal Constitution Act adopted. Article 23 includes provisions on language of education for minorities.	PEL enacted in New Jersey and West Virginia.
1983	Bill 52 is enacted, containing minor amendments to Bill 101.		PEL is enacted in Minnesota.
1984	—		Indiana, Kentucky, and Tennessee adopt English as official language. BEA is reauthorized and now allows for English-based alternatives to native language methods.

TABLE 6–1 (continued)

| Year | Canada | | United States |
	Quebec	English Canada	
1985			Montana adopts PEL.
1986	Bill 142, Health and Social Services Act, is adopted, providing for English services.	Bill 8, French Language Services Act, is adopted in Ontario.	California and Georgia adopt English as official language. EEOC issues a policy statement on discrimination based on accent or manner of speaking.
1987			Mississippi, North Carolina, North Dakota, and South Carolina adopt English as official language.
1988	Supreme Court strikes down French-only signs requirement of Bill 101.	Supreme Court rules that French has legal status in Saskatchewan and Alberta, based on 1905 law. Status is abrogated by both provincial governments. New official languages act, C-72, passed at federal level.	Arizona, Colorado, and Florida adopt English as official language. BEA is reauthorized.
1989	Bill 178 reinstates part of French-only signs requirement.		*Teresa P. v. Berkeley;* U.S. district federal court decision made on

(Table continues)

TABLE 6–1 (continued)

| Year | Canada | | United States |
	Quebec	English Canada	
			acceptability of English-based bilingual education.
1990		Mahé ruling; Supreme Court clarifies right of minorities to education in their own language.	

SOURCES: The main sources are *Federal and Provincial Linguistic Dates*, Language and Society, vol. 28, Summer 1989, R-31; *U.S. English Update File Facts*, November–December 1988; *Simply Stated*, vol. 38, August 1983 ("Plain Language Laws: Where We Stand"); *Simply Stated in Business*, vol. 15, May–June 1986, p. 1; "The Bilingual Education Act: Twenty Years Later," Gloria Stewzer-Manzanares, FFOCUS, National Clearinghouse for Bilingual Education, occasional paper in bilingual education, no. 6, Fall 1988.

starting year was chosen because in both Canada and the United States, language policies acquired greater salience after 1965 than they had in the earlier part of the twentieth century. This difference is evident if one looks at the date of adoption of various language laws. For example, of the seventeen U.S. states that have adopted English as their official language, one did so in the 1960s, one in the 1970s, and thirteen did so in the 1980s.

Looking first at the Canadian part of table 6–1, one notes that the major language laws at the federal level, in Quebec and in New Brunswick, were all adopted during an eight-year interval, from 1969 to 1977. Since then, one has witnessed mainly some fine tuning of these legislations, with two exceptions. These are the adoption of Article 23 of the Constitutional Act (federal) in 1982, which created minority schooling rights, and of the French Language Services Act in Ontario in 1986, implemented in 1989. The thrust of these policies is to strengthen the status of French in both Quebec and Canada.

Turning to the American part of table 6–1, one notes that federal language policies were formulated in the 1960s and 1970s. State policies on bilingual education were introduced in the 1960s,[1] while those on English as the official language and Plain English requirements were in the main products of the 1980s. Federal policies increased the rights of minority-language speakers, while recent state policies appear aimed at reducing these rights, with the target group often being the Hispanics.

The chronology of language policies presented in table 6–1 raises two questions: What accounts for these policies, and thus differences, between Canada and the United States? And why did they arise at that time? A complete answer to these questions would require time, resources, and space well beyond what is available here. The following points, however, may provide useful clues to what the answer could be.

• Most Francophones, inside and outside Quebec, believe that the 1760 conquest of New France by Great Britain was carried out in such a way that the distinct nature of French society—civil law, Catholic religion, French language—was respected by the conquerors. As a result, the Confederation of 1867 can be seen as a pact between the two founding nations. This pact did not have as its aim the assimilation of Francophones. It thus implicitly dismissed the policies advocated by Lord Durham in 1840, following the unsuccessful 1837 rebellion of Francophones.

• A majority of English-speaking Canadians agree with the view that Canada is a bilingual nation, with Ontarians, eastern Canadians, and Anglophones more likely to agree than Westerners and Canadians whose mother tongue is neither English nor French (allophones). Among those who disagree, the majority probably agrees with the use of French in Quebec.

• Almost no Hispanics or Americans believe the conquest of northern Mexico respected the distinctive nature of the Spanish territories, even though annexation treaties may have contained such clauses. Only a minority of Americans would view the United States as a bilingual nation.

• Most Francophones were born in Canada, and their share of Canada's population has been decreasing slowly since 1950, while only a minority of Hispanics were born in the United States, and their share of the U.S. population has been increasing since 1960. As a result, one is dealing with native citizens in one case, with immigrants in the other—a subgroup settling in the land of some of their forefathers.

• Historically, Francophones have been the group whose language rights and use were curtailed in Canada.

185

These facts can help us better understand the language policies in Canada and the United States. With respect to the timing of these policies, one should note the following:

• The late 1940s, the 1950s, and the 1960s saw the decolonization of Africa and part of Asia. The phenomenon was accompanied and perhaps in part explained by a change in ideology that may have been accelerated by the spread of television, which put great emphasis on the equality of all human beings.

• The 1950s and 1960s saw a steady rise in real incomes in Canada and the United States, thus facilitating the implementation of redistributive policies.

These changes in ideology and resources manifested themselves in the United States through the civil rights movement and through laws that targeted racial segregation and discrimination against blacks. In Canada there are no important racial minorities, but the ethnic and linguistic group of Francophones was seen as disadvantaged and was thus the target of language laws, particularly in Quebec; Quebec Francophones represent both about 80 percent of Quebec's population and 80 percent of Canada's Francophones. The exact timing depended in part on events such as the Kennedy presidency (1960–1963) and its legacy, or the election of the pro-independence Parti Québécois in Quebec in 1976.

In the case of Quebec it should also be pointed out that since 1960 the Quebec government has increased its power through various mechanisms, such as revenue and power-sharing agreements with the federal government and the creation of various public corporations.

Hence the timing of the affirmation of civil rights in the United States, including those of minority-language speakers, and of Francophone rights in Quebec and Canada as a whole, coincides in part because of common factors. Similarly, the affirmation of English speakers' rights in the 1980s also coincides in both countries.

Language Policies in Canada and the United States. To facilitate their presentation, language policies have been broken down into four components: language of education, language of work, language of business, and language of government services. For each, we describe the main features of the existing language policies using a comparative table and then review their emergence and evolution since 1965. The contents of Quebec's language laws (Bill 22 of 1974, and Bill 101 of 1977) and existing policies (Bill 101, Bill 142, Bill 178, and section 23 of the charter) are presented in appendix table 6-A1.

Language of education. As table 6–2 shows, education is the primary responsibility of subnational governments in Canada and the United States, although both countries have federal subsidy programs and a federal responsibility to Indians and to some federal employees, such as the armed forces. In Canada, the thrust of the language-of-education policies as manifested by constitutional requirements, federal spending programs, and provincial laws and regulations is the maintenance of both official language minorities and the learning of the second official language by both groups. In the United States, the thrust of language policies appears to be the promotion of English, as shown both by federal laws and programs and by state laws and regulations. One should note that it is argued by some that this aim has been replaced by the aim of maintaining the knowledge of the mother tongue of minorities—mainly Hispanics—rather than the learning of English, through maintenance rather than through transitional bilingualism.[2] What the means and aims of the teaching of English to nonnative speakers in the United States should be is thus the object of a continuing debate.

Language of work. As table 6–3 shows, the only jurisdiction that specifically regulates the language of work is Quebec. Two kinds of regulations are in effect. First, most employers, private and public, with fifty employees or more must obtain a certificate from the Office de la langue française, the Quebec language regulatory body. This certificate is granted after an analysis of the use of French in the work place has been carried out and such measures as the translation of documents, French language training for Anglophones, and the hiring of Francophones to increase the use of French have, if necessary, been implemented. Second, language requirements at the hiring, promoting, and firing stages are regulated in Quebec. In English Canada there are no equivalent regulations. In the United States, the Equal Employment Opportunity Commission (EEOC) enforces Title VII of the Civil Rights Act of 1964, which bans the federal government and other private or public employers with fifteen or more employees from employment discrimination based, among other grounds, upon national origin, with language treated as a national-origin trait. The main policy parameters affect the rights of employers to use English-only tests, to require English fluency if it can be shown to be job-related, to impose English-only rules when justified by safety or commercial reasons and not at all times, and to ask for bilingualism in some jobs.[3] In general, even language requirements in the manner of accents must be justifiable with respect to the specific jobs to which they are applied.[4]

187

TABLE 6–2: LANGUAGE OF EDUCATION, 1867–1990

| Topic | Canada | | United States |
	Quebec	English Canada	
Constitutional status	The original constitution of Canada (British North America Act, 1867) indicates that education is an exclusive provincial responsibility and provides for Catholic and Protestant schools in Quebec. Since 1982 the right of language minorities—Anglophones in Quebec, Francophones in English Canada—to instruction in their language where numbers warrant it is recognized in Article 23.		The Constitution of the United States leaves by default the control of education in the hands of the states.
Federal statutes and policies	Neither the Official Languages Act of 1969, amended 1988, nor other federal laws address this issue. Through the Official Languages in Education program, however, the federal government transfers money to provinces to pay for the schooling of language minorities in their own language and the teaching of the official language to the majority.		The Bilingual Education Act was passed in 1968, and has been reenacted since then. Its impact on access to non-English-language education by minority group members has varied through time depending on funding and regulations. In addition, the Lau decision of the Supreme Court (1974) strengthened the right to special language

| Provincial or state laws and policies | Bill 101 of 1977 required children of migrant parents who were not schooled in English in Quebec to attend French public or publicly subsidized elementary and secondary schools. After 1984 this requirement was imposed only on children whose parents were not schooled in English in Canada. Private, unsubsidized schools are open to all but are unimportant (fewer than 1 percent). Short-term visitors (less than 3 years) can be exempted from this requirement. | Provincial policies and laws on access to (where numbers warrant) and control of (separate or mixed school boards) French schools vary and are sometimes challenged under Article 23. A 1990 Supreme Court judgment strengthened these rights but left room for differences between provinces. There is no restriction on language of schooling of immigrants, and French immersion programs are offered to Anglophones. | education but did not specify the means nor provide funding.

State and local policies, including English as official language laws, and requirement for English competency in higher education have tended to favor English as the language of education. This has led to conflict with the federal laws. Various programs have been approved or mandated by the courts. Their official aim is to teach English to non-English students (transitional bilingualism), although some may be teaching both English and the mother tongue (maintenance bilingualism). |

SOURCE: Author.

TABLE 6–3

LANGUAGE OF WORK, PRIVATE SECTOR, 1969–1986

Topic	Canada			United States
	Quebec	English Canada		
Constitutional status	None	None		None
Federal statutes and policies	None. Some of the money spent as part of the Promotion of Official Languages program goes to volunteer and private-sector organizations to fund bilingualism (French). Some corporations may have set up bilingual services in response to but not as a requirement of the Official Languages Act of 1969.			The EEOC has issued guidelines and policy statements that require the employer to show that necessary language knowledge—bilingualism, level of fluency, accent—and policies—English-only, English tests—are job-related and not a discriminatory barrier against Hispanics.

| Provincial or state laws and policies | Bill 101, 1977, requires firms with fifty or more employees to hold a Francisation certificate, acquired when a satisfactory level of French is used in the work place. It also gives rights to workers with respect to language requirements at the hiring, promotion, and firing stages. | None | None. Official language laws do not address this issue except in the preamble of the 1986 Georgia law. |

SOURCE: Author.

Language of business. Both the oral language of service and the written language of signs and forms are examined here. As indicated in table 6–4, in the case of the language of service there are no legal requirements, but the language-of-work requirements of Bill 101 apply in large stores. In the language of signs, Quebec is the main intervener. Since Bill 178 of 1989, it mandates unilingual French exterior signs, except for a few exceptions, such as ethnic-oriented stores; but it allows interior bilingual signs, with French prominent in small stores. Finally, in Quebec the language of documents such as contracts is regulated by Bill 101, which requires French but allows the use of other languages, either alongside French as in instruction sheets for consumer goods, or in replacement of French, such as in contracts where both parties agree to use such a language (English). One should note that in the United States, a fair number of states now require the use of Plain English in various documents such as insurance contracts, while the language of service to customers is taken into account in EEOC policies and court decisions.

Language of government. As shown in table 6–5 the constitution of Canada provides for equal treatment of English and French at the federal level, and in Quebec in parliamentary and judicial institutions. In addition, the hiring and language-of-service policies of the federal government since 1969 reflect a commitment to an equal status of English and French in both Quebec and English Canada. Local governments and institutions have a certain amount of freedom in providing services in various languages. In general, the supply of services in English in Quebec, French in Canada, or Spanish in the United States depends on the demographic makeup of the area. Quebec municipalities, however, appear more likely than other municipalities in Canada to offer second-language services, everything else being equal.

General assessment of language policies. The following observations can be made about the language policies of Canada and the United States. First, Canadian language policies are usually the explicit results of language laws, while American language policies are sometimes derived implicitly from various statutes. As a result, it is more difficult to describe the latter's policies.

In both cases, a tension exists between the central government, which acts as a protector of language minorities, and the provincial or state governments, which restrict minority-language rights. In Canada, the role of the federal government derives from its status as an arbitrator between the two language groups; in the United States, it

TABLE 6-4

LANGUAGE OF BUSINESS, 1977–1988

Topic	Canada			United States
	Quebec	English Canada		
Constitutional status				None
Federal statutes and policies	None	None		None
	Private businesses operating on some federal premises (such as airports) may be required to provide services in both official languages.			
Provincial or state laws and policies	Bill 101 of 1977 and Bill 178 of 1988 regulate the use of French and other languages on signs and forms. Language of oral service is not regulated, although it is referred to in Bill 101.	None		A few local governments regulate the language of signs. Many states require the use of Plain English in their documents. The EEOC and the courts take it into consideration when assessing language requirements set by employers.

SOURCE: Author.

TABLE 6–5
LANGUAGE OF GOVERNMENT, 1867–1986

Topic	Canada		United States
	Quebec	English Canada	
Constitutional status	The British North America Act of 1867 provides for equal status of English and French in the federal parliament and courts and in the Quebec parliament and courts. The Manitoba Act of 1870 provides for the same treatment in Manitoba.		None. But note that the Constitution is written in English.
Federal statutes and policies	Provisions of the Criminal Code, a federal responsibility, provide for the right to a trial in the English or French mother tongue of the accused in the provinces where it has been proclaimed. Voting at the federal level is covered by the Official Languages Act. The federal government is committed to provide services in both official		The Voting Rights Act of 1965, amended in 1975, makes provisions for bilingual voting materials in areas with at least a 5 percent uneducated language minority. There

| Provincial or state laws and policies | languages and attains that goal with a varying degree of success according to the region or department. Bill 101 provides for the use of French as the language of government, but does permit for services in English to the population. These are offered in almost all cases. Bill 142 of 1986 creates rights to English-language services in some social services and health organizations. | Both New Brunswick and Ontario provide for some services in French in various public institutions. Municipalities are exempted from these requirements, but some do offer bilingual services. Manitoba offers limited services in French, while other provinces do not. | is an English-language requirement for nationalization. Some states have literacy requirements for voting, but they have often been suspended by federal laws or declared unconstitutional by the Supreme Court. |

SOURCE: Author.

results from its status as a defender of individual civil rights. Charter rights have become more important in recent years in Canada, however.

In general, the Canadian language policies recognize and support the notion of a bilingual country, while American policies are those of a unilingual state. As Lemco states, "The provisions for minority language services in Canada and the United States are based predominantly on two different principles."[5]

The Theory of the Economic Impact of Language Policies

Language policies are usually introduced in the context of a political entity, such as a nation or region, where two or more languages and language groups vie with one another. They aim either at increasing or at least maintaining the use of a given language, or at reducing or at least preventing the increased use of a language. In Quebec, Bill 101 is an example of the first kind of policy; English-only laws in the United States are an example of the second. Hence, it seems appropriate to examine language policies in a demand-and-supply framework where policies can be classified into two groups: policies that have an impact on demand and policies that have an impact on supply. We first present this framework, which was initially developed by Vaillancourt, and then classify the policies presented above so as to yield a prediction as to their impact.[6]

The Demand-and-Supply Framework. To use a demand-and-supply framework, one must identify quantities and prices. In this case, the quantity is the percentage of time that a given language is used in market-related activities, defined here as consumption and work activities, at a minimum level of fluency. We chose the percentage of time in use rather than the share of population, or absolute number of speakers of a given language, because while the knowledge of a language is a necessary condition for its use, it is not a sufficient one, and because we believe that language use is the relevant dimension in market-related activities. We excluded nonmarket activities such as the language of family life or friendships because these choices are less amenable to quantification. We excluded the language of education because it is often a tool of language policies rather than a goal. The impact of policies in that area, however, will be examined below. Finally, we specify an implicitly minimal level of fluency, which can be seen as a level ensuring comprehension, if not style.

While the percentage of time a language is used can be measured through either direct observation or survey data, the price of a language is not directly observed. It must be calculated, using hedonic

FIGURE 6–1
QUANTITY AND PRICE OF A GIVEN LANGUAGE
AT A GIVEN TIME, IN MARKET USE

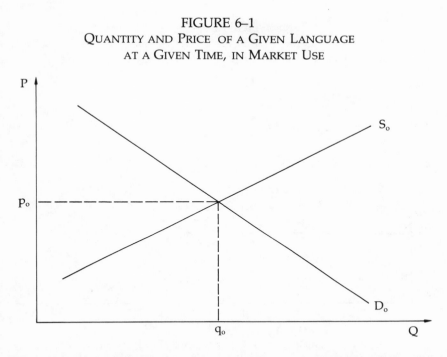

NOTES: P = price, Q = quantity, D = demand, and S = supply. Quantity refers to use and price refers to return.

SOURCE: Author.

methods, from data on either earnings or prices of goods and services. It is the implicit return to a given language. Figure 6–1 shows the equilibrium for a language in a society at a given time.

The location of the demand and supply curves depends on both past and current factors. In the case of the demand curve, the relevant factors include (1) the language of the existing instruments of work (forms, manuals, or operating instructions) that depends on the technology used and on its suppliers; (2) the language of the markets served by the employees; and (3) the language of the owners of firms. In the case of the supply curve, its position depends mainly on the language skills of the population (work force) at a given time, which depend on demographic (fertility, mortality, mobility), linguistic (assimilation), and educational (language acquisition) factors.

It is interesting to note that this model, which takes the use of language in one market as the quantity variable, is similar in its

197

FIGURE 6–2
IMPACT OF SUPPLY-ENHANCING
AND DEMAND-INCREASING POLICIES ON LANGUAGE USE

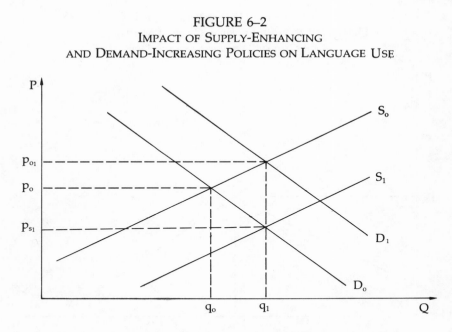

NOTES: P = price, Q = quantity, D = demand, and S = supply. D_0 and $S_0 \rightarrow S_1$ refer to supply-enhancing policies; $D_0 \rightarrow D_1$ and S_0 refer to demand-increasing policies.
SOURCE: Author.

structure and implications to the model put forward by Bloom and Grenier, which uses the quantity of labor in two language markets.[7] Both indicate the same determinant of demand and supply. One should point out, however, two interesting features of their model. First, it allows for adjustment in the supply of labor between the two markets. Second, it raises the issue of the feedback between the supply and demand of workers of one language, pointing out in particular the possibility of discontinuous change.

Both supply-enhancing and demand-increasing policies will increase the use of a given language, as shown in figure 6–2. In the first case, however, its price (return) will diminish, while in the second it will increase.

This distinction is important, because its redistributive implications are not the same. For example, assume that one wants to increase the use of French in managerial activities in Quebec. One

198

policy to attain this would be to increase the supply of well-trained French-speaking managers, either by ensuring that Anglophone management graduates speak French through immersion programs or by increasing the enrollment of Francophones in management programs. Both approaches would lead to an increased supply of French-speaking managers and, for a given demand, to a lower price for these managers. A second policy could be to impose hiring and promotion quotas for French-speaking managers. This policy would increase the demand for these individuals and, at least in the short term, increase their wages and thus the implicit return to their language skills.

The Nature of the Language Policies in Canada and in the United States. In table 6–6 we indicate the nature of the Canadian (Quebec and English Canada) and American language policies and their plausible impacts. It is mainly in Quebec that language policies are most developed and, as a result, most likely to have a measurable impact. Since in that case there are both demand-increasing and supply-enhancing policies, their impact in terms of efficiency and equity is not obvious.

One should also note that the lack of an official language policy does not imply a lack of economic impact of language choices. For example, the lack of an official status for English in the United States does not prevent this language from being the de facto language of common use. As a result, individuals who do not speak it properly, such as some Hispanics, usually earn less than other Americans.

The Impact of Language Policies in Canada and the United States

In the preceding section, we established the plausible impact of American and Canadian language policies. In this section, we present for Quebec, English Canada, and the United States the empirical evidence of the impact of language policies, both at the micro (specific policy) and macro (social) level. We examine each region in turn, in recognition of the interaction of language policies in their impacts, and of Quebec's application of a much broader range of language policies than the other two jurisdictions'. As a result they have been the object of more studies than other language policies.

The Impact of Language Policies in Quebec. *Language of education.* The expected direct impact of this policy is to increase the share of allophones and Anglophones attending French-language schools. In the case of allophone immigrants, this increase is a legal requirement.

199

TABLE 6-6
Expected Impact of Language Policies on the Returns to Language

Language of	Canada		United States
	Quebec	English Canada	
Education	An enhanced supply of French speakers, through increased French schooling of allophones and Anglophones, would reduce returns to French in Quebec in the long run.	Through increased French schooling of Francophones, recent changes should reduce the decrease in the number of French speakers attributable to assimilation. Changes will also increase the supply of bilingual Anglophone workers in the 1990s, through immersion programs. Both trends will reduce returns to French in English Canada in the long run.	Policies should enhance the supply of competent English speakers through the bilingualism program, although some argue that these programs will not do this. No economic impact is expected.

Work		Increased demand for French at work through francisation programs for firms with fifty or more employees and hiring, promoting, firing requirements will cause a demand-shift increase in returns to French.	EEOC policies are based on objective job requirements and should not affect the returns to English.
Business		Increased use of French in signs and documents should have no impact.	Increased use of Plain English in documents should have no impact.
Government	Increased use of French as the language of work and services should cause an increased demand for French speakers.	Increased demand for French through increased use of French as the language of work should bring increased returns to French.	The availability of some government services in Spanish should increase the returns to Spanish.

SOURCE: Author.

201

TABLE 6–7

ANGLOPHONE AND ALLOPHONE STUDENTS AT THE PRIMARY AND
SECONDARY LEVEL, BY TYPE OF LANGUAGE OF SCHOOLING,
IN QUEBEC, 1971–1986
(percent)

| Language of Schooling | Anglophones | | | Allophones | |
| | French | | | | |
	School	Immersion[a]	English	French	English
1971	9.6	5.0	85.4	15.0	85.0
1977	6.3	11.9	81.9	19.9	80.1
1981	12.8	16.6	70.6	40.7	59.3
1986	17.6	17.9	64.5	58.7	41.3

a. All immersion students are assumed to be Anglophones.
SOURCES: For columns 1, 4, and 5, as follows: 1971—*La situation linguistique dans les écoles primaires et secondaires: 1971–1972 à 1978–1979*, by Claude Saint-Germain (Québec: Conseil de la langue française, 1980, Dossier #3, table A-3). 1977—*Statistiques de l'enseignement, clientèles scolaires 1977–1978* (Québec: Ministère de l'Education, table 5.1). 1981—*Statistiques de l'enseignement effectifs scolaires 1981–1982* (Québec: Ministère de l'Education, table 10). 1986—*Statistiques de l'éducation préscolaire, primaire et secondaire, 1986–1987* (Québec: Ministère de l'Education, table 2.3.3).
For column 2, as follows: 1971—Assumed to be 5 percent, given data for later years. 1977—Numerator taken from *La cohabitation linguistique en milieu scolaire au Québec*, Edith Bédard and Claude Saint-Germain (Québec: Conseil de la langue française, 1980. Notes and documents #1, table 5). 1981 and 1986—The numerator is set at 18,000, as stated in *Minority and Second Language Education: Elementary and Secondary, 1985–1986*, Statistics Canada, no. 81–257, p. 11. From a conversation held with R. Maheu of the Ministry of Education on March 3, 1988, we were able to ascertain that this is a reasonable number. 1977, 1981, and 1986—Denominators (the numbers of students) are found in the sources of column 1 above.
For column 3, the figures represent $100 - [(1) + (2)]$.

In the case of Anglophones, it is a legal requirement for those schooled outside Quebec (1977–1984) or Canada (1984 and after). Table 6–7 shows that the percentage of both Anglophones and allophones schooled in French increased from 1970 to 1986. More recent data not reported here show that this trend has continued until 1989.

Language of work. The expected direct impact of this policy is to increase the demand for and use of French at work. This should

TABLE 6-8

USE OF FRENCH IN THE WORK PLACE IN QUEBEC, 1970 AND 1979
(percent of work time)

	Francophones	Anglophones	Total
1970	87	17	77
1979	90	37	85

NOTE: Individuals are categorized by their mother tongue. Calculations are based on data collected by the Gendron Commission in 1971 and the Conseil de la langue française in 1979.
SOURCE: François Vaillancourt, "Le statut socioéconomique des francophones et du français au Québec à la fin des années 1970," *Revue de l'ACELF*, 1982, pp. 9-12.

increase the returns to French in the work place. The direct impact can be ascertained using data either on the use of French or on the need to speak French to obtain employment. Table 6-8 presents evidence on the use of French in the workplace in Quebec in 1970 and 1979. It shows that the use of French increased in Quebec in the 1970s mainly because of an increased use by Anglophones. One should note the widespread use of French by Francophones in 1970 before the introduction of language policies. In the 1980s the use of French in the workplace increased slightly.

Table 6-9 shows that the percentage of management and engineering jobs that were advertised in newspapers in the Montreal area for which a knowledge of French is required increased from 1964 to 1979; it then remained stable or slightly decreased from 1979 to 1984. The impact on the returns to French can be ascertained by examining earnings. Table 6-10 presents data on the average earnings of Anglophones, Francophones, and allophones with given language skills. The data show a narrowing of the earnings gap between Anglophones and Francophones from 1970 to 1980 and little change from 1980 to 1985. This finding, however, could derive from a change in nonlanguage skills. For this reason we present data in table 6-11 on the net return to language skills, having standardized for schooling, experience, and weeks worked.

These data clearly show that the relative return to French with respect to English increased in the Quebec labor market, markedly from 1970 to 1980 and less dramatically from 1980 to 1985. Bloom and Grenier have also calculated the net returns to language skills for Quebec for 1970, 1980, and 1985.[8] We report some of their results in

TABLE 6–9

LANGUAGE SKILLS REQUIRED IN NEWSPAPER ADS FOR MANAGERS AND ENGINEERS, MONTREAL, 1964–1984
(percent)

Language Skills Required	French Only		English and French		English Only	
	Managers	Engineers	Managers	Engineers	Managers	Engineers
1964	31	12	40	16	29	72
1970	27	27	39	21	34	52
1979	36	43	44	37	20	20
1984	31	35	49	29	20	36

SOURCES: For 1964–1979, François Vaillancourt and Alain Daneau. "L'évolution des exigences linguistiques dans les postes de cadres et d'ingénieurs au Québec de 1970 à 1979, *Gestion*, April 1981, p. 25. For 1984, "Offres d'emploi annoncées dans les quotidiens et exigences linguistiques requises à l'embauche," Yves Archambault (Québec: Conseil de la langue française, 1988, mimeo), p. 85.

TABLE 6–10

AVERAGE ANNUAL EMPLOYMENT INCOME FOR MEN AND WOMEN IN QUEBEC, 1970–1985

Mother Tongue	Men						Women					
	1970		1980		1985[a]		1970		1980		1985[a]	
	Dollars	RRC[b]	Dollars	RRC	Dollars	RRC	Dollars	RRC	Dollars	RRC	Dollars	RRC
Unilingual Anglophones	8,171	1.59	17,635	1.22	23,924	1.24	3,835	1.24	10,271	1.17	14,335	1.21
Bilingual Anglophones	8,938	1.74	19,562	1.36	26,078	1.36	3,956	1.28	10,759	1.22	14,449	1.22
Unilingual Francophones	5,136	—	14,408	—	14,235	—	3,097	—	8,801	—	1,802	—
Bilingual Francophones	7,363	1.43	19,547	1.36	25,923	1.35	3,842	1.24	11,195	1.27	14,718	1.25
English-speaking allophones	6,462	1.26	15,637	1.09	20,504	1.07	3,329	1.07	9,753	1.11	12,927	1.10
French-speaking allophones	5,430	1.06	13,287	0.92	17,664	0.92	3,241	1.05	8,191	0.93	9,918	0.84
Bilingual allophones	7,481	1.46	17,946	1.25	23,729	1.23	3,881	1.25	10,868	1.23	14,060	1.19
Other allophones	4,229	0.82	10,003	0.69	12,666	0.66	2,343	0.76	7,539	0.86	8,539	0.72
Anglophones or Francophones	—	—	—	—	21,705	1.13	—	—	—	—	13,182	1.12

a. In the 1986 census database, some individuals are classified as having two mother tongues, English and French. This is not the case for the 1971 or 1981 database.

b. RRC: Ratio-to-reference category (unilingual Francophone). For example, 1970 earnings of unilingual male Anglophones were 59 percent higher than those of unilingual Francophones.

SOURCE: For 1970 and 1980, François Vaillancourt, *Langue et Disparités de Statut Economique au Québec, 1970–1980* (Québec: Conseil de la langue française, 1988), table 3.1. For 1985, calculations made by the author, using the 1986 Census Individual Microdata File.

TABLE 6–11

EFFECTS OF INDIVIDUAL ATTRIBUTES ON EMPLOYMENT INCOME FOR MEN AND WOMEN IN QUEBEC, 1970–1985
(percent)

Factors	Men			Women		
	1970	1980	1985	1970	1980	1985
Linguistic (reference: unilingual Francophones)						
Unilingual Anglophones	10.11	−7.16	−12.76	0	−4.60	0
Bilingual Anglophones	16.99	0	−3.53	0	0	0
Bilingual Francophones	12.61	5.11	5.91	9.73	7.50	9.07
English-speaking allophones	0	−16.27	−21.01	0	0	0
French-speaking allophones	0	−20.03	−25.11	22.82	0	−9.47
Bilingual allophones	6.025	−6.41	−9.08	11.10	0	5.32
Other allophones	−17.64	−45.11	−33.12	0	0	0
Anglophones/Francophones	—	—	−9.87	—	—	0

Standardization

Education						
Primary (5–8 years)	5.87	−13.25	0	0	−11.48	−14.47
Secondary (9–10 years)	19.98	−6.44	7.43	0	0	−8.79
Secondary (11–13 years)	35.61	13.46	31.20	35.06	22.71	19.30
University (1–2 years)	68.34	25.82	49.09	73.66	58.08	50.58
University (3–4 years)	119.3	63.41	90.25	135.05	86.51	89.14
University (5 years or more)	140.35	90.74	130.93	152.27	128.70	114.68
Experience (years)	6.15	5.95	7.11	2.06	2.00	4.86
Experience^2	−0.093	−0.09	−0.11	−0.03	−0.03	−0.08
Weeks worked (each additional week)	3.37	3.53	3.64	4.10	4.35	4.27
Percentage of variance explained (R^2)	49.10	49.54	50.87	46.71	50.26	49.04

NOTES: The equation is a log-linear equation with employment income as the dependent variable. It was estimated using the 1971 and 1981 Census Microdata File for individuals with a positive employment income. 0 indicates a coefficient not significant from zero, using as a cut-off point a t-statistic of 1.65. In the 1986 census database, some individuals are classified as having two mother tongues, English and French. This is not the case for the 1971 or 1981 database.

SOURCES: For 1970 and 1980, François Vaillancourt, *Langue et Disparités de Statut Economique au Québec, 1970–1980* (Québec: Conseil de la langue française, 1988), table 3.2. For 1985, calculations by the author, using the 1986 Census Individual Microdata File.

TABLE 6–12

EFFECTS OF LANGUAGE SKILLS ON EARNINGS FOR MALES, 25–64 YEARS
OF AGE, IN QUEBEC AND ENGLISH CANADA, 1970–1985, AND IN THE
UNITED STATES, 1969–1980
(logarithmic differences in earnings)

	1969–1970	1979–1980	1985
Quebec			
Francophones with respect to Anglophones	− 13	0	0
Unilingual Francophones with respect to unilingual Anglophones	− 18	0	0
Canada			
Francophones with respect to Anglophones	0	0	0
United States			
In high Spanish areas	− 21	− 20	—

NOTES: The dependent variable is the logarithm of earnings. Other independent variables are weeks worked, hours worked, age and age squared, marital status, region, education, and for the United States, year of immigration. The high Spanish areas include the states of Arizona, California, Colorado, New Mexico, Texas, and the metropolitan areas of the states of Florida and New York. 0 indicates a nonsignificant difference at the 5 percent level.
SOURCE: David E. Bloom and Gilles Grenier, "The Earnings of Linguistic Minorities," chapter 9 in this volume, tables 9–3 and 9–5.

table 6–12, as well as results for English Canada and the United States. Their results for Quebec are similar to our findings.

To explain this increase in the profitability of French relative to English from 1970 to 1985, we must examine the changes in the supply or demand of English and French over that period. Let us first look at the supply. Since the ratio of English-speaking to French-speaking workers diminished in Quebec between 1970 and 1985, if the demand were constant, this supply shift should have decreased rather than increased the profitability of French. It appears, then, that supply changes are not the determining factor. Therefore, it must be a shift in demand that determined changes in the relative profitability of

English and French from 1970 to 1985. In our opinion, the increased demand for French and the decreased demand for English can be attributed to the following four factors:

• the growth (measured in numbers of employees) of the public and parapublic sectors (see appendix table 6-A2)

• the growth of employment under Francophone control in the private sector (see appendix table 6-A3), due in part to the transfer of some head office functions outside Quebec for various reasons

• the growth in the disposable income of Francophones (table 6–10) who prefer to spend their money in French, explained in significant part by an increase in their education

• language legislations that encouraged some firms to implement Francisation programs. These laws had little impact on the economic status of Quebec's two language groups for two reasons. First, by 1970 a substantial proportion of Francophones were already working in French (see table 6–8). Second, many decisions to implement Francisation programs were made before the language legislation was enacted.[9]

While the direct impact of language laws may explain only about one-fourth of the change in the economic status of Francophones from 1970 to 1980, one should note that the other three factors are in good part the result of policies of the Quebec government, whose aim was the improvement of the economic status of Francophones. As for the relative lack of change from 1980 to 1985, one should note that the growth in the public and quasi-public sector was much less from 1980 to 1985 than from 1970 to 1980, that the growth in disposable income was also smaller,[10] and that language legislations were, if anything, relaxed over the 1980–1985 period.

Language of business. The expected direct impact is an increased use of French in signs and documents. Little information exists in this area, but the one study that attempted to make a comparison of the situation between 1970 and 1985 concluded that there was a marked increase in the use of French-only outside signs in Quebec.[11] In the Montreal area, this use would have increased from 35.3 percent in 1970 to 78.5 percent in 1984.[12] One can also note that the percentage of Francophones who reported having had difficulties in being served in French by salespeople decreased from 13 percent in 1970 to 9 percent in 1979 in Quebec.[13]

Language of government. No empirical evidence exists on this point, perhaps because French was widely used before language legislations.

Macro impacts. In addition to the specific micro-impacts, the language policies pursued in Quebec have been alleged in political and popular discourse to have affected the employment and income, both wages and profits, of Francophone and non-Francophone residents alike, along with former residents of the province. It is difficult, however, to assess the exact impact of language policies. Their introduction coincided with an increase in the promotion of Quebec Francophone economic power. This increase came about through such means as the creation of publicly owned corporations, the assistance of a semicapitalized public pension plan, making funds available to Francophone entrepreneurs, and preferential procurement policies. Additionally, nationalist, independence-seeking political activity increased, culminating in the election of the Parti québécois in 1976.

Vaillancourt puts forward a framework that complements earlier work and provides a *partial* estimate of the cost of Quebec language laws.[14] This analytical framework distinguishes between psychic costs and resource costs, with the latter divided into expensed costs and output losses.

Psychic costs are the result of the imposition of constraints on individual behavior that prevent individuals from carrying out their welfare-maximizing behavior. For example, the requirement imposed on allophones to send their children to French schools constrains them, reduces their access to English schools, and thus reduces their welfare (see table 6–13). No evidence exists that measures the importance of these costs in willingness-to-pay valuation, but as shown in table 6–13, non-Francophones are in much less agreement with the requirements of Quebec's language law than Francophones.

Resource costs include both expenses and immediate output losses due to the language laws. Amounts spent can be ascertained with some degree of precision by using both public documents and surveys of private firms. Output losses are more difficult to determine because they depend both on productivity effects and on displacement effects. Resource costs are presented in table 6–14.

The key finding of table 6–14 is that the quantifiable cost of Quebec's language policies for the whole 1974–1984 period was somewhere between one-fourth and one-half of 1 percent of Quebec's GDP. This figure is comparable to the estimates of costs of other socioeconomic policies, such as affirmative action or environmental, in various jurisdictions, which can be found in the relevant literature.

Finally, one should remember that the long-term impact, positive or negative, on the growth path of the Quebec economy is not accounted for in these calculations. On the positive side, the increase in the use of French in the work place could increase the productivity of

TABLE 6–13

RESIDENTS IN AGREEMENT WITH VARIOUS STATEMENTS ON BILL 101,
QUEBEC, 1983
(percent)

Statement: *In Quebec. . .*	Mother Tongue of Respondent		
	French	English	Other
. . . *outside signs of businsses should be in French only.*	47	5	18
. . . *children of new immigrants must attend French schools.*	67	24	40
. . . *the language of work must be French.*	79	25	48
. . . *the language of business must be French.*	68	20	35

SOURCE: *La question linguistique: l'état de l'opinion publique,* Daniel Monier (Québec: Conseil de la langue française, 1984), table I.3.

Francophone workers and thus the output of the Quebec economy. On the negative side, one should note that out-migration more than doubled from the 1971–1976 period (59,415) to the 1976–1981 period (141,760). In particular, the English-speaking migrants' inflow went from 39,515 to 25,220, their outflow from 89,595 to 131,530, and their net out-migration from 50,080 to 106,310.[15] While part of this increased net out-migration may be due to nonlinguistic factors, a part can surely be traced to the anticipated impact of Bill 101.

In addition to efficiency costs to Quebec as a whole, language and nationalist policies also have an impact on the relative position of various language groups. Indeed, such authors as Breton would argue that this is their main intent.[16] Redistribution may occur through various mechanisms, such as changes in access to management jobs or transfers of wealth through changes in the prices of such assets as houses. We do not have data on wealth impacts. We can calculate, however, the change in the share of employment income between Francophones and non-Francophones from 1970 to 1980 using mean employment income from table 6–10 and data from Vaillancourt on the share of employment.[17] The results are presented on table 6–15.

Table 6–15 shows that while the Francophone's share of employment grew by 3.04 percentage points from 1970 to 1980, their share of employment income grew by 5.48 percentage points over the same

TABLE 6–14

RESOURCE COSTS OF QUEBEC'S LANGUAGE POLICIES, CUMULATED OVER
THE 1974–1984 PERIOD
(millions of 1984 dollars and percent of GDP)

Costs	Minimum	Maximum
Direct expenses		
Governmental		
language agencies	171.9[a]	232.1[b]
Employer Francisation		
programs	804.6	928.7
Individual language		
training	106.7[c]	249.7[d]
Language of business[e]	35.0	70.0
Total expenses	1,118.2	1,480.5
(percent of GDP)	(0.11)	(0.15)
Output loss	1,652.0[f]	3,303.0[g]
(percent of GDP)	(0.17)	(0.33)
Total cost, as	2,770.2	4,783.5
(percent of GDP)	(0.28)	(0.48)
Total GDP, 1974–1984	997,662.0	997,662.0

a. Direct spending by the relevant agencies as established in the *Public Accounts* of Quebec.

b. Minimum plus central agency cost (10 percent), administratives, and compliance costs of taxes (5 percent) and the excess burden of taxes (20 percent). It is presumed that all governmental spending on the item is financed through taxes.

c. Nonimmigrant related public spending from Archambault Ariane, and Jean-Claude Corbeil, *"L'enseignement du français, langue seconde aux adultes"* (Québec: Conseil de la langue française, Notes et documents 23, 1982); private spending calculated from expenditure survey data.

d. Minimum plus immigrant language training from Archambault and Corbeil.

e. Arbitrary amounts of 5 million per year (minimum) and 10 million (maximum) were used in both cases. Their choice reflect the results of Econosult, *Etude sur les avantages et les coûts de la francisation* (Montréal: Office de la langue française, 1980).

f. One half of output loss due to direct loss of 6,800 jobs is compensated for by remaining firms; Allaire, Yvan, and Roger Miller, *L'enterprise canadienne et la loi sur la francisation du milieu de travail* (Montréal: Institut C.D. Howe, 1980).

g. No compensation by remaining firms.

SOURCE: François Vaillancourt, "The Benefits and Costs of Language Policies in Quebec, 1974–1984," in *The Economics of Language Use*, Proceedings of the 1986 Conference Center for Research and Documentation on World Language Problems, 1987, table 4.

TABLE 6–15

EMPLOYMENT AND EMPLOYMENT INCOME FOR FRANCOPHONES AND
NON-FRANCOPHONES IN QUEBEC, 1970 AND 1980
(percent)

	1970		1980	
	Share of Employment	Share of Employment Income	Share of Employment	Share of Employment Income
Francophone	78.35	74.95	81.39	80.43
Non-Francophone	21.65	25.05	18.01	19.57

NOTE: Similar results were not calculated for 1985 because of the existence of the Anglophone/Francophone category.
SOURCES: For share of employment: Vaillancourt, *Langues et Disparités*, tables B-1, B-3, B-5, and B-7; see source note for table 6–11. For share of employment income: *Share of Employment × Mean Employment Income* (table 6–10).

period, indicating a shift in both employment and income in favor of Francophones. This can be explained in part by a better access to managerial jobs, since in 1970, 64.9 percent of these jobs were held by Francophones, while in 1980 this percentage rose to 75.8 percent.[18]

English Canada and the United States. In English Canada, the most important direct impact of language policies can be expected in the field of education.

Table 6–16 presents information on school enrollment in English Canada. Its results show a slight decrease in the attendance of French school by French minorities and a strong increase in the enrollment in the French immersion program by Anglophones.

As to the civil service, table 6–17 shows an increase in the proportion of Francophone employees from 1965 to 1988, which can be attributed to the increase in the use of French as the language of work, mandated by the Official Languages Act.

In the United States, the most important direct impact of language policies can be expected in the field of education. Data on federal spending on bilingual education programs from Fiscal Year 1970 onward are reported for selected years in table 6–18. They show that spending on bilingual education increased in the 1970s, peaked in the early 1980s (in 1981, at $172,833,000), and subsequently decreased in nominal and real dollars. It has also decreased as a share of federal spending on elementary and secondary education programs. Enroll-

TABLE 6–16
Elementary and Secondary School Enrollment in English Canada, 1977–1988

Year	Total Enrollment	French School Total	%	French Immersion Total	%
1977–1978	3,917,770			20,081	0.5
1981–1982	3,440,528	157,734	4.6	42,927	1.2
1987–1988	3,657,868	153,390	4.2	202,564	5.5

Sources: For 1977–1978 and 1987–1988, *Annual Report 1988*, Commissioner of Official Languages, table C–2. For 1981–1982, *Annual Report 1982*, Commissioner of Official Languages, table B–5.

TABLE 6–17
Share of Francophones in the Federal Civil Service of Canada, 1965–1988
(percent)

1965	1975	1988
21.5	25.6	28.3

Sources: For 1965 and 1975, *Annual Report 1979*, Commissioner of Official Languages, table A–5. For 1988, *Annual Report 1988*, Commissioner of Official Languages, table B–2.

TABLE 6–18
Bilingual Education Expenses in the U.S. Federal Government, 1970–1985
(thousands of dollars)

1970	1975	1980	1985
26,192	62,829	169,540	157,539

Note: All figures are in current dollars.
Sources: For 1970 and 1975, *Digest of Educational Statistics 1982* (Washington: National Center for Education Statistics), table 155. For 1980 and 1985, *Digest of Educational Statistics 1988* (Washington: National Center for Education Statistics), table 257.

ment in bilingual education programs appears to have increased from about 1,350,000 in 1983, to 1,460,000 in 1985, to 1,534,000 in 1986.[19] We say "appears" because data on enrollment in these programs seem unreliable. For example, education department enrollment figures were 1,387,536 for school year 1985–1986, while the General Accounting Office figures were 1,515,406.[20]

Finally, using the relevant results of table 6–12, one notes with interest that no change has occurred in the relative returns of English to French in English Canada from 1970 to 1985, or in the relative returns of Spanish to English in the United States from 1969 to 1979—a result in accord with the absence of change in language policies in these labor markets.

Evaluation of Language Policies

In this section we address the issue of which language policies would be appropriate for Canada and the United States from an economic perspective, putting aside legal, political, and sociolinguistic considerations. We first put forward general principles and then address the case for each area in turn.

Economic Analysis and Language Policies. The standard economic reason for the state's intervention in a given area is that a failure of the market has occurred because of such phenomena as externalities or myopia. In the case of language, such market failures will depend, in part, on the nature of the geopolitical institutions. If the borders of each autonomous state corresponded to those of only one language group, then such market failure would be unlikely; the language of the state and of its citizens or residents would be the same.

In many states, countries, and empires, however, more than one language community resides in intermingled fashion with others. In these political entities languages vie with one another, but one language is usually dominant because its speakers control one or more of the economic, military, or political spheres of activity, often for historical reasons. In some cases, these speakers will choose to impose their language as the common and often sole language to be used in the territory. A language imposition policy brings about both costs and benefits. In costs it means that the nondominant language capital will first lose value and will eventually also decrease in quantity, by assimilation. In benefits, it increases the use of the dominant language and thus reduces communication costs in the same way that new physical means of communications, such as railroads or canals, would do.

Of course, it could be argued that the dominant language will spread naturally without government intervention. The cost of learning a language is smaller, however, the earlier it is learned in life, both for a psychopedagogical (ease-of-learning) reason and for an opportunity-cost reason. As a result the state may need to intervene to correct myopic choices by parents with respect to language, in a way similar to the introduction of compulsory schooling in the nineteenth century. This intervention would result in the promotion of the dominant language. Note that the preservation of minority languages for their value in international relations and trade could also result from state intervention. It is unlikely, however, that states would want to preserve a minority language to ensure greater language diversity.

Since in many cases the language or languages used in a given territory at a given time result not from the interplay of private choices but rather from past policies, this policy may lead to rigidities and to a minority's deriving rent from the use of its language. The minority would then object to changing a language use that is economically efficient. The group may even be able to prevent the change because of its socioeconomic position. Breton and Mieszkowski have argued that in that case state intervention to reverse historical rigidity may be appropriate.[21]

Finally, language policy can also be used simply to redistribute economic power and wealth from one language group to another.[22]

Having established the possibility of an economic foundation for intervention by the state in language matters, the goal is to determine what kind of policy is appropriate. The answer depends on the setting for the policy. In general, however, the following three rules should apply:

• Language policies can require the learning of a common language, but they should not prohibit the learning of other languages. The imposition of a common-language requirement can be justified by the impact on the size of the common market. The prohibition against learning another language has no economic basis, and it reduces both the human capital stock and the welfare of the group thus affected. It is usually imposed to bring about cultural assimilation rather than economic integration. The funding of such activities can be public or private, depending on the usefulness of the language, the degree of local demand, and the school-funding arrangements.

• Language policies should not prohibit the use of more than one language in signs and documents, but they may require that the common language be used. Bilingual or multilingual written material offers a choice that does not detract from one language or another but adds to the welfare of the consumer.

• Language policies may prescribe the right to use a language in interactive settings such as the language of oral services in stores, but it should not prohibit the use of other languages, both parties willing.

The first rule states that a supply-increasing policy for one language does not imply a supply-reducing policy for others. The other two rules state that demand enhancement for one language does not imply demand suppression for others. Indeed, language policies, legal or customary, should not prohibit the use of a language but can indicate what language will be used in cases of disagreement.

These three rules are aimed at taking into account both the previous discussion on state intervention in language matters and the general principle that economic agents should always be allowed the greatest possible degree of choice, since additional constraints usually reduce society's welfare.

Let us now turn to language policies in Quebec, English Canada, and the United States.

Language Policies in Quebec, English Canada, and the United States. The economic basis for Quebec's language policy was the perception of a continuing overuse of English by Quebec's Anglophone minority, as a result of rent-seeking behavior. In our opinion, the existing language policy is flawed in its prohibitive components. We have therefore proposed that the objectives of Quebec's language policies should be as follows:

• to ensure that French is the common language of oral communication in the internal Quebec market
• to allow the use of other languages in combination with French for written communication (for example, on forms and signs)
• to allow companies to use the optimal combination of languages to serve their external market
• to promote the learning of English by all Francophones
• to require or promote the learning of French by all non-Francophones, depending on their place of birth and age[23]

These objectives are compatible with the aforementioned rules on language acquisition, the written use of language, and the interactive use of language.

The ultimate objective of such a policy is the optimal use of French in Quebec. The two most important dimensions of the policy are the first and fourth listed; since the first requires individual employees of private and public enterprises serving the internal Quebec market to know French, and the fourth requires compulsory French schooling in many cases.

In the case of English Canada and the United States, we would recommend that schooling for minority (Francophone or Hispanic) children aim at ensuring the knowledge of both their mother tongue and English. In the case of English Canada, this policy would ensure a supply of employees capable of dealing with Quebec customers in their own language. In the United States it ensures a supply of employees capable of dealing with most Central and South Americans in their own language. In both cases it is a low cost option. We would also recommend, in both cases, that no prohibition be placed on the language of signs and documents but that the common oral language be English.

The thrust of our recommendations is to adopt a territorial vision of language policies. Such a vision is at odds with Canada's federal language policies but is in agreement with quite a few European language policies. We believe it yields an acceptable language environment at a lower resource cost.

Conclusion

This chapter presents Canadian and American language policies, examines their impact, and reflects on their adequacy. Our main conclusions are:

- that language policies in North America are most developed in the area of education and that Quebec is outstanding, given the scope of its policies
- that it is possible to predict some of the specific impacts of language policies by using a supply-and-demand framework and that these predictions are supported by the empirical evidence
- that it is possible to use economic analysis to make recommendations with respect to language policies

In closing, let us note that we examined existing language policies with respect to English-French and English-Spanish interaction in Canada and the United States, respectively. A more general analysis would lead us to inquire about the policies that these countries should carry out with respect to all language skills. Should they, for example, take into account their language portfolio in selecting immigrants and help them to retain their native languages over time so as to better serve all markets? Or should they use their resources to ensure the spread of a world language? If so, should it be an artificial (Esperanto) or natural one, and if a natural one, which one? English is the leading contender.

APPENDIX 6–A1

A COMPARISON OF THE MAIN FEATURES OF BILL 22, BILL 101, AND 1990 LANGUAGE POLICIES IN QUEBEC

	Bill 22 (1974)	*Bill 101 (1977)*	*Status in 1990*
Language of business	French or bilingual documents (bills, instructions) and store signs	French or bilingual documents and French-only signs for stores	Bill 178 (1989) allows a greater use of English on indoor signs
Language of education	Access to English language schools is on the basis of language tests administered to children	Access to English schools is restricted to children of parents who attended English elementary schools in Quebec	Article 23 of the 1982 Constitutional Act (federal) includes children whose parents attended English schools in Canada
Language of work	Increased use of French through Francisation programs and hiring of "Francophones" is required of firms doing business with the Quebec government	Increased use of French through Francisation programs that firms of fifty employees or more must implement	Unchanged

Language requirements for professionals		Members of professional corporations (nurses, engineers, M.D.'s) must demonstrate proficiency in French to attain the right to practice	Unchanged
Language of public services		Individuals may be served in languages other than French	Bill 142 (1986) extends services in English
Main language bodies	Régie de la langue française	Office de la langue française, Conseil de la langue française, Commission de protection de la langue française	Unchanged

SOURCE: Adapted from "The Cost and Benefit of Language Policies in Quebec, 1974–1984: Some Partial Estimates," by François Vaillancourt, in *The Economics of Language Use*, H. Tomkin and K.M. Johnson-Weiner, eds., New York, CRDWLP, 1987, p. 71–94, at 76 table 1.

APPENDIX 6–A2

Ownership by Language Groups and Employment, Various Sectors of the Quebec Economy, 1961, 1978, and 1987
(number and percent of employment in sector)

	1961	1978	1987
Private number	1,365,621	1,920,400	2,242,400
percent	81.6	76.3	75.6
Public number	307,553	596,000	722,800
percent	18.4	23.7	24.4
Total number	1,673,174	2,516,400	2,965,200

NOTES: For comparability, the public sector includes government, health, education, religious, and domestic employment. Each of the last two categories represents less than 1% of all employment in 1987 and has been decreasing through time.
SOURCES: For 1961, Raynauld, "La propriété des entreprises au Québec," tables II-17A and II-21. For 1978, Raynauld and Vaillancourt, "L'appartenance des enterprises," tables II-24 and II-26. For 1987, Vaillancourt, "Demolinguistic Trends and Canadian Institutions," tables 2.9 and 3.3.

APPENDIX 6–A3

OWNERSHIP BY LANGUAGE GROUPS OF VARIOUS SECTORS OF THE QUEBEC ECONOMY, 1961, 1978, AND 1987

(percent of total employment)

Sector	Francophone Controlled			Anglophone Controlled			Foreign Controlled		
	1961	1978	1987	1961	1978	1987	1961	1978	1987
Agriculture	91.3	91.8	87.5	8.7	8.2	12.2	0[a]	0[a]	0.3
Forestry	–[b]	33.4	92.3	–[b]	28.9	7.7	–[a]	37.7	0
Mining	6.5	17.0	35.0	53.1	18.1	40.4	40.4	64.9	24.6
Manufacturing	21.7	27.8	39.3	47.0	38.6	38.2	31.3	33.5	22.5
Construction	50.7	74.4	75.5	35.2	18.5	21.8	14.1	7.1	2.7
Transportation, communications, and public services	36.4	42.2	44.9	55.3	53.4	50.2	8.3	4.4	4.9
Commerce	50.4	51.0	57.8	39.5	32.0	34.0	11.5	17.0	8.2
Finance, insurance, and real estate	25.8	44.8	58.2	53.1	43.1	34.6	21.1	12.1	7.2
Services	71.4	75.0	75.7	28.6	21.2	21.6	0[a]	3.8	2.7
Government	51.8	67.2	67.0	47.7	32.8	33.0	0.5	0[a]	0[a]
Total	47.1	54.8	61.6	39.3	31.2	30.8	13.6	13.9	7.8

a. Hypothesis.
b. Not calculated. Note that the data for this sector vary in such a manner that intertemporal comparisons are difficult.
SOURCE: Vaillancourt and Carpentier, *Le contrôle de l'économie du Québec*, table 3.2.

TABLE 6–A4: Main Sources and Calculations Used in Estimating the Resource Costs of Quebec Language Policies for Employees

Minimum: This study was carried out in 1977 and its results used by Allaire and Miller.[24] Various types of employers were surveyed, and the results on the expected cost of Francisation are of particular interest to us. Per employee, the annual Francisation costs are $60 in 1977 ($105 in 1984 dollars) for large firms (500 employees or more), and $50 in 1977 ($88 in 1984 dollars) for small firms (50–99 employees). In total, Quebec employers incur once-and-for-all set-up costs for Francisation activities of $139.7 million in 1977 dollars, (243.8 millions in 1984 dollars) and annual costs of $96.2 millions in 1977 dollars, ($167.9 million in 1984 dollars). The annual costs are divided as follows: 32 percent to translation, 3 percent to moving, and 5 percent to language training expenses. Using data on set-up costs, assuming that Francisation activities began in 1979 (after the set-up period), that their intensive phase lasted for three years and thus cost $503.7 million in 1984 dollars (167.9 × 3), and that the maintenance phase is made up mainly of translation activities and thus represents 32 percent of the intensive phase that is $53.7 million (1984 dollars) on an annual basis, or $161.2 million (1984 dollars) for the 1982–1984 period, one obtains a figure for total expenses of Francisation equal to $804.6 million in 1984 dollars for the 1974–1984 period.

Maximum: To obtain the maximum cost we combined information from CLE on per employee costs, from Denise Daoûst on the number of employees affected by Francisation, and from Econosult on the length of Francisation. See table 6–2 in Vaillancourt for details.

Costs per employee are established as follows: The Centre de linguistique de l'entreprise surveyed its members, which are large firms (500 employees or more), and it provided information on the expenses on linguistic counselors, translation,[25] and language training. For the 1978–1982 period, the reported per employee cost was $425. Dividing it by five, we obtain an annual cost of $85; using the midpoint of the time span as the representative year yields a 1984-dollar cost of $114. One notes, however, that the CLE argues that the per employee annual cost is of the order of $200 for the 2–3 year period of intensive Francisation. Assuming that this figure holds in 1980 yields a 1984-dollar annual cost of $268. The CLE also notes that some costs (such as printing, and traveling) have been neglected in their survey. Their inclusion would increase Francisation costs by about 50%.

The large firm (500 employees or more) basic intensive cost is reported in the CLE study. The small firm cost is set equal to ⁵⁄₆ of the large firm cost, using the ratio reported by Allaire and Miller.[26] The maintenance costs are set equal to 32% of the intensive phase, as reported by Allaire and Miller. This reflects the fact that maintenance costs are mainly translation costs, as result in part from the hiring requirements of Bill 101. Total costs are obtained by multiplying basic costs by 1.5 to account for unstated cost.[27]

	Number of Employees Affected		Basic Cost per Employee per Year		Number of Years		Basic Costs
Public or semipublic employees							
Intensive phase	86,000	×	$246	×	3	=	63,468,000
Maintenance phase	86,000	×	$79	×	4	=	27,176,000
Private firms, 50–99 employees							
Intensive phase	110,000	×	$223	×	3	=	73,590,000
Maintenance phase	110,000	=	$71	×	4	=	31,240,000
Private firms, 100 and more employees							
Intensive phase	402,000	×	$246	×	3	=	296,670,000
Maintenance phase	402,000	×	$79	×	4	=	127,030,000

Sources: The source for the minimum costs is SECOR, 1977. The maximum cost has been calculated by combining information from the Centre de linguistique de l'enterprise (CLE), "Mémoire sur la charte de la langue française," from Denise Daoust, "Francisation and Terminology Change in Quebec Business Firms," and from Econosult, *Etude sur les avantages et les coûts de la francisation*." See François Vaillancourt, "The Benefits and Costs of Language Policies in Quebec, 1974–1984," *The Economics of Language Use*, Proceedings of the 1986 Conference Center for Research and Documentation on World Language Problems, 1987, table 2.

225

Bibliography

Allaire, Yvan, and Roger Miller. *L'entreprise canadienne et la loi sur la francisation du milieu de travail.* Montréal: Institut C.D. Howe, 1980.

Anonymous. "Official English: Federal Limits on Effort to Curtail Bilingual Services in the States." Note in *Harvard Law Review* 100 (1987): 1345–62.

Archambault, Ariane, and Jean-Claude Corbeil. *L'enseignement du français, langue seconde aux adultes.* Québec: Conseil de la langue française, Notes et documents 23, 1982.

Beaty, Stuart. "Official Languages in Education: The Way Ahead." *Language and Society* 21 (Winter 1987): 23–24.

Beaty, Stuart, and Jean Claude Le Blanc. "Applying Minority Education Rights." *Language and Society* 24 (Fall 1988): 33–34.

Bennett, William J. *The Condition of Bilingual Education in the Nation, 1988.* U.S. Department of Education, 1988.

Bloom, David E., and Gilles Grenier. "The Economic Position of Linguistic Minorities: French in Canada and Spanish in the United States." Chapter 9 in this volume.

Breton, Albert. "The Economic of Nationalism." *Journal of Political Economy* 72 (August 1964): 376–86.

Breton, Albert, and Peter Mieszkowski. "L'investissement linguistique et la francisation du Québec." In *Economie et langue*, ed. François Vaillancourt. Québec: Conseil de la langue française, 1985, pp. 83–100.

Carazos, Laura F. *Annual Evaluation Report, Fiscal Year 1988.* Department of Education.

Centre de linguistique de l'enterprise (CLE). "Mémoire sur la charte de la langue française." Montréal, October 1983, mimeo.

Daoûst, Denise. "Francisation and Terminology Change in Quebec Business Firms." *Conflict and Language Planning in Quebec*, ed. R. Y. Bourhis. Clevedon, United Kingdom: Multilingual Matters, 1984.

Econosult. *Etude sur les avantages et les coûts de la francisation.* Montréal: Office de la langue française, 1981.

Hood, Sarah. "Corporate Language Policies." *Language and Society,* 21 (Winter 1987): 29.

Imhoff, Gary. "The Position of U.S. English on Bilingual Education." *Annals of the American Academy of Political and Social Sciences* 508 (March 1990): 48–61.

Institut Gamma. *Prospective de la langue française au Québec.* Québec: Conseil de la langue française, Document 25, 1986.

Kohl, John P., and David P. Stephens. "The Increasing Use of Bilingual Requirements in Classified Advertisement: A Questionable or Illegal Personnel Practice." *Labor Law Journal* (November 1987): 307–11.

Lacroix, Robert, and François Vaillancourt. "Les revenus et la langue au Québec (1970–1978)." Québec: Conseil de la langue française, 1981.

Larson, Arthur, and Lex K. Larson. *Employment Discriminations, vol. 3, Race, Religion, and National Origin* (June 1989) Cumulative Supplement, Matthew Bender.

Leibowitz, Arnold H. "The Official Character of Language in the United States: Literacy Requirements for Immigration, Citizenship, and Entrance into American Life." *Aztlan* 15 (1984): 25–70.

Lemco, Jonathan, "Official Language Legislation in the United States and Canada: A Route to National Disharmony." Forthcoming in *Public Policy in Canada and the United States*, ed. M. Lubin. Greenwood Press, 1990, mimeo, p. 4.

Maurais, Jacques, and Philippe Plamondon. "Le visage français du Québec—Enquête sur l'affichage." Québec: Conseil de la langue française, Notes et documents 54, 1986.

Moran, Rachel F. "Bilingual Education as a Status Conflict." *California Law Review*, vol. 75, 1987, pp. 321–62.

Olsen, Roger E. W.-B. *Report of the Limited English (LEP) Student Enrollment Survey*, 1989. Mimeo.

Raynauld, André. *Le propriété des entreprises au Québec, les années 60.* Montréal: PUM, 1974.

Raynauld, André, and François Vaillancourt. *L'appartenance des entreprises: le cas au Québec en 1978.* Québec: Conseil de la langue française, 1984.

Schmidt, Carol. "Language and Education Rights in the United States and Canada." *International and Comparative Law Quarterly* 36 (October 1987): 903–08.

Scott, Stephen A. "Judicial Guarantees." *Language and Society*, vol. 17. March 1986, pp. 29–33.

Secor. "La charte de la langue française et son impact." Québec: Journal des débats, commission permanente de l'éducation des affaires culturelles et des communications, Assembleé Nationale, June 27, 1977.

Sloan, Tom. "Transfers and Subsidies for Official Language Programs." *Language and Society* 24 (Fall 1988): 35.

Special Issues Analysis Center (SIAC). "States' Activities Related to the Education of LEP Students." OBEMLA, mimeo, 1989.

Strong, Charles. "Bilingual Municipal Services: A New Initiative." *Language and Society* 28 (Fall 1989): 11.

Sutherland, Alfred J. "National Origin Discrimination Based on Accent or Manner of Speaking." Prentice Hall, Personal Management Series, 1987.

Thernstrom, Abigail M. "Bilingual Miseducation." *Commentary* vol. 89, February 1990, pp. 44–48.

Vaillancourt, François. "The Benefits and Costs of Language Policies in Quebec, 1974–1984." *The Economics of Language Use*, Proceedings of the 1986 Conference Center for Research and Documentation on World Language Problems, 1987, pp. 71–91.

————. "La Charte de la langue française: un essai d'analyse." *Canadian Public Policy/Analyse de Politique*, Summer 1978, pp. 284–308.

————. "Demolinguistic Trends and Canadian Institutions: An Economic Perspective." In *Demolinguistic Trends and the Evolution of Canadian Institutions*, Canadian Issues. Association for Canadian Studies, 1989.

————. "The Economics of Language and Language Planning." *Language Problems and Language Planning*, vol. 7, Summer 1983, pp. 162–78.

————. *Langue et Disparités de Statut Economique au Québec, 1970–1980.* Québec: Conseil de la langue française, 1988.

————. "Langue et statut économique au Québec, 1980–1985." Québec Conseil de la langue française, 1992.

————. "Pour un nouveau pacte linguistique." *L'Actualité Economique* 64, 1988, pp. 486–88.

————. "Le statut socioéconomique des francophones et du français au Québec à la fin des années 1970." *Revue de l'ACELF*, 1982.

Vaillancourt, François, and Josée Carpentier. *Le contrôle de l'économie du Québec: la place des francophones en 1987 et son évolution depuis 1961.* Montréal: Office de la langue française, 1989.

Vaillancourt, François, and Alain Daneau. "L'évolution des exigences linguistiques dans les postes de cadres et d'ingénieurs au Québec de 1970 à 1979." *Gestion* (April 1981): 25.

7

Language in the Immigrant Labor Market

Barry R. Chiswick and Paul W. Miller

Spoken language skill, the ability to communicate verbally, is the most basic form of human capital. It is the first type of human capital to be acquired among children, and usually the last to be lost by the aged. Spoken language skills are acquired primarily in the home as infants learn to imitate older children and adults. The initial learning by imitating is quickly followed by a learning by doing.

Spoken language skills are so basic that they are usually taken for granted. Yet it is clear that the ability to communicate verbally through a common language must have substantial economic value. Economic transactions can take place without verbal communication, but the cost of these transactions is sharply increased, and their frequency sharply decreased, when this communication cannot occur.[1]

International immigrants are perhaps the group most acutely sensitive to the importance of language capital. Moving to a country where a different language is spoken results in a depreciation of the value of this catalyst for economic and social interaction. The decision to migrate, the choice of destination, and the success of adjustment in the destination all depend, in part, on language skills.

Two key questions are addressed in this study. First, what are the determinants of the extent to which immigrants not fluent in the dominant language acquire dominant-language skills? The adjustment process may vary systematically with the immigrant's economic, human-capital, and demographic characteristics. Second, what are the impacts of dominant-language fluency on labor market outcomes, such as earnings? Economic theory predicts that, ceteris paribus, those less fluent in the dominant language of the destination will have lower earnings. The more difficult issue is determining the extent to which earnings are lower.

These research questions are important for several reasons. First, their answers will provide a better understanding of how labor markets operate and of the earnings determination process. Such understanding, of course, is important for public policy regarding efficiency, income distribution, and poverty. Another reason is that the answers shed light on the economic and noneconomic incentives for, and determinants of, an important aspect of skill formation. Third, an understanding of these issues will provide better insights regarding public policy toward the maintenance of minority languages. As is shown by the Vaillancourt chapter, public policies of the United States and Canada differ regarding minority languages and regarding the dominant languages—English in the United States and, English and French in Canada. Finally, language skills can have explicit and implicit roles in immigration policy and naturalization policy. The role of language in immigration policy differs in the two countries, as is shown by the Reimers and Troper chapter. Fluency in one or the other of the two official languages of Canada is explicitly considered in the Canadian immigration system. Proposals for explicitly incorporating English-language skills in U.S. immigration policy were under debate in the development of the 1990 Immigration Amendments, and most assuredly will emerge again in the future.

The following section of this chapter addresses the issue of the determinants of dominant-language fluency among immigrants. After developing the theoretical framework, empirical analyses are performed for adult male immigrants in the United States, using microdata from the 1980 Census of Population, and in Canada, using microdata from the 1981 Census of Canada. The section closes with a comparative analysis of the U.S.-Canadian findings.

The next section is an analysis of the role of dominant-language fluency in determining earnings in the two countries. The interaction of language fluency with other determinants of earnings is also analyzed. The theoretical discussion is followed by earnings analyses for adult male immigrants in the two countries, again using microdata from the 1980 and 1981 censuses.

The last section is a summary and conclusion, with implications for public policy. The appendixes include the language questions used in the 1980 U.S. and 1981 Canadian censuses, a detailed discussion of the variables used in the statistical analysis, and tables of the means and standard deviations of these variables.

The Determinants of Dominant-Language Proficiency

This section presents comparative analyses of the determinants of dominant-language proficiency in both Canada and the United

States. These analyses are based on census data for each country: the 1981 Census of Canada and the 1980 Census of Population, for the United States. These sources include questions on fluency in speaking the dominant languages: English in the United States, English or French in Canada. Data are not available in these sources for reading or writing skills in the dominant language. Furthermore, although there are data in the censuses on nondominant languages spoken in the home, there is no information on the degree of proficiency in speaking, reading, or writing nondominant languages.

Special emphasis is placed on defining variables that are broadly comparable across the two data sets, and this emphasis has a bearing on the manner in which the investigations are conducted. While the 1981 Census of Canada contains three questions on language, only one can be used as an indicator of fluency in a dominant language: the so-called official language question on the census permits respondents to be distinguished on the basis of their ability to speak one or both of the official languages of Canada well enough to carry on a conversation.[2]

It is not possible to construct for Canada a measure of dominant-language fluency with finer gradations from these data. In the U.S. Census, however, individuals who spoke a language other than English in the home were asked to report their level of proficiency in English. Responses were coded into four categories: very well, well, not well, and not at all. To facilitate the Canadian–U.S. comparisons, individuals who spoke only English in the home and those who spoke a language other than English in the home but spoke English very well or well are distinguished from those less fluent in English.

Previous research suggests that factors such as mother tongue, educational attainment, country of origin, duration of residence, age at arrival, and region of residence are important determinants of dominant-language proficiency.[3] To this list it seems reasonable to add variables—indicating the presence of young children in the family; whether the individual has been in the armed forces; measuring a minority group concentration; and indicating marital status and country of marriage. The relationships expected between these factors and dominant-language fluency are described below.

Country of birth may affect proficiency in the dominant language through an exposure factor. Countries differ in the extent to which particular languages are used as the dominant language, as a second language, or as the language of commerce. For example, individuals born in a predominately English-speaking country presumably know, or at least have been exposed to, the English language. Thus, immigrants from Britain, Canada, the United States, Australia, New Zealand, the British West Indies, and Ireland, for example, are arguably proficient in the English relevant for the United States and Canada—in spite of differences in accents and minor differences in terminology, idioms, and spelling.[4] For many North Europeans (such as the Dutch and Scandinavians) English is a second language, and hence English-language fluency is presumably both greater at arrival and easier to acquire than it is for others. Similarly, because of colonial experiences, among immigrants in Canada fluency in the French language may be greater or easier to acquire for those born in Vietnam or Lebanon than among those born in Korea or Turkey.

Immigrants arriving as youths are likely to gain greater fluency in the destination language than older immigrants with the same number of years in the destination. Children have a facility for acquiring new spoken-language skills that diminishes sharply as they become adults—that is, their production function for acquiring dominant-language skills is more efficient. In addition, youths gain a more intensive exposure to the dominant language through schools than adults gain at home or in the labor market, and thus youths rapidly acquire fluency in the primary language of the destination country.[5] Moreover, the benefits accruing to language skills will tend to be greater among youths, due to the complementarity between dominant-language skills and other human capital (such as schooling) and their longer payoff period. Hence, from the human capital perspective, one also would expect that immigrants arriving as youths are more likely to undertake the investments necessary to become proficient in the dominant language.

Dominant-language proficiency should vary directly with years since migration. The longer the individual has been in the host country, the more likely it is that he would have been exposed to the dominant language and hence would have acquired some language skills or would have improved existing skills. This adjustment factor has been emphasized in studies of the economic adjustment of immigrants that focus on the determinants of earnings and occupational status. The present study attempts to model the process explicitly. There may also be important interactions between levels of schooling and years since migration. Chiswick, for example, argues that in a population that initially has a very low level of fluency, the impact of education on immigrants' dominant-language fluency should increase with duration of residence.[6] His empirical evidence was consistent with this proposition.

Incentives to invest in dominant-language skills also vary with the expectation of remaining in the destination. Other factors being equal, the higher the probability of return migration in the near term, the weaker the incentives for investment in destination-specific skills, including dominant-language skills. Therefore, the greater the expectation is of return migration, the poorer the fluency in the dominant language. While data are not available on the probability of return migration for specific individuals, it is known that return migration rates are much higher for some groups than for others. In the U.S. context it is very high for Mexican immigrants but very low for another group of Hispanics—the Cubans. In the Canadian context, it is much higher for Italian and Greek immigrants than for the Vietnamese.

Although the exact causal process is open to debate, it is generally assumed that there will be a positive relationship between educational attainment and proficiency in the dominant language for immigrants from countries in which the dominant-destination language is not the primary language. For these immigrants the positive effect on fluency of preimmigration schooling may reflect the curriculum of the school attended, with second-language skills being learned only in the more advanced grades. More generally, it is likely that there is a complementarity between schooling and dominant-language proficiency. That is, those with more schooling would be more proficient in acquiring other forms of human capital, including language capital. Also, the language of instruction is generally the dominant language, and language capital perhaps more than other capital is enhanced by exposure and usage. Causality, however, may also go in the opposite direction because of the complementarity of forms of human capital. Those with greater dominant-language skills, other factors being equal, may have a greater productivity from additional schooling in the destination. The positive relationship between educational attainment and dominant-language proficiency could also be the outcome of a third process. For example, those with higher levels of ability may both acquire more schooling and be more capable of mastering other skills, such as a second language.

It has been suggested above that an individual's incentive to acquire dominant-language skills will be inversely related to the extent to which his native tongue is used in his present environment. DeVries and Vallee report that the language composition of the individual's environment is important to understanding the distribution of bilingualism in Canada.[7] Similarly, Chiswick suggests that for inhabitants of the Los Angeles area, the presence of a sizable Spanish-speaking, Mexican-origin enclave community may reduce the incentive to acquire English-language skills, as compared with other immigrants.[8] Some insights into this issue can be gained by adding statistical controls to the estimating equation for the fraction of the regional population that has the same origin-language as the individual concerned; for example, Spanish is relevant for many countries of origin. This minority-language concentration measure is similar in motivation to Veltman's battery of dummy variables for region of residence, constructed with reference to concentrations of minority-language groups within geographic units in the United States.[9]

The presence of children in the household may affect the language-acquisition process. First, children are expected to learn the dominant language more readily than their parents, in part because children have superior language-acquisition skills and in part because they are placed in circumstances that facilitate this—in school and in association with native-born children who speak the dominant language. Such skills may then be passed on to the parents within the home environment, so that parents learn the dominant language from the children.[10] Alternatively, where young children are present, parents may attempt to facilitate the assimilation of the young by learning and then speaking only the dominant language in the household. Finally, having children in the household, rather than leaving them in the origin or being childless, may reflect a stronger permanent attachment to the destination. Thus, in households where there are or have been young children, the older members of the household are expected to be more proficient in the dominant language. This effect can be expected to be larger if there is more than one child because of the language interaction between or among the children and the longer period and greater intensity of parental exposure.

Marital status could also affect dominant-language fluency, although the most important influence may come from the timing of the marriage. If the individual was married prior to migration, it is more likely that the spouse is of the same language group. It is hypothesized that this circumstance would weaken the incentive to become proficient in the language of the host country. On the other hand, marriage after migration is more likely to be with a dominant-language speaker. This suggests a differential effect of being married, depending on whether it is pre- or post-migration.

Finally, veteran status is expected to be associated with an increase in the probability that the individual is proficient in the dominant language, mainly through the remedial courses and dominant language exposure that the armed forces offer for individuals deficient in language skills.

The next subsection contains the analysis of the determinants of English-language proficiency in the United States. Following this, dominant-language (English or French) fluency in Canada is studied.

The section concludes with a comparison of the major findings from the analyses of dominant-language fluency in the two countries.

Dominant Language Proficiency in the United States. The study of dominant-language fluency in the United States is based on the 1980 U.S. Census of Population Public Use Microdata Sample C. All foreign born twenty-five to sixty-four-year-old males employed in 1979 in this 1/100 random sample of the population are included in the analysis. Further details on the data are presented in appendix 6–B. This appendix also contains descriptive statistics for the variables included in the estimating equation. Fully 80 percent of those in the sample are proficient in the English language, although this figure varies appreciably across birthplace regions. English-language fluency is almost universal (99.2 percent) among immigrants from English-speaking countries, while for immigrants from non-English-speaking countries the fluency rate is 76.6 percent. The mean age of the sample is forty-one years and the average immigrant has been in the United States for sixteen years and has twelve years of education. The distribution of the population across birthplace groups reveals that 17 percent of the sample are from Mexico, 28 percent from Europe, 6 percent from Canada, 9 percent from Asia (South Asia, Vietnam, or Other Asia), and 10 percent from South and Central America.

Table 7–1 presents results from Ordinary Least Squares (OLS) estimation of equations with the language-proficiency measure *GOODENG* as the dependent variable.[11] *GOODENG* equals unity when the person speaks only English in the home or, if another language is also spoken in the home, when English is spoken either very well or well. *GOODENG* equals zero for those whose English-speaking skills are not well or nil. These results are for the total adult, male, foreign-born work force. The estimates in column a of table 7–1 are for a simple specification of the language model that includes neither the minority-language concentration measure that is one of the features of this study nor interaction terms between variables. This specification permits some comparisons with earlier research. Column b includes the minority-language concentration variable. Column c adds two interaction terms to the estimating equation.

The estimates in the linear probability model presented in column a have a number of distinguishing features. Each additional year of education increases the probability of being proficient in English by 2.9 percentage points.[12] This partial effect is quite large. It implies, for example, that a person who attended college for three years would have a predicted probability of being proficient in Eng-

235

TABLE 7–1

REGRESSION ESTIMATES OF ENGLISH-LANGUAGE FLUENCY AMONG
ADULT FOREIGN-BORN MEN, UNITED STATES, 1980

	a	b	c
Constant	0.549	0.568	0.514
	(45.20)	(47.13)	(27.31)
Education	0.029	0.027	0.040
	(60.75)	(58.08)	(53.20)
Age	−0.004	−0.004	−0.007
	(16.00)	(16.33)	(15.66)
Years since	0.019	0.020	0.026
migration (YSM)	(33.72)	(34.51)	(30.83)
YSM squared/100	−0.028	−0.028	−0.035
	(22.98)	(23.93)	(25.39)
Married	0.012	0.012	0.011
	(2.30)	(2.38)	(2.04)
Married overseas	−0.035	−0.035	−0.028
	(6.86)	(6.89)	(5.43)
Child < 6 years only	0.001	0.004	0.007
	(0.20)	(0.60)	(1.07)
Child 6–17 years only	−0.003	−0.001	0.007
	(0.62)	(0.13)	(1.50)
Children < 6 & 6–17			
years	0.003	0.009	0.018
	(0.45)	(1.35)	(2.78)
Veteran	0.013	0.010	0.023
	(3.22)	(2.45)	(5.86)
Rural location	−0.013	−0.018	−0.018
	(2.20)	(3.06)	(3.12)
South	0.003	0.018	0.017
	(0.66)	(3.89)	(3.80)
Minority-language	N.E.	−0.014	−0.014
concentration		(20.59)	(20.84)
Birthplace			
Europe	−0.099	−0.092	−0.089
	(25.65)	(24.07)	(24.02)
Vietnam	−0.131	−0.135	−0.150
	(5.59)	(5.76)	(6.44)
Philippines	−0.018	−0.008	−0.026
	(2.54)	(1.19)	(3.64)
China	−0.212	−0.207	−0.211
	(21.20)	(20.65)	(21.38)
South Asia	−0.046	−0.047	−0.079
	(7.02)	(7.28)	(11.93)

TABLE 7–1 (continued)

	a	b	c
Other Asia	−0.156	−0.156	−0.169
	(16.70)	(16.71)	(18.38)
Mexico	−0.314	−0.151	−0.142
	(44.35)	(14.25)	(13.41)
Cuba	−0.282	−0.191	−0.181
	(27.19)	(16.81)	(16.04)
Other America	−0.162	−0.083	−0.080
	(22.38)	(10.76)	(10.42)
Africa	−0.028	−0.028	−0.050
	(3.53)	(3.55)	(6.57)
Middle East	−0.052	−0.053	−0.053
	(5.13)	(5.35)	(5.38)
Not reported	−0.105	−0.061	−0.061
	(12.50)	(7.80)	(7.91)
Age * YSM/100	n.e.	n.e.	0.015
			(9.52)
Education * YSM/100	n.e.	n.e.	−0.082
			(23.86)
Sample size	32,255	32,255	32,255
Adj R^2	.3540	.3660	.3813

n.e. = variable not entered.
NOTES: The dependent variable is GOODENG. The t statistics in parentheses were derived using the White, "Heteroskedasticity-consistent Covariance Matrix Estimator."
SOURCE: 1980 Census of Population, Public Use Sample, 1/100 sample of the foreign-born.

lish 14.5 percentage points higher than that of a comparable individual who left school following the completion of the tenth grade.

A higher fraction of the young than of the old have an adequate command of the English language, other things being the same.[13] As these effects emerge when controlling for duration of residence in the United States, the age variable can be interpreted as a measure of age at migration. From this perspective, the results suggest that immigrants arriving as youths are more likely to become proficient in English.[14] This feature of the language-proficiency model is also evident when the age variable is replaced by an age-at-arrival measure.

Language skills increase with years since migration, but at a decreasing rate, until thirty-four years of residence.[15] This finding is consistent with the explanation often advanced in studies of earnings determination where the curvilinear relationship between earnings and duration of residence is often associated with adjustment factors such as the acquisition of language skills. It is worth noting that the Anglicization process reflected in these data continues twenty years longer than suggested by Veltman's analysis (fifteen years). This difference could reflect the different focus (all immigrants versus Veltman's Spanish mother-tongue immigrants) or the different statistical approaches (multivariate versus Veltman's bivariate analysis). The first of these explanations is investigated below.

Birthplace is also seen to matter to the explanation of the distribution of language skills. The ranking in order of skills is: English-speaking origin (the benchmark), the Philippines, Africa, South Asia, the Middle East, Europe, Not Reported, Vietnam, Other Asia, Other America, China, Cuba, and Mexico. The relatively low ranking of the Chinese and Spanish-speaking groups is consistent with findings reported by Veltman.[16] The Asian countries fall into two groups. English proficiency is greater among immigrants from the Philippines and South Asia, both of which are multilingual areas in which a legacy of the American and British administrations is the acceptance of English as a lingua franca. The much poorer English proficiency of those from China, Vietnam, and Other Asia (primarily Korea and Japan) may be attributable to the greater linguistic distance between their native languages and English.

This argument, of course, cannot be used for the Spanish-speaking Mexican and Cuban immigrants. The similarity in the ranking, ceteris paribus, of Cuban and Mexican immigrants is somewhat surprising. Cuban immigrants have a lower probability of return migration and hence would be expected to have a greater propensity to invest in U.S.-specific human capital, including language capital. The greater incentive to invest that derives from this source, however, may be offset by the fact that refugees are less likely to be favorably selected for migration. For these immigrants, the compelling factors may be the adverse effects on English-language acquisition caused by many of the Mexicans' view of themselves as temporary migrants, by the Cubans being refugees, and, as is shown below, by both the Mexicans and the Cubans being more likely to live in large minority-language enclaves.

The results in table 7–1 indicate that individuals who were married in the United States are more likely to be proficient in English than are those who never married, other things being the same.[17] Marriage prior to migration, however, reduces the probability of being proficient in English below the level of those who married after migration, and even below that of the unmarried. This result can be viewed as a simple extension of the language-group enclave argument; those married prior to migration are more likely to have a spouse fluent in the same immigrant language and to speak this language at home.

Veteran status is a statistically significant determinant of English-language proficiency, and it has the expected positive sign. Thus, individuals who have been in the U.S. armed forces are more likely to be proficient in English, ceteris paribus.[18] Grenier and Vaillancourt report a similar finding.[19]

The presence of young children in the household affects the level of language proficiency, but not in table 7–1, columns a or b. The variable for the presence of Children under six and from six to seventeen is stastically significant in table 7–1, column c, but the variables indicating the presence of one or more children under six or between ages six and seventeen are not. That is, only the variable that unambiguously indicates the presence of at least two children is statistically significant. Perhaps it is the linguistic interaction between or among children that enhances parental fluency.[20]

There is also an interaction on English-language fluency between the effect of children in the household and duration of residence. Using a specification similar to the one in table 7–1, column a and a one-in-fifty sample, the equation was recomputed for those who immigrated after 1965. The dichotomous variable for the presence of one or more children in the household has a statistically significant partial effect (coefficient, 0.0093, t-ratio $= 1.98$) on the English-language fluency variable.[21] Thus it appears that the presence of children has a larger effect on enhancing parental English-language fluency among the more recent immigrants.

Rural residence is associated with a marginally significant lower level of fluency, while southern residence is associated with greater reported fluency. The latter effect, however, is significant only when the minority-language concentration variable is held constant. By implication, fluency is least in the rural non-South and greatest in the urban South, other things being the same.

Column b in table 7–1 adds the minority-language concentration measuring to the estimating equation. This variable is defined as the percentage of the population in the state speaking the same foreign language as the respondent for the twenty numerically most populous languages. If the respondent speaks only English at home or a language not in the top twenty, the variable is defined to be zero. There is a very strong effect of minority-language concentration. Immigrants living in states that have a relatively high representation of their language group are less likely to be fluent in English, other things being the same. Comparing, for example, a state where 1 percent of the population speaks Spanish at home with a state where 10 percent speak Spanish at home, Spanish-background workers in the second state would have a rate of English-language fluency 13 percentage points lower than similar workers in the first state.[22]

The inclusion in the estimating equation of the minority-language concentration variable has a marked impact on the Mexican, Cuban, and Other-America birthplace dummy variables. The partial effect of being born in Mexico or Other America falls by one-half, and that of being born in Cuba by one-third. As is discussed below, this enclave effect also operates within individual birthplace regions, and therefore the minority-language concentration measure does not appear to be acting simply as a surrogate for birthplace.

Table 7-1, column c adds several interaction terms to the basic estimating equation. The coefficient on the interaction term between age and years since migration is positive, and this reinforces a finding discussed earlier. That is, immigrants who arrive at an older age have less fluency initially but a more rapid improvement.

The second interaction term included in the table 7-1, column c specification is between education and years since migration. The negative coefficient here reveals that the positive partial effect of educational attainment on English-language fluency diminishes with duration of residence in the United States. The implication is that it takes a longer duration in the United States for those with less schooling to acquire the same level of English-language proficiency. This finding contrasts with the finding reported by Chiswick for a study of low-skilled illegal aliens in the United States for a short period of time.[23] Chiswick held constant fluency at immigration, however, a variable not available in the census and positively correlated with level of education. The finding here is consistent with some other analyses of earnings determination. Another study by Chiswick, for example, reported that the partial effect of education on earnings among immigrants from English-speaking countries declines the longer they have been in the United States.[24] In other words, the complex pattern of effects that education appears to have on earnings may originate from the adjustment process associated with the learning of the dominant language.

Table 7-2 develops the analysis of the minority-language concentration effect by incorporating interaction terms into the model between the minority-language variable and education, age, and years since migration. The inclusion of these interaction terms does not affect the coefficients on other variables in any material way. The estimates listed in table 7-2 show that the language-concentration effect varies significantly with education, age, and years since migra-

TABLE 7–2

Selected Regression Coefficients for English-Fluency Model
with Minority-Language-Concentration Interaction Terms,
Adult Foreign-born Men, United States, 1980

	a	b	c	d
Education	0.027	0.021	0.021	0.021
	(58.08)	(40.21)	(40.37)	(41.23)
Years since	0.020	0.019	0.019	0.017
migration (YSM)	(34.51)	(33.99)	(34.09)	(28.31)
YSM squared/100	− 0.028	− 0.028	− 0.028	− 0.026
	(23.93)	(23.61)	(23.68)	(21.41)
Age	− 0.004	− 0.004	− 0.003	− 0.003
	(16.33)	(16.21)	(14.86)	(10.99)
Minority-language	− 0.014	− 0.030	− 0.027	− 0.022
concentration	(20.59)	(26.62)	(13.84)	(11.24)
(CONC)				
CONC * Education	n.e.	0.002	0.002	0.001
		(19.84)	(19.33)	(16.04)
CONC * Age/100	n.e.	n.e.	− 0.007	− 0.036
			(1.90)	(8.70)
CONC * YSM/100	n.e.	n.e.	n.e.	0.060
				(14.85)
Sample size	32,255	32,255	32,255	32,255
Adj R^2	.3660	.3765	.3766	.3829

n.e. = variable not entered.
Notes: Same as for table 7–1.
In addition to the variables listed, all other control variables used in table 7–1
are included in these equations:
Partial derivatives, from column d, evaluated at sample means are:
$\delta GOODENG/\delta EDUC = 0.021 + 0.001\ CONC = 0.025$
$\delta GOODENG/\delta Age = 0.026 − 0.00036\ CONC = −0.027$
$\delta GOODENG/\delta YSM = 0.017 − 0.00052\ YSM + 0.0006\ CONC = 0.011$
$\delta GOODENG/\delta CONC = −0.022 + 0.001\ EDUC − 0.00036\ Age + 0.0006\ YSM$
$= −0.015$
Source: Same as for table 7–1.

tion. The adverse effect on English-language skills of living in an
ethnic-language enclave is greater for those with less skill—that is,
less schooling, or for more recent arrivals who immigrated at an older
age. These are the immigrants with the lowest language facility,
ceteris paribus.

Further insights into the determination of English-language proficiency among immigrants can be gained by disaggregating the analysis by birthplace region. Of particular interest are the analyses,

summarized in table 7–3, for the major birthplace groups, especially the Spanish-speaking groups that have attracted the most attention in previous research.

Educational attainment exercises a strong positive influence on language fluency in each birthplace region. The effect is greatest for immigrants from Vietnam, China, Cuba, and Mexico, and lowest for immigrants from Africa, South Asia, the Middle East, the Philippines, and Europe. The former groups are characterized by relatively low language fluency at the time of arrival in the United States, and the latter groups by relatively high language fluency at arrival (see table 7–1). It appears, therefore, that while education can help overcome language handicaps, its impact depends on the extent of initial language deficiency; education is more important the lower the initial level of proficiency.

The number of years since migration also has a strong positive influence on language fluency for all birthplace regions. The speed of language adjustment is greater among immigrants from Mexico, Cuba, and Other America than for the remaining birthplace groups.[25] These are the least endowed with respect to language skills at arrival. Hence, the story here is akin to that reported in the earnings determination literature: immigrants having the lowest skill level upon arrival in the United States will be characterized by a relatively rapid adjustment. This consistent pattern is suggestive of an underlying structure, common to both language-capital accumulation and all forms of human capital relevant for the destination, which gets translated in the labor market into earnings.

The minority-language concentration measure is significant and negative in six of the twelve disaggregated analyses and negative but not statistically significant in four others (table 7–3). The estimated effects for Mexico, Cuba, and Other America are all of the same order of magnitude, suggesting that the Spanish-language groups are fairly homogeneous with respect to the language-enclave effect. As noted earlier, the fact that this enclave variable is significant within birthplace regions for the Spanish-origin groups indicates that it is more than a proxy for country of birth.[26] The insignificance of the language-concentration measure in other birthplace regions (Vietnam, the Philippines, China, Other Asia, the Middle East) may arise because the concentration of those speaking these languages is too small for linguistic enclaves to retard English-language fluency.[27]

Finally, the partial effect of the married-overseas variable is nearly consistently negative (table 7–3). It is negative and significant (at the 5 percent level) in the case of immigrants from Europe, Mexico, and Cuba, and negative but not significant for most other birthplace groups.[28] The insignificance of this variable for the small sample of Vietnamese immigrants is not surprising: 92 percent of Vietnamese immigrants entered the United States after 1975, and thus few would have married in the United States prior to census enumeration in 1980. Moreover, the concentration of this wave of migration in such a short period implies that the foreign marriage variable may be measured imprecisely (see appendix 7–B).

Dominant-Language Proficiency in Canada. The analysis of dominant-language fluency in Canada is based on the 1981 Census of Canada. Two data files are available: the one-in-one hundred Household and Family File and the one-in-fifty Individual File. The relevant features of these two files are reported in table 7–4.

The relative strength of the Individual File lies in the more detailed information available on home-language usage, its larger sample size, and the availability of data on citizenship. The four additional categories of home language coded in the Individual File should allow the impact of the important minority-language concentration variable to be measured more precisely. Where the focus of attention is on whether the impact of this and other variables differ between birthplace groups, the larger sample size (23,741 observations as compared with 11,382) of the Individual File provides a superior basis for analysis. Finally, the data on citizenship permits the estimation of a model of earnings determination in the next section that corresponds to that estimated using the U.S. data.

The comparative strength of the Household and Family File is that it contains data on the number and age structure of children, the language usage of children, the birthplace of spouse, and spouse's language usage that are not available from the Individual File. Therefore, only the Household and Family File permits an investigation of the key issue of whether the language attainment of adult males is related to characteristics of their spouse and children.

Full use was made of both sets of data. In the first instance a preliminary analysis was conducted using the one-in-one hundred sample from the Household and Family File to estimate the impact of children and of spouse's birthplace in the model of dominant-language proficiency in Canada. The one-in-fifty Individual File is then used to obtain a more accurate measure of the minority-language concentration effect and to examine whether this effect differs among birthplace groups.

The striking feature of the data is the very high rate of dominant-language fluency. Almost 97 percent of immigrants report themselves as able to speak English or French well enough to conduct a con-

TABLE 7-3

SELECTED REGRESSION COEFFICIENTS FOR ENGLISH-LANGUAGE FLUENCY BY PLACE OF BIRTH, ADULT FOREIGN-BORN MEN, UNITED STATES, 1980

Birthplace (% fluent)	Education	YSM	YSM Squared[a]	Minority Concentration	Married Overseas	Sample Size
Non-English total (76.63)	0.029 (57.28)	0.022 (33.59)	−0.031 (22.13)	−0.013 (19.74)	−0.035 (6.13)	27,850
Europe (87.54)	0.022 (27.00)	0.023 (21.10)	−0.034 (16.31)	−0.019 (7.53)	−0.049 (5.16)	8,971
Vietnam (70.75)	0.053 (7.01)	0.017 (1.27)	−0.031 (0.55)	0.012 (1.01)	0.016 (0.29)	335
Philippines (95.09)	0.021 (7.55)	0.004 (1.50)	−0.005 (0.83)	−0.009 (1.59)	−0.003 (0.17)	1,181
China (75.56)	0.039 (18.71)	0.018 (5.25)	−0.018 (2.47)	−0.009 (0.57)	−0.048 (1.63)	1,289
South Asia (98.11)	0.012 (3.94)	0.002 (0.91)	0.003 (0.49)	0.012 (2.84)	0.015 (1.48)	1,007

Other Asia (80.83)	0.034 (12.98)	0.023 (7.48)	−0.039 (4.80)	−0.013 (1.22)	−0.030 (1.23)	1,575
Mexico (48.30)	0.037 (26.86)	0.025 (13.60)	−0.035 (7.94)	−0.012 (9.32)	−0.069 (4.57)	5,602
Cuba (64.71)	0.039 (17.32)	0.031 (6.97)	−0.034 (3.36)	−0.009 (3.76)	−0.059 (2.26)	1,649
Other America (75.62)	0.033 (18.99)	0.030 (13.32)	−0.049 (9.68)	−0.013 (10.85)	−0.004 (0.24)	3,121
Africa (97.31)	0.011 (3.74)	0.007 (3.20)	−0.013 (2.27)	−0.014 (1.90)	0.036 (2.36)	670
Middle East (90.67)	0.017 (6.63)	0.012 (3.73)	−0.017 (2.30)	−0.001 (0.08)	−0.040 (1.52)	804
Not reported (83.84)	0.021 (9.82)	0.015 (6.55)	−0.021 (4.45)	−0.020 (10.90)	−0.008 (0.34)	1,646

NOTES: Additional control variables are: age, married, child<6 only, child 6–17 only, children < 6 and 6–17, rural, south, and veteran status. The *t* statistics in parentheses were derived using White's "Heteroskedasticity-consistent Covariance Matrix Estimator."

a. Variable divided by 100.

SOURCE: Same as for table 7–1.

TABLE 7–4

CHARACTERISTICS OF 1981 CENSUS OF CANADA DATA FILES

Variables Available in Data	Household/ Family File	Individual File
Foreign marriage	Yes	Yes
Citizenship	No	Yes
Spouse's home language	Yes	No
Children's home language	Yes	No
Presence/age of children	Yes	No
Minority language	4 groups	8 groups
Sample size (adult foreign-born men)	11,382	23,741

Source: Statistics Canada: Census of Canada, 1981, Public Use Sample Tapes, User Documentation.

versation. There is some variation in dominant-language proficiency across the major birthplace regions. Immigrants from the English- or French-speaking countries have a rate of fluency, for all practical purposes, of 100 percent (two respondents in the sample reported a dominant-language deficiency), while immigrants from Chinese Asia, Southern Europe, and South and Central America have relatively lower rates of dominant-language fluency (87 percent, 92 percent, and 95 percent, respectively). The much higher rate of dominant-language fluency in Canada as contrasted with the United States (where 80 percent of immigrants are classified as fluent in the dominant language) reflects in part the different definitions used; see appendix 7–B.[29] It arises in part also because of the use in Canada of knowledge of one or both of the official languages in the immigration selection procedure.[30]

The examination of the influence of family environment factors on dominant-language proficiency in Canada based on the Household and Family File (not reported here) can be summarized succinctly. First, children do not appear to affect the dominant-language fluency of their parents. This finding may be attributable to the fact that dominant-language fluency is virtually universal in Canada, implying that the exposure factor associated with children's conversations is likely to be of minor importance.[31] Second, foreign marriage reduces the probability of dominant-language fluency in the destination country, and this effect persists when variables for the birthplace of the spouse, her home language, or her mother tongue are included in the estimating equation. This finding suggests that the foreign-marriage variable captures influences on the language out-come other than merely the country of origin of the partner or the language usage within the home.[32] Included here may be custom, cultural factors, and larger family networks in the country of origin. These factors promote a greater propensity to identify with the coun-try of origin through both origin-language retention and eschewal of the dominant language of the destination country.

The remainder of this subsection is based on the Individual File. These analyses have a starting point similar to the analysis of the U.S. labor market presented in table 7–1. Thus, the results of a baseline specification of a linear probability model of language fluency are presented in column a of table 7–5. In this equation, dominant-language proficiency is related to education, age, years since migra-tion and its square, marital status, overseas marriage, birthplace, and province and region of residence. In the column b specification, the minority-language concentration measure is added to the basic esti-mating equation. Columns c through e list results for specifications that include interaction terms between the minority-language con-centration measure and educational attainment, age, and duration of residence.

The general pattern of results in table 7–5, column a is remark-ably similar to the results for the United States. The magnitudes of individual estimated effects differ considerably between the two analyses, however, and these differences are discussed in the follow-ing subsection.

Years of education and age exercise major influences on domi-nant-language skill, with each additional year of education being associated with about one percentage point of improvement in the rate of dominant-language fluency.[33] A negative relationship exists between age and language fluency when other factors, including years since migration, are the same. That is, the older an individual at the time of migration, the less likely he is to acquire dominant-language skills.

The influence of years since migration on dominant-language proficiency is nonlinear. The partial effect of this variable on the probability of being proficient in the dominant language is given by $\delta GOODLANG/\delta YSM = 0.006\text{-}0.00018YSM$. Evaluated at ten, twenty (approximately the mean), and thirty years' residence in Canada, the partial effect is 0.4, 0.2, and 0.1 percentage points, respectively. While these partial effects may appear small, the years-since-migration fac-tor has a substantial impact on the pattern of dominant-language fluency. There is, for example, an 8 percentage point difference be-tween the rates of dominant-language proficiency of a recent arrival

TABLE 7–5
Regression Estimates of Dominant-Language Fluency among Adult Foreign-born Men, Canada, 1981

	a	b	c	d	e
Constant	0.909 (106.53)	0.909 (107.10)	0.929 (114.59)	0.919 (129.90)	0.932 (134.75)
Education	0.007 (18.90)	0.006 (16.73)	0.004 (12.13)	0.004 (12.80)	0.003 (11.61)
Age	−0.002 (10.98)	−0.001 (10.16)	−0.001 (9.43)	−0.001 (9.47)	−0.001 (5.69)
Years since migration (YSM)	0.006 (13.46)	0.007 (13.99)	0.007 (14.66)	0.007 (14.85)	0.005 (10.89)
YSM squared/100	−0.009 (9.68)	−0.009 (10.39)	−0.010 (11.32)	−0.010 (11.56)	−0.008 (9.27)
Married	−0.001 (0.29)	−0.001 (0.30)	0.001 (0.55)	0.001 (0.63)	0.003 (1.57)
Married overseas	−0.016 (5.32)	−0.013 (4.48)	−0.013 (4.37)	−0.012 (4.27)	−0.009 (3.18)
CMA	−0.009 (4.61)	−0.002 (0.99)	−0.001 (0.78)	−0.001 (0.77)	−0.001 (0.33)
Province Atlantic	−0.001 (0.01)	−0.001 (0.30)	0.001 (0.33)	0.001 (0.32)	0.001 (0.20)

	(1)	(2)	(3)	(4)	(5)
Quebec	0.012 (3.80)	0.010 (3.05)	0.011 (3.36)	0.011 (3.35)	0.009 (2.92)
Prairie	0.009 (3.58)	0.005 (2.09)	0.005 (2.13)	0.005 (2.21)	0.003 (1.44)
British Columbia	0.007 (3.11)	0.007 (2.77)	0.004 (1.56)	0.004 (1.58)	0.006 (2.81)
Minority-language concentration (CONC)	n.e.	−0.018 (11.49)	−0.059 (13.46)	−0.038 (3.84)	−0.048 (4.95)
Birthplace					
Western Europe	−0.013 (9.60)	−0.011 (8.65)	−0.015 (11.96)	−0.015 (11.86)	−0.007 (6.94)
Eastern Europe	−0.004 (1.65)	−0.003 (1.42)	−0.009 (3.70)	−0.009 (3.98)	−0.007 (2.86)
Southern Europe	−0.057 (17.66)	−0.029 (9.22)	−0.032 (10.21)	−0.032 (10.11)	−0.029 (9.57)
Chinese Asia	−0.095 (11.02)	−0.065 (7.31)	−0.095 (10.29)	−0.094 (10.28)	−0.064 (7.14)
Other Asia	0.003 (1.06)	0.004 (1.40)	0.006 (2.03)	0.006 (2.31)	−0.003 (1.15)
Mexico, South & Central America	−0.024 (2.53)	−0.021 (2.21)	−0.023 (2.33)	−0.022 (2.26)	−0.029 (2.92)
Africa	0.010 (3.77)	0.011 (4.23)	0.013 (4.67)	0.013 (4.93)	0.005 (1.89)

(Table continues)

TABLE 7–5 (continued)

	a	b	c	d	e
Other	-0.003 (0.79)	-0.004 (0.95)	-0.006 (1.52)	-0.005 (1.42)	-0.007 (1.83)
CONC * Education	n.e.	n.e.	0.005 (11.62)	0.004 (9.39)	0.004 (9.43)
CONC * Age/100	n.e.	n.e.	n.e.	-0.039 (2.37)	-0.179 (9.62)
CONC * YSM/100	n.e.	n.e.	n.e.	n.e.	0.351 (15.63)
Sample size	23,741	23,741	23,741	23,741	23,741
Adj R²	.1058	.1214	.1386	.1395	.1840

n.e. = variable not entered.

NOTES: The dependent variable is GOODLANG. The t statistics in parentheses were derived using White, "Heteroskedasticity-consistent Covariance Matrix Estimator." Partial derivatives from column e evaluated at sample means are:

$$\delta GOODLANG / \delta Education = 0.003 + 0.004 \, CONC = 0.005$$
$$\delta GOODLANG / \delta Age = -0.001 - 0.002 \, CONC = -0.002$$
$$\delta GOODLANG / \delta YSM = 0.005 - 0.00016 \, YSM + 0.004 \, CONC = 0.004$$
$$\delta GOODLANG / \delta CONC = -0.48 + 0.004 \, EDUC - 0.002 \, Age + 0.004 \, YSM = -0.009$$

SOURCE: 1981 Census of Canada, Public Use Sample, Individual File, 1/50 sample of the foreign-born.

and of a comparable immigrant with the mean duration of residence in Canada. The process of adjustment captured by the years-since-migration variable continues for thirty-five years. Even though the United States and Canada differ greatly in terms of the relative size of their immigrant stock (6 percent versus 25 percent of their work forces, respectively), the nature of their dominant languages (English only versus English and French), and the definition of fluency, the relationship between years-since-migration and dominant-language fluency is remarkably similar.

Marital status per se does not exercise an independent influence on language skills. For individuals who were married prior to migration, however, there is a statistically significant reduction in the probability of dominant-language fluency.

Province of residence appears to exercise an independent impact. Residents of Quebec, British Columbia, and the Prairie provinces have rates of dominant-language skills that are significantly higher than those in the other provinces, but the estimated differences are quite small—about 1 percentage point in each instance.

Finally, the birthplace controls indicate that immigrants categorized as Chinese Asians have a rate of dominant-language proficiency 10 percentage points lower than that of the benchmark groups of immigrants from English-speaking countries, other variables being the same. South Europeans are also distinguished by a lower level of language skills, 5.7 percentage points lower than that of the benchmark group. Three other birthplace groups are characterized by small, statistically significant differences in the level of language skills: East Europeans (at the 10 percent level), West Europeans, and South and Central Americans. Immigrants from Africa are shown to have a rate of dominant-language fluency significantly greater than that of the benchmark group of immigrants from English-speaking countries, but this result appears to derive from the application of OLS to a bounded variable having a mean close to a bound.[34] The relatively high rate of dominant-language deficiency among the South Europeans is broadly consistent with previous analyses by deVries and Vallee, who report that immigrants from Mediterranean countries have a high propensity to retain their origin language.[35]

The position of the Chinese Asians, however, does not appear to have emerged as a focal point in previous discussion. The larger coefficient for this group is consistent with the greater linguistic distance between Chinese and the dominant languages and the refugee nature of much of the migration of Chinese from Asia to Canada.

Column b in table 7–5 adds the minority-language concentration variable to the analysis. As is outlined in appendix 7–B, this variable measures the percentage of the population in the region (twenty-three localities, defined by using the Census Metropolitan Area and Province variables) that has the same nondominant, home language as has the respondent. The estimated impact of the language-concentration variable is sizable (-0.018) and is highly significant ($t = 11.49$).[36] Thus, in a region with a concentration 5 percentage points above the national average of people speaking the same nondominant home language as the respondent, the respondent's probability of being fluent in a dominant language would fall by 9 percentage points. The inclusion of the minority-language concentration variable in the analysis has a negligible impact on the estimated effects of the other regressors, other than for the South European birthplace variable. The disadvantage, ceteris paribus, of a South European birthplace declines by around 3 percentage points from -0.057 to -0.029. This decline probably reflects the explicit identification of the Greek language in the language-enclave measure used in table 7–5.

The estimated impact of the minority-language concentration variable in table 7–5 (-0.018) is stronger than that reported in the study of language attainment in the U.S. labor market (-0.014), a difference that is small but statistically significant ($t = 2.35$). It is possible that this impact is associated with a difference in the method of constructing the variable for the two countries. For the United States, the variable is defined with reference to the state in which the respondent lives. For Canada, however, for approximately one-half of all respondents, the variable is defined with reference to the particular city (Census Metropolitan Area) of residence. The Canadian variable, even though defined for fewer language categories than the U.S. equivalent (eight as compared with twenty), may nevertheless provide a more accurate proxy of the underlying language-enclave effect, and this may be what is reflected in the larger estimated coefficient.

Columns c through e of table 7–5 examine the interactions between the minority-language concentration measure and education, age, and years since migration. The findings are similar to those for the U.S. labor market: the minority-language-enclave effect is strongest among recent, adult immigrants who have below-average levels of education. The analysis of the Canadian data reveals these to be the groups possessing fewest dominant-language skills, ceteris paribus.

Table 7–6 presents results from estimation of the model of dominant-language fluency for each of the major non-English- or French-speaking birthplace groups. A number of differences are evident in the relationships between dominant-language fluency and education, duration of residence in Canada, foreign marriage, and the language-enclave variable.

A strong positive association exists between educational attainment and dominant-language fluency for most birthplace groups. The impact is largest for the Chinese Asians, the group with the lowest level of language proficiency upon arrival in Canada. Conversely, for the two groups with the highest level of initial language fluency, West Europeans and Africans, the education variable is insignificant. Hence the conclusion from this analysis parallels that for the United States: education is an important determinant of dominant-language fluency, but its importance is greater at the lower initial level of proficiency.

The impact of years since migration is generally positive, but it differs considerably across the birthplace groups. The ranking of birthplaces in terms of the impact of years since migration on language fluency is approximately the inverse of their ranking in terms of mean level of language fluency. Thus, the impact of years since migration is greatest for immigrants from Chinese Asia and Southern Europe, the two groups with the lowest mean levels of language fluency. Levels of language fluency do not vary significantly with years since migration for immigrants from Northern Europe, Africa, or the "Other" birthplace groups, each of which has a relatively high level of language skill.

As expected, the performance of the minority concentration variable is mixed because of the limited number of languages (eight) separately identified in the 1981 Census. For example, since Spanish is not separately identified, it is not surprising that the variable shows no statistical significance for the Latin American group of countries. The minority concentration variable is generally negative, but it is significant only for the East European and South European birthplace regions—which constitute 48 percent of the nondominant language sample. While the estimated language-enclave effect for Eastern Europe is close to that derived on the basis of the aggregated data (see table 7–5), the effect for Southern Europe is twice that reported earlier. This result may reflect the better quality of the data—that is, the use of three important language groups (Italian, Greek, and Portuguese) in the construction of the language-enclave variable relevant to the South European region.

Finally, the foreign marriage variable is significant for three birthplace groups and insignificant for the remaining five. For the cases where it is statistically significant the estimated impact is negative, but it differs by birthplace region. Marriage overseas, for example, re-

TABLE 7-6

Selected Regression Coefficients for Dominant-Language Fluency by Place of Birth, Adult Foreign-born Men, Canada, 1981

Birthplace (% fluent)	Education	YSM	YSM Squared[a]	Minority-Concentration[b]	Married Overseas	Sample Size
Nondominant language total (95.91)	0.008 (16.28)	0.010 (13.87)	−0.014 (9.74)	−0.017 (10.48)	−0.017 (3.86)	16,092
W. Europe[c] (99.94)	0.001 (1.37)	0.001 (0.96)	−0.001 (0.97)	−0.003 (0.83)	−0.000 (0.07)	3,248
E. Europe (99.01)	0.012 (2.17)	0.004 (2.39)	−0.006 (1.99)	−0.014 (1.99)	−0.014 (2.13)	2,229
S. Europe (91.96)	0.010 (9.67)	0.021 (9.82)	−0.032 (6.73)	−0.015 (8.31)	−0.035 (3.52)	5,511

Chinese Asia (88.60)	0.024 (8.81)	0.019 (4.74)	−0.025 (2.25)	−0.008 (1.59)	0.002 (0.10)	1,132
Other Asia (98.63)	0.004 (4.02)	0.005 (3.89)	−0.008 (2.96)	−0.022 (1.27)	0.001 (0.14)	2,040
Africa (99.72)	0.002 (1.33)	0.001 (1.24)	−0.002 (0.84)	−0.001 (0.40)	0.003 (0.39)	703
Mexico, South & Central America (95.00)	0.010 (3.67)	0.014 (2.79)	−0.026 (2.01)	0.002 (0.13)	−0.012 (0.49)	480
Other (98.93)	0.003 (2.30)	0.002 (0.95)	−0.001 (0.42)	−0.008 (0.65)	−0.028 (2.29)	749

NOTE: Additional control variables are: age, married, province, and resident of metropolitan area. The t statistics in parentheses were derived using White's "Heteroskedasticity-consistent Covariance Matrix Estimator."

a. Variable divided by 100.

b. The eight identifiable languages used in the minority-language-concentration variable are Chinese, German, Italian, Ukrainian, Greek, Netherlandic languages, Polish, Portuguese.

c. Computed F value for equation of 1.778 is at the margin of statistical significance.

SOURCE: Same as for table 7–5.

255

duces the probability of dominant-language fluency by 1.4 percentage points for immigrants from Eastern Europe, but by 3.5 percentage points for immigrants from Southern Europe.

The study of the dominant-language attainment process within each birthplace group yields a pattern of results that is broadly consistent with the aggregate analysis. The aggregate results are not dominated by one birthplace or by subtle country-of-origin interactions. Education, years since migration, foreign marriage, and minority concentration exercise important influences on dominant-language fluency. The larger impact of the human-capital variables (education and years since migration) for birthplace regions with lower initial levels of dominant-language proficiency emerges as a major finding of the disaggregated analysis.

U.S.-Canadian Comparisons. Canada and the United States differ appreciably in terms of the fraction of the population who are foreign-born, the source countries of immigrants, and the methods used by the authorities for selecting immigrants. About one-quarter of the Canadian work force is foreign-born, as compared with 6 percent of the U.S. work force. In Canada the immigrant stock is largely of U.K. or European origin (66 percent), although there is a sizable group of recent Asians (13 percent). In the United States the largest immigrant group comes from Latin America. Canada has a skill-based points system for entry, whereas most of the stock of immigrants in the United States enter on the basis of kinship. Under the definitions used for this study, 97 percent of Canada's immigrants report that they are fluent in a dominant language, whereas only 80 percent of immigrants in the United States are fluent in English.[37]

Despite these differences, the immigrant experience in dominant-language fluency is remarkably similar in the United States and in Canada. Education, age at arrival, years since migration, foreign marriage, minority-language concentration, and country of birth affect dominant-language fluency in the hypothesized direction in each country. Dominant-language fluency among adult men increases with years of education and duration in the destination, and it decreases with age at arrival, foreign marriage, and minority-language concentration. Fluency also varies with country of origin in accordance with the extent to which the dominant language of the destination country is used in the origin country.

The magnitudes of the estimated effects of the explanatory variables on language fluency differ between Canada and the United States. Comparing columns a and c in table 7–7 indicates that while the model of dominant-language fluency performs similarly in the

TABLE 7-7

PARTIAL EFFECTS OF SELECTED VARIABLES ON LANGUAGE FLUENCY,
UNITED STATES, 1980, AND CANADA, 1981

Variable	United States	United States (assuming Canada definition)	Canada
Education	0.027	0.009	0.006
Age	−0.004	−0.001	−0.001
Years since migration[a]	0.014	0.006	0.005
Years since migration[b]	0.009	0.003	0.003
Married	0.012	0.009	−0.001[c]
Married overseas	−0.035	−0.012	−0.013
Minority-language concentration	−0.014	−0.005	−0.018

a. Evaluated at 10 years of residence.
b. Evaluated at 20 years of residence.
c. Estimated effect not significant at the 5 percent level.
SOURCE: Table 7-1, column b and table 7-5, column b.

two countries, the estimated impacts for the United States are consistently two to three times larger than those computed for Canada. The one exception is the impact of minority-language concentration on dominant-language fluency, where the impacts estimated for each country are similar. The differences between the United States and Canada may be substantive or may merely reflect the different definitions of dominant-language usage. To ascertain the weights that should be attached to these explanations, the language-fluency variable for the United States was redefined so that only individuals who spoke English "not at all" are in the not-fluency category. This gives a level of dominant-language fluency for the United States of 95 percent, which is comparable to the 97 percent fluency rate for Canada. Results from the estimation of the language-fluency model using this alternative definition of the dependent variable are summarized in column b of table 7-7.

For all variables other than the minority-language concentration variable, the column b results for the United States are of the same order of magnitude as for Canada. This suggests that the differences in results between table 7-5 for Canada and table 7-1 for the United States are largely definitional.

One implication is that the category for fluency in an official language is too broad in the Canadian Census, being equivalent to the "well," "very well," and "not well" categories in the U.S. data. This suggests the desirability of using a question that determines more precisely the degree of language fluency in Canada, comparable to question 13c in the 1980 United States Census (see appendix 7–A).

A striking difference characterizes the language-enclave effects between the two countries. In contrast to the other findings, the estimated impact is considerably stronger for Canada than for the United States. This difference is likely to reflect the information on city of residence used in the construction of this variable for one-half of the respondents and just province for the other half in the Canadian data, as compared with state of residence for all respondents in the U.S. analysis.

Dominant-language fluency, therefore, is amenable to statistical analysis, and such analysis yields consistent patterns for the U.S. and Canadian labor markets.

Language Proficiency and Earnings

This section examines the importance of proficiency in the dominant language for the explanation of variations in earnings within and across labor market groups. The framework for the analysis follows that developed in the previous section. Initially, statistical analysis of the 1980 U.S. Census of Population is conducted. Then a similar investigation of the 1981 Canadian Census is undertaken. The section concludes with a series of comparisons between the roles of dominant-language proficiency in the two North American labor markets.

The model of earnings determination employed is a human-capital earnings function in which the natural logarithm of earnings is related to years of schooling, labor market experience, weeks worked, marital status, region of residence, and a series of immigrant variables that includes birthplace, duration of residence, proficiency in the dominant language, and citizenship. In this characterization of the earnings-determination process, the duration-of-residence, proficiency-in-the dominant-language, and citizenship variables capture dimensions of the economic adjustment process among immigrants.

The relationship between earnings and duration of residence is generally held to reflect the following: learning about the institutions and idiosyncrasies of the labor market of the host country; cultural adjustment factors; the development of networks of labor market contacts; and investments in country-specific human-capital skills that lead to labor market success. Included in these actions would be the acquisition of citizenship. Citizenship may open doors to better paying jobs, and it would be expected to lead to a monetary reward sufficient to offset such nonmonetary costs as the forfeiture of citizenship of the country of origin. Naturalization generally requires the demonstration of at least a minimum level of fluency in the dominant language. It also reflects a commitment to the host country. Similarly, learning the language of the host country reflects a commitment to the adopted country and an adaptation to the circumstances of that country. As has been noted previously, learning the language may provide access to better jobs and hence may be associated with higher earnings.

The rates at which different immigrant groups adjust to the labor market have been found to vary considerably. Immigrants who enter North America with relatively few internationally transferable skills (for example, immigrants from non-English speaking countries) or who are less favorably selected for migration (for example, refugees) have fewer destination-specific skills at arrival, ceteris paribus, and consistent with expectations they are typically characterized by a lower earnings profile but a relatively more rapid earnings growth with duration of residence.

Greater dominant-language fluency enhances earnings. Dominant-language fluency, however, is also expected to be related to the gains in earnings associated with language-skill acquisition. In these circumstances, because of correlation between the language-choice variable and the disturbance term, estimation of the earnings equation by least squares would in principle result in inconsistent estimates.

This feature of the data may be accommodated using either an instrumental-variable (IV) estimator or the sample selectivity methods developed by Heckman, whereby the inverse Mills ratio is added to the estimating equation.[38] The use of the instrumental-variables estimator facilitates a test of endogeneity using the Hausman test, while the significance of the inverse Mills ratio term provides a similar test with the alternative estimator.[39] Both tests suggest that the language variable is endogenous in the earnings equations estimated for both the United States and Canada. That is, the empirical results suggest that better language skills affect earnings, and that the greater the economic return to language skills, the greater the language fluency.

The United States. Results from study of the earnings of foreign-born workers in the United States are presented in table 7–8. Most of the variables listed in table 7–8 were introduced in the previous section, and the definitions and measurements presented there are retained here. The new variable LNWW is the natural logarithm of the number of weeks worked in 1979, and the citizen variable distinguishes immigrants who became U.S. citizens from those who did not. The race variable distinguishes black immigrants from all other racial groups.

TABLE 7–8: REGRESSION ESTIMATES OF EARNINGS EQUATIONS, ADULT FOREIGN-BORN MEN, UNITED STATES, 1980

	Total Sample			Fluent in English		Not Fluent in English	
	OLS a	OLS b	IV c	OLS d	Selectivity bias corrected e	OLS f	Selectivity bias corrected g
Constant	4.268 (58.07)	4.197 (57.40)	4.028 (59.63)	4.114 (46.87)	3.918 (38.70)	4.922 (27.79)	4.653 (17.19)
Education	0.050 (39.12)	0.046 (34.99)	0.037 (13.05)	0.053 (36.12)	0.057 (32.73)	0.015 (5.29)	0.010 (2.02)
Experience	0.030 (18.55)	0.030 (19.18)	0.033 (19.73)	0.036 (19.72)	0.035 (19.16)	0.012 (2.97)	0.013 (3.21)
Experience squared/100	−0.046 (15.99)	−0.046 (16.15)	−0.047 (16.79)	−0.056 (16.32)	−0.056 (16.23)	−0.020 (3.17)	−0.021 (3.20)
Years since migration (YSM)	0.023 (16.19)	0.020 (14.02)	0.013 (5.71)	0.018 (10.77)	0.021 (11.28)	0.030 (8.30)	0.025 (4.86)
YSM squared/100	−0.043 (13.52)	−0.039 (12.23)	−0.029 (7.25)	−0.033 (9.32)	−0.037 (9.91)	−0.062 (6.31)	−0.056 (5.20)
LNWW	1.062 (60.08)	1.057 (59.88)	1.046 (97.15)	1.084 (49.97)	1.088 (50.24)	0.969 (33.36)	0.969 (33.37)
Married	0.207 (17.64)	0.207 (17.62)	0.205 (17.76)	0.222 (16.80)	0.222 (16.86)	0.117 (4.62)	0.116 (4.54)
Citizen	0.054 (4.94)	0.043 (3.92)	0.016 (1.26)	0.045 (3.70)	0.044 (3.62)	0.030 (1.17)	0.030 (1.14)
Race (black)	−0.224 (9.08)	−0.245 (9.95)	−0.297 (10.66)	−0.259 (10.15)	−0.242 (9.35)	−0.136 (1.35)	−0.151 (1.49)
Rural location	−0.070 (3.76)	−0.068 (3.68)	−0.065 (3.92)	−0.081 (3.80)	−0.081 (3.82)	−0.056 (1.54)	−0.055 (1.52)

	(1)	(2)	(3)	(4)	(5)	(6)	(7)
South	−0.065 (5.43)	−0.065 (5.42)	−0.064 (5.53)	−0.062 (4.68)	−0.061 (4.60)	−0.087 (3.25)	−0.085 (3.20)
Birthplace							
Ireland	−0.178 (4.14)	−0.180 (4.21)	−0.186 (4.05)	−0.163 (3.81)	−0.160 (3.70)	n.e.	n.e.
Canada	−0.087 (3.15)	−0.086 (3.14)	−0.085 (2.98)	−0.074 (2.69)	−0.074 (2.72)	n.e.	n.e.
West Indies	−0.157 (4.14)	−0.160 (4.20)	−0.165 (3.98)	−0.126 (3.30)	−0.123 (3.22)	−0.494 (0.92)	−0.463 (0.86)
Europe	−0.140 (6.21)	−0.126 (5.59)	−0.092 (3.66)	−0.120 (5.32)	−0.131 (5.77)	0.077 (0.61)	0.126 (0.95)
Vietnam	−0.297 (6.43)	−0.281 (6.10)	−0.242 (4.85)	−0.268 (5.05)	−0.287 (5.37)	−0.125 (0.86)	−0.073 (0.48)
Philippines	−0.310 (10.55)	−0.310 (10.51)	−0.309 (9.67)	−0.328 (10.91)	−0.326 (10.87)	0.110 (0.81)	0.131 (0.95)
China	−0.364 (11.87)	−0.332 (10.81)	−0.253 (6.80)	−0.289 (8.85)	−0.315 (9.43)	−0.303 (2.30)	−0.231 (1.62)
South Asia	−0.144 (4.29)	−0.141 (4.19)	−0.133 (3.94)	−0.159 (4.69)	−0.161 (4.77)	−0.136 (0.65)	−0.128 (0.62)
Other Asia	−0.244 (7.80)	−0.222 (7.10)	−0.169 (5.14)	−0.218 (6.60)	−0.238 (7.16)	−0.001 (0.01)	0.060 (0.42)
Mexico	−0.333 (13.45)	−0.286 (11.47)	−0.173 (4.43)	−0.273 (10.32)	−0.319 (11.04)	−0.188 (1.51)	−0.105 (0.75)

(Table continues)

TABLE 7–8 (continued)

	Total Sample			Fluent in English		Not Fluent in English	
	OLS a	OLS b	IV c	OLS d	Selectivity bias corrected e	OLS f	Selectivity bias corrected g
Cuba	-0.325 (11.31)	-0.280 (9.77)	-0.174 (4.26)	-0.263 (8.72)	-0.299 (9.51)	-0.089 (0.68)	-0.002 (0.02)
Other America	-0.335 (13.01)	-0.308 (11.99)	-0.245 (7.73)	-0.265 (9.93)	-0.288 (10.60)	-0.247 (1.94)	-0.181 (1.30)
Africa	-0.195 (5.07)	-0.186 (4.84)	-0.165 (4.21)	-0.181 (4.66)	-0.187 (4.82)	-0.142 (0.57)	-0.120 (0.48)
Middle East	-0.219 (5.72)	-0.213 (5.57)	-0.199 (5.55)	-0.199 (5.15)	-0.203 (5.27)	-0.128 (0.73)	-0.099 (0.56)
Not Reported	-0.298 (9.75)	-0.281 (9.17)	-0.239 (7.51)	-0.266 (8.19)	-0.279 (8.55)	-0.121 (0.91)	-0.061 (0.43)
Proficient in English	n.e.	0.169 (12.52)	0.571 (5.43)	n.e.	n.e.	n.e.	n.e.
Lambda	n.e.	n.e.	n.e.	n.e.	0.399 (3.74)	n.e.	-0.216 (1.38)
Sample size	32,255	32,255	32,255	25,713	25,713	6,542	6,542
Adj R^2	.3856	.3886		.3632	.3635	.3176	.3177

n.e. = variable not entered.

NOTES: Dependent variable is natural logarithm of earnings in 1979. The t statistics in parentheses were computed using White's "Heteroskedasticity-consistent Covariance Matrix Estimator."

SOURCE: Same as for table 7–1.

262

Table 7–8, column a presents results for a conventional specification of the human-capital-earnings function in which the explanatory variables comprise years of schooling, years of labor market experience and its square, marital status, locality, weeks worked, birthplace, duration of residence and its square, and citizenship. These results are reasonably standard, and only brief comments are provided.

There is a strong positive relationship between earnings and years of schooling. Each extra year of education is associated with 5.0 percent higher earnings, other things being the same. This coefficient is low relative to that estimated for the native-born (around 7 percent), but consistent with previous analyses of immigrants' earnings.[40]

The impact of labor market experience on earnings differs according to whether the experience was accumulated in the country of origin or in the United States. The partial effect of labor market experience in the country of origin, EXP, is given by the coefficients on the experience variables. Hence, $\delta \ln EARN / \delta EXP = 0.030 - 0.0009$ EXP. Evaluated at $EXP = 10$ years this equals 2.1 percent, while after 20 years of labor market activity the earnings growth associated with experience is 1.2 percent.

Under the assumption that the cross section may be used to make longitudinal conjectures, the return to experience in the United States (that is, experience in the origin plus the differential effect of pre-immigration experience) is given as $\delta \ln EARN / \delta EXPUS = 0.053 - 0.00178 EXPUS$. Assuming all labor market activity takes place after migration, the earnings growth with an additional year of experience is 3.5 percent when evaluated at $EXPUS = 10$, and 1.7 percent when evaluated at $EXPUS = 20$. This is larger than the effect of pre-immigration experience.

There is considerable variation in earnings across birthplace regions. In this analysis, Britain is used as the reference group. Each of the fifteen birthplace-dichotomous variables is negative and statistically significant, indicating that members of the particular birthplace have earnings lower than immigrants from Britain. The ranking of birthplaces in terms of decreasing earnings is: Canada, Europe, South Asia, Ireland, the Middle East, Other Asia, Vietnam, Africa, the Phillippines, Not Reported, Cuba, Mexico, West Indies, Other America, and China. The estimated coefficients range from -0.09 to -0.38, indicating a percentage earnings differential of between 7 percent and 32 percent.

The estimating equation (table 7–8, column a) shows that married (spouse present) men have earnings considerably higher than those in other marital statuses, that citizens have a small (5 percent) earnings advantage, and that residents of southern states or of rural areas each have earnings 5 percent lower than residents of other localities, ceteris paribus. Black immigrants have earnings about 20 percent lower than other immigrants (coefficient -0.22), even after controlling for schooling and country of origin. It is not clear to what extent the race differential reflects discrimination, and if so whether it is discrimination in the origin or the destination.

The elasticity of earnings with respect to weeks worked is 1.062, and this is significantly different from one. In other words, full-year workers receive 6 percent higher weekly earnings than part-year workers, ceteris paribus. This difference may reflect dimensions of human capital accumulation by those with a greater attachment to the labor market not captured by the proxy for labor market experience. It may also reflect the effects of an upward-rising labor supply curve (that is, those with higher wages working more weeks) and the positive correlation of hours worked per week and weeks worked per year.

One attribute that has not been accounted for in the table 7–8, column a specification is knowledge of the English language. This knowledge is expected to play a major role in explaining variations in earnings. There is a difference of .611 in the mean logarithmic earnings of foreign-born residents of the United States who are fluent in English and those who have an English-language deficiency, implying an earnings differential of approximately 46 percent. The relatively short period of time those with an English-language deficiency have been in the United States (ten years versus seventeen years), the fewer years of schooling that they possess (eight years versus thirteen years), and the fact that they work, on average, three weeks per year fewer than other immigrants who are fluent in English are factors likely to contribute to the difference in observed earnings.

To isolate the impact on earnings of variables other than English-language deficiency so that the effect of fluency can be estimated, the dichotomous English-fluency variable used in the previous section is added to the conventional human-capital earnings function. Results are presented in column b of table 7–8. Individuals who are fluent in English have 16.9 percent higher earnings than other groups, ceteris paribus. This earnings advantage is of the same order of magnitude as that reported by Fishback and Terza for all workers.[41] As the unadjusted earnings differential was 46 percent, this suggests that differences in measurable endowments account for two-thirds of the observed, unadjusted earnings differential between the two levels of fluency.

When the GOODENG variable is included in the estimating equation, there are minor changes to some other coefficients (table

7–8, column b. Several birthplace coefficients fall by moderate amounts—for example, China by 3 percentage points, Cuba and Mexico by 5 percentage points—and the partial effect of duration of residence in the United States is reduced and is given by $\delta \ln EARN/\delta YSM = 0.020 - 0.00078 YSM$. Evaluated at $YSM = 10$ this yields 1.2 percent, as compared with 1.4 percent when GOODENG is excluded from the model. While this decline can be noted, it is important to emphasize that even when the language-proficiency variable is included in the model, years since migration still exercise a pronounced impact on earnings.[42] This is consistent with other studies of immigrant earnings.[43]

A number of other specifications of the earnings equation (not reported here) were estimated. They included interaction terms between duration of residence and the human-capital variables for years of schooling and for experience in the country of origin. Both of these variables were significant and positive. Thus the earnings growth with years in the United States is greater for the better educated than for the less educated, and also greater for immigrants possessing greater levels of overseas labor market experience. The interaction terms therefore provide evidence of complementarity between the human capital represented by schooling and years of preimmigration experience and that represented by the duration-of-residence variable.

The remainder of table 7–8 focuses on the potential endogeneity of proficiency in the English language. Column c presents results derived using an instrumental-variables (IV) estimator. The instruments for the GOODENG variable are all the explanatory variables in table 7–1, with the identifying instruments being the veteran status, children, foreign-marriage and minority-language concentration measures. There are a number of differences between the OLS and instrumental variables estimates, and as would be expected, the most pronounced change occurs in the GOODENG variable. This increases from .169 in OLS to .571 with the instrumental variables approach. Although this is a dramatic change, it is noted that similar changes have been reported elsewhere. In Robinson's analysis of the 1981 Canadian Census, for example, the coefficient recording the wage premium to bilingualism increased by a factor of 2.5 when an instrumental-variables estimator was used instead of OLS.[44] The increase in the wage premium to dominant-language fluency is associated with a reduction in the apparent rewards to other (complementary) types of human-capital investment, such as formal education, labor market experience, and years since arrival.

These results are open to a number of interpretations. They could

265

derive from the endogeneity of dominant-language attainment in earnings determination and thus indicate that the notion of endogeneity should be treated seriously. Alternatively, the dominant-language fluency variable may be measured with considerable random error, which results in a downward bias in the OLS estimates when compared with the value of 0.571 derived using instrumental variables. If so, the self-reported measures of language fluency in the census should be viewed with considerable skepticism. Finally, the large difference between the OLS and instrumental-variables estimates may reflect in part the quality of the instruments available for *GOODENG:* where the instruments have a low correlation with *GOODENG,* the instrumental-variables estimates will be consistent but will have a large variance relative to OLS. This caveat to the method should be kept in mind when interpreting the results.

Further evidence of the endogeneity of dominant-language attainment in earnings determination is found in table 7–8, columns d through g. Here the sample is separated according to language proficiency, and separate equations are estimated for each language group, with and without a correction for sample selection bias.[45] There are a number of minor differences between the results for the sample of workers who are fluent in English and the results discussed above, the marginally higher earnings growth associated with both formal education and labor market experience being the most important. The statistical significance of the inverse Mills ratio term (lambda) provides one test of the exogeneity of the language-attainment variable. This sample selection term is significant ($t = 3.11$) and positive. That is, workers become fluent in English if their unobservable skills are more highly rewarded when they are fluent.

The equation estimated for the sample reporting an English-language deficiency table 7–8, columns f and g has a number of features. The earnings growth associated with both formal education and labor market experience is markedly lower than for comparable workers possessing English-language fluency. This suggests a degree of complementarity between types of human-capital skills. The premium to labor market experience in the United States, however, as compared with experience in the country of origin, is higher for workers who are not fluent in English. Evaluated at ten years of residence, for example, the partial effect of years since migration on earnings is 1.2 percentage points for individuals with English-language fluency, but 1.8 percentage points for individuals not fluent (see table 7–8, columns d and f). The third characteristic of these results is that the earnings differences across birthplace groups is smaller within each of the two broad fluency groups than it is for the sample as a whole.

Finally, among the immigrants with an English-language deficiency, the sample selection term is negative but statistically insignificant ($t = 1.38$). As the lambda variable for this equation is constructed to be negative, the negative sign indicates positive self-selection in this instance. That is, individuals who are not fluent in the dominant language have above-average levels of the unobserved skills that determine earnings in the nonfluent language market. This provides further support for the hypothesis that English language fluency is endogenous.

A summary of the exogeneity issue may be provided by pooling the two samples and estimating an equation that includes the two sample selection terms.[46] The F test on the incremental contribution of the two auxiliary regressors is 29.859, which is significant at the 5 percent level. This indicates that exogeneity of the English-language fluency variable is rejected.[47]

Thus, there is a consistent set of evidence: immigrants in the United States who are proficient in English have higher earnings than individuals with an English-language deficiency, ceteris paribus, and English-language fluency appears to be the outcome of a choice process, determined in part by the economic returns from acquiring language skills. Hence the acquisition of language capital, as with other forms of human capital, is responsive to economic incentives.

Canada. The average annual earnings of immigrant workers in Canada who are fluent in a dominant language are 49 percent higher than the earnings of immigrant workers who lack this skill. Individuals who possess dominant-language skills are also relatively well endowed in most other skills associated with higher earnings. Their average level of schooling is 11.8 years and their average duration of residence in Canada 19.7 years, as compared with the averages of 7.1 and 11.9 years for workers who lack fluency in a dominant language. While workers with a dominant-language deficiency have more years of labor market experience (34 as compared with 26), two-thirds of this experience was accumulated in the country of origin.

The independent effect on earnings associated with dominant-language fluency is analyzed in this section using the earnings functions presented in table 7–9. These estimates are derived for twenty-five to sixty-four-year-old foreign-born male workers in the one-in-fifty sample Individual File of the 1981 Census of Canada. The approach followed is similar to that adopted to study earnings deter-

TABLE 7-9
Regression Estimates of Earnings Equations, Adult Foreign-born Men, Canada, 1980

	Total Sample			Fluent in a Dominant Language		Not Fluent in a Dominant Language	
	OLS a	OLS b	IV c	OLS d	Selectivity bias corrected e	OLS f	Selectivity bias corrected g
Constant	4.447 (44.26)	4.347 (39.44)	4.105 (15.37)	4.402 (43.54)	4.207 (27.58)	5.011 (8.94)	6.345 (6.95)
Education	0.045 (19.63)	0.044 (19.37)	0.043 (16.73)	0.045 (19.83)	0.046 (19.92)	−0.014 (0.70)	0.006 (0.27)
Experience	0.026 (10.23)	0.026 (10.20)	0.026 (10.07)	0.027 (10.56)	0.027 (10.57)	0.012 (0.53)	−0.001 (0.01)
Experience squared/100	−0.050 (10.51)	−0.050 (10.40)	−0.048 (9.99)	−0.052 (10.69)	−0.052 (10.81)	−0.025 (0.76)	−0.023 (0.69)
Years since migration (YSM)	0.025 (8.37)	0.024 (8.14)	0.023 (7.78)	0.025 (8.27)	0.026 (8.46)	0.003 (0.11)	0.030 (1.07)
YSM squared/100	−0.042 (6.37)	−0.042 (6.27)	−0.04 (6.68)	−0.042 (6.29)	−0.043 (6.42)	−0.024 (0.35)	−0.052 (0.74)
LNWW	1.031 (42.64)	1.029 (42.54)	1.025 (59.87)	1.036 (42.30)	1.039 (42.29)	0.949 (9.02)	0.988 (9.28)

Married	0.210 (11.70)	0.211 (11.75)	0.213 (12.34)	0.214 (11.83)	0.212 (11.75)	0.029 (0.21)	0.001 (0.01)
Citizen	0.071 (4.12)	0.067 (3.89)	0.058 (2.98)	0.065 (3.74)	0.066 (3.79)	0.148 (1.25)	0.153 (1.30)
CMA	0.077 (4.82)	0.078 (4.90)	0.081 (5.15)	0.080 (4.99)	0.078 (4.87)	−0.121 (0.81)	−0.195 (1.26)
Province Atlantic	0.038 (0.80)	0.038 (0.80)	0.037 (0.83)	0.039 (0.81)	0.039 (0.81)	−0.101 (0.18)	−0.136 (0.24)
Quebec	−0.047 (2.48)	−0.049 (2.56)	−0.053 (2.62)	−0.036 (1.90)	−0.034 (1.78)	−0.388 (2.65)	−0.303 (2.00)
Prairie	0.104 (5.46)	0.103 (5.39)	0.100 (5.12)	0.110 (5.74)	0.112 (5.82)	−0.080 (0.40)	−0.037 (0.19)
British Columbia	0.115 (6.36)	0.114 (6.31)	0.112 (5.97)	0.110 (6.03)	0.111 (6.10)	0.534 (3.35)	0.572 (3.60)
Birthplace Ireland	−0.162 (1.61)	−0.162 (1.61)	−0.163 (1.88)	−0.162 (1.61)	−0.162 (1.61)	—	—
United States	−0.123 (3.93)	−0.123 (3.93)	−0.124 (4.02)	−0.124 (3.94)	−0.124 (3.97)	—	—
West Indies	−0.225 (6.92)	−0.228 (6.99)	−0.234 (6.73)	−0.225 (6.90)	−0.220 (6.76)	0.783 (3.77)	0.816 (3.93)
France	−0.115 (2.51)	−0.114 (2.48)	−0.110 (2.08)	−0.124 (2.70)	−0.125 (2.73)	1.787 (6.92)	1.876 (7.04)

(Table continues)

TABLE 7–9 (continued)

	Total Sample			Fluent in a Dominant Language		Not Fluent in a Dominant Language	
	OLS a	OLS b	IV c	OLS d	Selectivity bias corrected e	OLS f	Selectivity bias corrected g
W. Europe	-0.138 (6.35)	-0.136 (6.29)	-0.133 (5.83)	-0.137 (6.33)	-0.139 (6.39)	0.821 (1.34)	1.042 (2.13)
E. Europe	-0.182 (6.86)	-0.182 (6.84)	-0.181 (7.03)	-0.184 (6.88)	-0.184 (6.90)	0.962 (4.62)	1.121 (5.18)
S. Europe	-0.140 (6.86)	-0.133 (6.49)	-0.117 (4.30)	-0.138 (6.73)	-0.148 (6.97)	0.750 (4.26)	0.812 (4.53)
Chinese Asia	-0.344 (10.16)	-0.332 (9.85)	-0.304 (6.75)	-0.286 (8.41)	-0.301 (8.70)	n.e.	n.e.
Other Asia	-0.237 (8.95)	-0.237 (8.95)	-0.237 (8.69)	-0.234 (8.86)	-0.234 (8.83)	0.206 (0.75)	0.477 (1.61)
Mexico, South & Central America	-0.296 (6.66)	-0.294 (6.60)	-0.286 (5.90)	-0.291 (6.56)	-0.296 (6.67)	0.484 (1.56)	0.643 (2.05)
Africa	-0.130 (3.73)	-0.131 (3.75)	-0.133 (3.27)	-0.134 (3.82)	-0.132 (3.76)	0.906 (3.06)	1.331 (4.34)

Other	−0.103 (2.67)	−0.103 (2.67)	−0.103 (2.68)	−0.105 (2.73)	−0.106 (2.73)	0.973 (3.64)	1.146 (4.10)
Dominant-language proficiency	n.e.	0.122 (2.43)	0.414 (1.34)	n.e.	n.e.	n.e.	n.e.
Lambda	n.e.	n.e.	n.e.	n.e.	0.577 (1.71)	n.e.	1.160 (1.92)
Sample size	23,741	23,741	23,741	23,081	23,081	660	660
Adj R²	.2217	.2220		.2161	.2162	.2131	.2157

n.e. = variable not entered.

NOTES: Dependent variable is natural logarithm of earnings in 1980. The t statistics in parentheses were computed using White's "Heteroskedasticity-consistent Covariance Matrix Estimator."

SOURCE: Same as for table 7-5.

mination in the U.S. labor market. Hence column a presents results for a conventional specification of the augmented human-capital earnings equation, in which the natural logarithm of annual earnings is related to years of schooling, years of labor market experience and its square, marital status, locality, weeks worked, duration of residence and its square, citizenship, and birthplace. The general patterns that emerge from this analysis are consistent with those highlighted in the study of the U.S. labor market.

Earnings increase more than proportionately with weeks worked—the elasticity of earnings with respect to weeks worked is 1.031. This elasticity is considerably higher than that reported in earlier studies, but this difference can be linked to the treatment of workers who reported nonpositive earnings.[48] When this group is excluded from the analysis, the elasticity coefficient drops to 0.917, a level consistent with previous research on Canada.[49]

Earnings increase by 4.5 percent with each additional year of education, and by 1.6 percent with each additional year of labor market experience in the country of origin (evaluated at $EXP = 10$). Labor market experience in Canada is associated with an earnings premium compared with experience prior to migration. Evaluated at ten years of residence in Canada, the premium is a sizable 1.7 percent. Even after twenty years of residence in Canada, an extra year of Canadian labor market experience is worth 0.8 percentage points more in earnings than is experience in the country of origin.

Region of residence exercises an important influence on earnings. Residents of Census Metropolitan Areas have earnings approximately 8 percent higher than those of workers who live outside the major cities. The ranking of immigrants' earnings across provinces is similar to that reported by Chiswick and Miller.[50] Thus the earnings of residents of Quebec are 5 percent lower and the earnings of residents of the Prairie provinces and British Columbia are about 10 percent higher than the earnings of residents of the other provinces. The earnings disadvantage associated with residence in Quebec among immigrants may explain why immigrants tend to avoid this province.

Country of origin is very important for understanding variation in earnings in the Canadian labor market. Each of the birthplace groups has earnings significantly lower than the earnings of immigrants from Britain, ceteris paribus, although the Irish coefficient is at the margin of significance. The ranking of earnings in decreasing order is: Britain (the benchmark), Other, France, the United States, Africa, Western Europe, Southern Europe, Ireland, Eastern Europe, West Indies, Other Asia, South and Central America, Chinese Asia. At the lowest end of the spectrum, the earnings of immigrants from

South and Central America and Chinese Asia are approximately 30 percentage points lower than those of the British. The earnings of immigrants from the United States are 12 percentage points lower than those of the British.[51]

The earnings of immigrants who have become Canadian citizens are 7 percent higher than those for noncitizens, other variables being the same. This sizable earnings premium may reflect in part the use of citizenship status as a screen for access to higher paying jobs, or the greater motivation and commitment to the Canadian labor market of individuals seeking citizenship.

In table 7–9, column b the dominant-language proficiency measure is included in the estimating equation. Individuals who are proficient in a dominant language have earnings 12.2 percentage points higher than individuals who lack this skill, other things being the same. The inclusion of the dominant-language proficiency variable has a negligible impact on all other estimated coefficients. In particular, the partial effect of years since migration on earnings is not affected in any material way (a reduction from 1.7 percentage points to 1.6 percentage points, evaluated at ten years of residence in Canada). This finding is consistent with the evidence reported in Abbott and Beach and Chiswick and Miller for quite different specifications of the language-fluency variable.[52] It appears, therefore, that the economic progress of immigrants in Canada reflected in the duration-of-residence variable arises from a source other than merely the accumulation of language capital.

The results listed in table 7–9, column c are derived using an instrumental-variables method of estimation. In this model the foreign-marriage and minority-language-concentration measures are used as the identifying instruments for the dominant-language proficiency variable. The comparison between the OLS and instrumental-variables coefficients in table 7–9 is similar to that found in the U.S. data. Hence the coefficient on the dominant-language proficiency variable increases threefold. In this case, however, it is statistically insignificant. In the U.S. study, the language variable was highly significant in the instrumental variables model ($t = 5.43$).

This difference may indicate that the problems of errors in variables and endogeneity are less serious in the analysis for Canada, where the language question is less subjective (see appendix 7–A) and the level of dominant-language fluency considerably higher. The finding could simply be caused, however, by the identifying instruments' being less suitable in the analysis of earnings determination in Canada than in the same model applied to the U.S. labor market. In the U.S. labor market, the coefficient of determination (adjusted R^2)

273

in the model of dominant language fluency was .37 (see table 7–1). For the study of Canada, however, the coefficent of determination is only .12 (see table 7–5). As there is an inverse relationship between the asymptotic variance of the instrumental-variables estimator and the asymptotic correlation between the instruments and the variable instrumented, the instrumental variables would be expected to be less successful when applied to the Canadian data than to the U.S. data.

The application of the control function method (table 7–9, columns d through g yields results that are more consistent with the findings reported previously for the United States. Columns d and e list estimates of earnings equations for the portion of the sample reporting that they are fluent in a dominant language, while columns f and g list estimates for immigrants who are not fluent. Both OLS and selectivity corrected estimates are presented.

Individuals who are fluent in a dominant language make up 97 percent of the total sample. Consequently, the OLS estimates for this group do not differ appreciably from those listed for the total sample. The coefficient on the sample selectivity correction term is positive and at the margin of statistical significance ($t = 1.71$). Thus some, although not overwhelming evidence suggests that the sample of dominant-language speakers is nonrandom. The high representation of this group in the total sample (97 percent) may have an important bearing on this outcome. Correction for sample selectivity does not affect the estimated coefficients in the model.

Columns f and g in table 7–9 list results for the portion of the sample that lacks fluency in a dominant language. The sample here is relatively small (660 observations), and the human-capital variables (education, pre- and post-immigration labor market experience) are statistically insignificant. There is considerable variation, however, in earnings across birthplace groups. Because the British birthplace group is not represented in this sample, the Chinese Asia immigrants serve as the benchmark. Compared with this group, all birthplace regions except Other Asia, South and Central America, and Western Europe have higher earnings. The selectivity correction term (lambda) is positive and has a t of 1.92. This provides support for the hypothesis of endogeneity of language skills in the model of earnings determination. Correction for sample selection does not affect the other coefficients, but it is associated with a widening of the earnings differences across birthplace groups; all birthplace variables other than those for Other Asia are significant once the nonrandom nature of the sample is taken into account.

The evidence contained in table 7–9, while not as conclusive as for the study of the U.S. labor market, suggests that dominant-

TABLE 7–10
PARTIAL EFFECTS ON EARNINGS OF SELECTED VARIABLES, UNITED
STATES, 1980, AND CANADA, 1981

Variable	United States	Canada
Education	0.046	0.044
Experience in origin[a]	0.021	0.016
Experience in origin[b]	0.012	0.006
Experience in destination[a]	0.033	0.032
Experience in destination[b]	0.016	0.013
Weeks worked	1.057	1.029
Married	0.207	0.211
Citizen	0.043	0.067
Proficiency in dominant language(s)	0.169	0.122
Proficiency in dominant language(s)[c]	0.127	0.122

a. Evaluated at experience of 10 years.
b. Evaluated at experience of 20 years.
c. Canadian definition for the United States.
SOURCE: Table 7–8, column b and table 7–9, column b.

language fluency is endogenous: that is, it is in part determined by earnings. Further evidence to this effect is provided by the estimation of pooled equations for the two language groups that contain both sample selection correction terms used in the analyses discussed above. In this analysis the F-test on the incremental contribution of the lambda terms was 7.327, which is statistically significant. Hence this summary measure of the endogeneity issue suggests that it is important. Consistent with this finding, the Addison and Portugal test returned an F-statistic of 10.882.[53]

U.S.-Canadian Comparisons. The main feature of the comparative study of the determinants of earnings among immigrants in Canada and the United States is the overwhelming similarity of the findings, as summarized in table 7–10.

In both of the North American labor markets, the earnings growth associated with an extra year of schooling is roughly 4.5 percent. The increase in earnings associated with labor market experience differs according to whether the experience was accumulated in the country of origin or in the destination labor market. An extra year of labor market experience results in earnings roughly 2 percent higher (evaluated at experience of ten years) if the experience was accumulated in the country of origin, and 3.3 percent higher earnings if it was accumulated in the destination. Citizens earn more than noncitizens in each country. Although the U.S. and Canadian labor markets are contiguous, the similarity of these effects in the earnings model is remarkable.

Individuals who are proficient in the dominant language in the United States have earnings 16.9 percent higher than those who lack this skill. In Canada, however, the earnings premium associated with dominant-language fluency is only 12.2 percent. This difference is not statistically significant. When earnings equations are estimated for the United States using the Canadian definition of dominant-language fluency, the earnings premium associated with language skills in the United States is 12.7 percent. When the instrumental variables approach is used, however, the effects of dominant-language fluency are 57.1 percent and 41.4 percent for the U.S. and Canadian labor markets, respectively, but the coefficient is less statistically reliable in the Canadian analysis. The analyses also demonstrate that in each country, dominant-language skills are endogenous with respect to labor-market earnings.

Conclusion

This chapter has explored the determinants and labor market implications for immigrants of proficiency in speaking the dominant language in the country of destination. The statistical analysis uses the microdata files on adult foreign-born men in the 1980 and 1981 censuses of the United States and Canada, respectively. The languages treated as dominant are English in the United States and English and French in Canada. The analyses are based on the self-reported responses to questions on spoken-language fluency.

The findings in the analysis of the determinants of language proficiency for the United States and Canada are remarkably similar, and the findings are similar when the analysis is done separately by country of origin for the immigrants. It is shown that in both countries dominant-language fluency varies systematically with exposure, efficiency, and economic variables. Language skills are shown to be determined endogenously with earnings.

Dominant-language fluency can be viewed as produced by the individual. This process is more efficient the greater the exposure is to the dominant language prior to immigration and the younger the age at immigration, apparently because younger people are more efficient in creating language capital. Greater fluency is also achieved by those who have more schooling, presumably because of the complementarity of various types of human capital. The advantageous position of those with more schooling diminishes but does not disappear, however, with a longer duration of residence.

Learning by doing is particularly important for language skills, and a longer duration in the destination enhances fluency. The effect of duration of residence on language skills is larger for those who immigrate at an older age and with less schooling. In general, immigrants with the poorest fluency at arrival undergo the most rapid improvement with experience in the destination.

Family characteristics also appear to matter. Those who are less likely to speak the dominant language at home (for example, because their spouses speak the same nondominant language and there are no children in the households) have lower levels of fluency.

A very important determinant of dominant-language proficiency is the extent to which others in the area in which the respondent lives speak the same nondominant language. That is, immigrants living in communities where their nondominant language of origin is spoken with greater frequency have a lower level of fluency in the dominant language. The adverse effect of a language enclave, however, is not neutral. It is more intense during the initial years in the destination for less educated immigrants and for those who immigrated as adults. These are the very immigrants with the lowest level of language fluency.

The statistical analysis of earnings in the two countries uses as the starting point the standard human-capital earnings function, augmented for immigrant analyses. A dichotomous variable for being fluent in the dominant language is then added to the analysis. Yet the self-reported language variable may be subject to much random measurement error, and language fluency may be determined endogenously with earnings. That is, those who have a greater economic incentive to acquire fluency in the dominant language may have a higher degree of fluency. As a result, the analysis explores alternative statistical methodologies for the two countries, including ordinary least squares, instrumental variables, and sample selectivity techniques.

The determinants of earnings among immigrants are remarkably similar in the United States and Canada; it is as if there is one earnings determination process for the two countries. Using the ordinary least-squares methodology, those in the United States who speak English well or very well have 17 percent higher earnings than those with less fluency, while in Canada those who can carry on a conversation in English or French have 12 percent higher earnings than those who cannot. Converting the U.S. data to a close approximation of the less satisfactory Canadian definition, those who are fluent in English also have 12 percent higher earnings. The instrumental-variables approach indicates an even larger effect of dominant-language fluency—roughly 50 percent.

The sample selectivity test addresses the issue of the endogeneity of fluency. The test indicates that workers are more likely to become fluent in the dominant language if their unobservable characteristics are more highly rewarded when they are fluent. Thus, the acquisition of language capital appears to be responsive to the economic incentives for acquiring language skills.

The addition of the language-proficiency variable to the earnings equation, whether using the observed value or an instrumental-variables approach, has little effect on the size or statistical significance of the coefficients for the other variables in the analysis. In the instrumental-variables analysis, however, there is a diminution in the partial effect of duration of residence, an important determinant of language fluency. But it remains large and highly significant.

The analysis demonstrates that spoken dominant-language proficiency is an important determinant of earnings and presumably of other measures of economic success among immigrants. This suggests the importance of selecting immigrants who have or who can be expected quickly to acquire this proficiency, if the successful economic adjustment of immigrants is an important policy objective.

Canadian immigration policy explicitly recognizes the importance of this issue by awarding points in their point system for English or French fluency. Current U.S. immigration policy ignores language skills. Even the language requirements for illegal aliens to obtain permanent amnesty under the provisions of the 1986 Immigration Reform and Control Act are so meaningless as to be useless.

The analysis demonstrates the potential counterproductive nature of efforts to shelter immigrants from the economic consequences of inadequate proficiency. Immigrants respond positively to the economic incentives for fluency, thereby making the investment and becoming fluent. The analysis also demonstrates the importance of schooling, age at immigration, and other variables in determining fluency. These findings need to be explicitly recognized in immigration policy and in programs to facilitate immigrant adjustment. Again, the Canadians seem to have done a better job in this regard than the Americans.

This study also generates recommendations regarding the questions asked in the census. The language-related questions in the 1980 U.S. Census are superior to those in the 1981 Canadian Census. In the U.S. data, individuals who speak a language other than or in addition to English at home are asked to report the non-English language and the degree of their spoken fluency in English on a four-point scale (very well, well, not well, not at all). In the Canadian data, however, only those who cannot carry on a conversation in English or French are identified; these are the equivalent of the "not at all" English speakers in the United States. Furthermore, instead of the long list of non-English languages and countries of birth as provided in the U.S. data, the Canadian Census data permit the specific identification of only a handful. This coarseness in the Canadian data hampers the analysis of language. Both countries are repeating their language questions in the 1990–1991 censuses.

On a final note, the knowledge that dominant-language skills are very important for the economic success of immigrants for two countries with different immigration policies suggests the fundamental role of language capital in the labor market. In general, language capital is too obvious to be noticed. Immigration research highlights its role. This research also suggests that even among the native-born, fluency is important, and degrees of fluency, not discerned in current data, may be important determinants of economic attainment.

Appendix 7–A
The Census Language Questions

UNITED STATES: 1980 CENSUS

13a. Does this person speak a language other than English at home?

    ○ Yes   ○ No, only speaks English
                             (skip to 14)

b. What is this language?

(For example—Chinese, Italian, Spanish, etc.)

c. How well does this person speak English?

    ○ Very well   ○ Not well
    ○ Well   ○ Not at all

NOTE: The respondents were instructed to report "yes" to Q.13a if a language other than English is spoken at home, even if English is spoken more frequently than the other language. Those who speak

279

only English at home include those who may speak another language at school, work, or elsewhere, but not at home, and those whose use of another language at home is limited to a few expressions or slang.

Those respondents speaking two or more non-English languages at home were asked to report the language spoken most often, or if this could not be determined, the first language learned. The write-in entries were coded into 387 language categories.

SOURCE: US Bureau of the Census, *Census of Population and Housing, 1980: Public Use Microdata Sample, Technical Documentation* (Washington, D.C.: 1983), pp. K26 and K65.

CANADA: 1981 CENSUS

QUESTION 12.
WHAT IS THE LANGUAGE YOU FIRST LEARNED IN CHILDHOOD AND STILL UNDERSTAND?

|_____| ENGLISH

|_____| FRENCH

|_____| GERMAN

|_____| ITALIAN

|_____| UKRAINIAN

|_____| OTHER (SPECIFY)

QUESTION 18.
WHAT LANGUAGE DO YOU YOURSELF SPEAK AT HOME NOW?
(IF MORE THAN ONE LANGUAGE, WHICH LANGUAGE DO YOU SPEAK MOST OFTEN?)
MARK ONE BOX ONLY

|_____| ENGLISH

|_____| FRENCH

|_____| GERMAN

|_____| ITALIAN

|_____| Ukrainian

|_____| Other (specify)

Question 19.
Can you speak English or French well enough to conduct a conversation?
Mark one box only

|_____| English only

|_____| French only

|_____| Both English and French

|_____| Neither English nor French

Note: The responses to "Other," specified in Q.12 and Q.18, were coded and reported in the Household/Family File as Chinese and Other, whereas Chinese, Greek, Netherlandic languages, Polish, and Portuguese are identified as separate languages in the Individual File.

Source: Form 3: Individual Census Questionnaire. Statistics Canada, *Summary Guide, Total Population*, Catalogue No. 99-902.

Appendix 7–B
Definitions of the Variables

The variables used in the analysis are defined below. Mnemonic names are also listed where relevant.

Analysis of 1980 U.S. Census of Population:

Definition of Population: Foreign-born men aged twenty-five to sixty-four who worked during 1979.

Earnings (LNEARN): The natural logarithm of the sum of wage or salary income and self-employment income (either non-farm or farm). Income data refer to 1979.

Weeks Worked (LNWW): The natural logarithm of the number of weeks the respondent worked in 1979.

Years of Education (EDUC): This variable records the total years of full-time education.

Years of Experience (EXP): This is computed as age minus years of education minus 5 (that is, $EXP = AGE - EDUC - 5$). A quadratic specification is used.

Years since Migration (YSM): The categorical Census information on year of migration is converted to a continuous measure using the following values: 1975–1980 = 2 years, 1970–1974 = 7 years, 1965–1969 = 12 years, 1960–1964 = 17 years, 1951–1959 = 24.5 years, prior to 1950 = 40 years. A quadratic specification is used for this variable.

Birthplace (BIRTH): A number of birthplace regions were considered in the analyses: Britain, Ireland, Other Europe, Canada, West Indies, Mexico, Cuba, Other America, China, the Philippines, Vietnam, South Asia (which comprises the regions of British influence, namely India, Pakistan, Sri Lanka, Bangladesh, Bhutan and Nepal), Other Asia (for example, Korea and Japan), the Middle East, Africa, and Not reported. For the study of language proficiency, immigrants from Britain, Ireland, Canada, Australia, New Zealand, and the West Indies comprise the omitted English-speaking category, whereas for the study of earnings, the omitted category is restricted to immigrants from Britain.

English Language Proficiency (GOODENG): GOODENG is set to one for individuals who speak only English at home, or if a language other than English is spoken in the home, who speak English either "very well" or "well." The GOODENG variable is set to zero where a language other than English is spoken in the home and the respondent speaks English either "not well" or "not at all."

Citizenship (CITIZEN): This is a dichotomous variable, set to one for individuals who were either naturalized citizens or were born abroad of American parents.

Minority Group Concentration (CONC): Each respondent is assigned a measure equal to the percentage of the population aged eighteen to sixty-four in the state in which he lives, which reports the same non-English language group as the respondent. In the construction of this variable only the twenty largest nationwide language groups are considered. In descending order, these are: Spanish, Italian, German, French, Polish, Chinese, Tagalog, Greek, Portuguese, Japanese, Yiddish, Korean, Arabic, Vietnamese, Hungarian, Russian, Dutch, Hindi, Ukrainian, Czech. These constitute 92 percent of all valid responses. Representation in the other language groups is so small numerically that the proportions are approximately zero, and this value is assigned. Those who reported only English are also assigned a zero value. Table 7–B3 presents data on the percentage representation in the 8 largest language groups for each state.

Marital Status (MARRIED): This is a binary variable that distinguishes between individuals who are currently married, spouse present (equal to 1), and all other marital states.

Married Overseas (FORMAR): This variable is defined only for the foreign-born who have been married only once. It is constructed from information on age at first marriage and age at arrival in the United States. Individuals currently in their first marriage for whom age at first marriage is lower than age at arrival in the United States are assumed to have married in the country of origin. The variable is zero for all other individuals.

Children: Three variables are included in the estimating equations. The first records whether one or more children aged younger than six years were living in the family, and there were no older children. The second records whether one or more children aged between six and seventeen years, inclusive, were living in the family, and there were no younger children. The third variable records the presence of children aged younger than six years and between six and seventeen years.

Veteran Status (VETSTAT): This is a dichotomous variable, set to one where the respondent is a veteran of the U.S. Armed Forces; otherwise it is set to zero.

Location: The two location variables record residence of a rural area (Rural) or of the South Atlantic, East-South Central, or West-South Central geographic divisions (South). These variables are not mutually exclusive.

Race: This is a dichotomous variable, set to one if the individual is Black, and set to zero for all other racial groups (White, Asian and Pacific Islander groups, other groups).

NOTE: All variables for the United States are dichotomous except earnings, education, total experience, duration in the destination, weeks worked, and minority-language-group concentration. The means and standard deviations of the variables used in the analyses for the United States are reported in appendix table 7–B1.

Analysis of 1981 Canadian Census:

Definition of Population: Foreign-born men aged twenty-five to sixty-four who worked during 1980.

283

Earnings (LNEARN): The natural logarithm of the sum of wage or salary income and self-employment income. Income data refer to 1980.

Weeks Worked (LNWW): The natural logarithm of the number of weeks worked by the respondent in 1980.

Years of Education: This variable records the total years of full-time education.

Years of Experience (EXP): This is computed as age minus years of education minus 5 (EXP = AGE − EDUC − 5). A quadratic specification is employed.

Years since Migration (YSM): The census information on year of arrival in Canada is recorded in individual years between 1971 and 1980, and in intervals of varying length for pre-1971 arrivals. The categorical information was converted to a continuous measure of years since migration using the following values: 1967–70 = 12.5 years, 1966 = 15 years, 1961–65 = 18 years, 1956–60 = 23 years, 1946–55 = 30.5 years, and pre-1946 = 42 years. A quadratic specification is employed.

Birthplace (BIRTH): Previous studies (Meng, "Earnings of Canadian Immigrants," and Chiswick and Miller, "Earnings in Canada") have proposed a range of birthplace groupings for inclusion in analyses of earnings. The present study uses a set of birthplace regions that facilitates comparisons with the study of the U.S. labor market. The following birthplace groups are recognized in this study: Britain (including Northern Ireland), Republic of Ireland, the United States, France, Western Europe (which includes Belgium, Luxembourg, West Germany, the Netherlands, and Austria), Southern Europe (which includes Greece, Italy, Portugal and Yugoslavia), Eastern Europe (which includes Hungary, Poland, the USSR, and Czechoslovakia), Chinese Asia, Other Asia, South and Central America, English-origin West Indies, Africa, and Other. These regions are identified based on the birthplace, ethnic origin, and mother-tongue information in the Census Files. Mother tongue is used to separate immigrants from South and Central America from English-origin immigrants from the Caribbean. Ethnic origin is used to allocate some of the responses to birthplace coded as "Other Europe" to the categories of Northern and Western Europe, Southern Europe, and Eastern Europe, and also to distinguish Chinese Asia from other regions of Asia. For the study of dominant-language proficiency, immigrants from Britain, Ireland, the United States, and the British West Indies make up the omitted dominant-language-speaking category, while for the study of earnings, the omitted category is restricted to immigrants from Britain.

Dominant-Language Proficiency (GOODLANG): Individuals who reported that they could speak English or French well enough to conduct a conversation were classified as proficient in the dominant language.

Minority-Group Concentration (CONC): Each respondent is assigned a measure equal to the percentage of the population aged eighteen to sixty-four in the region (defined using information on residence in a Census Metropolitan Area and province of residence) in which he lives that reports the same home language as the respondent. The nondominant-language groups Chinese, German, Italian, and Ukrainian are identified on the Household and Family File, and Chinese, German, Italian, Ukrainian, Greek, Netherlandic languages, Polish, and Portuguese are identified on the Individual File. The first four language groups constitute 46 percent of nondominant-language responses, and the final four a further 20 percent. Table 7–B4 presents data on the percentage in each language group for the twenty-three regions distinguished in the construction of the variable.

Marital Status (MARRIED): This is a binary variable that distinguishes between individuals who are married, spouse present (equal to 1), and all other marital states.

Married Overseas (FORMAR): This variable is computed from information on age at first marriage and age at arrival in Canada. Individuals for whom age at first marriage is lower than age at arrival in Canada, and for whom the date of marriage corresponds to that of their spouses, are assumed to have married their present spouses in the country of origin. The variable is unity for this group and zero for all others.

Location: Two location variables are used in the study. The first records province of residence. This information was grouped as follows: Ontario, Atlantic provinces (Newfoundland, Nova Scotia, New Brunswick, Prince Edward Island), Quebec, Prairie provinces (Manitoba, Saskatchewan, Alberta), and British Columbia. The second locality variable records the size of the place of residence. Here, individuals residing in Census Metropolitan Areas (defined as places having 100,000 or more in population) are distinguished from other individuals.

Citizenship (CITIZEN): Individuals who hold Canadian citizenship are distinguished from immigrants who have not yet become Canadian citizens. This information is available only from the Individual File.

285

Note: All variables for Canada are dichotomous except earnings, education, total experience, duration in the destination, weeks worked, and minority-language-group concentration. The means and standard deviations of the variables used in the analyses for Canada are reported in appendix table 7–B2.

APPENDIX 7–C1

MEANS AND STANDARD DEVIATIONS OF VARIABLES BY REGION OF ORIGIN FOR ADULT FOREIGN-BORN MEN, UNITED STATES, 1980

| | Total Sample | | Country of Origin | | | |
| | | | English-speaking | | Non-English speaking | |
	Mean	Standard deviation	Mean	Standard deviation	Mean	Standard deviation
Education	11.981	4.949	13.174	3.598	11.792	5.104
Age	41.108	11.007	44.049	11.493	40.539	10.851
Experience	24.038	12.539	25.876	12.680	23.748	12.492
YSM	15.751	11.994	20.033	13.213	15.074	11.647
Married	0.807	0.394	0.802	0.398	0.808	0.394
Married overseas	0.360	0.480	0.330	0.470	0.365	0.481
Child <6 only	0.144	0.351	0.101	0.301	0.150	0.357
Child 6–17 only	0.277	0.448	0.294	0.456	0.275	0.446
Children < 6 & 6–17	0.137	0.344	0.085	0.279	0.145	0.352
Veteran	0.167	0.373	0.237	0.425	0.156	0.363
Rural location	0.078	0.269	0.125	0.331	0.071	0.257
South	0.194	0.396	0.163	0.369	0.199	0.399
Minority concentration	3.808	5.781	0.262	1.305	4.368	6.012
Citizenship	0.482	0.500	0.540	0.498	0.473	0.499
Birthplace						
Britain	0.039	0.194	0.292	0.455	—	—
Canada	0.060	0.237	0.437	0.496	—	—
Ireland	0.012	0.108	0.086	0.281	—	—

(Table continues)

APPENDIX 7-C1 (continued)

	Total Sample		Country of Origin			
			English-speaking		Non-English speaking	
	Mean	Standard deviation	Mean	Standard deviation	Mean	Standard deviation
West Indies	0.025	0.157	0.185	0.388	—	—
Europe	0.278	0.448	—	—	0.322	0.467
Vietnam	0.010	0.101	—	—	0.012	0.109
Philippines	0.037	0.188	—	—	0.042	0.202
China	0.040	0.196	—	—	0.046	0.210
South Asia	0.031	0.174	—	—	0.036	0.187
Other Asia	0.049	0.216	—	—	0.057	0.231
Mexico	0.174	0.379	—	—	0.201	0.401
Cuba	0.051	0.220	—	—	0.059	0.236
Other America	0.097	0.296	—	—	0.112	0.315
Africa	0.021	0.143	—	—	0.024	0.153
Middle East	0.025	0.156	—	—	0.029	0.167
Not reported	0.051	0.220	—	—	0.059	0.236
Earnings	17,279	16,559	21,362	19,161	16,633	16,015
Log (earnings)	9.391	0.991	9.639	0.939	9.351	0.994
Weeks worked	46.405	10.893	47.468	10.005	46.237	11.018
Log (weeks worked)	3.779	0.431	3.811	0.399	3.774	0.436
GOODENG	0.797	0.402	0.992	0.088	0.766	0.423
Sample size	32,255		4,405		27,850	

NOTES: The English-speaking regions include Britain, Canada, Ireland, the British West Indies.
SOURCE: 1980 Census of Population, Public Use Sample, 1/100 Sample of the Foreign-born.

APPENDIX 7-C2

MEANS AND STANDARD DEVIATIONS OF VARIABLES BY REGION OF ORIGIN FOR ADULT FOREIGN-BORN MEN, CANADA, 1981

	Total Sample		Country of Origin			
			Dominant language		Nondominant language	
	Mean	Standard deviation	Mean	Standard deviation	Mean	Standard deviation
Education	11.689	3.851	12.950	3.220	11.090	3.979
Age	42.645	10.542	42.724	10.738	42.608	10.447
Experience	25.956	12.035	24.773	11.706	26.518	12.149
YSM	19.452	10.626	19.725	11.344	19.323	10.266
Married	0.827	0.378	0.814	0.389	0.833	0.373
Married overseas	0.272	0.445	0.280	0.449	0.269	0.443
Child < 6 only	0.129	0.335	0.108	0.311	0.138	0.345
Child 6–17 only	0.430	0.495	0.410	0.492	0.444	0.497
Children < 6 & 6–17	0.112	0.315	0.091	0.288	0.122	0.327
Metropolitan (CMA)	0.744	0.436	0.694	0.461	0.768	0.422
Atlantic province	0.021	0.145	0.041	0.198	0.012	0.110
Prairie provinces	0.139	0.346	0.134	0.341	0.142	0.349
Quebec	0.143	0.350	0.105	0.306	0.161	0.367
British Columbia	0.159	0.365	0.181	0.385	0.148	0.355
Minority concentration	0.540	1.395	0.009	0.174	0.793	1.631
Citizenship	0.743	0.437	0.679	0.467	0.773	0.419
Birthplace						

(Table continues)

289

APPENDIX 7-C2 (continued)

| | Total Sample | | Country of Origin | | | |
| | | | Dominant language | | Nondominant language | |
	Mean	Standard deviation	Mean	Standard deviation	Mean	Standard deviation
Britain	0.200	0.400	0.621	0.485	—	—
United States	0.056	0.230	0.174	0.379	—	—
Ireland	0.005	0.073	0.017	0.128	—	—
West Indies	0.044	0.206	0.137	0.344	—	—
France	0.016	0.127	0.051	0.220	—	—
W. Europe	0.137	0.344	—	—	0.202	0.401
E. Europe	0.094	0.292	—	—	0.139	0.345
S. Europe	0.232	0.422	—	—	0.342	0.475
Chinese Asia	0.048	0.213	—	—	0.070	0.256
Other Asia	0.086	0.280	—	—	0.127	0.333
Africa	0.030	0.170	—	—	0.044	0.204
South & Central America	0.020	0.141	—	—	0.030	0.170
Other	0.032	0.175	—	—	0.047	0.211
Earnings	20,218	13,391	22,797	14.427	18,991	12,687
Log (earnings)	9.595	1.096	9.752	1.009	9.521	1.128
Weeks worked	46.472	10.446	47.471	9.607	45.996	10.789
Log (weeks worked)	3.789	0.391	3.819	0.352	3.774	0.408
GOODLANG	0.972	0.164	1.000	0.016	0.959	0.198
Sample size	23,741		7,649		16,092	

NOTE: The dominant-language regions of origin include Britain, the United States, Ireland, British West Indies, and France. The children-variables were

SOURCE: 1981 Census of Canada, Public Use sample, Individual File, 1/50 sample of the foreign-born.

APPENDIX 7-C3

Representation of Major Minority-Language Groups by State, United States, 1980
(percent)

State	Spanish	Italian	German	French	Polish	Chinese	Tagalog	Greek
Alabama	0.40	0.03	0.18	0.38	0.00	0.05	0.03	0.10
Alaska-Hawaii	1.72	0.07	0.79	0.22	0.14	1.08	3.66	0.00
Arizona	17.82	0.20	0.43	0.18	0.18	0.23	0.00	0.13
Arkansas	0.30	0.00	0.17	0.08	0.04	0.04	0.04	0.00
California	13.97	0.47	0.71	0.38	0.08	1.08	0.92	0.13
Colorado	6.69	0.27	1.09	0.61	0.10	0.27	0.00	0.00
Connecticut	3.35	2.90	0.73	2.33	1.37	0.13	0.10	0.32
District of Columbia	2.61	0.33	0.65	1.79	0.00	0.65	0.16	0.65
Florida	8.48	0.66	0.83	0.71	0.22	0.06	0.10	0.15
Georgia	0.68	0.11	0.34	0.41	0.05	0.02	0.00	0.13
Illinois	5.02	0.80	0.87	0.31	1.20	0.24	0.20	0.42
Indiana	1.41	0.04	0.75	0.26	0.33	0.04	0.02	0.07
Kentucky	0.47	0.11	0.28	0.28	0.00	0.00	0.03	0.03
Louisiana	1.14	0.26	0.19	6.68	0.02	0.02	0.02	0.07
Maine	0.55	0.20	0.20	6.52	0.35	0.08	0.04	0.12
Maryland	1.18	0.37	0.52	0.45	0.33	0.14	0.17	0.35
Massachusetts	1.91	1.94	0.39	2.90	0.78	0.41	0.02	0.36
Michigan	1.26	0.46	0.63	0.31	0.95	0.12	0.06	0.12
Minnesota	0.76	0.08	1.30	0.24	0.10	0.06	0.04	0.08
Mississippi	0.52	0.00	0.12	0.32	0.00	0.08	0.00	0.00

(Table continues)

APPENDIX 7–C3 (continued)

State	Spanish	Italian	German	French	Polish	Chinese	Tagalog	Greek
Montana	2.28	0.18	0.87	0.18	0.05	0.09	0.00	0.00
New Jersey	5.97	2.59	1.10	0.41	1.00	0.25	0.32	0.34
New York	8.12	3.19	0.80	0.94	0.78	0.73	0.15	0.58
North Carolina	0.97	0.07	0.29	0.51	0.03	0.08	0.05	0.12
Ohio	1.02	0.42	0.71	0.31	0.31	0.07	0.05	0.13
Oklahoma	1.04	0.06	0.36	0.26	0.03	0.16	0.00	0.13
Oregon	1.85	0.18	0.78	0.33	0.07	0.22	0.04	0.07
Pennsylvania	1.22	1.10	0.84	0.30	0.64	0.09	0.00	0.17
South Carolina	0.45	0.13	0.32	0.48	0.03	0.00	0.00	0.06
Tennessee	0.61	0.00	0.33	0.35	0.00	0.07	0.00	0.02
Texas	18.23	0.08	0.57	0.34	0.07	0.16	0.10	0.04
Utah-Nevada	2.90	0.14	0.68	0.50	0.05	0.05	0.27	0.05
Virginia	0.78	0.20	0.43	0.56	0.02	0.06	0.22	0.19
Washington	2.00	0.17	0.92	0.39	0.00	0.36	0.46	0.00
West Virginia	0.51	0.25	0.35	0.10	0.20	0.05	0.00	0.00
Wisconsin	1.37	0.38	1.50	0.11	0.80	0.04	0.04	0.00

NOTES: These percentages are defined for the population aged 18 to 64 in each state or group of states. Maine includes Maine, New Hampshire, and Vermont; Massachusetts includes Massachusetts and Rhode Island; Minnesota includes Minnesota, Iowa, Missouri, Kansas, Nebraska, South Dakota, and North Dakota; Maryland includes Maryland and Delaware; Montana includes Montana, Idaho, and Wyoming; Arizona includes Arizona and New Mexico.

SOURCE: 1980 Census of Population, Public Use Sample, C sample, 1/1,000 sample of the population.

APPENDIX 7–C4

REPRESENTATION OF MAJOR MINORITY-LANGUAGE GROUPS BY REGION, CANADA, 1981
(percent)

Region	Chinese	German	Greek	Italian	Netherlandic	Polish	Portuguese	Ukrainian
Newfoundland	0.1	0.0	0.0	0.0	0.0	0.0	0.0	0.0
Nova Scotia								
Halifax	0.1	0.2	0.3	0.1	0.0	0.0	0.1	0.0
Other	0.1	0.0	0.0	0.0	0.0	0.0	0.0	0.0
New Brunswick	0.2	0.1	0.0	0.0	0.0	0.0	0.0	0.0
Quebec								
Quebec City	0.1	0.1	0.0	0.1	0.0	0.0	0.0	0.0
Montreal	0.4	0.2	1.3	3.6	0.0	0.2	0.7	0.2
Other	0.0	0.1	0.0	0.1	0.0	0.0	0.0	0.0
Ontario								
Ottawa-Hull	0.7	0.3	0.1	1.3	0.1	0.2	0.4	0.1
Toronto	2.1	0.6	1.3	5.9	0.1	0.7	2.1	0.5
Hamilton	0.5	0.8	0.4	3.8	0.1	0.7	0.8	0.5
St. Catherines	0.2	0.8	0.2	3.5	0.2	0.8	0.0	0.6
Kitchener	0.5	2.8	0.3	0.4	0.2	0.3	3.0	0.2
London	0.6	0.3	0.8	1.2	0.1	0.2	1.0	0.2
Other	0.3	0.6	0.1	1.2	0.2	0.3	0.3	0.2

(Table continues)

APPENDIX 7–C4 (continued)

Region	Chinese	German	Greek	Italian	Netherlandic	Polish	Portuguese	Ukrainian
Manitoba								
Winnipeg	0.7	1.4	0.2	0.6	0.1	0.5	0.9	1.4
Other	0.2	5.0	0.0	0.1	0.1	0.1	0.1	2.1
Saskatchewan	0.4	1.1	0.1	0.1	0.1	0.0	0.0	1.0
Alberta								
Calgary	1.9	0.6	0.2	0.8	0.3	0.1	0.2	0.2
Edmonton	1.6	0.8	0.0	0.7	0.2	0.4	0.3	0.8
Other	0.3	1.3	0.0	0.1	0.2	0.1	0.0	0.7
British Columbia								
Vancouver	4.5	0.9	0.3	0.9	0.2	0.1	0.4	0.1
Other	0.5	0.8	0.1	0.4	0.2	0.0	0.2	0.1
Pr. Edward Is.	0.3	0.0	0.0	0.0	0.0	0.0	0.0	0.0

SOURCE: 1981 Census of Canada, 1/50 Public Use Sample, Individual File.

Bibliography

Abbott, Michael G., and Charles M. Beach. "Immigrant Earnings Differentials and Cohort Effects in Canada." Institute for Economic Research, Queen's University, discussion paper no. 705, 1987.

Addison, John T., and Pedro Portugal. "The Endogeneity of Union Status and the Application of the Hausman Test." *Journal of Labor Research* 10 (1989): 437–41.

Breusch, T. S., and A. R. Pagan. "A Simple Test for Heteroskedasticity and Random Coefficient Variation." *Econometrica* 47 (1979): 1287–94.

Chiswick, Barry R. "The Effect of Americanization on the Earnings of Foreign-born Men." *Journal of Political Economy* 85 (1978): 897–921.

———. "Soviet Jews in the United States: A Preliminary Analysis of their Linguistic and Economic Adjustment." *International Migration Review*, forthcoming.

———. "Speaking, Reading and Earnings among Low-skilled Immigrants." *Journal of Labor Economics* 9 (April 1989): 149–70.

Chiswick, Barry R., and Paul W. Miller. "Earnings in Canada: The Roles of Immigrant Generation, French Ethnicity and Language." *Research in Population Economics* 6 (1988): 183–224.

DeVries, John, and Frank G. Vallee. *Language Use in Canada.* Ottawa: Statistics Canada, 1980.

Fishback, Price V., and Joseph V. Terza. "Are Estimates of Sex Discrimination by Employers Robust? The Use of Never Marrieds." *Economic Inquiry* 27 (1989): 271–85.

Greenwood, Michael J., and John M. McDowell. "The Factor Market Consequences of U.S. Immigration." *Journal of Economic Literature* 24 (1986): 1738–72.

Grenier, Gilles, and François Vaillancourt. "An Economic Perspective on Learning a Second Language." *Journal of Multilingual and Multicultural Development* 4 (1983): 471–83.

Hausman, J. A. "Specification Tests in Econometrics." *Econometrica* 46 (1978): 1251–71.

Heckman, James J. "Sample Selection Bias as a Specification Error." *Econometrica* 47 (1979): 153–62.

Lee, Lung-Fei. "Generalized Econometric Models with Selectivity." *Econometrica* 51 (1983): 507–12.

McManus, Walter, William Gould, and Finis Welch. "Earnings of Hispanic Men: The Role of English-Language Proficiency." *Journal of Labor Economics* 1 (1983): 101–30.

Meng, Ronald. "The Earnings of Canadian Immigrants and Native-born Males." *Applied Economics* 19: 1107–19.

Reimers, David M., and Harold Troper. "Canadian and American Immigration Policy since 1945." Chapter 2 in this volume.

Robinson, Chris. "The Joint Determination of Union Status and Union Wage Effects: Some Tests of Alternative Models." *Journal of Political Economy* 97 (1989): 639–67.

―――――. "Language Choice: The Distribution of Language Skills and Earnings in a Dual-Language Economy." *Research in Labor Economics* 9 (1988): 53–90.

―――――. "Union Endogeneity and Self-Selection." *Journal of Labor Economics* 7 (1989): 106–12.

Vaillancourt, François. "Language and Public Policy in Canada and the United States: An Economic Perspective." Chapter 6 in this volume.

Veltman, Calvin. *Language Shift in the United States.* Berlin: Mouton Publishers, 1983.

―――――. "Modelling the Language Process of Hispanic Immigrants." *International Migration Review* 22 (1988): 545–62.

White, Halbert. "A Heteroskedasticity-consistent Covariance Matrix Estimator and a Direct Test for Heteroskedasticity." *Econometrica* 48 (1980): 817–38.

Commentary on Part Three

Linda Chavez

Chapters 6 and 7 present a great deal of information about the role of language and earnings, and François Vaillancourt's chapter is particularly instructive about the Canadian experience. Neither chapter, however, addresses an issue that I believe to be especially important in the United States: namely, the role of public policy in exerting countervailing pressures to that of the marketplace, which encourages the acquisition of English-language skills.

Officially, the United States has no language policy. Unofficially, the people of the United States have chosen English as the dominant language of the overwhelming majority of the population. More recently, some seventeen states have adopted legislation or constitutional amendments declaring English their official language. Voters in these states did not act in a vacuum but rather responded to a gradual erosion of a de facto policy that encouraged all immigrants in this country to adopt English as the language of their public discourse, whatever language they chose to speak in their homes. Accurate or not, the perception is that some groups are not adapting to English as quickly as did previous immigrant groups. I believe that government action—not necessarily the actions of the groups in question, mostly Hispanics—is responsible for this widely held perception.

More than any other public policy, bilingual education encourages retention of the native language. The federal program that began in 1968 has proliferated, and now most states also have bilingual programs to teach children who have limited proficiency in English. The original aim of such programs was to teach children in their native language for a limited period while they gradually learned English. The assumption was that children placed in such programs would have English vocabularies that were too limited to compete with their English-speaking peers in a mainstream classroom. Today the program has clearly shifted its goals and in many parts of the country has become a native-language maintenance program.

In some school districts in California, for example, tests used to place children in bilingual programs do not assess whether they are English- or Spanish-dominant; rather, they assume that a child who comes from a home where Spanish is spoken and who performs poorly on a standardized test of language skills will benefit from native-language instruction. Recently in New York a task force of the State Board of Regents recommended that native-language instruction be made available to so-called "language minority" students through the twelfth grade. Moreover, the panel recommended that graduation exams be given to immigrant children in their native language rather than in English.

The standard method of determining who should be placed in a native-language or bilingual program and who should graduate from such a program is one of percentile ranking. In New York, for example, the Regents' task force recommended that all children from Spanish-speaking homes should be placed in the program if they scored below the fortieth percentile on a standardized achievement test. The problem is that by definition 40 percent of all students score below the fortieth percentile. Since Hispanic students tend to come from low-income families, a greater proportion of them will have lower-than-average scores on standardized tests, irrespective of their language dominance.

The chapter by Chiswick and Miller suggests that the presence of children in an immigrant's home is likely to have a positive effect on the adult immigrant's acquisition of English. That certainly has been the traditional immigrant model, and indeed it occurs today in many immigrant households. But if the children of such immigrants spend their day being instructed in their native language, they will be far less helpful in their parents' acquisition of the new language.

These issues are particularly important to the Hispanic community in the United States. For most of this century, the overwhelming majority of Hispanics—especially Mexican-Americans—were U.S.-born. In 1960, 85 percent of the Mexican-American population was born in the United States. Today, however, the tremendous increase in the Latin immigrant population has transformed the Hispanic population. In 1988, only about 55 percent of the adult Mexican-origin population was born in the United States. The majority of Mexican-origin persons living in the United States today are either immigrants or the children of immigrants. The Chiswick-Miller chapter strongly suggests that the failure to learn English has negative effects on the earnings of immigrants. If Hispanic immigrants and their children are not acquiring English as quickly as previous groups of immigrants did, the consequences in terms of lost earnings will be disastrous for future generations of Hispanics.

Some Hispanic leaders have suggested that the solution is to move to a model similar to the Canadian one, in which Spanish would become a second officially recognized language in the United States. I will not comment on the wisdom of Canada's policy, but it is clearly not appropriate to the American experience. For more than two hundred years the United States has welcomed immigrants with the intention of integrating them into its society. The acquisition of a common language has been a vital element in that process. Certainly the social benefits of being able to communicate with each other in a common language are apparent. Chiswick and Miller have shown that the economic rewards are great as well.

Walter S. McManus

The chapters by Vaillancourt and by Chiswick and Miller are excellent studies of the impact of language skills on earnings. Both studies demonstrate that knowledge of the dominant language is associated with a significant earnings premium. Vaillancourt focuses on Quebec while Chiswick and Miller compare the United States to Canada as a whole. The basic agreement between the two chapters over the earnings effects of language skills gives their findings additional credibility. Chiswick and Miller's unique contributions are the findings that the United States and Canada have very similar human-capital-earnings functions and that skills in the dominant language have quite similar effects in these two countries that have followed dissimilar language policies. Vaillancourt's unique contribution is the finding that changes in language policies have large and predictable effects.

Chiswick and Miller examine the determinants of dominant-language skills and the effects of dominant-language skills on earnings in a parallel analysis for the United States and Canada. For the United States English is the obvious dominant language, but for Canada Chiswick and Miller define a person as being fluent in the dominant language if he speaks either English or French or both. Using these definitions of fluency in the dominant language, Chiswick and Miller find that both the determinants of dominant-language skills and the determinants of earnings, including the effects of dominant-language skills, are remarkably similar. This result is surprising given the differences between the United States and Canada with respect to language and language policy.

The U.S. essentially has an English-speaking economy, but Canada is composed of an English-speaking economy and a French-speaking economy in uneasy union. Officially, Canada attempts to be a bilingual and bicultural society, though exactly what that means is not clear. In addition the U.S. language policies are not explicit, whereas Canada's, and especially Quebec's, are. The similarity of the

299

Chiswick and Miller results for the United States and Canada are quite surprising. These similarities at the national level, however, may mask underlying differences between the United States and Canada. For example, suppose the returns to English fluency were in fact much higher than the returns to French fluency in Canada. Defining dominant-language fluency as Chiswick and Miller do would then result in estimated returns to dominant-language fluency somewhere between the actual returns to English and to French. This average return is what Chiswick and Miller show to be equal to U.S. returns to English. Thus Canadian returns to English skills could be very different from U.S. returns, even though measured returns to dominant-language skills are identical.

By focusing on dominant-language fluency as they define it Chiswick and Miller limit the policy application of the study. The policy implication that Chiswick and Miller emphasize is that U.S. immigration policy, being less skills-oriented than Canada's, may help to make the United States less competitive. The policy of promoting two languages in Canada, which they cannot address, is probably far more significant for economic growth and competitiveness than is immigration policy.

Chiswick and Miller's estimates of the determinants of dominant-language fluency are broadly sensible and believable. The major difference between the U.S. and Canadian equations is that the estimated impact of minority concentration is larger in Canada than it is in the United States. Chiswick and Miller suggest this difference may be due to the more refined Canadian measure: concentration is defined at the city level in Canada and at the state level in the United States. An alternative explanation could be that Canada's clear promotion of English and French as official languages makes enclaves more attractive there than in the United States, which does not promote English as vigorously as Quebec promotes French.

Chiswick and Miller focus on the language skills and earnings of immigrants. This is very sensible, as they are the ones likely to be the most sensitive to language policy. This focus means, however, that they are working with self-selected samples that suffer from the well-known selectivity bias. Thus their estimates of the impact of language on earnings and of the impact of years since immigration on language skills provide only upper limits on the true effects.

Vaillancourt begins his chapter with a very useful comparison of language policies in the United States, Canada, and Quebec. The comparison is comprehensive and brings out the areas of major differences. One distinction he draws, however, is less clear. In Canada, he claims, the federal government's role in language policy derives from its role as the arbitrator between the two language groups, while in the United States it derives from the federal government's role as the defender of individual civil rights. In recent decades, however, U.S. affirmative action and civil rights policies have tended to define and defend protected groups rather than individual persons. Thus the only remaining distinction is that in Canada only two groups are protected, while in the United States the number of protected groups is limited only by the ethnic, racial, and sexual composition of the population. Practical policy implications follow: in Canada allophone immigrants are encouraged to acquire English or French, but in the United States, because of a tendency to protect minority group rights, there is less official encouragement to acquire English.

Vaillancourt's theoretical model looks at the language market in isolation. It is thus a partial equilibrium analysis that limits the generality of the equity and efficiency implications that can be derived. For example, increasing the supply of French has resource costs that can be measured in the context of his model, but the costs of increasing French demand cannot. To consume more French, consumers must forgo consumption of English or some other good, but the simple, single-market model cannot reflect this cost.

Vaillancourt's empirical study focuses on the effects of Quebec's language policies. The magnitude of the effects of changes in language policy on earnings of various language groups strongly supports this approach, as opposed to the more aggregate approach of Chiswick and Miller. Vaillancourt's estimates of the returns to language skills indicate that demand factors dominated in Quebec. Allophones were hardest hit by the policies; even French-speaking allophones experienced a 20 percent relative earnings drop between 1971 and 1981.

In 1971, 14.6 percent of Anglophones in Quebec and 15 percent of allophones attended French schools. Because of the policy changes, in 1986 35.5 percent of Anglophones were in French or immersion schools, while 58.7 percent of allophones were in French schools. The costs of the constraints on allophone choices are not merely psychic. Presumably, if they were free to choose in 1986 they would have come closer to matching the Anglophones, as they did in 1971. Quebec could suffer productivity losses because fewer allophones were willing to migrate to Quebec, and French schools incur the excessive costs of training reluctant students.

One interesting change in the Quebec earnings structure documented by Vaillancourt is a decline in the average returns to schooling from 9 percent to 6 percent. A large body of literature tries to account for a similar phenomenon in the United States, largely focusing on demographic factors. Is the decline in the returns to schooling in Quebec an unintended consequence of language policy?

Vaillancourt's policy recommendations propose a retreat from suppression of English to more moderate promotion of French. On the whole his recommendations are sound and reasonable, especially given his empirical estimates of the impact that more extreme policies have had on the structure of earnings in Quebec. Some issues remain unresolved by his recommendations, however—most notably, the appropriate level of government that should determine language policy. Implicitly he assumes that the national is the right level, and that Canada has two "nations." But Canada's recent experience with the Meech Lake accords suggests there is not unanimous agreement that Canada has two nations. As Europe moves toward political and economic integration, should they look to Canada or to the United States as a model for their language policy?

PART FOUR

Language, Women, and Minorities

8

Gender Issues in Immigration and Language Fluency

Monica Boyd

The phrase "a nation of immigrants" often is used to describe the birth and continued vitality of U.S. life. It is an even more appropriate depiction of Canada. With a population roughly one-tenth that of the United States, Canada had until recently an immigration flow approximating one-quarter of all movement into the North American continent. Nearly one in five of the Canadian population is foreign born, compared with about one in twenty in the United States.

Both countries share a similar history of legal migration flows and immigration policies. In the decades following World War II, migrant flows to both countries shifted from European countries to third world countries, and they now include substantial family-based migration. These changes in migration composition reflect fundamental alterations in North American immigration legislation. Starting in the 1960s, both Canada and the United States revised postwar immigration policies, discarding national origin as the main criterion of admission and instead invoking social, humanitarian, and economic criteria.

Third world migration and family migration challenge existing views on immigration in at least four ways. First, family reunification contrasts with perceptions of migrants as young men, recruited on the basis of labor market skills. Second, third world migration renews concern over how host societies socially and economically incorporate newcomers who are not members of charter groups or of earlier (but now accepted) immigrant groups. Third, both family migration and third world migration influence socioeconomic heterogeneity and socioeconomic stratification within the foreign population as well as between foreign- and native-born groups. Fourth, both family migration and third world migration provide the impetus for increased attention to immigrant women. Until recently many North American and European studies focused either on the male immigrant population or on the total immigrant population, undistinguished by sex. These analyses of migrants and their families frequently had three characteristics: (1) they ignored the sizable flow of female migration, often assuming that migrants equaled males and families equaled dependent women and children; (2) they perpetuated the invisibility of migrant women by ignoring their economic activities; and (3) they implicitly generalized findings regarding adaptation from male or total populations to females.[1] The latter two features were especially common, often indicated by the generic use of "immigrants" in titles and texts of research on male immigrants or male migration flows.

Throughout the 1970s and 1980s in North America, female participation in the labor force increased alongside the development and consolidation of the women's movement. These events led to critiques regarding the invisibility of women in social science research, and they stimulated investigations into female-male differences in economic, social, and legal positions. The field of international migration was not immune to these developments, which also coincided with increased family migration and third world migration. Early calls for sex-specific data and analyses became less unusual, and during the 1980s researchers increasingly studied the situation of migrant women in North America and in Europe.[2]

The incorporation of women into migration research adds the dimension of gender to knowledge about the socioeconomic stratification of immigrant groups. North American research shows differences in nativity between foreign-born and native-born with respect to economic location and labor market rewards. A foreign birthplace is associated with socioeconomic status partly because immigrants bring with them the imprint of their former society. Differences in the countries of origin with respect to racial and ethnic composition, educational systems (type, coverage, and level), economic structure (agrarian or nonagrarian; industrial composition), urbanization, and kinship systems generate differences among immigrants with respect to race or color, educational attainment, occupational skills, knowledge of the host society's language, urban-rural experiences, and expectations regarding family size, composition, and life. At the same time, the foreign-born population is further diversified and stratified by host country characteristics, which include economic demand for certain kinds of labor and not for others; the existence or nonexistence of ethnic, racial, or birthplace-based stereotypes; and perceptions of migrants as temporary workers or as permanent residents.

Gender further stratifies the foreign-born population. Gender stratification in countries of origin often means that women are less well-educated than men or receive different employment-related training. As well, sex roles and occupational stereotypes in the receiving society can affect the type of employment obtained. The socioeconomic situation of migrant women, however, cannot be viewed only as the outcome of labor market characteristics and considerations. Gender stratification outside the labor market has important consequences. Researchers in areas of women and work observe that in general women's roles within the family shape and constrain employment. When combined with paid employment, family responsibilities can result in the double-duty or the double-day syndrome, hampering efforts to invest further in human capital such as host languages. In his 1981 remarks concerning the possible enrollment of immigrant women in language training classes provided by the secretary of state as part of citizenship instruction, Lloyd Axworthy, the minister of employment and immigration, Canada, observed that for such women "working long hours, caring for a family, and attending part-time classes often proves impossible."[3]

Yet language is a key variable affecting the socioeconomic position of all immigrants. As several chapters in this volume note, language represents social and human capital, and it shapes labor market experiences. Knowing the language of the host society enhances the ability to obtain information about the new society: information about schools, health care, social programs, housing, and employment opportunities. Knowing the language also means the ability to participate in those labor markets where the host language is essential to the completion of tasks. Conversely, not knowing the language of the host society limits the degree to which individuals can utilize their education and work experience in a broad array of jobs. The social and economic participation of such individuals is constrained to settings in which their language is the norm, such as in ethnic enclaves[4] or where it is not required for job performance (for example, cleaning occupations). In turn, the participation of individuals in language-specific labor markets both creates and maintains a defined labor supply. In particular, female immigrants, many with limited fluency in host languages—Asian and Southern Europeans in Montreal and Toronto and Puerto Ricans in New York—represent the backbone of the garment industry.[5]

The level of language skill thus is an important factor in understanding the socioeconomic situations of immigrant women as well as immigrant men. As a complement to the many investigations of language skill among foreign-born males, the research presented in this essay has two objectives: (1) to show the considerable presence of women in North American migration and (2) to examine the stratifying role played by language in the social and economic adaptation of foreign-born women, using the most recent data available. The first section shows that females are well represented in migration flows to North America. Women, however, are more likely than men to cross borders as accompanying family members or for purposes of family reunification. The flow data also show temporal shifts in the country of origin for foreign-born women, away from European countries to third world countries. Compared with other groups, women who are members of new origin groups or who are recent arrivals are less likely to know the host language.

Subsequent sections explore the social and economic correlates of language knowledge in Canada and in the United States. Although some differences exist between Canada and the United States, the general conclusions are remarkably consistent across borders. For women, not knowing a host country language is associated with low education, low labor force participation, employment in manufacturing, and low wages. In terms of employment earnings, immigrant women who do not know the host language earn less than other foreign-born women or foreign-born men, and they experience lower earnings returns to their education. The chapter concludes with a discussion of policy perspectives and programs that pertain to these empirical findings.

Women Are Immigrants Too

Migration patterns of the nineteenth century and early twentieth century underlie the demographic axiom that males predominate in long-distance moves.[6] As shown in table 8-1, males substantially outnumbered females in international migration flows to Canada and to the United States before the 1930s.[7] This imbalance, however, disappeared in later decades. Despite fluctuations in the ratio of females to males, females in fact represent an important component of migratory flows to the North American continent during most of the twentieth century.[8] Most enter Canada and the United States as adults. From 1962 to 1987 approximately three of four female and male immigrants were fifteen or older (table 8-2).

Canadian and U.S. immigration regulations and laws of the 1960s and 1970s included family ties among the criteria for immigration. Most immigrants now enter under the auspices of family reunification or under humanitarian principles. Indeed even in Canada, which has a much discussed point system used in admitting more distant relatives (assisted relatives) and economic migrants (other independent migrants), the majority of migrants do not enter under this labor market–oriented system. Of all permanent residents admitted to Canada between 1980 and 1987, only 19.9 percent were principal applicants to whom the point system applied (table 8–3, column 5). The remaining migrants in the assisted relatives and other independent migrant classes include selected groups, such as retirees, who do not have the point system applied and spouses and dependents of principal applicants, who are admitted as members of the immediate family. Migrants in the family class or refugee and designated-group class represent 60 percent of all permanent residents admitted between 1980 and 1987 (calculated from table 8–3).

Females are more likely than males to enter on the basis of family ties. In Canada 56 percent of all females and 46 percent of all males were admitted in the two categories of family class (immediate family) and assisted relatives class between 1980 and 1987 (table 8–3). In the United States females outnumbered males as immigrants in the immediate relatives class, representing spouses, children, and parents of U.S. citizens. Among the six major preference categories, family-based migration far exceeds the numbers entering on the basis of labor market criteria for both men and women (table 8–4).

Canadian and U.S. immigration laws permit permanent migrants to be accompanied by their immediate family regardless of the admission class of the principal applicant. This also is a type of family migration—and it affects females and males differently. In Canada females are more likely than males to enter as spouses of the principal applicant. They are less likely to be principal applicants[9] (table 8–3, columns 2–4). A similar situation exists in the United States, although the preference system makes the pattern less apparent.[10]

The participation of females in international migration flows and their admission on the basis of family ties mean that popular descriptions of increased third world origins characterize female immigrants as well as male immigrants. Census data show the changing birthplace origins of immigrants in Canada and in the United States by sex and period of arrival[11] (tables 8–5 through 8–8). In Canada 97 percent of the women who entered before 1951 were born in Europe or in the United States, compared with 35 percent arriving between 1981 and 1986 (table 8–5). Birthplace origins changed with each period of immigration, moving from the United States, the United Kingdom, and East Europe (including the USSR) as major source countries before 1951 to Southern European countries in the 1950s and 1960s to Asian, African, South and Central American, and Caribbean countries in the 1970s and 1980s. The upswing in migration from Asian countries was especially pronounced. Of women entering Canada between 1981 and 1986, two in five were born in Asia. This figure approximated and

TABLE 8–1
Immigration to Canada and the United States, by Sex, 1911–1987

Period[a]	Canada			United States		
	Females	Males	Sex ratio[b]	Females	Males	Sex ratio[b]
1911–15	n.a.	n.a.	n.a.	1,565,894	2,893,937	541
1916–20	n.a.	n.a.	n.a.	526,497	749,483	702
1921–25	n.a.	n.a.	n.a.	1,145,790	1,493,123	767
1926–30	n.a.	n.a.	n.a.	678,431	789,865	859
1931–35	n.a.	n.a.	n.a.	130,341	89,868	1,450
1936–40	40,720	31,586	1,289	168,940	139,282	1,213
1941–45	37,448	23,484	1,595	100,801	70,151	1,437
1946–50	217,231	213,157	1,019	516,251	347,836	1,484
1951–55	349,134	442,796	788	584,003	503,635	1,160
1956–60	376,020	406,891	924	776,055	651,786	1,191
1961–65	256,443	242,347	1,058	804,675	645,637	1,246
1966–70	447,563	463,274	966	1,029,391	844,974	1,218
1971–75	415,364	419,080	991	1,032,459	903,822	1,142
1976–79	240,433	222,319	1,081	1,070,914	955,480	1,208
1980	71,178	71,939	989	205,436[c]	192,660[c]	1,066[c]
1981	65,496	63,122	1,038	242,065[c]	224,184[c]	1,079[c]
1982	61,649	59,498	1,036	284,576	287,874	989
1983	47,652	41,505	1,148	264,975	271,966	974
1984	47,295	40,944	1,155	269,007	274,896	979

1985	44,036	40,266	1,094	283,868	286,141	992
1986	50,099	49,120	1,244	300,931	300,777	1,001
1987d	75,123	76,975	976	301,278	300,238	1,003

n.a. = not available.

a. From 1912 through 1976, data are for fiscal years ending June 30. For 1977 on, data are for fiscal years ending September 30.

b. Number of females per 1,000 males.

c. Excludes 132,543 and 130,351 persons for whom sex is not reported in the 1980 and 1981 statistics, respectively.

d. Provisional statistics as of April 1988.

SOURCES: For Canada: F. H. Leacy, ed., *Historical Statistics of Canada*, 2d ed. (Ottawa: Canada, Supply and Services, 1983. Statistics Canada Catalog no. CS11-516E) Series A369-384; Canada, Employment and Immigration, *Immigration Statistics* (Ottawa: EI, annual reports for 1976–1986. Unpublished tabulations for 1987 supplied by Employment and Immigration, April 1988.

For the United States: Houston, Marion F., Roger G. Kramer, and Joan Mackin Barrett. "Female Predominance in Immigration to the United States Since 1930: A First Look." *International Migration Review* 18 (Winter 1984): 908–963, Appendix A-1. Houston, Kramer, and Barrett (1984), appendix A-1; U.S. Department of Justice, Immigration and Naturalization Service, *1988 Statistical Yearbook of the Immigration and Naturalization Service* (Washington, D.C.: Government Printing Office), table 11. Unpublished statistics supplied to the author by INS for 1980, 1981 (December 1988).

311

TABLE 8–2
Age Distribution and Sex Ratios for Immigration to Canada and the United States, 1962–1987

Sex and Period	Canada				United States			
	Total	<15	15–64	65 plus	Total	<15	15–64	65 plus
Number[a]								
Females								
1962–71	725,878	162,971	539,775	23,132	1,882,003	410,271	1,421,452	50,280
1972–79/81[b]	792,471	177,493	575,860	39,120	1,905,423	430,406	1,398,307	76,710
1982–87	325,854	62,697	241,027	22,130	1,704,607	349,477	1,296,336	58,794
Males								
1962–71	733,960	172,993	547,352	13,615	1,538,716	422,016	1,084,687	32,013
1972–79/81[b]	776,468	188,724	561,150	26,594	1,686,774	436,731	1,199,425	50,618
1982–87	308,308	66,735	225,213	16,360	1,721,850	365,144	1,303,450	53,256
Percent								
Females								
1962–71	100.0	22.4	74.4	3.2	100.0	21.8	75.5	2.7
1972–79/81[b]	100.0	22.4	72.7	4.9	100.0	22.6	73.4	4.0
1982–87	100.0	19.2	74.0	6.8	100.0	20.5	76.1	3.4

Males								
1962–71	100.0	23.6	74.6	1.8	100.0	27.4	70.5	2.1
1972–79/81[b]	100.0	24.3	72.3	3.4	100.0	25.9	71.1	3.0
1982–87	100.0	21.7	73.0	5.3	100.0	21.2	75.7	3.1
Sex ratios (females per 1,000 males)								
1962–71	989	942	986	1,699	1,223	972	1,310	1,571
1972–79/81[b]	1,020	940	1,026	1,471	1,130	986	1,166	1,515
1982–87	1,057	939	1,070	1,353	990	957	994	1,104

a. Nonresponses to age are are omitted from the total numbers.
b. Series extends to 1981 for Canada and to 1979 for the United States. U.S. data by age and sex are not available for 1980 and 1981.

SOURCES: For Canada: Canada, Employment and Immigration, *Immigration Statistics* (Ottawa: EI, annual reports for 1962–1986). Data for 1987 are from unpublished tabulations to the author provided by Employment and Immigration, April 1988.
For the United States: Houston, Marion F., Roger G. Kramer, and Joan Mackin Barrett. "Female Predominance in Immigration to the United States Since 1930: A First Look." *International Migration Review* 18 (Winter 1984): 908–963, tables 6 and 7; U.S. Department of Justice, Immigration and Naturalization Service, *1971 Annual Report* (Washington, D.C.: Government Printing Office, 1971), table 10; *1988 Statistical Yearbook of the Immigration and Naturalization Service* (Washington, D.C.: Government Printing Office, 1988), table 11.

TABLE 8–3

PERMANENT RESIDENTS ADMITTED TO CANADA IN PRINCIPAL APPLICANT–SPOUSE–DEPENDENT STATUS,
BY SEX, 1980–1987
(percent)

| | Total Number[a] | Principal Applicant | Spouse | Dependent | Admitted under Point System[b] | |
					All immigrants	Sex specific
Total female immigrants	461,448	46.3	27.6	26.1	5.8	11.4
Family class	217,814	64.4	17.2	18.2	n.a.	n.a.
Refugee and designated	66,054	26.1	35.3	38.6	n.a.	n.a.
Assisted relatives	40,484	34.8	31.0	34.0	1.6	3.1
Retirees	9,150	37.6	48.2	14.2	n.a.	n.a.
Other independents[c]	127,946	30.1	38.6	31.3	4.3	8.3

Total male immigrants	442,433	68.3	1.8	29.9	13.1	26.6
Family class	160,337	72.1	0.9	26.8	n.a.	n.a.
Refugee and designated	92,766	67.5	0.7	31.6	n.a.	n.a.
Assisted relatives	41,202	60.3	4.0	35.7	2.8	5.6
Retirees	7,692	76.7	3.8	19.5	n.a.	n.a.
Other independents[c]	140,428	66.2	2.6	31.2	10.3	21.0
Total immigrants[d]	903,881	57.1	14.9	28.0	19.9	—

n.a. = not available.

a. Numbers vary slightly from published numbers because persons with no designated status are omitted and 1987 figures are preliminary.

b. Calculated as the number of principal applicants in the assisted relatives and other independent categories divided by total immigrants (column 5) or by total female or total male immigrants (column 6). Although included in the independent classification, retirees are not evaluated on any of the assessment unit standards.

c. This includes entrepreneurs, businessmen, investors, and all other independent categories.

d. For 1980–1986, the few cases where sex was not reported were assigned to the male category.

SOURCES: Unpublished tabulations supplied to author by Canada: Employment and Immigration Canada, Immigration Policy branch, January 30, 1987, February 6, 1987, and August 4, 1988.

315

TABLE 8–4
IMMIGRANTS TO THE UNITED STATES BY MAJOR ENTRY CATEGORIES AND BY SEX, 1972–1987

	Number[a]		Percent Admitted as Spouses[b]	
	1972–79	1980–87	1972–79	1980–87
Immediate relatives				
Females	566,329	756,080	58.4	57.7
Males	368,979	655,561	64.7	66.3
1st preference (unmarried adult sons and daughters of U.S. citizens)				
Females	6,603	28,801	88.1	82.1
Males	8,461	33,160	90.4	83.4
2nd preference (spouses and unmarried sons and daughters of permanent resident aliens)				
Females	240,177	437,686	49.9	39.4
Males	211,670	425,699	32.0	28.2
3rd preference (members of the professions or persons of exceptional ability in the arts and sciences)				
Females	64,856	82,777	31.6	49.8
Males	65,067	97,537	16.3	0.7
4th preference (married sons and daughters of U.S. citizens)				
Females	25,336	67,735	22.0	22.5
Males	26,618	69,233	23.1	22.7
5th preference (brothers and sisters of U.S. citizens)				
Females	243,489	287,645	19.8	22.7
Males	268,924	292,614	16.6	17.9
6th preference (skilled and unskilled workers in short supply)				
Females	51,288	102,281	42.2	30.7
Males	61,239	94,862	5.1	11.4

a. Numbers include persons whose status was adjusted to immigrant in any given year.
b. Totals include persons in the principal migrant category where the preference designates the spouse as the principal migrant, as in preferences 1 and 2.
SOURCES: 1971–1979: calculated from Houston, Marion F., Roger G. Kramer, and Joan Mackin Barrett. "Female Predominance in Immigration to the United States Since 1930: A First Look." *International Migration Review* 18 (Winter 1984): 908–63, figure II and table 7; 1980–1987 calculated from unpublished tabulations provided to the author by the U.S. Immigration and Naturalization Service, Statistics Branch, December 1988.

TABLE 8–5

Birthplaces of Female Foreign-born Population in Canada, Aged Fifteen and Older, 1986

Birthplace[a]	Number in Sample[b]	Percent of Total	Percent by Period of Immigration				
			<1951	1951–70	1971–75	1976–80	1981–86
United States	2,952	7.7	14.8	5.0	8.3	7.0	7.7
United Kingdom	8,352	21.9	41.6	22.1	13.7	11.4	8.6
West Europe	4,148	10.9	9.5	16.8	3.5	3.9	4.3
South Europe	6,363	16.7	4.6	27.1	14.9	7.1	3.5
East Europe, USSR	3,569	9.4	22.3	7.9	2.6	4.1	7.9
Other Europe	1,464	3.8	4.4	4.5	2.4	2.9	2.8
East Asia	2,286	6.0	0.7	3.7	10.5	11.2	14.1
Southeast Asia	2,020	5.3	0.2	1.4	7.0	17.1	17.5
South Asia	1,410	3.7	0.2	1.7	8.6	7.9	7.3
West Asia	614	1.6	0.3	1.0	1.4	3.9	4.6
North Africa	332	0.9	0.0	1.1	1.6	1.8	1.6

(Table continues)

TABLE 8–5 (continued)

Birthplace[a]	Number in Sample[b]	Percent of Total	Percent by Period of Immigration				
			<1951	1951–70	1971–75	1976–80	1981–86
Other Africa	644	1.7	0.1	0.6	4.4	2.5	2.6
South and Central America	1,364	3.6	0.3	1.8	6.5	7.3	9.7
Caribbean	2,066	5.4	0.4	3.9	12.8	10.1	5.9
Other	304	0.8	0.3	0.7	1.3	1.2	1.0
Other, residual	239	0.6	0.3	0.7	0.5	0.6	0.9
Total[b]	38,127	100.0	100.0	100.0	100.0	100.0	100.0

a. See appendix 8–A1 for specific countries included in these areas.
b. Numbers exclude foreign-born who are Canadian citizens by birth.
SOURCE: Statistics Canada, Electronic Data Dissemination Division, 1986 Census Public Use Microdata File on Individuals, June 1990.

TABLE 8-6

BIRTHPLACES OF FEMALE FOREIGN-BORN POPULATION IN THE UNITED STATES, AGED FIFTEEN AND OLDER, 1980

Birthplace[a]	Number in Sample[b]	Percent of Total	<1950	Percent by Period of Immigration 1950–69	1970–74	1975–80
Canada	4,645	7.2	12.9	7.0	1.9	2.7
United Kingdom	3,862	6.0	9.2	6.3	2.7	2.7
West Europe	7,485	11.6	16.3	15.1	2.9	3.4
South Europe	6,855	10.6	16.0	10.4	8.8	3.8
East Europe, USSR	6,216	9.6	20.5	6.4	2.6	4.8
Other Europe	3694	5.7	11.0	5.2	1.7	1.7
East Asia	4,634	7.2	1.6	6.9	11.7	13.0
Southeast Asia	3,895	6.1	0.6	3.4	10.9	16.4
South Asia	946	1.5	0.1	0.7	3.4	3.7
West Asia	1,505	2.3	1.1	1.6	2.5	5.8
North Africa	262	0.4	0.2	0.2	0.4	0.7

(Table continues)

TABLE 8–6 (continued)

Birthplace[a]	Number in Sample[b]	Percent of Total	Percent by Period of Immigration			
			<1950	1950–69	1970–74	1975–80
Other Africa	438	0.7	0.2	0.5	1.0	1.5
Mexico	8,793	13.6	6.5	13.4	21.9	18.8
Other Central America	1,821	2.8	0.6	2.8	4.7	5.0
South America	2,602	4.0	0.6	4.7	6.3	6.2
Cuba	3,180	4.9	0.6	8.9	7.0	1.7
Dominican Republic	800	1.2	0.1	1.9	1.9	1.8
Other Caribbean	2,552	4.0	1.2	4.1	7.1	5.5
Other	397	0.6	0.7	0.5	0.6	0.8
Total	64,582	100.0	100.0	100.0	100.0	100.0

a. See appendix 8–A2 for specific countries included in these areas.
b. Numbers exclude foreign-born who are born to American parents and persons born in Puerto Rico, in outlying U.S. areas or at sea.

SOURCE: Census of Population and Housing, 1980. Public Use Microdata Sample C (machine readable data file prepared by the Bureau of the Census, Washington, D.C. [producer and distributor], 1983).

TABLE 8–7: BIRTHPLACES OF MALE FOREIGN-BORN POPULATION IN CANADA, AGED FIFTEEN AND OLDER, 1986

Birthplace[a]	Number in Sample[b]	Percent of Total	Percent by Period of Immigration				
			<1951	1951–70	1971–75	1976–80	1981–86
United States	2,149	5.9	12.0	4.2	6.6	5.4	4.2
United Kingdom	7,083	19.5	34.4	20.3	14.2	11.4	7.8
West Europe	4,141	11.3	9.7	17.2	3.4	3.9	3.9
South Europe	6,981	19.2	7.3	29.4	15.3	7.5	4.8
East Europe, USSR	3,564	9.8	27.0	8.4	2.0	3.4	8.1
Other Europe	1,565	4.3	5.4	4.9	2.9	3.3	2.8
East Asia	2,166	5.9	1.6	3.4	10.3	12.4	12.9
Southeast Asia	1,697	4.7	0.1	0.8	6.5	17.2	15.7
South Asia	1,596	4.4	0.3	2.3	9.4	7.9	10.7
West Asia	753	2.1	0.2	1.2	2.3	4.6	6.7
North Africa	418	1.2	0.0	1.3	1.6	1.6	1.1
Other Africa	744	2.1	0.2	0.7	5.4	4.3	4.4
South and Central America	1,223	3.4	0.4	1.4	7.6	6.3	9.0
Caribbean	1,669	4.6	0.5	3.1	10.6	8.5	5.9
Other	288	0.8	0.4	0.6	1.2	1.4	1.0
Other, residual	276	0.8	0.5	0.8	0.7	0.9	1.0
Total	36,303	100.0	100.0	100.0	100.0	100.0	100.0

a. See appendix 8–A1 for specific countries included in these areas.
b. Numbers exclude foreign-born who are Canadian citizens by birth.
SOURCE: see table 8–5.

TABLE 8–8

BIRTHPLACES OF MALE FOREIGN-BORN POPULATION IN THE UNITED STATES, AGED FIFTEEN AND OLDER, 1980

Birthplace[a]	Number in Sample[b]	Percent of Total	Percent by Period of Immigration			
			<1950	1950–69	1970–74	1975–80
Canada	3,382	6.1	11.6	6.4	1.8	2.4
United Kingdom	2,363	4.3	6.8	4.7	1.9	2.4
West Europe	4,689	8.4	14.8	10.7	1.7	2.2
South Europe	6,739	12.1	18.2	13.7	10.0	4.2
East Europe, USSR	4,935	8.9	19.1	7.6	2.3	4.4
Other Europe	2,859	5.1	11.3	4.6	1.7	1.6
East Asia	3,397	6.1	2.6	4.8	8.8	10.4
Southeast Asia	3,479	6.3	2.5	3.6	7.4	14.1
South Asia	1,238	2.2	0.1	1.6	4.7	4.0
West Asia	2,259	4.1	1.3	2.7	4.4	9.3

	Count	%	%	%	%	%
North Africa	343	0.6	0.2	0.6	0.7	1.0
Other Africa	704	1.3	0.4	0.7	1.8	2.8
Mexico	9,874	17.8	7.8	16.6	27.2	24.3
Other Central America	1,327	2.4	0.6	2.2	3.6	3.9
South America	2,338	4.2	0.8	5.0	6.5	5.1
Cuba	2,712	4.9	0.6	9.3	5.9	1.4
Dominican Republic	628	1.1	0.1	1.3	1.9	1.4
Other Caribbean	2,029	3.6	1.3	3.5	6.9	4.2
Other	299	0.5	0.3	0.4	0.7	0.9
Total	55,594	100.0	100.0	100.0	100.0	100.0

a. See appendix 8–A2 for specific countries included in these areas.
b. Numbers exclude foreign-born who are born to American parents and persons born in Puerto Rico, in outlying U.S. areas or at sea.

SOURCE: Census of Population and Housing, 1980, Public Use Microdata Sample C (machine readable data file prepared by the Bureau of the Census, Washington, D.C. [producer and distributor], 1983).

replaced the two of five born in the United Kingdom for women migrating before 1951.

Similar trends exist for the United States although its common land border with Mexico makes the pre-1950 immigration cohort slightly less European or Canadian in birthplace origins (87 percent). The Mexican border coupled with American historical and political ties to the Caribbean underlies the higher proportion of women from Mexico, Latin America, and the Caribbean in the 1950s and thereafter (table 8–6, columns 4–6). Forty-nine percent of women immigrating to the United States from 1970 to 1974 were from these regions as were 40 percent of women entering between 1975 and 1980.

Asia also became an important source for male and female immigrants to the United States during the 1970s (tables 8–5 through 8–8). The percentage of foreign-born women from Asian countries (including West Asia) rose from nearly 13 percent for the 1951–1970 cohort to 28 percent and 39 percent of women entering in 1970–1974 and 1975–1980, respectively. Remarkably, the percentages of the Asian-born among women entering the United States in the 1970s are virtually identical to the percentages entering Canada during that period[12] (table 8–5 through 8–8, columns 5–6). This similarity between the two countries, however, is offset by differences in the mix of European versus Western Hemisphere immigrants. Compared with Canada, lower percentages of women entering the United States in the 1970s were born in Europe, and higher percentages were from Western Hemisphere countries (excluding Canada).

New Immigrants and Language Skill

Changing origin composition of recent immigrants means changing language composition. Many of the recent or new immigrants are from countries or regions where the main language is not the charter language of Canada (English and French) and the United States (English). Tables 8–9 and 8–10 show language fluency and knowledge for foreign-born men and women by origin and period of arrival. In Canada, the measure is derived from the 1986 census question on knowledge of official languages. This question asked if the respondent and each member of the household knew English or French well enough to carry on a conversation.[13] In the 1980 U.S. census, one question asked if English was the language spoken at home. If the home language was not English, a second question probed the ability to speak English, with precoded responses ranging from very well, well, not well, to not at all. In this chapter, both questions are combined into one variable with five categories (speaks English at home;

TABLE 8–9

FOREIGN-BORN POPULATION IN CANADA, AGED FIFTEEN AND OLDER,
WITHOUT CONVERSATIONAL ABILITY IN ENGLISH OR FRENCH, BY SEX,
BIRTHPLACE, AND PERIOD OF IMMIGRATION, 1986
(percent)

	Female	Male	Female-Male Ratio
Birthplace			
United States	0.1[a]	0.1[a]	n.c.
United Kingdom	0.1[a]	0.1[a]	n.c.
West Europe	1.2[a]	0.2[a]	n.c.
South Europe	18.5	8.7	2.1
East Europe, USSR	5.4	2.2[a]	2.5
Other Europe	2.3[a]	1.2[a]	n.c.
East Asia	29.4	15.7	1.9
Southeast Asia	12.4	6.4	1.9
South Asia	11.5	4.1[a]	2.8
West Asia	9.0[a]	3.6[a]	n.c.
North Africa	3.6[a]	0.5	n.c.
Other Africa	3.2[a]	0.5	n.c.
South and Central America	6.7	4.7[a]	1.4
Caribbean	0.6[a]	0.5[a]	n.c.
Other	3.3[a]	1.0[a]	n.c.
Other residual	3.8[a]	0.3[a]	n.c.
Period of immigration			
<1951	1.6[a]	0.9[a]	n.c.
1951–60	4.7	2.0	2.3
1961–65	8.6	3.6	2.4
1966–70	7.2	2.9	2.5
1970–75	7.4	3.8	1.9
1976–80	11.0	5.8	1.9
1981–86	17.6	11.7	1.5
% of total population	7.2	3.7	1.9

n.c. = not calculated when the percentage of one group was 1.0 percent or less.
a. Estimates are based on small numbers and should be treated with caution. See the guidelines appearing in the 1990 codebook for the 1986 Canadian census for the Public Use Sample Tape of individuals.
SOURCE: Statistics Canada. Electronic Data Dissemination Division. 1986 Census Public Use Microdata File on Individuals, June 1990.

TABLE 8–10

FOREIGN-BORN POPULATION IN THE UNITED STATES, AGED FIF-
TEEN AND OLDER, WITH POOR OR NO ABILITY TO SPEAK ENGLISH,
BY SEX, BIRTHPLACE, AND PERIOD OF IMMIGRATION, 1980
(percent)

	Female		Male		Female–Male Ratio	
	Not very well	Not at all	Not very well	Not at all	Not very well	Not at all
Birthplace						
Canada	1.9	0.2	1.4	0.1	1.4	n.c.
United States	0.1	—	0.2	—	n.c.	n.c.
West Europe	2.4	0.3	1.9	0.2	1.3	n.c.
South Europe	20.9	7.1	16.0	4.0	1.3	1.8
East Europe, USSR	13.3	2.9	10.2	2.0	1.3	1.5
Other Europe	5.3	2.0	5.9	1.2	0.9	1.7
East Asia	23.0	9.6	22.2	4.9	1.0	2.0
Southeast Asia	14.3	5.2	16.7	3.2	0.9	1.6
South Asia	6.8	3.0	2.7	0.5	2.5	n.c.
West Asia	17.1	6.2	9.7	1.5	1.8	4.1
North Africa	14.9	3.8	3.8	—	3.9	n.c.
Other Africa	5.3	0.9	3.0	0.3	1.8	n.c.
Mexico	28.8	40.8	31.6	20.2	0.9	2.0
Other Central America	23.2	12.7	22.8	8.7	1.0	1.5
South America	19.0	8.6	15.1	3.8	1.3	2.3
Cuba	22.7	23.1	21.2	15.2	1.1	1.5
Dominican Republic	32.6	28.9	28.0	18.2	1.2	1.6
Other Caribbean	4.7	2.1	4.1	0.9	1.1	n.c.
Puerto Rico	22.4	11.6	17.9	4.3	1.9	4.2
Other territories	6.4	3.1	3.3	0.6	1.9	n.c.
Other	2.3	1.3	3.0	0.7	0.8	n.c.
Born at sea	7.8	5.7	9.6	5.1	0.8	1.11
Total	14.5	8.5	14.5	6.0	1.0	1.4

TABLE 8–10 (continued)

	Female		Male		Female–Male Ratio	
	Not very well	Not at all	Not very well	Not at all	Not very well	Not at all
Period of immigration						
<1950	7.9	2.1	6.5	1.2	1.2	1.8
1950–59	9.3	3.3	8.8	2.1	1.1	1.6
1960–64	12.9	5.4	11.3	3.7	1.1	1.5
1965–69	15.8	10.4	15.6	5.9	1.0	1.8
1970–74	19.0	13.6	19.3	8.3	1.0	1.6
1975–80	23.1	19.1	24.1	14.4	1.0	1.4
Total	14.0	8.4	14.4	6.2	1.0	1.4

n.c. = not calculated if the numerator or denominator was 1.0 percent or less.
— = no cases in that cell.
NOTE: Verbal ability is based on a constructed variable comparing persons who indicate English is the language spoken at home with persons whose home language is not English.
Birthplace excludes persons born abroad to American parents.
Excludes persons in Puerto Rico and other U.S. territories for whom period of immigration is not collected and excludes foreign-born who are born to American parents.
SOURCE: Census of Population and Housing, 1980. Public Use Microdata Sample C (machine readable data file prepared by the Bureau of the Census, Washington D.C. [producer and distributor], 1983).

English is not the home language, but speaks English very well; well; not well; and not at all).

In Canada, third world origin groups and recent arrivals have higher percentages of their populations who cannot converse in English or French than do immigrants born in the United Kingdom, Western Europe, or the United States (table 8–9). Southern European migrants (born in Greece, Italy, Portugal, and Yugoslavia) have relatively high percentages who do not know Canada's charter languages. Women also are more likely than men not to be able to converse in English or French. The percentage of immigrant women who lack official language fluency is approximately twice that of men. This finding characterizes both the foreign-born population as a whole and those immigrants born in Southern Europe, East Asia, Southeast Asia, and South Asia. Between one in ten and three in ten women from these areas do not know English or French well enough to carry on a conversation. Although many of these women are recent arrivals (see table 8–5), the data for women from Southern Europe indicate that the inability to converse in the official language persists for some groups long after entering Canada.

Similar conclusions exist for language fluency in the United States (table 8–10). The percentages who speak English not very well or not at all are higher for women than for men, although the magnitude of the gender gap differs by region of birth, year of arrival, and degree of language fluency. Percentages also are highest for the recent immigrants to the United States and for third world immigrants compared with persons born in Canada, the United Kingdom, or Western Europe. Percentages who speak English not very well or not at all are high for persons born in most Latin American, South American, and Caribbean countries: ranging from two of ten (for South American–born men) to seven of ten (for women born in Mexico).

Social Correlates of Not Knowing the Language

Knowing or not knowing the language of the receiving society affects social and economic integration of immigrants in their adopted country. The impact of language knowledge for foreign-born women can be gauged by asking two related questions. First, what are the sociodemographic characteristics of those foreign-born women who lack fluency in the host society language compared with those who do? Second, what are the economic consequences of not knowing the host language? North American research that documents considerable socioeconomic inequality by sex prompt a third question. How do the socioeconomic characteristics of foreign-born women who do not know the host country language compare with the characteristics of foreign-born males?[14]

Answers to these questions are based on analyses of the foreign-born population aged fifteen to sixty-four. The age group of sixty-five and older is excluded for two reasons. First, since many persons older than sixty-five are in their retirement years and may have lived in the receiving country for some time, the correlates and consequences of not knowing the host language are less easily determined. Second, although the migration of elderly persons is growing, these recent immigrants have quite distinctive language skills, incomes, and living arrangements compared with their younger counterparts and with other elderly foreign-born groups.[15] A separate analysis of their situation is advised.

The association between language fluency, birthplace, and period of immigration is documented in earlier tables. Table 8–11 extends the findings for the age group fifteen to sixty-four. Foreign-born women who cannot converse in English or French in Canada are primarily from Southern Europe, East Asia, Southeast Asia, and Southern Asia. Nearly three-fourths immigrated to Canada between 1971 and 1986. Their region of residence is not very different from the residential patterns of foreign-born women who can converse in English or French, but women with no conversational fluency are more likely to live in central metropolitan areas (CMAs), especially Toronto. This residential concentration in Canada's megacities is not surprising. Perceived economic opportunities and the existence of ethnic communities and kin in Montreal, Toronto, and Vancouver, make these areas the final destination for most of Canada's recent immigrants.

Compared with foreign-born women who can converse in English or French, immigrant women who cannot are older and more likely to be married. They also have a higher percentage of their population who are widowed and a higher percentage who live in households without children.[16] Such characteristics are consistent with the older age distribution of these women who cannot converse in English or French.

Educational attainment differs between the two groups of foreign-born women. As shown in table 8–11, nearly 75 percent of those women who cannot converse in English or French have less than a ninth-grade education compared with less than 20 percent for foreign-born women with a conversational fluency. Not knowing a host language of Canada is strongly linked to low educational attainment and functional illiteracy.[17] This association has two interconnected implications for any attempts to increase language skills. First, many strategies of learning languages either assume or are enhanced by literacy. Thus a population with poor language fluency and a low literacy rate will not necessarily learn a host language quickly. Relatively high percentages of women born in Southern Europe do not know English or French although many of these women immigrated to North America in the 1950s and 1960s (tables 8–9 and 8–10). These women also have low levels of education.[18] A second implication, then, of the education-language association is that recent arrivals to Canada or to the United States may not readily acquire English or French on their own if they are poorly educated.[19]

The sociodemographic correlates of language fluency that exist for Canada also characterize foreign-born women in the United States (table 8–12). Compared with women whose language at home is English or who speak English very well or well, foreign-born women who do not speak English very well or at all are more likely to have immigrated during the 1970s, to have been born in third world re-

TABLE 8–11
DEMOGRAPHIC AND SOCIAL CHARACTERISTICS OF FOREIGN-BORN IN CANADA, AGED FIFTEEN TO SIXTY-FOUR, BY SEX, 1986
(percent with conversational ability)

Characteristic	Female			Male		
	Total	Yes	No	Total	Yes	No
Percent	100.0	94.4	5.6	100.0	97.1	2.9
Birthplace	100.0	100.0	100.0	100.0	100.0	100.0
United States	7.2	7.6	0.1	5.5	5.7	—
United Kingdom	19.0	20.1	0.1	17.5	18.0	0.1
West Europe	11.1	11.8	0.3	11.7	12.0	0.5
South Europe	18.1	16.6	44.1	20.5	19.8	44.3
East Europe, USSR	7.2	7.4	3.6	7.4	7.5	3.8
Other Europe	3.7	3.9	0.8	4.0	4.1	1.0
East Asia	6.3	5.2	23.7	6.3	5.8	25.6
Southeast Asia	6.2	5.8	12.1	5.3	5.2	10.7
South Asia	4.3	4.1	6.6	4.9	4.9	4.7
West Asia	1.8	1.8	2.0	2.3	2.3	1.9
North Africa	0.9	1.0	0.4	1.3	1.3	0.1
Other Africa	2.0	2.1	0.8	2.4	2.4	0.5
South and Central America	4.3	4.3	4.4	3.9	3.8	5.7
Caribbean	6.3	6.6	0.2	5.3	5.5	0.7

Other	0.9	1.0	0.5	0.9	0.9	0.1
Other, residual[a]	0.7	0.7	0.3	0.8	0.8	0.3
Period of immigration						
<1951	100.0	100.0	100.0	100.0	100.0	100.0
	8.9	9.3	0.7	7.9	8.1	1.0
1951–60	23.7	24.4	10.4	26.0	26.5	9.5
1961–65	9.6	9.6	10.2	9.1	9.1	7.7
1966–70	17.2	17.3	15.1	18.0	18.1	13.0
1971–75	16.9	17.0	15.6	16.7	16.8	15.8
1976–80	12.4	12.1	17.6	11.9	11.7	17.3
1981–86	11.3	10.2	30.4	10.4	9.7	35.7
Region of residence						
Maritimes	100.0	100.0	100.0	100.0	100.0	100.0
	2.1	2.2	0.3	2.0	2.0	0.2
Quebec	13.4	13.3	15.2	14.1	14.1	13.0
Ontario	54.9	54.8	56.4	54.0	53.9	59.1
Prairies	13.9	13.9	12.5	14.2	14.3	11.3
British Columbia	15.7	15.7	15.7	15.6	15.6	16.3
Yukon, Northwest Territories	0.1	0.2	0.0	0.1	0.1	0.1
Place of residence						
Montreal	100.0	100.0	100.0	100.0	100.0	100.0
	12.0	11.8	14.5	12.3	12.3	12.0
Toronto	33.3	32.6	44.4	33.1	32.7	46.4
Vancouver	10.0	9.8	12.6	10.1	10.0	13.8
Other major CMAs[a]	20.8	21.1	18.4	21.2	21.3	17.9
Other area[a]	23.9	24.7	10.1	23.3	23.7	9.9

(Table continues)

331

TABLE 8–11 (continued)

Characteristic	Female			Male		
	Total	Yes	No	Total	Yes	No
Age	100.0	100.0	100.0	100.0	100.0	100.0
15–24	13.4	13.8	6.2	13.9	14.0	7.7
25–34	20.7	21.2	12.9	18.9	19.0	15.8
35–44	26.3	26.7	18.9	27.0	27.3	17.1
45–54	19.8	19.5	25.4	21.4	21.3	25.1
55–64	19.8	18.8	36.6	18.8	18.4	34.3
Marital status	100.0	100.0	100.0	100.0	100.0	100.0
Never married	16.9	17.6	5.0	21.3	21.6	13.2
Currently married	71.4	70.9	80.0	72.7	72.4	83.1
Separated, divorced	7.5	7.8	2.6	5.2	5.2	2.3
Widowed	4.2	3.7	12.4	0.8	0.8	1.4
Presence of children in household						
At least 1 (younger than age 2)	4.8	4.9	4.2	n.a.	n.a.	n.a.
Some (age 2–5)	4.4	4.5	3.0	n.a.	n.a.	n.a.
At least 1 (younger than age 6, some age 6+)	8.2	8.3	7.3	n.a.	n.a.	n.a.
Some (age 6–14)	19.4	19.3	20.0	n.a.	n.a.	n.a.
No children (younger than age 15)	21.0	20.3	33.3	n.a.	n.a.	n.a.
No children present	42.2	42.7	32.2	n.a.	n.a.	n.a.

Education					
	100.0	100.0	100.0	100.0	100.0	100.0
<grade 5	5.8	3.8	40.0	3.8	3.0	29.6
Grades 5–8	14.2	13.0	34.4	11.8	11.1	35.7
High school	36.8	37.8	20.0	32.2	32.4	24.5
Post–high school	43.2	45.4	5.6	52.2	53.5	10.2
Mean years of education	11.6	11.9	6.2	12.5	12.7	7.1
Total in PUST sample	30,744	29,036	1,708	30,465	29,593	872

n.a. = not available.

NOTE: Data on presence of children in households are not provided for males.

a. "Other CMA" consists of Hamilton, Kitchener and St. Catherines–Niagara, Winnipeg, Regina, Saskatoon, Calgary, and Edmonton. "Other area" consists of all areas other than Montreal, Toronto, Vancouver, and other CMA.

SOURCE: Statistics Canada. Electronic Data Dissemination Division. 1986 Census Public Use Microdata File on Individuals, June 1990.

TABLE 8–12

FLUENCY IN ENGLISH AND DEMOGRAPHIC AND SOCIAL CHARACTERISTICS OF FOREIGN-BORN FEMALES IN THE UNITED STATES, AGED FIFTEEN TO SIXTY-FOUR, 1980

(percent)

		English Proficiency				
	Total	English at home	Speaks very well	Speaks well	Not very well	Not at all
Birthplace						
Total	100.0	100.0	100.0	100.0	100.0	100.0
Canada	5.4	16.5	2.6	1.1	0.5	0.1
United Kingdom	4.8	17.3	0.6	0.1	0.1	—
West Europe	9.0	12.6	15.1	5.8	0.8	0.0
South Europe	7.4	2.7	8.5	10.3	10.0	6.5
East Europe, USSR	4.8	3.8	5.7	6.6	4.1	1.5
Other Europe	3.3	5.8	3.9	2.2	0.8	0.5
East Asia	7.5	3.5	6.9	11.7	10.8	5.6
Southeast Asia	6.5	2.0	9.8	9.4	5.8	3.4
South Asia	1.6	0.6	3.2	2.0	0.7	0.5
West Asia	2.2	0.7	2.9	3.5	2.6	1.2
North Africa	0.4	0.2	0.7	0.5	0.4	0.2
Other Africa	0.7	1.0	1.0	0.6	0.2	0.1

Mexico	13.9	1.3	9.8	13.7	26.6	44.9
Other Central America	3.0	1.3	3.1	3.3	4.6	4.2
South America	4.3	2.2	4.6	6.1	5.4	3.6
Cuba	4.7	0.4	5.7	5.3	7.0	8.9
Dominican Republic	1.4	0.1	0.9	1.2	2.9	4.4
Other Caribbean	4.1	11.4	1.5	1.7	1.3	0.8
Puerto Rico	7.9	1.5	9.3	10.6	11.7	9.5
Other territories	0.6	1.2	0.5	0.3	0.2	0.0
Other area	0.6	1.5	0.6	0.3	0.1	0.1
Born at sea	5.9	12.4	3.2	3.7	3.4	4.1
Period of immigration						
Total	100.0	100.0	100.0	100.0	100.0	100.0
<1950	12.1	24.2	11.1	6.9	3.6	2.3
1950–59	17.6	24.7	20.2	16.1	8.7	4.5
1960–64	12.9	14.3	15.7	12.1	10.4	5.6
1965–69	16.4	13.8	18.5	16.9	17.3	15.3
1970–74	18.1	10.4	18.3	21.4	23.3	25.4
1975–80	22.9	12.6	16.2	26.6	36.7	46.9
Region of residence						
Total	100.0	100.0	100.0	100.0	100.0	100.0
New England	6.4	7.4	6.4	6.0	5.9	4.6
Middle Atlantic	28.3	28.0	28.6	29.3	29.3	23.9
East North Central	11.5	12.6	12.3	12.2	9.5	7.1
West North Central	2.0	3.3	2.0	1.7	1.0	0.4

(Table continues)

TABLE 8–12 (continued)

	Total	English at home	Speaks very well	Speaks well	Not very well	Not at all
			English Proficiency			
South Atlantic	12.1	14.3	12.8	11.6	9.4	9.5
East South Central	1.2	2.4	1.2	0.8	0.4	0.2
West South Central	7.2	5.7	6.6	6.9	7.6	13.4
Mountain	3.3	4.3	3.2	2.9	2.5	3.3
Pacific	28.0	22.0	26.9	28.6	34.4	37.6
Place of residence						
Total	100.0	100.0	100.0	100.0	100.0	100.0
6 major cities[a]	50.4	37.8	49.9	53.4	62.8	61.8
Other urban areas	24.2	28.4	25.4	24.3	19.6	14.3
Nonurban	25.4	33.8	24.7	22.3	17.6	23.9
Age						
Total	100.0	100.0	100.0	100.0	100.0	100.0
15–24	19.3	17.6	23.1	19.1	15.9	18.1
25–34	26.6	21.7	30.0	28.2	27.6	24.5
35–44	22.0	20.9	22.2	23.2	22.4	20.5
45–54	17.7	19.4	14.6	17.5	20.3	19.5
55–64	14.4	20.4	10.1	12.0	13.8	17.4

Marital status						
Total	100.0	100.0	100.0	100.0	100.0	100.0
Never married	19.7	20.0	24.0	18.2	15.2	15.2
Currently married	65.2	62.6	63.8	67.9	68.0	67.0
Separated, divorced	10.4	11.9	9.1	9.5	11.0	10.7
Widowed	4.7	5.5	3.1	4.2	5.8	7.1
Presence of own children						
Total	100.0	100.0	100.0	100.0	100.0	100.0
Younger than age 6	14.3	9.7	14.9	15.3	16.4	18.9
6–17	35.6	36.8	37.1	35.7	33.9	30.8
<6 and 16–17	13.9	9.1	13.1	14.6	17.7	20.9
No children of own	36.2	44.4	34.9	34.4	32.0	29.4
Education						
Total	100.0	100.0	100.0	100.0	100.0	100.0
<grade 4	7.9	1.3	2.1	5.9	17.4	35.6
5–8	17.5	7.9	8.7	20.3	34.4	40.7
9–12	44.3	55.0	45.1	45.5	36.3	19.6
Post–high school	30.3	35.8	44.1	28.3	11.9	4.1
Mean years of education	10.8	12.1	12.4	10.7	8.2	5.9
Total	56,499	14,893	16,450	11,778	8,542	4,836
Percent	100.0	26.4	29.1	20.8	15.1	8.6

NOTE: Excludes persons born abroad to American parents.

a. These are Boston, Chicago, Los Angeles, Miami, New York, and San Francisco.

SOURCE: Census of Population and Housing, 1980. Public Use Microdata Sample C (machine readable data file prepared by the Bureau of the Census, Washington, D.C. [producer and distributor], 1983).

gions, to live in one of the six largest cities in the United States, and to concentrate in the middle Atlantic, the west south central, and the Pacific regions. Contained in these geographic distributions are birth-place-specific concentrations. Women born in Asia and in Latin America (including Mexico) concentrate in the Pacific region. Table 8–12 and unpublished 1986 Public Use Sample tabulations for urban areas reveal that women born in Puerto Rico or the Dominican Republic reside in the middle Atlantic areas, gravitating especially to New York City, while Cuban women tend to reside in Florida (Miami). These geographical concentrations of specific birthplace groups also are found in other recent studies.[20]

As in Canada, foreign-born women who live in the United States and who have low or nonexistent English language fluency are older and more likely to be married or widowed. They also are substantially less educated than other foreign-born women with some English language fluency. These women who lack fluency in English, however, are less likely to be single and more likely to be separated or divorced than their Canadian counterparts. They also are more likely to have children present compared with foreign-born women with language skills. To a considerable degree, these sociodemographic characteristics reflect the profiles of the large Hispanic foreign-born female population in the United States.[21]

In general, the social correlates of language knowledge for foreign-born women in Canada and in the United States also describe foreign-born men (tables 8–11, 8–12, and 8–13). In Canada, however, the association between not knowing the host language and a low education is considerably greater for women than for men (table 8–11). Furthermore, gender differentials in both Canada and the United States increase markedly when economic correlates of language knowledge are considered.

Language Skill and Characteristics of the Labor Force

Quite apart from its social correlates, knowing or not knowing the language of the host society influences labor market participation and economic integration of immigrants in North America. As shown in tables 8–14 through 8–16, lower rates of labor force participation characterize foreign-born men and women who lack fluency in the dominant languages of Canada and the United States. In both countries this lower participation rate holds across all educational levels. In addition, no knowledge or limited knowledge (for example, not very well) affects the relation between education and labor force participation rates. Higher rates of labor force participation for the better-

TABLE 8–13

FLUENCY IN ENGLISH AND DEMOGRAPHIC AND SOCIAL CHARACTERISTICS OF FOREIGN-BORN MALES IN THE UNITED STATES, AGED FIFTEEN TO SIXTY-FOUR, 1980

			English Proficiency			
	Total	English at home	Speaks very well	Speaks well	Not very well	Not at all
Birthplace						
Canada	4.7	15.8	2.2	0.9	0.3	0.0
United Kingdom	3.2	12.6	0.6	0.2	0.0	—
West Europe	6.1	11.5	8.7	2.8	0.5	0.2
South Europe	8.9	4.4	10.2	12.0	9.6	6.3
East Europe, USSR	4.8	4.7	5.2	6.2	3.4	1.5
Other Europe	3.1	5.8	3.2	2.1	1.1	0.2
East Asia	6.0	2.3	5.9	9.1	8.2	3.6
Southeast Asia	6.0	1.9	8.0	8.4	6.4	2.7
South Asia	2.4	1.2	5.2	1.8	0.4	0.1
West Asia	4.0	1.9	5.9	5.9	2.3	0.5
North Africa	0.6	0.4	1.1	0.7	0.2	—
Other Africa	1.3	1.7	2.1	0.9	0.2	0.1
Mexico	17.8	1.8	11.6	18.9	37.2	57.9
Other Central America	2.5	1.3	2.6	2.5	3.8	3.4
South America	4.4	2.7	5.2	5.5	4.4	2.2

(Table continues)

TABLE 8–13 (continued)

	Total	English at home	Speaks very well	Speaks Well	Not very well	Not at all
			English Proficiency			
Cuba	4.7	0.7	6.2	4.8	6.1	8.3
Dominican Republic	1.2	0.1	0.9	1.4	2.2	3.2
Other Caribbean	3.7	11.0	1.6	1.5	1.0	0.4
Puerto Rico	7.3	1.9	9.5	10.1	8.3	4.2
Other territories	0.6	1.2	0.6	0.4	0.1	0.1
Other area	0.5	1.2	0.5	0.4	0.1	0.1
Born at sea	6.2	13.9	3.3	3.5	4.2	5.1
Period of immigration						
Total	100.0	100.0	100.0	100.0	100.0	100.0
<1950	10.5	22.8	9.3	6.0	3.3	1.5
1950–59	16.0	24.3	18.3	13.5	7.2	3.7
1960–64	11.9	13.3	15.1	10.6	7.8	5.7
1965–69	15.8	13.8	18.2	16.4	15.5	11.1
1970–74	19.0	11.5	19.2	22.8	23.8	21.7
1975–80	26.8	14.3	19.9	30.7	42.4	56.3
Region of residence						
Total	100.0	100.0	100.0	100.0	100.0	100.0
New England	6.2	7.7	6.7	5.7	4.8	4.0

Middle Atlantic	26.6	27.4	27.9	28.4	24.5	15.4
East North Central	12.2	13.9	13.1	13.0	10.5	6.7
West North Central	2.0	3.2	1.9	1.7	1.4	0.3
South Atlantic	11.5	13.6	13.0	10.0	8.2	9.7
East South Central	1.1	2.1	1.0	0.8	0.3	0.1
West South Central	7.6	5.3	6.3	7.6	10.6	15.2
Mountain	3.3	4.2	2.9	2.9	2.9	3.5
Pacific	29.5	23.2	27.2	29.9	36.8	45.1
Place of residence						
Total	100.0	100.0	100.0	100.0	100.0	100.0
6 major cities[a]	50.8	39.3	51.2	55.0	59.4	55.6
Other urban areas	24.5	29.0	26.1	23.4	19.5	15.8
Nonurban	24.7	31.7	22.7	21.6	21.1	28.6
Age						
Total	100.0	100.0	100.0	100.0	100.0	100.0
15–24	23.0	21.3	25.0	22.0	21.7	28.1
25–34	27.6	24.5	29.8	28.5	27.2	26.3
35–44	20.6	19.0	21.9	21.5	20.8	16.6
45–54	15.7	16.3	13.8	16.4	17.5	15.4
55–64	13.1	18.9	9.5	11.6	12.8	13.6

(Table continues)

341

TABLE 8–13 (continued)

	Total	English at home	English Proficiency			
			Speaks very well	Speaks well	Not very well	Not at all
Marital status						
Total	100.0	100.0	100.0	100.0	100.0	100.0
Never married	28.6	27.5	31.3	27.3	25.7	31.5
Currently married	64.3	63.0	61.8	66.5	68.2	63.1
Separated, divorced	6.4	8.5	6.3	5.6	5.3	4.7
Widowed	0.7	1.0	0.6	0.6	0.8	0.7
Presence of own children						
Total	100.0	100.0	100.0	100.0	100.0	100.0
Younger than age 6	15.6	11.9	15.9	17.2	17.1	18.5
6–17	34.2	35.4	35.8	34.6	31.1	27.6
<6 and 16–17	14.1	9.5	14.0	15.3	17.7	18.0
No children of own	36.0	43.2	34.3	32.9	34.1	35.9
Education						
Total	100.0	100.0	100.0	100.0	100.0	100.0
<grade 4	7.8	1.6	2.2	6.1	19.5	36.1
5–8	17.1	7.9	8.4	20.0	35.4	38.9
9–12	37.4	43.5	35.6	41.4	31.8	19.7
Post–high school	37.7	47.0	53.8	32.5	13.3	5.3

Mean years of education	11.2	12.8	13.1	10.9	8.0	5.9
Total	51,229	12,319	15,543	12,313	7,849	3,205
Percent	100.0	24.1	30.3	24.0	15.3	6.3

NOTE: Excludes persons born abroad to American parents.

a. These are Boston, Chicago, Los Angeles, Miami, New York, and San Francisco.

SOURCE: Census of Population and Housing, 1980. Public Use Microdata Sample C (machine readable data file prepared by the Bureau of the Census, Washington, D.C. [producer and distributor], 1983).

343

TABLE 8–14

ECONOMIC CHARACTERISTICS OF FOREIGN-BORN IN CANADA, AGED FIFTEEN TO SIXTY-FOUR, BY SEX, 1986

(percent conversant in English or French)

Characteristic	Female			Male		
	Total	Yes	No	Total	Yes	No
Labor force participation rate	65.5	66.7	45.8	88.2	88.5	77.7
Education						
<grade 5	46.8	49.9	41.7	80.5	80.9	79.1
Grades 5–8	49.7	49.9	48.2	84.2	84.8	78.1
High school	61.7	62.1	49.7	83.0	83.1	74.8
Post–high school	76.5	76.7	45.8	92.7	93.0	79.8
Unemployment rate	9.3	9.1	13.7	7.6	7.5	11.4
Occupation						
Manager	7.3	7.5	1.7	13.5	13.8	2.4
Upper white-collar	18.5	19.2	2.1	15.7	16.0	0.9
Clerical	28.1	29.1	3.5	5.9	6.0	2.0
Sales	8.8	9.1	2.3	7.3	7.4	3.2
Service	17.7	17.2	31.0	11.7	11.4	26.7
Primary	2.4	2.3	5.3	3.4	3.3	5.3
Processing	2.4	2.2	6.8	4.6	4.5	8.1
Machinery production	10.8	9.6	39.6	17.9	17.9	19.6
Construction, transportation	0.6	0.6	0.6	14.0	13.8	22.2
Other	3.4	3.2	7.1	6.0	5.9	9.6

Industry						
Extractive	3.2	3.1	6.0	4.4	4.4	4.0
Manufacturing	19.0	17.7	51.0	26.4	26.3	31.0
Other goods	7.6	7.8	3.7	23.5	23.3	28.5
Retail	13.3	13.6	5.9	9.8	9.8	8.9
Finance, business	12.9	13.2	3.5	9.2	9.5	2.5
Social service	21.7	22.4	4.2	9.0	9.1	2.9
Public administration	4.3	4.5	0.2	5.0	5.1	0.9
Other service	18.0	17.7	25.5	12.7	12.5	21.3
1985 work status						
Full time	72.0	71.6	83.4	91.4	97.5	98.1
Part time	28.0	28.4	16.6	8.6	2.5	1.9
Hours worked in 1986 reference week	35.4	35.3	38.4	43.0	43.1	42.1
Weeks worked in 1985	40.6	40.7	39.9	43.6	43.7	41.9
Weekly wage, 1985[a]						
Average	355	357	284	606	610	425
Full time	397	402	287	630	635	430
Part time	245	245	271	338	338	338
Annual wage[a]	14,106	14,247	10,246	25,882	26,094	16,840

a. These include only individuals who arrived in Canada by 1983 and who are wage and salary earners. See text note 25.
SOURCE: Statistics Canada. Electronic Data Dissemination Division. 1986 Census Public Use Microdata File on Individuals, June 1990.

TABLE 8–15: Economic Characteristics of Foreign-born Females in the United States, Aged Sixteen to Sixty-four, by Fluency in English, 1980
(percent)

	Total	English as Language at Home	Speaks Very Well	Well	Not Very Well	Not at All
Labor force participation rate	54.6	58.9	58.9	53.8	47.7	40.8
Education						
<grade 5	44.0	42.0	46.4	51.9	46.3	38.6
Grades 5–8	47.6	50.2	47.7	49.3	48.4	42.8
Grades 9–12	52.7	56.0	53.2	52.7	47.0	40.2
Post–high school	63.9	65.9	67.3	59.0	50.2	42.2
Unemployment rate	7.7	5.9	6.0	8.4	11.1	15.1
Class of worker						
Private salary	81.1	78.7	77.3	82.1	88.4	91.7
Government worker	13.8	15.8	17.3	12.4	7.3	5.6
Other	5.1	5.5	5.4	5.5	4.3	2.7
Occupation						
Managers	5.6	7.3	7.6	4.0	1.9	1.4
Professionals, semi-professionals	13.4	16.4	18.9	10.3	4.3	1.9
Clerical	23.2	29.7	29.6	19.6	9.2	4.6
Sales	10.0	12.3	11.5	9.1	5.9	3.7

Service	19.9	21.6	15.8	22.4	22.4	18.6
Primary	1.9	0.8	0.9	1.7	3.3	9.0
Product, craft	3.7	2.2	3.1	5.1	5.2	5.8
Operatives	18.1	7.2	10.1	22.7	39.8	45.1
Transport, construction	0.7	0.7	0.6	0.9	0.9	0.8
Handlers	3.5	1.8	1.9	4.2	7.1	9.1
Sector						
Extractive	2.3	1.2	1.3	1.9	3.7	9.8
Transformative	27.8	16.5	20.5	32.1	48.9	55.1
Distributive	5.8	6.1	6.7	5.5	4.6	4.3
Producer	12.4	15.9	15.1	10.2	6.3	3.2
Social services	23.0	28.9	28.2	20.7	10.0	7.0
Public administration	3.1	3.5	4.0	2.5	1.8	0.9
Personal service	8.2	8.2	6.1	9.3	10.8	10.2
Retail	17.4	19.7	18.1	17.8	13.9	9.5
Hours worked weekly	35.8	35.0	35.3	36.3	37.2	37.3
Weeks worked in 1979	40.3	41.2	40.8	40.3	38.9	36.9
Mean weekly wage, 1979	192	200	209	181	165	150
Mean wage income, 1979	7,590	8,155	8,496	7,179	5,938	5,037

NOTE: Excludes persons born abroad to American parents.
SOURCE: Census of Population and Housing, 1980. Public Use Microdata Sample C (machine readable data file prepared by the Bureau of the Census, Washington, D.C. [producer and distributor], 1983).

347

TABLE 8–16: Economic Characteristics of Foreign-born Males in the United States, Aged Sixteen to Sixty-four, by Fluency in English, 1980
(percent)

	Total	English as Language at Home	Speaks Very Well	Well	Not Very Well	Not at All
Labor force participation rate	83.2	84.2	83.4	82.2	83.1	82.2
Labor force rate by education						
<grade 5	83.5	72.5	81.2	83.9	85.6	83.0
Grades 5–8	86.8	80.9	85.7	88.8	87.7	86.4
Grades 9–12	80.9	80.5	80.1	82.9	80.5	75.4
Post–high school	83.7	88.4	85.3	76.9	73.0	71.3
Unemployment rate	6.4	5.2	5.3	6.3	8.4	11.2
Class of worker						
Private salary	77.3	73.1	72.3	78.7	86.4	90.6
Government worker	12.0	15.2	15.3	10.4	5.9	4.4
Other	10.7	11.7	12.4	10.9	7.7	5.0
Occupation						
Managers	10.1	14.6	13.4	8.1	3.5	1.3
Professionals, semi-professionals	14.2	19.0	21.8	10.0	3.2	1.4
Clerical	6.6	8.0	8.2	6.4	3.4	1.8
Sales	6.7	8.8	8.1	5.9	3.6	1.6

	1	2	3	4	5	6
Service	13.3	10.1	11.2	15.3	18.2	16.2
Primary	4.9	2.2	2.3	4.0	9.5	19.8
Product, crafts	12.4	12.0	11.7	14.3	12.5	9.6
Operatives	13.2	7.8	8.8	15.7	22.0	23.8
Transport, construction	11.5	12.3	9.6	12.8	12.3	11.0
Handlers	7.1	5.2	4.9	7.4	11.6	13.5
Sector						
Extractive	5.3	2.7	2.9	4.2	9.8	20.7
Transformative	39.7	36.8	34.5	42.4	47.6	46.2
Distributive	10.2	12.3	10.6	9.9	8.1	6.2
Producer	11.3	13.7	13.5	9.9	7.5	6.2
Social services	10.5	12.9	14.5	8.9	4.3	2.9
Public administration	3.0	4.3	4.0	2.2	1.1	1.0
Personal service	4.2	3.8	4.0	4.9	4.8	3.1
Retail	15.8	13.5	16.1	17.6	16.8	13.7
Hours worked weekly	41.2	41.3	41.3	41.0	41.2	41.1
Weeks worked in 1979	44.6	45.3	45.2	44.6	43.5	41.6
Mean weekly wage, 1979	315	378	352	290	228	187
Mean wage income, 1979	14,183	17,443	16,125	12,827	9,580	7,478

NOTE: Excludes persons born abroad to American parents.
SOURCE: Census of Population and Housing, 1980. Public Use Microdata Sample C (machine readable data file prepared by the Bureau of the Census, Washington, D.C. [producer and distributor], 1983).

educated compared with the less-educated characterize persons with fluency in the host language. But this almost disappears for the foreign-born who live in Canada and who have no conversational ability in English or French (table 8–14). This pattern also describes foreign-born women in the United States (table 8–15). The degree of interaction, however, is much stronger for foreign-born males in the United States (table 8–16, column 2 versus columns 5 and 6).

To a large extent, these variations in labor force participation by language fluency are not surprising. Persons with little or no speaking ability in the host language of Canada and the United States will not have the language skills required for many jobs. The gap between employment based on other human capital skills and actual employment and earnings opportunities may be quite large and may deter labor market participation. The magnitude of the gap and thus the costs of not knowing the language presumably would be greater for immigrants who have high levels of human capital, such as education. One consequence, then, of not knowing the host language is reduced participation in the labor force.[22]

Despite the depressant effect of language on labor force participation, more than four of ten women who have low or nonexistent speaking ability in the host language are in the Canadian and United States labor force. How do these women without knowledge of the host language economically fare relative to women who are more fluent? The answer is remarkably similar across countries. Women who cannot converse in English or French in Canada, or who speak English poorly or not at all in the United States, have the highest unemployment rates of all groups. They are employed primarily in service and in the manufacturing occupations (machining, production, and fabrication occupations in Canada and such industries in the United States). Studies find that many of these women in manufacturing occupations are employed in the garment industry.[23]

Given the occupational profiles, it is not surprising that about half of the foreign-born women who lack fluency in the host language are employed in the manufacturing sector of the Canadian and U.S. economies. When they participate in the service sectors, they do so largely in the retail or personal service industries (subsumed in table 8–14 by the category of other service). A much lower percentage are in the social service sector or in government employment, represented by the public administration sector[24] (tables 8–14 and 8–15).

Compared with other foreign-born women, women who cannot speak the host language work more hours per week. In response to a question on the Canadian census form, a higher percentage of these women also indicated that their 1985 employment was full time.

These women also worked more hours in the reference week preceding the 1986 census (table 8–14). Compared with others, however, women who cannot converse in the host language or speak it poorly worked fewer weeks in the year preceding the census (1979 for the United States and 1985 in Canada). This difference was especially pronounced in the United States. The weeks- and hours-worked data are consistent with the high concentration of women with no or low language knowledge in manufacturing and service jobs.

Lower earnings is an important correlate of the economic location of women who cannot speak the host language. Regardless of whether employment earnings are depicted annually or weekly,[25] women in Canada who cannot converse in English or French receive lower wages and salaries than do women who can converse in one or both of the official languages. In the United States, as knowledge of English declines, so do wages and salaries. Women who do not speak English very well or at all earn less weekly and annually than do women whose language at home is English or who speak English very well.

Comparisons between foreign-born men and women further show that women who cannot converse in English or French (Canada) or cannot speak English (United States) not only earn less than other women but also earn less than their male counterparts (table 8–14, columns 1–3 versus columns 4–6; table 8–15 versus table 8–16). Foreign-born women without knowledge of host languages have the lowest earnings of all sex and language fluency groups.

Language and Earnings of Immigrant Women

Three possible explanations exist for the findings that women without language fluency have low earnings. First, the association between language fluency and earnings may arise because knowing or not knowing the host language is related to other variables that are known to influence earnings. Women with low levels of fluency in the host language, for example, often are poorly educated (these levels of education could reflect the educational systems in the non-English- or non-French-speaking countries of origin as well as practices that favor educating males rather than females). Second, not knowing the host country language may mean a devaluation of earning-related skills. Women who have higher levels of education or whose work experience has provided job training may find that the worth of these human capital investments is reduced by the linguistic inability to participate in large labor markets. Third, low language fluency might reduce earnings for foreign-born women for other, less easily meas-

351

ured reasons. Such women might have low earnings because they represent cheap labor used in low-wage industries. Not knowing the host language means that such women form a readily identifiable labor pool that is employable only in a limited range of jobs. The imbalance between supply and demand suggests that wage rates should be low in such circumstances. Such low wages can become institutionalized. Several analysts note the complex relationships between immigrant labor supply and labor demand.[26] One tenet is that immigrants in North America represent cheap labor because (1) they take low-wage jobs as a result of their drive to achieve in the new country; (2) this maintains the viability of low-wage industries, thus perpetuating the demand for low-wage labor; and (3) as a consequence of these two factors, select immigrant groups become defined as low-wage labor.

Some insights into the first two interpretations are obtained by regressing the logarithm of wage and salary earnings on the socioeconomic characteristics of foreign-born women in the Canadian and the U.S. labor force. Because both countries field their censuses partway into the year, earnings data are collected for the year preceding the census to capture a full twelve-month period. Four types of regression models are presented using dummy variable analysis in which the effects of not knowing the host language are expressed as deviations from parameters for women who do indicate language knowledge (table 8–17). Model 1 represents the differences in earnings between women grouped by language knowledge without any statistical adjustments for the influence of other variables also associated with language knowledge or with earnings.[27] Model 2 shows the effect of not knowing the host language after adjusting for age, region of birth, period of migration, region of residence, residence in large cities or urban areas, and marital status.[28] For both Canada and the United States, the results indicate that not knowing the host language reduces earnings. Since the models represent semilogarithmic equations, the effects can be interpreted as percentage decrements. For foreign-born women in the U.S. labor force, for example, the inability to speak English means about a 36 percent reduction in earnings compared with women who know at least some English.[29] After statistical adjustments are made for differences in sociodemographic characteristics, not knowing English means about a 20 percent loss in earnings for foreign-born women in the U.S. labor force (table 8–17, column 6).

Model 3 invokes a frequent strategy in studies of migrants. It indicates the effect of language after adjusting for associations between language knowledge, education, and earnings. This model shows that net of education and other sociodemographic variables, the effect of not knowing the host language on earnings is statistically insignificant from the effect of knowing the host language. This finding exists in other studies, where it is viewed with puzzlement.[30]

In model 3, however, the influence of education on earnings is assumed to be the same across language knowledge groups. In fact the influence of education on earnings is conditioned by language knowledge, as shown in model 4 (table 8–17, columns 4 and 8), which presents three regression coefficients: the effects of not knowing the host language on earnings, the effect of education for women who do know the host language, and the effect of education on earnings for women who do not, controlling for other sociodemographic variables.[31] Results of this model indicate that in Canada and in the United States, respectively, the inability to speak the host language means a 3 percent reduction in earnings per year of education relative to foreign-born women who are familiar with the host language.[32] Simply put, not knowing the host language reduces the capacity of immigrant women in the labor force to convert human capital in the form of education into earnings.

Somewhat paradoxically model 4 indicates that not knowing the host language has a positive effect on earnings, after statistical adjustments for education and sociodemographic variables. This is observed in other studies.[33] One empirical interpretation is that the lower returns to education observed for women without language knowledge depress total earnings only for better-educated foreign-born women in the labor force. In Canada this negative impact affects the foreign-born female labor force with an eighth-grade education or more, and in the United States it reduces the earnings of women with a sixth-grade education or higher.

While initially paradoxical, these findings in fact are less puzzling when substantive and methodological reasons are considered. Substantively credentialism in North America means that education is a labor market resource only above some minimum level of attainment. In North American labor markets today, some high school increasingly is an entry requirement for most jobs. At lower levels of schooling, education may not matter much as a form of human capital that influences earnings of foreign-born women in the labor force. Instead participation in ethnic enclaves, as well as other variables not included in the regression models, may increase the earnings of foreign-born women who are without host language skills and who have low educational capital.

Methodologically the regression models depict the relationship between education and language on earnings for foreign-born women

353

TABLE 8–17

Regression Estimates of Language Knowledge and Education on Wage and Salary Earnings (L_N) for Foreign-born Women in the Labor Force, in Canada, 1985, and the United States, 1979

	Canada[a]				United States[b]			
	Model 1	Model 2[c]	Model 3[c]	Model 4[c]	Model 1	Model 2[c]	Model 3[c]	Model 4[c]
Does not know host language	−.171***	−.208***	−.003	+.245*	−.357***	−.195***	−.012	+.194**
	(.044)	(.044)	(.006)	(.086)	(.026)	(.027)	(.028)	(.050)
Education	n.i.	n.i.	.055***	n.i.	n.i.	n.i.	.049***	n.i.
			(.002)				(.002)	
Combined Education, knows host language	n.i.	n.i.		.056***	n.i.	n.i.		.051***
				(.002)				(.002)
Education, does not know host language	n.i.	n.i.		−.029*	n.i.	n.i.		−.033***
				(.012)				(.007)
Intercept	9.141	9.225	8.432	8.413	8.551	8.601	7.954	7.923
R^2	.001	.105	.131	.132	.006	.102	.124	.125

n.i. = variable was not included in the regression model for column.

a. Age fifteen to sixty-four; 1986 labor force.

b. Age sixteen to sixty-four; 1980 labor force; excludes Puerto Rico and other territory birthplaces, where year of immigration is not applicable and excludes persons born abroad to American parents.

c. See appendix 8–3 for the details on the sociodemographic variables.

*$P \leq .05$

**$P \leq .01$

***$P \leq .001$

SOURCES: For Canada, Statistics Canada. Electronic Data Dissemination Division. 1986 Census Public Use Microdata File on Individuals, June, 1990. For United States, Census of Population and Housing, 1980. Public Use Microdata Sample C (machine readable data file prepared by the Bureau of the Census, Washington D.C. [Producer and distributor]), 1983.

who are currently in the labor force. But better-educated women who do not know the host language have reduced participation in the labor force compared with women with greater language fluency (tables 8–14 and 8–15). To the extent that sample selectivity exists whereby women who receive low returns to education remain out of the labor force, the data in table 8–17 will not provide estimates of the total impact of language fluency on the relation between education and earnings. Although data in table 8–17 do portray the situation for foreign-born women currently in the labor force, future analysis is desirable if we are to unravel and extend the results presented in table 8–17.

Policy Prescriptions

Data presented in this chapter show that women represent an important share of past and current migrant flows to North America. The origins of these women, like their male counterparts, have shifted over time away from traditional sources in Europe and from Canadian–U.S. flows. Many migrant women now come from third world countries where English or French is not the normal language of conversation, education, or business. The percentage of women who lack language fluency is far higher among these new immigrant groups—new because they hail from nontraditional source countries and new because they are recent arrivals. And the percentage of women who cannot converse in the host language or do not speak it well is higher than that of men.

For both men and women, the knowledge of the host language, or lack thereof, is a basis of socioeconomic differentiation among immigrants. But gender is a factor as well. The combined impact of knowledge of the host language and gender is evident for labor force participation rates, unemployment rates, and occupational and industrial location. Compared with other foreign-born women, and their male counterparts, immigrant women who do not know the host language have the lowest labor force participation rates and the highest unemployment rates in Canada and the United States. Such women in Canada are more likely than other groups to hold jobs in service, machining, and production occupations and to work in manufacturing or other service (including personal services) industries. In the United States, a similar pattern holds with respect to the percentages found in service and industrial occupations and in manufacturing and personal service industries. In both Canada and the United States, foreign-born women who do not know the host language have the lowest average wage and salary earnings compared with their male counterparts and with foreign-born women with at least some language fluency. Among foreign-born women in the labor force, not knowing the host language means a reduced return to income, especially for the better-educated.

At least three policy-related questions emerge from the findings. First, what policy alternatives exist and on what basis? Second, what policies in Canada and in the United States have as their objective the learning of the host language by groups that lack knowledge or fluency? And third, given the existence of gender stratification, how well are migrant women incorporated into existing programs?

There are numerous possible policy responses to empirical findings on language fluency. All are part of larger debates over whether to increase, to preserve, or to decrease current levels of immigration to Canada and the United States.[34] Linguistic fluency characteristics of migrants in general, however, and migrant women in particular, emphasize gender and language components of these debates and policy responses. One policy alternative in both Canada and the United States modifies immigration policies to select more aggressively highly skilled migrants. Such a policy could include language requirements that favor the admission of immigrants who know or can rapidly acquire host language. The impact of such policy on language characteristics of immigrants likely is modest, however, because of persisting family-based migration. As shown in table 8–3, family-related migration is sizable, even in Canada, where a labor market–oriented point system already exists. Neither country is likely to deny the right of family reunification to their citizens and permanent residents, thus ensuring that future migration streams will reproduce the linguistic mix of past migration flows.

Moreover, selecting migrants on the basis of language skill would not necessarily reduce the gender gap in language knowledge for two reasons. First, gender stratification in the origin country usually means that women are less likely than men to receive higher levels of education and nonhome language instruction. Second, since women often migrate as family members, and not as principal applicants to whom language criteria can be applied, future North American immigration flows would continue to include women without language knowledge of the host country.

Altering the volume and composition of migrant flows requires adjustments to immigration policy. Policy prescriptions directed at immigrants who are already in North America commonly are called migrant policies. What kind of policy prescriptives regarding language skills are possible? One stance is noninterventionist, often based on the assumption that learning the host language will occur

357

naturally over time. Another is more proactive, consisting of the development of, or even enlargement of, programs that provide language training to target populations. The exact policy formulations and program implications, however, tend to differ according to disciplinary paradigms, value judgments, and country-specific emphases.

The dominant paradigms in economics, sociology, and political science emphasize different inputs into human behavior. This was summarized succinctly thirty years ago by James Duesenberry's observation that "the difference between economics and sociology is very simple. Economics is all about how people make choices. Sociology is all about why they don't have any choices to make."[35] While this remains a fundamental distinction between neoclassical economics and much of sociology, Duesenberry also could have contrasted neoclassical attentiveness to markets, efficiency, and individualism against sociological and pluralist emphases on structural constraints, social community, equality, and social goods.[36]

These paradigms generate different policy prescriptions regarding language training. The assumptions of neoclassical economics favor policies that leave learning a language up to the individual or propose language training programs for targeted labor market participants because of the risk of reduced productivity. Proponents of readily available language training to all individuals start from different premises. For them, knowledge of the host language is a social right, which like education is essential for the full participation of individuals in their society and for the well-being of the next generation. In neither approach are claims of scientific or value-free theories tenable. Conrad Waligorski argues that "conservative" economics represents a political theory despite its claims to the contrary.[37] In sociology, earlier preoccupations with the development of a value-free science have been replaced by the realization that all models contain assumptions and value judgments.

Policy responses are shaped not only by disciplinary paradigms but also by country-specific institutions and histories. Seymour Martin Lipset, an American sociologist, argues that Canadians look to the government as providing solutions more than Americans. Along similar lines, Lars Osberg, a Canadian economist, notes the support by all three major parties for federal involvement in universal social programs during the free trade debate. He also cites the widespread perception that this limiting of the role of market forces was not characteristic of U.S. political and economic life and represented a major difference between the two countries.[38] One implication of these observations is that the Canadian government may be more actively involved in the formulation and implementation of language training for immigrants.

Policy Responses in Canada and the United States

Are there in fact country differences in policy responses to the language needs of immigrants? The answer is both no and yes, for while Canada and the United States do have many points of similarity, modest differences also exist.

Canada and the United States share a long history as countries of immigration and countries of settlement. As "liberal" welfare states, they also are similar in their principles of rights and stratification.[39] This is evident not only in the general development of social assistance policy but also in the general stance taken toward immigrant integration and adaptation. Both Canada and the United States admit immigrants as permanent residents and extend social and civic rights relatively quickly to them. Even legal citizenship can be obtained after several years. Alongside this ready extension of rights is the laissez-faire expectation that immigrants will make their own way and integrate on their own.[40] As a result, in both Canada and the United States, few programs are targeted explicitly at immigrants. Even when policies and related programs do designate immigrants as clients, the coverage often is limited to types of migrants, such as refugees, or to certain geographical areas.

Language training policies are shaped within this context. In the United States, most discussions regarding learning English focus on bilingual education efforts. These efforts are considered important because poor linguistic ability of children is associated with demotion in school, with higher dropout rates, and ultimately with unequal educational opportunities.[41] Bilingual education is a much debated topic in the United States, partly because of differences in educational approaches and partly because of the question whether the United States is, or should be, a monolingual or bilingual (English and Spanish) society.[42] For the purposes of this essay, it is enough to note that programs of bilingual education rest on two premises: they are directed to all children who do not know English, not just the foreign-born, and it is assumed that children of the foreign-born, like those of the native-born, partake of the universal right to attend school.

Less focused attention is paid by the U.S. federal and state governments to the provision of English language training to adults. Existing programs are aimed at different clients and have different objectives and coverage.[43] In addition to programs for children, for example, some schools do offer adult programs in English as a second language. The federally funded orientation program for Southeast Asian refugees includes twenty weeks of cultural orientation and English as a second language. Some programs are offered through nongovernmental organizations including volunteer agencies. Further, a limited program authorized under the Bilingual Vocational Training Act of 1984 provides vocational training to out-of-school youth and adults with little English. On the whole, however, language training for adults is not extensive and not based on national policy.

Compared with the United States, Canada experienced a more proactive immigration policy in the post–World War II years, and the state played a slightly more positive role in the adaptation of newcomers. Language training assistance to incoming migrants is varied, but at the federal level it primarily is tied to labor market training policies. Numerous reports review Canada's language training programs and outline their shortcomings.[44] As of 1990, most federal language training programs are developed and funded under the auspices of the Canada Employment and Immigration Commission (CEIC).[45] Two types of programs are funded through CEIC: (1) programs, such as the Settlement Language Program (SLP), that fund immigrant service agencies to provide basic coping language skills for adults not destined for the labor force, primarily immigrant women at home with child care responsibilities, and (2) programs offered by the CEIC through the programs of the Canadian Job Strategy (CJS). The latter have a larger budget than the former. They are directed at persons either who are destined for the labor market or who are already in the labor force. The direct purchase option (DPO) for example, under the Job Entry Program of the CJS allows for the purchase of language training places at provincial educational institutions for persons destined to the labor force. Job Entry also allows for combined language and skills training projects. Under the new Language and Orientation Initiative, announced May 28, 1990, Language at Work (LAW), an option of the Skills Investment Program of the Canadian Jobs Strategy, provides funding for language training in the work place. It is directed at persons already in the labor force.

What do these programs say about country differences in policy initiatives? As is true in the United States, language training in Canada is not comprehensive in coverage, although unlike the United States, federal labor market policies include a language training component, and some funds are allocated toward language training of persons not in the labor market through SLP. The fact that the Canadian federal government provides language training programs and on a modest scale targets immigrants outside the labor force indicate policies that are somewhat more proactive than in the United States and slightly less driven by market-based arguments.

Conclusion

Data presented in this chapter shows that a higher percentage of foreign-born women do not know the host languages of Canada and the United States than men and that language is a powerful stratifying variable affecting the social and economic situation of immigrant women. Do the two countries differ in the extent to which immigrant women benefit from language training policies and programs? Two responses exist. First, the Canadian Settlement Language Training Program, offered through CEIC, emerged from pressures and concerns regarding the difficulties that migrant women at home face in learning English or French. No equivalent federal program exists in the United States. This difference, however, is minimized by coverage and acessibility issues. The Canadian SLT program is limited in funding and coverage. And in both countries foreign-born women more than men may be handicapped in gaining access to other programs. In his report on the status of foreign-born women in the United States, Roger Kramer notes that while access to training programs is theoretically the same for both sexes, there may be biases against women in the administration of the programs.[46]

In Canada the CEIC labor market–based language training programs do not explicitly discriminate on the basis of sex. Recent statistics supplied by Employment and Immigration show that women and men participate in the DPO training program in nearly equal numbers. But numerical equality in participation does not necessarily mean equal rates of participation when calculated by the number of enrollments divided by the population at risk (those who do not know English or French). If one group has a larger population at risk, the rate of participation will be lower even if the numbers of participants equal those of another group. Although this argument is made by immigrant women's advocacy groups, estimates of populations at risk and rates of participation are difficult to produce because of the varied programs in place, the need to match program users to populations in surrounding geographical areas, and costs of obtaining the necessary statistics.

At least two features of the Canadian CEIC labor market–based programs may reduce the usefulness of these programs for immigrant women. First, persons not destined for the labor force are not eligible for language training under the direct purchase options of the Canadian Jobs Strategy program, and persons who are not in the labor force are not eligible for the newly initiated LAW program. Yet foreign-born women who cannot converse in English or French are most likely not to be in the labor force (table 8–14) and thus not to be eligible for either program.

Second, the CEIC Job Entry Program provides five types of income support: basic training allowances, which include training allowances and unemployment insurance benefits to assist the unemployed worker in continuing to meet prior financial obligations; and supplemental allowances, including dependent care allowance, trainee travel assistance, and the living away from home allowance. For sponsored immigrants in the family and assisted-relatives classes, the basic training allowances are eliminated, the argument being that sponsors have agreed to provide economically for these immigrants. But because women more than men are sponsored immigrants, they are more likely than men not to be receiving basic training allowances even if they are eligible for participating in the CEIC program. This curtailment of income increases the likelihood that sponsored immigrant women will not participate in the program.[47]

In sum, even when language training is incorporated into governmental policies, foreign-born women in North America are neglected constituents as a result of eligibility criteria and program objectives. Yet not knowing the host language has both social and economic implications for immigrant women. One social result is the potential for intensified isolation and dependency on those who act as linguistic brokers.[48] As this essay shows, the economic correlates are lower earnings, reduced returns to education, and employment in service and manufacturing jobs.

Thus far the Canadian response highlights subtle but possibly important differences between Canada and the United States regarding grounds for policy action. Various groups, including the coalition-based National Organization for Visible Minority and Immigrant Women in Canada, actively pressure the Canadian federal government to increase services targeted at immigrant women. Language training is high on the list. The rationales for such services do not rest on market efficiency claims but rather emphasize social citizenship aspects to language training, the need to eradicate the lower socioeconomic position of women who lack knowledge of English or French, and the importance of providing immigrant women with resources when marriages dissolve. The establishment of Canada's Settlement Language Program partly reflects such lobby efforts. For many critics, current programs and new initiatives still are inadequate in meeting the language needs of immigrant women. Yet from a comparative perspective, these developments suggest that in the area of language training the Canadian state is slightly more responsive than the United States to claims based on social citizenship and gender inequality.

APPENDIX 8–A1

Nations Constituting Regional Birthplaces, as Defined for Canadian Immigration

West Europe
  Belgium and Luxembourg
  France
  Germany
  Netherlands
  Austria

South Europe
  Greece
  Italy
  Portugal
  Yugoslavia

East Europe, USSR
  Czechoslovakia
  Hungary
  Poland
  USSR

Other Europe
  Other European countries not
    specified above, including
    Republic of Ireland.

Eastern Asia
  Mongolia
  People's Republic of China
  Hong Kong
  Japan
  North Korea
  South Korea
  Macao
  Taiwan

Southeast Asia
  Brunei
  Burma
  Indonesia
  Kampuchea
  Laos
  Malaysia
  Philippines
  Singapore
  Thailand
  Vietnam

South Asia
  Bangladesh
  Bhutan
  India
  Republic of Maldives
  Nepal
  Pakistan
  Sri Lanka

Western Asia
  Turkey
  Afghanistan
  Bahrain
  Iran
  Iraq
  Israel
  Jordan
  Kuwait
  Lebanon
  Oman
  Qatar

(Table continues)

363

Appendix 8–A1 (continued)

Saudi Arabia
Syria
United Arab Emirates
People's Democratic Republic
  of Yemen
Yemen Arab Republic

Northern Africa
  Egypt
  Libya
  Algeria
  Morocco
  Tunisia

West Sahara
Sudan

Other Africa
  Other countries not listed in
    Northern Africa.

Other
  Includes countries and regions
    not elsewhere identified.

Other residual

NOTE: These regional birthplace areas are referred to in tables 8–5 and 8–7. In order to maximize the level of detail in the birthplace variable while preserving the anonymity of respondents to the census who live in sparsely settled areas of Canada, Statistics Canada employed two procedures in the preparation of the birthplace variable for release on the 1986 Public Use Sample Tape of Individuals. The first approach was to generate a list of countries or region of birth for provinces: Quebec, Ontario, Manitoba, Saskatchewan, Alberta, and British Columbia. Countries not included in the categories fell into the "Other" category. For the three Atlantic provinces—Prince Edward Island, Nova Scotia, and New Brunswick—and for the Yukon and Northwest Territories, less detail was provided. Other than Canada, separate birthplace data were provided only for respondents who were born in the United States, Germany, and the United Kingdom. All other places were collapsed into what is called the "other residual" category.
SOURCE: Statistics Canada, Electronic Data Dissemination Division. 1986 Census Public Use Microdata File of Individuals. *Documentation and Users Guide.* Ottawa: Statistics Canada, June 1991.

APPENDIX 8–A2

NATIONS CONSTITUTING REGIONAL BIRTHPLACES, AS DEFINED FOR U.S. IMMIGRATION

Canada

United Kingdom

West Europe
  Austria
  Belgium
  France
  Luxembourg

Netherlands
Germany

South Europe
  Greece
  Italy
  Portugal
  Azores
  Madeira Islands

Appendix 8–A2 (continued)

San Marino
Vatican City
Yugoslavia

East Europe, USSR
Czechoslovakia
Hungary
Poland
Romania
USSR

Other Europe
All other countries not specified above, incuding the Republic of Ireland
East Asia
China
Hong Kong
Japan
North and South Korea
Macao
Mongolia
Taiwan
Other East Asia, not listed above

Southeast Asia
Brunei
Burma
East Timor
Indonesia
Kampuchea
Laos
Malaysia
Philippines
Singapore
Thailand
Vietnam
Other Southeast Asia, not listed above

South Asia
Bangladesh
Bhutan
India

Maldives
Nepal
Pakistan
Sri Lanka
Other South and Southwest Asia, not listed above

West Asia
Turkey
Afghanistan
Iran
Bahrain
Cyprus
Gaza Strip
Iraq
Jordan
Kuwait
Lebanon
Neutral Zone
Oman
Qatar
Saudi Arabia
Syria
United Arab Emirates
People's Democratic Republic of Yemen
Yemen Arab Republic

North Africa
Algeria
Egypt
Libya
Morocco
Sudan
Tunisia
Western Sahara
Other North Africa not listed above

Other Africa
Areas other than listed in North Africa

Mexico   *(Table continues)*

365

Appendix 8–A2 (continued)

Central America	excluding Cuba and the Dominican Republic
Cuba	Puerto Rico
Dominican Republic	Other Areas All countries not listed above
Other Caribbean All other Caribbean countries	Born at Sea

NOTE: These regional birthplace areas are referred to in tables 8–6 and 8–8.
SOURCE: Bureau of the Census, Data User Services Division, Census of Population and Housing. *Public Use Microdata Samples*. Washington, D.C.: Bureau of the Census, 1980.

APPENDIX 8–A3
SOCIODEMOGRAPHIC VARIABLES, MODELS 2–4, TABLE 8–17

Canada (1986 PUST)	*United States* (1980 PUM, C Tape)
	Birthplace[a]
USA	Canada
UK	UK
West Europe	West Europe
	Birthplace
South Europe	Other Europe
East Europe, USSR	East Asia
Other Europe	Southeast Asia
East Asia	South Asia
Southeast Asia	West Asia
South Asia	North Africa
West Asia	Other Africa
North Africa	Mexico
Other Africa	Other Central America
South and Central America	South America
Caribbean	Cuba
South Europe	Dominican Republic
East Europe, USSR	Other Caribbean

Appendix 8–A3 (continued)

Canada (1986 PUST)	United States (1980 PUM, C Tape)

Age

15–24	15–24
25–34	25–34
35–44	35–44
45–54	45–54
55–64	55–64

Period of Immigration

<1970	<1965
1971–1975	1965–1969
1976–1980	1970–1974
1981–1983	1975–1980

Province or Region

Quebec	Northeast
Ontario	North Central
Prairies	South
British Columbia	West

Live in a CMA / Size of Place

Live in a CMA	Size of Place
Yes	Nonurban
No	Urban
	Big city[b]

Marital Status

Single	Single
Married	Married
Separated, divorced, widowed	Separated, divorced, widowed

a. See appendix 8–A1 and appendix 8–A2 for countries that are grouped into each birthplace category.
b. Refers to residents of Boston, Chicago, Los Angeles, Miami, New York, and San Francisco.
Source: Author.

Bibliography

Acosta-Belen, Edna, and Barbara R. Sjostrom, eds. *The Hispanic Experience in the United States*. Westport, Conn.: Praeger Publishers, 1988.

Axworthy, Lloyd. "Multiculturalism: The Immigrant Woman in Canada: A Right to Recognition." In Canada, Secretary of State, Multiculturalism Directorate. *The Immigrant Women in Canada. Part 1. Report of the Proceedings of the Conference*, Ottawa: Minister of Supply and Services Canada, Catalog Ci 96-15/1981-1, 1981.

Badets, Janet. "Canada's Immigrant Population." *Canadian Social Trends*. Statistics Canada Catalogue 11-008E. No. 14 (Autumn 1989): 26.

Bailey, Thomas R. *Immigrant and Native Workers*. Boulder, Colo.: Westview Press, 1987.

Bean, Frank D., Jurgen Schmandt, and Sidney Weintraub, eds. *Mexican and Central American Population and U.S. Immigration Policy*. Austin: University of Texas at Austin, Center for Mexican-American Studies, 1989.

Bean, Frank D., and Marta Tienda. *The Hispanic Population of the United States*. New York: Russell Sage Foundation, 1987.

Bogen, Elizabeth. *Immigration in New York*. Westport, Conn.: Praeger Publishers, 1987.

Boyd, Monica. "At a Disadvantage: Occupational Attainments of Canadian Immigrant Women." *International Migration Review* 18 (Winter 1984): 1091–1119.

————. "Gender, Visible Minority and Immigrant Earnings Inequality: Reassessing and Employment Equity Premise." In *Deconstructing a Nation: Immigration, Multiculturalism and Racism in the 90s Canada*, edited by Vic Satzewich. Toronto: Garamond Press, 1992.

————. "Immigrant Women: Language, Socioeconomic Inequalities and Policy Issues." In *Ethnic Demography: Canadian Immigrant, Racial and Cultural Variations*, edited by Shiva Halli, Frank Trovato, and Leo Driedger. Ottawa: Carleton University Press, 1990.

————. "Immigration and Income Security Policies in Canada: Implications for Elderly Immigrant Women." *Population Research and Policy Review* 8 (January 1989): 5–24.

————. "Immigration and Living Arrangements: Elderly Women in Canada." *International Migration Review* 25 (Spring 1991): 4–27.

————. "Immigration Policies and Trends: A Comparison of Canada and the United States." *Demography* 13 (February 1976): 82–102.

————. "Migrant Women in Canada." In *International Migration: The Female Experience*, edited by Rita James Simon and Caroline Brettell. Totowa, N.J.: Rowman and Allanheld, 1986.

————. *Migrant Women in Canada: Profiles and Policies.* Immigration Research Working Paper, no. 2. Ottawa: Employment and Immigration Canada, Policy Analysis Directorate, Immigration Policy Branch, 1989.

————. "Occupations of Female Immigrants and North American Immigration Statistics." *International Migration Review* 10 (1976): 73–79.

————. "The Status of Migrant Women in Canada." *Canadian Review of Sociology and Anthropology* 12 (November 1975): 406–16.

Brettell, Caroline, and Rita J. Simon. "Immigrant Women: An Introduction." In *International Migration: The Female Experience*, edited by Rita James Simon and Caroline Brettell. Totowa, N.J.: Rowman and Allanheld, 1986.

Browning, Harley L., and Joachim Singelmann. "The Emergence of a Service Society: Demographic and Sociological Aspects of the Sectoral Transformation of the Labor Force in the U.S.A." Report prepared for the Manpower Administration, U.S. Department of Labor. Washington, D.C.: U.S. Department of Commerce, National Technical Information Service, 1975.

Bryce-Laporte, Roy S. "Introductions: The New Immigration: The Female Majority." In *Female Immigrants to the United States: Caribbean, Latin American and African Experiences*, edited by Delores M. Mortimer and Roy S. Bryce-Laporte. Research Institution on Immigration and Ethnic Studies. Occasional Papers, no. 2. Washington, D.C.: Smithsonian Institution, 1981.

Buchanan, Susan Huelsebusch. "Profiles of Haitian Migrant Women." In *Female Immigrants to the United States: Caribbean, Latin American and African Experiences*, edited by Delores M. Mortimer and Roy S. Bryce-Laporte. Research Institution on Immigration and Ethnic Studies. Occasional Papers, no. 2. Washington, D.C.: Smithsonian Institution, 1981.

Burnaby, B., M. Holt, N. Steltzer, and N. Collins. *The Settlement Language Training Program: An Assessment.* Ottawa: Employment and Immigration Canada, Immigration Group, Policy and Program Development Branch, Research Division, 1987.

Cafferty, Pastora San Juan. "Language and Social Assimilation." In *Hispanics in the United States,* edited by San Juan Cafferty and William C. McCready. New Brunswick, N.J.: Transaction Books, 1985.

Courtney, B. Cazden, and Catherine Snow, eds. "English Plus: Issues in Bilingual Education." *Annals of the American Academy of Political and Social Science* 508 (March 1990): 9–184.

Duesenberry, James S. "Comment" [on 'An Economic Analysis of Fertility' by Gary Becker]. In *Demographic and Economic Change in*

Developed Countries, edited by National Bureau of Economic Research. Princeton: Princeton University Press, 1960.

Esping-Anderson, Gosta. "The Three Political Economies of the Welfare State." *Canadian Review of Sociology and Anthropology* 26 (February 1989): 10–36.

Estable, Alma. "Immigrant Women in Canada-Current Issues." Background paper. Ottawa: Canadian Advisory Council on the Status of Women, 1986.

Evans, M. D. R. "Immigrant Entrepreneurship: Effects of Ethnic Market Size and Isolated Labor Pool." *American Sociological Review* 54 (December 1989): 950–62.

Fligstein, Neil, and Roberto M. Fernandez. "Hispanics and Education." In *Hispanics in the United States,* edited by Pastora San Juan Cafferty and William C. McCready. New Brunswick, N.J.: Transaction Books, 1985.

Foner, Nancy. "Introduction: New Immigrants and Changing Patterns in New York City." In *New Immigrants in New York* edited by Nancy Foner. New York: Columbia University Press, 1987.

Giles, Wenona. "Language Rights are Human Rights: Discrimination Against Immigrant Women in Canadian Language Training Policies." *Resources for Feminist Research* 17 (1988): 129–32.

Hawkins, Freda. *Canada and Immigration: Public Policy and Public Concern.* Montreal: McGill and Queen's University Press, 1972.

———. *Critical Years in Immigration: Canada and Australia Compared.* Montreal: McGill and Queen's University Press, 1989.

Houston, Marion F., Roger G. Kramer, and Joan Mackin Barrett. "Female Predominance in Immigration to the United States since 1930: A First Look." *International Migration Review* 18 (Winter 1984): 908–63.

Kirschten, Dick. "Come In! Keep Out!" *National Journal* (May 1990): 1206–11.

Kraly, Ellen. "Sources of Data for the Study of U.S. Immigration." In *Quantitative Data and Immigration Research,* edited by Stephen R. Couch and Roy S. Bryce-LaPorte. Research Institution on Immigration and Ethnic Studies. Research Note, no. 2. Washington, D.C.: Smithsonian Institution, 1979.

———. "U.S. Immigration Policy and the Immigrant Populations of New York." In *New Immigrants in New York,* edited by Nancy Foner. New York: Columbia University Press, 1987.

Kramer, Roger. "United States Government Policy in Relation to Women from Ethnic Minority Groups." Report submitted to the Monitoring Panel on Migrant Women. Paris: Organization for Economic Co-operation and Development, Directorate for Social Affairs, Manpower and Education, 1987.

Lee, Everett. "A Theory of Migration." *Demography* 3 (1966): 47–57.

Levine, Daniel, Kenneth Hill, and Robert Warren, eds. *Immigration Statistics: A Story of Neglect.* Washington, D.C.: National Academy Press, 1985.

Lipset, Seymour Martin. *Continental Divide.* New York: Routledge and Kegan Paul, 1989.

Marshall, Adriana. "New Immigrants in New York's Economy." In *New Immigrants in New York,* edited by Nancy Foner. New York: Columbia University Press, 1987.

McManus, Walter S. "Labor Market Assimilation of Immigrants: The Importance of Language Skills." *Contemporary Policy Issues* 3 (Spring 1985, pt. 1): 77–89.

—. "Labor Market Costs of Language Disparity: An Interpretation of Hispanic Earnings Differences," *American Economics Review* 75 (September 1985): 818–27.

McManus, Walter S., William Gould, and Finis Welch. "Earnings of Hispanic Men: The Role of English Language Proficiency." *Journal of Labor Economics* 1 (April 1983): 101–30.

Morokvasic, Mirjana. "Women in Migration: Beyond the Reductionist Outlook." In *One-Way Ticket: Migration and Female Labour,* edited by Annie Phizacklea. London: Routledge and Kegan Paul, 1983.

—. "Birds of Passage Are Also Women. . . ." *International Migration Review* 28 (Winter 1984): 886–907.

Mortimer, Delores M., and Roy S. Bryce-Laporte, eds. *Female Immigrants to the United States: Caribbean, Latin American and African Experiences.* Research Institution on Immigration and Ethnic Studies. Occasional Papers, no. 2. Washington, D.C.: Smithsonian Institution, 1981.

Myles, John F. "The Use of Nominal Categories in Regression Analysis." *Canadian Review of Sociology and Anthropology* 15 (February 1978): 97–101.

Ng, Roxanna, and Judith Ramirez. *Immigrant Housewives in Canada.* Toronto: The Women's Centre Press, 1981.

Noivo, Edite. *Migrations and Reactions to Displacement: The Portuguese in Canada.* M. A. thesis, Ottawa, Carleton University, 1984.

Osberg, Lars. "Distributional Issues and the Future of the Welfare State." In *Perspective 2000: Proceedings of a Conference Sponsored by the Economic Council of Canada, December 1988.* Edited by K. Newton, T. Schweitzer, and J. P. Voyer. Ottawa: Supply and Services.

Parai, Louis. *Immigration and Emigration of Professional and Skilled Manpower.* Special Study, No. 1, Economic Council of Canada. Ottawa: Queen's Printer, 1965.

Parcel, Toby L., and Charles W. Mueller. "Temporal Change in Occupational Earnings, 1970–1980." *American Sociological Review* 54 (August 1989): 622–34.

Paredes, Milagros. "Immigrant Women and Second Language Education." *Resources for Feminist Research/documentation sur la recherche feministe* 16 (March 1987): 23–27.

Pedraza-Bailey, Silvia. *Political and Economic Migrants in America: Cubans and Mexicans.* Austin: University of Texas Press, 1985.

Pessar, Patricia. "The Dominicans: Women in the Household and the Garment Industry." In *New Immigrants in New York,* edited by Nancy Foner. New York: Columbia University Press, 1987.

Richmond, Anthony H. "The Income of Caribbean Immigrants in Canada." In *Ethnic Demography: Canadian Immigrant, Racial and Cultural Variations,* edited by Shiva Hali, Frank Trovato, and Leo Dreidger. Ottawa: Carleton University Press, 1990.

Robinson, Patricia. "Language Retention among Canadian Indians." *American Sociological Review* 50 (August 1985): 515–29.

Sassen, Saskia. *The Mobility of Labor and Capital.* Cambridge, Eng.: Cambridge University Press, 1988.

Schwartz, Mildred, A. *The Environment for Policy Making in Canada and the United States.* Montreal: C. D. Howe Institute, 1981.

Seward, Shirley. "Immigrant Women in the Clothing Industry." In *Ethnic Demography: Canadian Immigrants, Racial and Cultural Variations,* edited by Shiva Hali, Frank Trovato, and Leo Dreidger. Ottawa: Carleton University Press, 1990.

Seward, Shirley, and Kathryn McDade. *Immigrant Women in Canada: A Policy Perspective.* Background paper. Ottawa: Canadian Advisory Council on the Status of Women, 1988.

Seydegart, K., and G. Spears. *Beyond Dialogue: Immigrant Women in Canada, 1985–1990.* Ottawa: Secretary of State, Multiculturalism, 1985.

Simon, Rita James, and Caroline Brettell, eds. *International Migration: The Female Experience.* Totowa, N.J.: Rowman and Allanheld, 1986.

"Situation and the Role of Migrant Women: Specific Adaptation and Integration Problems." *International Migration* 19 (Geneva, 1988): 1–292. "Women in Migration." Special issue.

U.S. Department of Labor, Bureau of International Labor Affairs. *The Effects of Immigration on the U.S. Economy and Labor Market.* Washington, D.C.: Government Printing Office, 1989.

Veltman, Calvin. "Testing the Effects of Language as Measured by the Canadian Census." Paper presented at the meeting of the Association International de Linguistique Applique, Brussels, August 9, 1984.

Waligorski, Conrad P. *The Political Theory of Conservative Economics.* Lawrence: University Press of Kansas, 1990.

"Women in Migration." Special issue. *International Migration Review* 18 (Winter 1984): 881–1382.

9

Earnings of the French Minority in Canada and the Spanish Minority in the United States

David E. Bloom and Gilles Grenier

The ability of economic agents to communicate contributes to the efficiency of many economic activities and transactions. Production and distribution activities that involve teamwork, supervision, and the interpretation of written or verbal instructions require that people communicate in a common language. In addition, the frequent inter-twining of language and culture suggests that economic agents may benefit from communicating in a particular language, independent of the value of that language in the production and distribution of goods and services.

The recognition of language as an economic variable was initiated in the seminal articles of Jacob Marschak, Toussaint Hocevar, and Albert Breton and Peter Mieszkowski and furthered by the contributions of François Vaillancourt, Gilles Grenier, and Chris Robinson.[1] In the past fifteen years or so, most of the research done on economic aspects of language has had an empirical orientation. Much effort has been devoted to testing the notion that the language abilities of individuals are a genuine component of their total human capital. A typical test involves fitting a standard wage equation—augmented with one or more variables that measure an individual's ability to communicate in the dominant language of the labor market—to cross-sectional survey data. By interpreting the estimated coefficients of the language variables as skill prices, one can use empirical results of this type to draw inferences about the economic value of different language skills.

Tables 9–1 and 9–2 summarize recent empirical research on the relationship between language skills and earnings in Canada and the United States. The different research methods used in the studies may be responsible for the discrepancies in the findings. The research

TABLE 9–1

Studies on Language Ability and Earnings
in the United States, 1978–1991

Study	Description	Major Findings
Gwartney and Long, 1978 (based on 1970 census)	Earnings regressions are estimated for males and females belonging to several ethnic minorities. Non–English mother tongue is a dummy regressor.	The results are mixed. Non-English mother tongue has a significant negative association with earnings for some groups, but for other groups the coefficient is either not significant or significant with a positive sign. Spanish mother tongue does not have a significant coefficient.
Carliner, 1980 (based on 1970 census)	Wage and earnings regressions are estimated for men of various ethnic groups. A dummy variable for non–English mother tongue is included among the regressors.	There is no significant effect of mother tongue on wages or earnings.
McManus, Gould, and Welsh, 1983 (based on 1976 Survey of Income and Education)	Earnings regressions are estimated for Hispanic men. An index of language ability is constructed from the various language questions available in the SIE. The index weights are estimated on the basis of their effect on earnings.	Language explains virtually all observed Hispanic wage differentials. This finding, however, appears to be the result of the authors' definition of the index of language ability, which is based on endogenous weights. This procedure may overestimate the effect of language (see Chiswick, 1991).

TABLE 9–1 (continued)

Study	Description	Major Findings
Reimers, 1983, 1984 (based on 1976 Survey of Income and Education)	Earnings regressions are estimated for men in the various Hispanic groups (Mexican, Puerto-Rican, Cuban, Central and South American, other Hispanic). A dummy variable for not speaking English very well is included in the regressions.	There is no significant effect on earnings of not speaking English very well.
Grenier, 1984 (based on 1976 Survey of Income and Education)	Wage regressions are estimated for Hispanic men. Various measures of language ability are defined and included in alternative specifications of the model.	Language variables are important and account for approximately one-third of the earnings differentials between whites and Hispanics.
McManus, 1985 (based on 1976 Survey of Income and Education)	Earnings regressions are estimated for Hispanic men. An index of language ability is defined, with endogenous weights as in McManus et al. (1983). The variables included in the index, however, are different.	The author estimates that the cost of English deficiency is between $1,000 and $2,000 a year (in 1976 dollars).
Kossoudji, 1988 (based on 1976 Survey of Income and Education)	Earnings and occupation choice are modeled simultaneously for immigrant men with various language	Immigrants who do not speak English are pushed down the occupational ladder.

(Table continues)

375

TABLE 9–1 (continued)

Study	Description	Major Findings
	skills. A simple measure of language ability is included in the regressions.	
Tainer, 1988 (based on 1976 Survey of Income and Education)	Earnings regressions are estimated for foreign born men. A simple index of English language proficiency is defined.	The effect of English language proficiency is significant, particularly among Hispanic and Asians.
McManus, 1990 (based on 1980 census)	Earnings regressions are estimated for Hispanic men. To assess the importance of Hispanic enclaves, the author includes the local proportion of Hispanics and the local proportion of Hispanics who speak English as independent variables.	Enclaves reduce the earnings losses associated with limited English skills. An increase in the proportion of Hispanic men who speak only English lowers the returns to English.
Rivera-Batiz, 1990 (based on 1985 National Assessment of Educational Progress (NAEP), Young Adult Literary Assessment Survey)	Earnings regressions are estimated for immigrant males and females ages 21–25 who speak various languages. A measure of English language ability is defined on the basis of scores from a reading test.	The test-based measure of proficiency has more effect on earnings than a self-assessed measure.
Chiswick, 1991 (based on 1986 Survey of illegal aliens apprehended	The sample is composed of about 800 males, most of whom are Spanish	Reading ability is more important than speaking ability in the explanation of

TABLE 9–1 (continued)

Study	Description	Major Findings
in the Los Angeles area)	speakers. Independent variables used in earnings regressions include a measure of speaking and reading ability at the time of the survey and a measure of speaking ability before coming to the United States.	earnings.

SOURCES: Refer to bibliography for complete listing.

TABLE 9–2

STUDIES ON LANGUAGE ABILITY AND EARNINGS IN CANADA, 1979–1988

Study	Description	Major Findings
Veltman, Boulet, and Castonguay, 1979 (based on 1971 census)	Earnings regressions (with earnings in dollars) are estimated for men in the Montreal metropolitan area. Dummy variables are included on the right-hand side for bilingualism and for language spoken at home.	For men whose mother tongue is French, there are monetary returns to both bilingualism and to speaking English at home. There are no such returns to speaking French for men whose mother tongue is English.
Boulet, 1980 (based on 1961 census; 1971 census; 1978 survey done by Bernard and Renaud of University of Montreal)	The study reports gross earnings differentials for men in the Montreal metropolitan area and also includes some earnings regressions (with earnings in dollars).	Gross earnings differentials between English and French mother tongue men decreased from 1961 to 1977. The differentials were 51% in 1961, 30% in 1970, and 15% in 1977. The differentials

(Table continues)

TABLE 9–2 (continued)

Study	Description	Major Findings
		appear to be caused mainly by the presence of a highly paid English-speaking elite.
Lacroix and Vaillancourt, 1980 (based on 1973 Survey of Highly Qualified Manpower)	Earnings regressions are estimated for men and women in Quebec. Language attributes are included on the right-hand side. Separate analyses are performed for age, industry, and occupation subgroups.	English has higher returns in the sectors of the economy with markets outside of Quebec. French has higher returns for internal sectors.
Vaillancourt, 1980 (based on 1971 census)	Earnings regressions are estimated for men in the province of Quebec and in the Montreal metropolitan area. Dummy variables are included for mother tongue and bilingualism. Separate analyses are performed for age, industry, and occupation subgroups.	Bilingualism has monetary returns for French-speaking men but not for English-speaking men.
Carliner, 1981 (based on 1971 census)	Earnings regressions are estimated for men in Quebec and English Canada. The language spoken at home is used to define language groups.	In Quebec there are subtantial economic returns to learning English for French speakers but no economic reward for English speakers to learn French. There are no significant returns to learning English for

TABLE 9–2 (continued)

Study	Description	Major Findings
		French speakers outside Quebec.
Lacroix and Vaillancourt, 1981 (based on 1971 census; 1971 survey by Quebec Commission on French Language; 1978 survey by Bernard and Renaud of University of Montreal; 1979 survey by the Quebec Conseil de la langue française)	Earnings regressions are estimated for men and women in Quebec. Various measures of language ability are used in addition to the usual ones from census data. Separate analyses are performed for age, industry, and occupation subgroups.	The return to speaking French increased between 1971 and 1978. Earnings disparities between English- and French-speaking men decreased between 1970 and 1980.
Shapiro and Stelcner, 1981 (based on 1971 census)	Earnings regressions are estimated for males and females in Canada, Quebec, and Ontario. The study focuses on the role of language in explaining male-female earnings differentials.	Language variables are important for determining male earnings but not female earnings.
Shapiro and Stelcner, 1982 (based on 1971 census)	Earnings regressions are estimated for males and females in Quebec.	For males, the return to learning English is much greater than the return to learning French. The difference between the returns to learning English and to learning French is less for women than for men.
Grenier, 1985 (based on 1979 survey by the Quebec Conseil de la langue française)	Earnings regressions are estimated for male and female Quebec residents. The study considers	Selectivity appears to be more important for French speakers who learn English than for English speakers who

(Table continues)

379

TABLE 9-2 (continued)

Study	Description	Major Findings
	selectivity in the decision to learn a language.	learn French.
Grenier and Lacroix, 1986 (based on 1981 census)	Earnings regressions are estimated for men residing in the Ottawa metropolitan area.	Returns to learning French are positive for men whose mother tongue is English primarily because of the presence of the federal government. The net effect of learning English for men whose mother tongue is French is not significant in the regressions, but this is probably because of the small number of unilingual French speakers in Ottawa.
Grenier, 1987 (based on 1981 census)	Earnings regressions are estimated for men who lived in Quebec in 1976 and subsequently moved. The returns to the knowledge of French and English are analyzed in relation to selectivity in emigration from Quebec from 1976 to 1981. Many men of English mother tongue migrated during this period.	Selectivity in migration appears to be important for English speakers. The returns to bilingualism for men whose mother tongue is English are underestimated when selectivity is ignored.
Shapiro and Stelcner, 1987 (based on 1971 census; 1981 census)	Earnings regressions are estimated for men and women living in Quebec.	There was an important reduction in earnings differentials between language groups from 1970 to 1980, especially for men.

TABLE 9–2 (continued)

Study	Description	Major Findings
Chiswick and Miller, 1988 (based on 1971 census; 1981 census)	Earnings regressions are estimated for men in Canada. Ethnicity rather than mother tongue is used to define the French group.	French ethnicity had a negative effect on earnings in 1971 and a positive effect in 1981. There was a positive return to bilingualism.
Grenier, 1988 (based on 1981 census)	Earnings regressions are estimated for women living in Quebec.	Language attributes are not important in explaining earnings differentials.
Robinson, 1988 (based on 1971 census; 1981 census; 1973 CARMAC; 1979 Quality of Life Survey)	Earnings regressions are estimated for men and women in Canada. The endogeneity of language choice is taken care of through fixed and random effects models.	French mother tongue is not a handicap in the earnings generation process. Bilingualism has positive returns.
Vaillancourt, 1988 (based on 1971 census; 1981 census)	Earnings regressions are estimated for men and women in Quebec. The samples are broken down according to various attributes, including age groups, occupations, and industries.	In general the return to speaking English was higher in 1971 than it was in 1981.

SOURCES: Refer to bibliography for complete listing.

methods vary in three main ways. First, in some studies the measure of an individual's language skills is a dummy variable for whether an individual's mother tongue is the same as the dominant language of the labor market; in other studies it is an ordinal index of an individual's ability to communicate in the dominant language of the labor market. Researchers may measure speaking or reading ability, and language skills may be self-assessed or measured objectively. Second, different human capital variables are held constant in assessing the marginal contribution of language skills to wages. Immigrant status and years since immigration, for example, may or may not be included as control variables. Third, studies may be national or regional in scope and may refer to different periods, gender groups, and linguistic groups.

Most Canadian studies concentrate on language-wage differentials in Quebec. These studies generally find that the return to ability in French increased in the 1970s for men. The few studies that examined the situation outside Quebec did not find strong language effects. The evidence reported in the U.S. studies is mixed. In some studies, language variables explain a significant portion of wage variation even after one controls for the effect of other standard human capital variables. But a sizable number of studies have failed to generate any convincing evidence that language has either a statistically significant or a substantively important effect on wages in the United States.

A fundamental premise of this study is that the return to language skills is determined by the interaction of the supply and demand for those skills *within* local labor and product markets. This framework suggests that the return to language skills may vary according to the total linguistic composition of local labor and product markets as well as in response to changes in other factors that may cause exogenous shifts in the supply or demand for particular language skills. We report empirical evidence based on this framework derived from 1971, 1981, and 1986 Canadian census data and from 1970 and 1980 U.S. census data. With the exception of the 1986 Canadian census, all of these sets of data have been used previously to study the wage effects of language skills, though not in as comparable a manner as reported here.

One of our principal aims is to test the view that a common economic framework can explain patterns and trends in the economic position of linguistic minorities in different national settings. Canada and the United States have similar economic structures, and English is the majority language in both countries. The countries' linguistic minorities, however, have little in common. Three important differences deserve mention. First, Canada's major linguistic minority—a French-speaking population—is not an immigrant group. The major linguistic minority in the United States—a Spanish-speaking population—is predominantly an immigrant group. Second, although the French-speaking population in Canada is a minority group nationally, it is a majority group in Quebec, a major province. In contrast, the Spanish-speaking population in the United States is a minority both nationally and in every state and SMSA. Finally, French is an official national language in Canada whereas Spanish is not an official language in the United States.

In the next section we briefly describe our theoretical framework. Our model suggests that markets with larger proportions of minority language speakers may value language skills differently than markets with smaller proportions. A large supply of minority language speakers may depress wages for workers who do not speak the dominant language. Alternatively the community of minority language speakers may create its own demand for services in the minority language, a situation that may lead to higher wages. Determining which of these two opposing forces has been stronger in Canada and the United States at different points during the past two decades is the main empirical issue addressed below.

In the following section we describe the five sets of data analyzed in this chapter. We also discuss the validity of our use of these sets of data to compare language-wage differentials over time and between Canada and the United States. In addition, we test the quality of U.S. data on ethnicity as a proxy for language ability.

The next section presents our major empirical results. In the United States the increasing supply of Spanish speakers appears to be responsible for the slight deterioration of relative wages received by Spanish workers in the 1970s. In Quebec, by contrast, the French-speaking community appears to have shifted out the demand for French language skills by more than the increased supply of French-speaking workers, thereby leading to a relative improvement in the value of French language skills. For Canada as a whole, the earnings gap between French and English speakers, which was sizable in the early 1970s, became substantially more narrow by the 1980s.

Theoretical Framework

Consider a local economy with two language communities and two corresponding labor markets, each with a set of labor supply and labor demand curves. Assume that workers in both markets have identical characteristics with the exception of the language they speak. It need not be assumed that the language an individual speaks is an exogenously fixed characteristic.

The location of the supply curve in each local labor market is determined largely by the number of individuals who speak each language. Outward shifts in the supply of labor can thus result from natural increase among a particular language community or from in-migration of individuals with similar language abilities, either from other local economies or from the other labor market within the same local economy.

Although our labor supply formulations for workers with different language characteristics are absolutely standard, our labor demand curves in one important respect are not. Our analysis permits the demand curves for workers with different language abilities to depend upon the number of consumers in local product markets with those same linguistic characteristics. In this way the demand for minority language employees is permitted to increase (not necessarily proportionately) with the relative size of the minority language community. The existence of such an effect seems especially plausible in certain industries, such as retail trade and health services. This formulation implies that the relative wages received by a linguistic minority may vary (probably positively) with the relative size of that minority community among all consumers.

In this model a language-wage differential is interpreted as reflecting some combination of labor supply and labor demand differences. In addition, varying the relative supply of workers who speak a particular language (for example, through in- or out-migration of individuals with certain language characteristics) or varying the relative demand (for example, by a shift in the language characteristics of participants in the relevant product market) may be expected to affect the relative wages received by the language group.

Two additional hypotheses suggest that the wages received by a linguistic minority are lower in regions with larger linguistic minority populations. First, given that individuals derive social and cultural benefits from living in communities where their language is used, minority language speakers may have a lower reservation wage in regions where they are more highly represented. Second, self-selection might reinforce these differentials insofar as out-migrants from areas with a high proportion of minority language speakers might place less value on these externalities or be more ambitious and aggressive in the labor market.

The nature of our data does not permit us to identify and to disentangle the effects of these various forces on language-wage differentials. They can, however, be used to perform some indirect tests. In addition, the model enriches our interpretation of the empirical results.

Language Data in Canada and the United States

Both Canadian and U.S. statistical agencies collect data on language and ethnicity. Language data may refer either to the first language learned and still spoken or understood (that is, the mother tongue) or to the language usually spoken at home. Data on ethnicity may also be a useful indicator of language ability.

Canadian Data. Most researchers define linguistic groups in Canada on the basis of mother tongue, a variable that is reported in the Canadian census and other survey data sets. Canadian censuses also report information on ethnicity, but this variable has generally not been used to study language because it is an error-ridden measure of language ability whose definition has not been stable over time.[2] In contrast, the definition of mother tongue has not changed over time.

The Canadian censuses also report information on the ability of respondents to speak English and French (with the same questions asked in the various Canadian censuses). Specifically respondents are asked to indicate whether they can conduct a conversation in English, French, both English and French, or neither English nor French. Only yes and no answers are allowed in response to these questions, and they represent a person's self-assessment of language ability. Although these data do not provide objective measures of language proficiency, they do distinguish two groups of people in a fairly comparable manner over time: those who consider themselves bilingual and those who do not.

Another useful language question has been included since Canada's 1971 census. It refers to the language that a person usually speaks at home. This question is sometimes preferred to mother tongue by those who are interested in measuring the size of different linguistic groups in Canada. Mother tongue, however, may be preferable to language used at home for some analytical purposes because it is an exogenous characteristic for a person.

We analyze three data sets for Canada: the public use samples of the 1971, 1981, and 1986 censuses. The two language categories used in our study of each Canadian census are French and English mother tongue (individuals who report having other mother tongues are excluded from our samples). For these two mother tongues, we consider individuals who are both unilingual and bilingual on the basis of their ability to carry a conversation in one or the other of the official languages. These language variables are the ones typically analyzed by those who study language-wage differentials in Canada.[3] We define Quebec as the region with a high proportion of French speakers; the rest of Canada constitutes the low-proportion region.

U.S. Data. Unlike the case for Canada, U.S. language data have not been consistent across censuses. A question on mother tongue appeared in the 1970 census but not in the 1980 census.[4] English-speaking ability was assessed in 1980 but not in 1970.[5] As a result, we explore the use of ethnicity data—which has been consistently reported for the United States—as a proxy for language ability.

We tested the quality of the variable for Spanish origin as an indicator of Spanish mother tongue using the 1976 Survey of Income and Education. This data set is unique among large survey data sets for the United States in that it reports information on both mother tongue and ethnic origin.[6] We exploited these overlapping data by fitting two sets of wage equations and comparing the results: the first set was specified to include a dummy variable with direct information on Spanish mother tongue as a regressor; the second set was specified identically except that the dummy variable of the Spanish mother tongue was replaced with a dummy variable for Spanish origin.

The estimates of these two specifications are reported in table 9–3. Comparing them reveals the coefficients of interest to be remarkably similar in both sets of equations. This apparently results because only 14 percent of the individuals who report their ethnic origin as Spanish in the survey of income and education also report English as their mother tongue. Thus our results suggest that the Spanish ethnic origin variable reflects much the same information as the Spanish mother tongue variable.[7]

We focus our attention on two data sets for the United States: the one-in-one-thousand public use samples of the 1970 and the 1980 censuses. Unfortunately no comparable national data set is yet available for a more recent year. The data on Spanish origin, which is defined similarly in both data sets, are used to identify the Spanish-speaking population.[8] In our study we compare individuals of Spanish origin to whites of non-Spanish origin; we exclude blacks and all other races from our comparison group. In addition, we divide the United States into regions of high and low proportions of people of Spanish origin. The distinction was made by examining the population of Spanish origin in each state and metropolitan area. Arizona, California, Colorado, New Mexico, Texas, and the metropolitan areas of New York state and Florida constitute the high Spanish-origin population region.[9] All other regions of the United States constitute the low Spanish-origin population.

In contrast to many earlier studies, we do not focus this analysis on earnings differences among various Hispanic ethnic groups (for example, Mexican, Puerto Rican, Cuban). Our analysis of the 1980 census, however, does in some cases distinguish people of Spanish origin according to their ability to speak English. Those individuals who reported that they can speak English well or very well are

TABLE 9–3
Relative Earnings for Males in the United States, by Spanish Origin, Spanish Mother Tongue, and Linguistic Region, 1975

	25–64 Age Group		25–34 Age Group	
	Spanish mother tongue	Spanish origin	Spanish mother tongue	Spanish origin
Earnings differentials (log points)[a]				
High Spanish[b]				
S to W	−.38	−.43	−.26	−.27
SM to W	−.81	−.89	n.r.	n.r.
SB to W	−.25	−.31	n.r.	n.r.
Low Spanish[b]				
S to W	−.29	−.24	−.24	−.20
SM to W	−.65	−.67	n.r.	n.r.
SB to W	−.14	−.11*	n.r.	n.r.
Regression corrected earnings differentials (log points)[c]				
High Spanish				
S to W	−.10	−.12	−.08*	−.11
SM to W	−.17*	−.19*	n.r.	n.r.
SB to W	−.10	−.12	n.r.	n.r.
Low Spanish				
S to W	−.06*	−.05*	−.03*	−.01*
SM to W	−.14*	−.15*	n.r.	n.r.
SB to W	−.03*	−.02*	n.r.	n.r.
Sample size[d]				
High Spanish	1,969	1,948	775	763
W	.891	.842	.897	.829
S	.108	.156	.103	.171
SM	.025	.032	n.r.	n.r.
SB	.082	.125	n.r.	n.r.
Low Spanish	5,396	5,377	1,969	1,961
W	.988	.985	.988	.985
S	.012	.015	.012	.015
SM	.004	.003	n.r.	n.r.
SB	.009	.010	n.r.	n.r.

* = The coefficient is not significantly different from zero at the 5 percent level.
n.r. = Results not reported because sample size is too small.
a. Definitions of symbols: S = Spanish, W = non-Spanish white, SM = Spanish monolingual, and SB = Spanish bilingual.

(Table continues)

TABLE 9–3 (continued)

---

b. High Spanish proportion regions include Arizona, California, Colorado, New Mexico, Texas, and the metropolitan areas of Florida and New York state. All other regions constitute the low Spanish proportion regions.

c. Variables included in regression: four dummies for weeks worked in previous year, six dummies for hours worked in the week preceding the census or the survey, two marital status dummies, three regional dummies, three period of immigration dummies, age, age squared, education, and education squared.

d. Whites are undersampled (8 percent of total), and observations are weighted accordingly. The proportions are those obtained after weighting the observations.

SOURCE: 1976 Survey of Income and Education, Public Use Sample, U.S. Department of Commerce, Bureau of the Census, Washington, D.C.

defined as bilingual for the purposes of this study, while those who reported that they do not speak English well or that they do not speak English at all are called monolingual.

Empirical Results

French-English Differentials in Canada. Table 9–4 first reports real earnings levels in 1970, 1980, and 1985 for males ages twenty-five to sixty-four and twenty-five to thirty-four with different linguistic characteristics.[10] These figures are reported separately for individuals who reside in different linguistic regions in Canada. Next come earnings differentials between individuals with different linguistic characteristics, again distinguishing between Quebec and the rest of Canada. The third set of figures describes the linguistic composition of the samples we analyze. For the sake of comparability with the regression results reported later, average earnings figures in table 9–4 are in the form of geometric (as opposed to arithmetic) averages, and earnings differentials are measured in log points (as opposed to percentage differentials).

We make two types of earnings comparisions: (1) between individuals with different language skills (for example, English speakers versus French speakers, unilingual English speakers versus bilingual English speakers, and unilingual French speakers versus bilingual French speakers) and (2) between individuals with comparable lan-

TABLE 9–4: REAL AND RELATIVE EARNINGS OF MALES IN CANADA, BY MOTHER TONGUE AND LINGUISTIC REGION, 1970, 1980, AND 1985

	25–64 Age Group			25–34 Age Group		
	1970	1980	1985	1970	1980	1985
Earnings in 1985 Canadian dollars (geometric mean)[a]						
Quebec						
English (all)	24,054	24,306	21,908	20,718	19,570	15,563
Unilingual	24,369	22,774	20,532	20,151	17,501	11,485
Bilingual	23,748	25,217	22,499	21,280	20,671	17,453
French (all)	17,820	22,012	19,600	16,994	19,971	16,083
Unilingual	15,605	19,544	17,209	15,445	18,769	14,704
Bilingual	20,564	25,144	22,483	19,024	21,413	17,853
Rest of Canada						
English (all)	21,248	24,035	21,623	20,009	21,248	17,895
French (all)	17,610	20,987	18,311	17,174	19,599	16,182
Unilingual	10,848	14,047	10,410	n.r.	n.r.	n.r.
Bilingual	18,457	21,605	19,110	n.r.	n.r.	n.r.
Earnings differentials (log points)[b]						
Quebec						
F to E	– .30	– .10	– .11	– .20	.02*	.03
EB to EU	– .02*	.10	.09*	.05*	.17	.41
FU to EU	– .45	– .15	– .18	– .27	.06*	.24
FB to EU	– .17	.10	.09*	– .06*	.20	.43

(Table continues)

TABLE 9-4 (continued)

	25-64 Age Group			25-34 Age Group		
	1970	1980	1985	1970	1980	1985
Rest of Canada						
F to E	−.19	−.14	−.17	−.15	−.08	−.10
FU to E	−.67	−.53	−.72	n.r.	n.r.	n.r.
FB to E	−.14	−.10	−.11	n.r.	n.r.	n.r.
Sample size						
Quebec	9,596	10,881	11,611	3,447	4,256	4,462
E	.153	.117	.106	.121	.105	.097
EU	.076	.042	.031	.059	.034	.026
EB	.077	.075	.075	.062	.070	.070
F	.847	.882	.894	.879	.895	.903
FU	.440	.466	.459	.476	.473	.486
FB	.407	.417	.435	.403	.422	.417
Rest of Canada	21,029	26,211	29,753	7,239	10,890	11,872
E	.922	.929	.934	.921	.931	.940
F	.078	.071	.066	.080	.069	.060
FU	.007	.005	.005	n.r.	n.r.	n.r.
FB	.071	.066	.061	n.r.	n.r.	n.r.

* = The coefficient is *not* significantly different from zero at the 5 percent level.

n.r. = Results not reported because sample size is too small.

a. Constant dollars are obtained from using CPI for Canada.

b. Definitions of symbols: F = French, E = English, EU = English unilingual, EB = English bilingual, FU = French unilingual, and FB = French bilingual.

SOURCES: Canadian censuses for 1971, 1981, and 1986; Public Use Samples, Individual Files, Statistics Canada, Ottawa.

guage skills who reside in different linguistic regions within Canada. We are also interested in analyzing trends in earnings differentials over time, especially in view of the social and political movement that has been active since the early 1970s to promote the use of French in Quebec.

We provide a separate set of figures for twenty-five- to thirty-four-year-olds because we expect their labor market outcomes to be more sensitive to exogenous shifts in the labor market. In contrast, the employment and earnings of older workers may reflect decisions and understandings that were established before the sample period. Females and youth are excluded from our analyses to avoid the well-known idiosyncrasies associated with their labor market behavior.

The figures in table 9–4 reveal sizable differences in average earnings among twenty-five- to sixty-four-year-old workers in all three censuses, with French-speaking workers having relatively low earnings in both linguistic regions (that is, within as well as outside Quebec). The earnings gaps are especially wide when one compares unilingual French workers to English-speaking workers in either linguistic region. This finding suggests that language skills can have an influence on earnings that is independent of any effects that might result from ethnic background.

Table 9–4 contains three other important results. First, language-earnings differentials were larger within Quebec than outside Quebec for both age groups in 1970, although the pattern is reversed in 1980 and 1985. The 1970 pattern is consistent with the model sketched in "Theoretical Framework" (that is, the supply effect outweighs the demand effect) as well as with the two alternative hypotheses that involve the positive externality of remaining in a language community and self-selection in out-migration. The 1970 data alone do not permit us to distinguish among these hypotheses.

Second, language-earnings differentials tended to decline between the 1970s and 1980s for both age groups. Although the decline was quite sharp within Quebec (where differentials actually reversed signs for twenty-five- to thirty-four-year-olds in 1980), it also occurred outside Quebec. This decline appears to have been caused by a sharp increase in the relative demand for French-speaking workers within Quebec during the 1970s and 1980s. One indicator of this demand shift is the association of the decline in earnings differentials in Quebec with a relative improvement in the employment-to-population ratio for Quebec's French-speaking workers. Yet the relative supply of French-speaking workers also increased in the 1970s. Indeed table 9–5 indicates that the linguistic composition of the Quebec work force shifted toward the French from 1970 to 1985—almost exclusively

TABLE 9–5

Employment-Population Ratios, Labor Force Participation, and Unemployment Rates for Males in Canada, by Mother Tongue and Linguistic Region, 1971, 1981, and 1986

	25–64 Age Group			25–34 Age Group		
	1971	1981	1986	1971	1981	1986
Employment-population ratio						
Quebec						
English	.912	.845	.793	.905	.855	.819
Unilingual	.911	.833	.733	.899	.862	.742
Bilingual	.913*	.852*	.820	.910*	.852*	.850
French	.830	.826*	.789*	.848	.865*	.817*
Unilingual	.802	.793	.746*	.823	.843*	.779*
Bilingual	.863	.866	.839	.879*	.890*	.865
Rest of Canada						
English	.929	.895	.856	.933	.922	.872
French	.873	.831	.788	.897	.895	.837
Unilingual	.801	.605	.582	n.r.	n.r.	n.r.
Bilingual	.881	.851	.806	n.r.	n.r.	n.r.
Labor force participation						
Quebec						
English	.949	.897	.865	.952	.929	.924
Unilingual	.950	.880	.824	.952	.910	.887
Bilingual	.949*	.907*	.883	.953*	.937*	.939

French	.882	.889*	.876*	.900	.938*	.928*
Unilingual	.862	.867*	.852*	.884	.924*	.912*
Bilingual	.904	.914	.904	.921*	.955	.949
Rest of Canada						
English	.963	.928	.923	.970	.963	.968
French	.928	.883	.872	.956	.947	.938
Unilingual	.878	.711	.701	n.r.	n.r.	n.r.
Bilingual	.933	.898	.887	n.r.	n.r.	n.r.
Unemployment rate						
Quebec						
English	.039	.058	.084	.050	.079	.114
Unilingual	.040	.053	.111	.055	.053	.164
Bilingual	.038*	.061*	.072	.045*	.091*	.096
French	.058	.070*	.100*	.058*	.079*	.119*
Unilingual	.069	.085	.125*	.068*	.088*	.146*
Bilingual	.045*	.052*	.073	.045*	.067*	.088
Rest of Canada						
English	.035	.036	.073	.038	.043	.091
French	.059	.059	.096	.062	.055*	.107*
Unilingual	.088	.148	.170	n.r.	n.r.	n.r.
Bilingual	.057	.053	.092	n.r.	n.r.	n.r.

* = Not statistically different from English (or English unilingual) at the 5 percent level.

n.r. = Results not reported because sample size is too small.

SOURCES: Canadian censuses for 1971, 1981, and 1986; Public Use Samples, Individual Files, Statistics Canada, Ottawa.

by replacing the unilingual English. Nonetheless, since relative earnings improved during the period, we may infer that the demand shift dominated the supply shift.

Third, language-earnings differentials are generally higher for twenty-five- to sixty-four-year-olds than for the subset of individuals aged twenty-five to thirty-four. The smaller language-wage differentials for younger workers is consistent with the decline of differentials among twenty-five- to sixty-four-year-olds and suggests a continuing trend toward overall wage parity between linguistic groups both outside Quebec and even more so in Quebec.

To further our understanding of the nature of these earnings differentials, we perform a simple analysis in which we examine the size of the estimated language-earnings differentials when one fits standard regression models that control for the effect on earnings of annual hours worked, marital status, age, education, and region (when appropriate). The results of this analysis, which are reported in table 9–6, indicate that the language-wage differentials that are reported in table 9–4 reflect in large measure, though not entirely, the correlation of language with other variables that determine annual earnings. The thirty–log point difference in annual earnings between French and English speakers in Quebec in 1970, for example, is reduced to thirteen points when one controls for annual hours worked, marital status, age, and educational attainment. But even more striking, in all other comparisons the French-English differentials are rendered small and insignificantly different from zero by the inclusion of these controls. Thus, although some genuine language-wage differentials are evident in Quebec in 1970, many of the sizable differentials reported in table 9–4 apparently result because English speakers work more hours per year (see table 9–7) and tend to have higher educational attainment than French speakers (see table 9–12).

Another striking finding in table 9–6 relates to the dramatic decline in wage differentials from 1970 to 1985 between Quebec workers who can speak at least some French and Quebec workers who speak only English. Indeed the considerable earnings disadvantage suffered by unilingual French workers in 1970—relative to comparable unilingual English workers—was entirely eliminated by 1985 and actually became a clear earnings advantage among twenty-five- to thirty-four-year-olds. Since the estimates reported in table 9–6 provide no evidence of a similar wage change outside Quebec, this finding constitutes further evidence of a strong outward shift in the demand for French language skills in Quebec between the 1970s and 1980s.[11]

TABLE 9–6
REGRESSION-CORRECTED RELATIVE EARNINGS OF MALES IN CANADA, BY MOTHER TONGUE AND LINGUISTIC REGION, 1970, 1980, AND 1985

Earnings Differentials[a]	25–64 Age Group			25–34 Age Group		
	1970	1980	1985	1970	1980	1985
Quebec						
F to E	−.13	−.01*	−.01*	−.08	.05*	.04*
EB to EU	.01*	.09	.04*	.06*	.12	.24
FU to EU	−.18	.02*	−.01*	−.11	.12	.19
FB to EU	−.09	.07	.04*	−.01*	.15	.25
Rest of Canada						
F to E	.01*	.02*	.01*	−.02*	.02*	.04*
FU to E	−.02*	.04*	.06	n.r.	n.r.	n.r.
FB to E	.01*	.03*	.00*	n.r.	n.r.	n.r.

n.r.: Results not reported because sample size is too small.
NOTE: Variables included in the regression: four dummies for weeks worked in the previous year, six dummies for hours worked in the week preceding the census, two marital status dummies, three regional dummies (for rest of Canada only), age, age squared, education, and education squared.
* = The coefficient is not significantly different from zero at the 5 percent level.
a. Log points. Definitions of symbols: F = French, E = English, EU = English unilingual, EB = English bilingual, FU = French unilingual, and FB = French bilingual.
SOURCES: Canadian censuses, 1971, 1981, and 1986; Public Use Samples, Individual Files, Statistics Canada, Ottawa.

Spanish-English Differentials in the United States. Tables 9–8 through 9–11 report statistics relating to the labor market outcomes experienced by Spanish- and English-speaking males in the United States in 1970 and 1980. To facilitate comparisons between the United States and Canada, we report statistics for the United States that are reasonably comparable to those reported above for Canada. Thus, we provide separate analyses for males aged twenty-five to sixty-four and twenty-five to thirty-four residing in different linguistic regions.

The results of tables 9–8 through 9–11 for the United States may be summarized as follows. First, the raw earnings differentials are sizable in both 1970 and 1980 but are relatively larger (1) for twenty-five- to sixty-four-year-olds and (2) in regions with a high proportion of Spanish-language workers. Second, monolingual Spanish workers fare less well in the labor market than bilingual Spanish workers.

TABLE 9–7

HOURS AND WEEKS WORKED BY MALES IN CANADA, BY MOTHER
TONGUE AND LINGUISTIC REGION, 1981 AND 1986

Time Worked	25–64 Age Group		25–34 Age Group	
	1981	1986	1981	1986
Hours per week				
Quebec				
English	42.3	42.3	43.2	42.2
Unilingual	41.5	42.2	42.2	43.3
Bilingual	42.7	42.4	43.6*	41.8*
French	42.1*	42.1	41.8	41.8*
Unilingual	42.5	42.3	42.3*	42.1*
Bilingual	41.6*	41.7	41.2*	41.4*
Rest of Canada				
English	44.4	45.0	44.2	44.8
French	43.6	44.4*	43.5*	44.7*
Unilingual	43.1*	41.4	n.r.	n.r.
Bilingual	43.6	44.6*	n.r.	n.r.
Weeks per year				
Quebec				
English	46.5	46.1	44.6	43.9
Unilingual	46.8	45.1	44.1	40.5
Bilingual	46.3*	46.5*	44.9*	45.1
French	45.2	44.6	44.7*	43.1*
Unilingual	44.0	43.2	44.3*	41.9*
Bilingual	46.6*	46.1*	45.2*	44.5
Rest of Canada				
English	46.5	45.5	45.6	44.1
French	44.2	42.7	43.9	41.5
Unilingual	36.6	31.4	n.r.	n.r.
Bilingual	44.7	43.5	n.r.	n.r.

*= Not statistically different from English (or English unilingual) at the 5 percent level.
n.r. = Results not reported because sample size is too small.
SOURCES: Canadian censuses, 1981 and 1986; Public Use Samples, Individual Files, Statistics Canada, Ottawa.

TABLE 9–8

REAL AND RELATIVE EARNINGS OF
MALES IN THE UNITED STATES, BY LANGUAGE
AND LINGUISTIC REGION, 1969 AND 1979

	25–64 Age Group		25–34 Age Group	
	1969	1979	1969	1979
Earnings in 1979 U.S. dollars (geometric mean)[a]				
High Spanish[b]				
White	16,190	15,726	14,395	13,092
Spanish (All)	9,970	9,548	10,104	8,918
Monolingual	n.a.	6,965	n.a.	n.r.
Bilingual	n.a.	10,522	n.a.	n.r.
Low Spanish[b]				
White	15,120	14,791	14,073	12,661
Spanish (All)	11,655	10,355	11,708	9,445
Monolingual	n.a.	7,526	n.a.	n.r.
Bilingual	n.a.	11,355	n.a.	n.r.
Earnings differentials (log points)[c]				
High Spanish				
S to W	− .48	− .50	− .35	− .38
SM to W	n.a.	− .81	n.a.	n.r.
SB to W	n.a.	− .40	n.a.	n.r.
Low Spanish				
S to W	− .26	− .36	− .18	− .29
SM to W	n.a.	− .68	n.a.	n.r.
SB to W	n.a.	− .26	n.a.	n.r.
Sample size[d]				
High Spanish	8,826	10,752	2,660	4,199
W	.882	.836	.853	.804
S	.118	.164	.147	.196
SM	n.a.	.038	n.a.	n.r.
SB	n.a.	.125	n.a.	n.r.
Low Spanish	21,892	24,314	6,675	9,199
W	.980	.979	.977	.976
S	.019	.021	.023	.024
SM	n.a.	.004	n.a.	n.r.
SB	n.a.	.017	n.a.	n.r.

n.a. = Information not available for that year.
n.r. = Results not reported because sample size is too small.
NOTE: Spanish origin is used as a proxy for Spanish mother tongue. White of
non-Spanish origin is used as a proxy for English mother tongue. All differen-

(Table continues)

TABLE 9–8 (continued)

tials reported in this table are significantly different from zero at the 5 percent level.
a. Constant dollars are obtained from using the CPI for the entire U.S.
b. High Spanish proportion regions include Arizona, California, Colorado, New Mexico, Texas, and the metropolitan areas of Florida and New York state. All other regions constitute the low Spanish proportion regions.
c. Definitions of symbols: S = Spanish, W = non-Spanish white, SM = Spanish monolingual, and SB = Spanish bilingual.
SOURCES: U.S. censuses, 1970 and 1980; Public Use Samples 1:1,000, U.S. Department of Commerce, Bureau of the Census, Washington, D.C.

TABLE 9–9

REGRESSION-CORRECTED RELATIVE EARNINGS OF
MALES IN THE UNITED STATES, BY LANGUAGE AND
LINGUISTIC REGION, 1969 AND 1979

Earnings Differentials[a]	25–64 Age Group		25–34 Age Group	
	1969	1979	1969	1979
High Spanish[b]				
S to W	−.21	−.20	−.13	−.16
SM to W	n.a.	−.29	n.a.	n.r.
SB to W	n.a.	−.19	n.a.	n.r.
Low Spanish[b]				
S to W	−.13	−.14	−.08	−.12
SM to W	n.a.	−.26	n.a.	n.r.
SB to W	n.a.	−.12	n.a.	n.r.

n.a. = Information not available for that year.
n.r. = Results not reported because sample size is too small.
NOTE: Variables included in regression are four dummies for weeks worked in previous year, six dummies for hours worked in the week preceding the census, two marital status dummies, three regional dummies, three period of immigration dummies, age, age squared, education, and education squared. Spanish origin is used as a proxy for Spanish mother tongue. All coefficients reported in this table are significantly different from zero at the 5 percent level.
a. Log points. Definitions of symbols: S = Spanish, W = non-Spanish white, SM = Spanish monolingual, and SB = Spanish bilingual.
b. High Spanish proportion regions include Arizona, California, Colorado, New Mexico, Texas, and the metropolitan areas of Florida and New York state. All other regions constitute the low Spanish proportion regions.
SOURCES: U.S. censuses, 1970 and 1980; Public Use Samples 1:1,000, U.S. Department of Commerce, Bureau of the Census, Washington, D.C.

TABLE 9–10

EMPLOYMENT-POPULATION RATIOS,
LABOR FORCE PARTICIPATION, AND UNEMPLOYMENT RATES FOR
MALES IN THE UNITED STATES, BY LANGUAGE AND
LINGUISTIC REGION, 1970 AND 1980

	25–64 Age Group		25–34 Age Group	
	1970	1980	1970	1980
Employment-population ratio				
High Spanish				
White	.897	.857	.913	.904
Spanish	.862	.846*	.876	.875
Monolingual	n.a.	.794	n.a.	n.r.
Bilingual	n.a.	.863*	n.a.	n.r.
Low Spanish[a]				
White	.895	.858	.927	.894
Spanish	.892*	.776	.910*	.754
Monolingual	n.a.	.777	n.a.	n.r.
Bilingual	n.a.	.776	n.a.	n.r.
Labor force participation				
High Spanish[a]				
White	.921	.889	.939	.945
Spanish	.903	.895*	.918*	.929*
Monolingual	n.a.	.864*	n.a.	n.r.
Bilingual	n.a.	.905	n.a.	n.r.
Low Spanish[a]				
White	.918	.899	.952	.949
Spanish	.923*	.847	.946*	.838
Monolingual	n.a.	.844	n.a.	n.r.
Bilingual	n.a.	.847	n.a.	n.r.
Unemployment rate				
High Spanish[a]				
White	.025	.036	.026	.043
Spanish	.045	.055	.046	.059
Monolingual	n.a.	.081	n.a.	n.r.
Bilingual	n.a.	.047	n.a.	n.r.
Low Spanish[a]				
White	.025	.046	.026	.057
Spanish	.033*	.083	.038*	.101
Monolingual	n.a.	.080*	n.a.	n.r.
Bilingual	n.a.	.084	n.a.	n.r.

* = Not statistically different from white at the 5 percent level.

(Table continues)

TABLE 9–10 (continued)

n.a. = Information not available for that year.
n.r. = Results not reported because sample size is too small.
NOTE: Spanish origin is used as a proxy for Spanish mother tongue.
a. High Spanish proportion regions include Arizona, California, Colorado, New Mexico, Texas, and the metropolitan areas of Florida and New York state. All other regions constitute the low Spanish proportion regions.
SOURCES: U.S. censuses, 1970 and 1980; Public Use Samples 1:1,000, U.S. Department of Commerce, Bureau of the Census, Washington, D.C.

TABLE 9–11

HOURS AND WEEKS WORKED BY
MALES IN THE UNITED STATES, BY LANGUAGE
AND LINGUISTIC REGION, 1980

Time Worked	25–64 Age Group	25–34 Age Group
Hours per week		
High Spanish[a]		
White	44.3	44.4
Spanish	42.1	42.1
Monolingual	41.3	n.r.
Bilingual	42.3	n.r.
Low Spanish[a]		
White	44.5	44.3
Spanish	43.0	43.1*
Monolingual	43.7*	n.r.
Bilingual	42.8	n.r.
Weeks per year		
High Spanish[a]		
White	47.9	47.2
Spanish	46.0	45.6
Monolingual	44.2	n.r.
Bilingual	46.6	n.r.
Low Spanish[a]		
White	48.1	47.4
Spanish	46.0	45.2
Monolingual	44.6	n.r.
Bilingual	46.4	n.r.

* = Not statistically different from white at the 5 percent level.
n.r. = Results not reported because sample size is too small.
NOTE: Spanish origin is used as a proxy for Spanish mother tongue.
a. High Spanish proportion regions include Arizona, California, Colorado, New Mexico, Texas, and the metropolitan areas of Florida and New York state. All other regions constitute the low Spanish proportion regions.
SOURCES: U.S. censuses, 1980; Public Use Samples 1:1,000, U.S. Department of Commerce, Bureau of the Census, Washington, D.C.

Third, Spanish workers became increasingly concentrated during the 1970s in regions that already had a large proportion of Spanish speakers, with only a small increase in the proportion of Spanish speakers outside these areas. Fourth, the earnings differentials between the Spanish- and English-speaking workers shrink when one controls for the effects on earnings of a standard set of control variables. Unlike the case of Canada, however, the language-earnings differentials in the United States do not vanish in size or significance when the controls are included. This finding suggests that language-wage differentials are a more deeply rooted phenomenon in the United States than in Canada.

Because of their general similarity with the results for Canada, the U.S. results further support the view that language-wage differentials are determined partly in the same way as any other garden-variety skill price and partly on the basis of the linguistic composition of a region. Indeed the slight deterioration in the relative earnings of Spanish-speaking workers in the United States during the 1970s is most likely explained by the increase in their relative supply. From 1970 to 1980, for example, the number of male Spanish workers increased at an annual rate of approximately 5.4 percent in regions with a high proportion of Spanish speakers, more than triple the rate of increase among non-Spanish workers in those areas. Similarly the number of Spanish male workers increased more than twice as fast as non-Spanish male workers in the regions with low proportions of Spanish speakers.

This conclusion about the importance of relative supply shifts in the United States contrasts with our reliance on a demand-shift explanation of the recent improvement in the relative earnings of French speakers in Canada. The relative supply of French speakers did in fact shift in Canada in the 1970s also, increasing in Quebec and declining outside Quebec. The difference in the relative growth rate of different linguistic groups in Canada and the United States highlights the fact that the main sources of additional French-speaking workers in Quebec were fertility and geographical redistribution within Canada, whereas the main source of additional Spanish workers in the United States was immigration.

Differences in Returns to Education. A linguistic minority might receive relatively low wages because its members earn a relatively low return on their investments in schooling. Indeed it seems reasonable to suppose that English-language schooling (throughout the United States as well as in Canada outside Quebec) contributes less per unit

TABLE 9–12

DIFFERENCES BETWEEN FRENCH AND ENGLISH MOTHER TONGUE
FOR MALES IN CANADA, BY LINGUISTIC REGION, IN YEARS OF
EDUCATION AND RETURNS TO EDUCATION, 1970, 1980, AND 1985

	25–64 Age Group			25–34 Age Group		
	1970	1980	1985	1970	1980	1985
Quebec						
Return to education[a]	− .009	− .003*	− .004*	− .008*	− .010*	− .002*
Years of education	− 2.2	− 1.5	− 1.2	− 1.9	− 1.0	− 0.5
Rest of Canada						
Return to education[a]	− .016	− .004*	− .018	− .013	− .009*	− .030
Years of education	− 1.9	− 1.5	− 1.5	− 1.5	− 0.9	− 0.6

* = The coefficient is not significantly different from zero at the 95 percent level.
a. Coefficient of French mother tongue interacted with years of education in an earning regression where the other independent variables are four dummies for weeks worked in the previous year, six dummies for hours worked in the week preceding the census, two marital status dummies, three regional dummies (for rest of Canada only), age, age squared, education, education squared, and one dummy for French mother tongue.
SOURCES: Canadian censuses, 1971, 1981, and 1986; Public Use Samples, Individual Files, Statistics Canada, Ottawa.

of time to the human capital of individuals for whom English is not the mother tongue than it does for native English speakers. Similarly the return to schooling received in a language other than English would also likely be relatively low in a labor market in which English is the dominant language.

To test this hypothesis, we fit a set of wage equations that allowed for interactions between the effects of mother tongue and years of schooling. The results are reported in tables 9–12 and 9–13. Although many of the estimated interaction effects are small and imprecise, they are all negative, indicating a lower schooling coefficient for members of linguistic minorities.

Tables 9–12 and 9–13 also report differentials in average educational attainment between different linguistic groups in Canada and the United States. The figures indicate that schooling gaps narrowed

TABLE 9–13

DIFFERENCES BETWEEN MALES OF SPANISH AND NON-SPANISH
ORIGIN, IN THE UNITED STATES, BY LINGUISTIC REGION, IN
YEARS OF EDUCATION AND RETURNS TO EDUCATION, 1969 AND
1979

	25–64 Age Group		25–34 Age Group	
	1969	1979	1969	1979
High Spanish				
Return to education[a]	−.007*	−.014*	−.007*	−.007
Years of education	−3.3	−3.5	−3.2	−3.3
Low Spanish				
Return to education[a]	−.020	−.002*	−.030	−.007*
Years of education	−1.4	−2.2	−1.4	−2.2

* = The coefficient is not significantly different from zero at the 95 percent level.
a. Coefficient of Spanish origin interacted with years of education in an earning regression where the other independent variables are four dummies for weeks worked in the previous year, six dummies for hours worked in the week preceding the census or survey, two marital status dummies, three regional dummies, three period of immigration dummies, age, age squared, education, education squared, and a dummy for Spanish origin.
SOURCES: U.S. censuses, 1970 and 1980; Public Use Samples 1:1,000, U.S. Department of Commerce, Bureau of the Census, Washington, D.C.

considerably in Canada from 1971 to 1986 for twenty-five- to sixty-four-year-olds and twenty-five- to thirty-four-year-olds both within and outside Quebec. In contrast, schooling gaps in the United States increased slightly in regions with a high proportion of Spanish speakers and sizably in regions with relatively low Spanish proportions.

Taken as a whole, the results of tables 9–12 and 9–13 suggest that changes in educational attainment and in the structure of returns to schooling are important to understanding the changing economic position of linguistic minorities in Canada and the United States. Neither set of changes, however, appears to follow a consistent pattern or to offer more than a partial explanation for the changes observed in the relative earnings of linguistic minorities.

Cohort Analyses. The estimates in table 9–6 indicate that the regression-corrected language-earnings differentials changed from $-.08$ log points in 1970 to $+.04$ log points in 1985 among the twenty-five- to thirty-four-year-olds in Quebec. Strictly speaking, this result indicates that the relative earnings in 1985 of French-speaking males born in the 1950s was larger than the relative earnings in 1970 of French-speaking males born between the mid-1930s and the mid-1940s. Insofar as this improvement in relative economic position could reflect a pure vintage effect associated with period of birth, it does not necessarily indicate an improvement over time in the relative economic position of any given population (that is, a true time effect).

To determine whether the comparison of cross-sectional results in tables 9–4 and 9–6 for Canada and in tables 9–8 and 9–9 for the United States reflect vintage effects or time effects (or both), we have calculated gross and regression-corrected earnings differentials for well-defined cohorts at different points in time. These results are presented in tables 9–14 and 9–15. In the case of Canada, both inside and outside Quebec, the gross- and regression-corrected cross-sectional and cohort results reveal similar patterns. These results suggest that the improved relative economic position of twenty-five- to thirty-four-year-old French speakers in Quebec was associated largely with labor market changes that occurred over time and only slightly with the entry into the labor market of cohorts that might be different in their latent relative quality. These results are consistent with the view that increased demand for French speakers from 1970 to 1985 has improved the relative economic position of French-speaking males in Quebec.

Our analysis for the United States suggests a different conclusion. From 1969 to 1979, the relative economic position of twenty-five- to thirty-four-year-old Spanish-speaking males deteriorated slightly (based on the regression-corrected differentials reported in table 9–9). In contrast, the relative economic position of Spanish-speaking males aged twenty-four to thirty-three deteriorated substantially by the time they reached ages thirty-four to forty-three in 1979. Although these results are a bit puzzling, our suspicion is that they reflect the strong inflow of Spanish-speaking males into the U.S. labor market during the 1970s. Given young Spanish-speaking workers are closer substitutes for older Spanish-speaking workers and for young English-speaking workers than they are for older English-speaking workers, a strong inflow of young Spanish-speaking workers would tend to result in larger language-earnings differentials for an older cohort as it aged but would not necessarily affect differentials among young cohorts entering the labor market. This hypothesis does imply, however, that earnings levels would be depressed for the recent labor

TABLE 9–14

RELATIVE EARNINGS OF THE MALE COHORT IN CANADA, AGED
25–34 IN 1971, BY MOTHER TONGUE AND LINGUISTIC REGION,
1970, 1980, AND 1985

	1970	1980	1985
Quebec			
Gross earning differential (log points)[a]			
F to E	− .20	− .12	− .06*
EB to EU	.05*	.23	− .04*
FU to EU	− .27	− .11*	− .23
FB to EU	− .06*	.18	.05*
Regression-corrected earning differentials[a,b]			
F to E	− .08	− .02*	.04*
FB to EU	.06*	.23	− .03*
FU to EU	− .11	.09	.00*
FB to EU	− .01*	.16	.02*
Rest of Canada			
Gross earning differential (log points)[a]			
F to E	− .15	− .17	− .21
Regression-corrected earning differential[a,b]			
F to E	− .02*	− .01*	− .02*

*= The coefficient is *not* significantly different from zero at the 95 percent
level.
a. Definitions of symbols: F = French, E = English, EU = English unilingual,
EB = English bilingual, FU = French unilingual, and FB = French bilingual.
b. Variables included in the regression: four dummies for weeks worked in
the previous year, six dummies for hours worked in the week preceding the
census, two marital status dummies, three regional dummies (for rest of
Canada only), age, age squared, education, and education squared.
SOURCES: Canadian censuses, 1971, 1981, and 1986; Public Use Samples,
Individual Files, Statistics Canada, Ottawa.

market entrants (both Spanish-speaking and English-speaking) relative to the older cohorts of English speakers. This pattern is exactly
what one observes in the first panel of table 9–8 in which the earnings
levels for twenty-five- to thirty-four-year-olds declined by substantially larger percentages from 1969 to 1979 than the earnings levels for
twenty-five- to sixty-four-year-olds. Thus supply-side shifts appear to
offer the most coherent explanation for the changing structure of
language-earnings differentials in the United States.

TABLE 9–15

RELATIVE EARNINGS OF THE MALE COHORT IN THE UNITED
STATES, AGED 25–34 IN 1970, BY LANGUAGE AND LINGUISTIC
REGION, 1969 AND 1979

	1969	1979
High Spanish		
Gross earning differential (log points)[a]		
S to W	−.35	−.58
Regression-corrected earning differentials[a,b]		
S to W	−.13	−.29
Low Spanish		
Gross earning differential (log points)[a]		
S to W	−.18	−.50
Regression-corrected earning differentials[a,b]		
S to W	−.08	−.21

NOTE: Spanish origin is used as a proxy for Spanish mother tongue.
All differentials reported in this table are significantly different from zero at
the 5 percent level.
a. Definitions of symbols: S = Spanish and W = non-Spanish white.
b. Variables included in the regression: four dummies for weeks worked in
the previous year, six dummies for hours worked in the week preceding the
census, two marital status dummies, three regional dummies, three period-
of-immigration dummies, age, age squared, education, and education
squared.
SOURCES: U.S. censuses, 1970 and 1980; Public Use Samples 1:1,000, U.S.
Department of Commerce, Bureau of the Census, Washington, D.C.

Summary and Conclusions

The foregoing analysis has measured and compared the relative earnings of the major linguistic minorities in Canada and the United
States. Although the two countries have the same dominant language
and are similar in many other respects as well, important differences
concern the situation of their linguistic minorities. Hispanics in the
United States are an immigrant group while French speakers in Canada are not; one major Canadian province has a French-speaking
majority while Hispanics in the United States are a minority in all
states; and French is an official language in Canada while Spanish is
not an official language in the United States.

Our empirical analysis is guided by the assumption that the
return to language skills in both Canada and the United States is
determined by the interaction of the supply and demand for those
skills within local labor and product markets. We examine data from

406

the 1971, 1981, and 1986 censuses for Canada and from the 1970 and 1980 censuses for the United States, thereby allowing us to measure changes over time in the relative earnings of the two linguistic minorities.

The empirical results for French speakers in Canada and Spanish speakers in the United States are similar in many respects. In both countries, there is evidence in the early 1970s that individuals who were unable to communicate in the dominant language of the labor market were penalized. The trends have been different between Canada and the United States, however, since the early 1970s. In Canada we find evidence of an important decrease in the earnings gap between French- and English-speaking men. In contrast, the earnings gap between Spanish- and English-speaking men in the United States remained large—and actually increased slightly—in the 1970s. This difference between Canada and the United States can be explained by differential supply-demand shifts in the two countries. The demand for French speakers seems to have increased in Canada during the 1970s (especially in Quebec) with relatively small changes in the supply of French speakers. In the United States the supply of Spanish-speakers increased during the 1970s because of rapid immigration, while there seems to be little evidence of a sizable outward shift in the relative demand for Spanish-speaking workers.

Bibliography

Boulet, Jac-André. *Language and Earnings in Montreal*. Ottawa: Economic Council of Canada, 1980.

Breton, Albert, and Peter Mieszkowski. "The Economics of Bilingualism." In *The Political Economy of Fiscal Federalism*, edited by Wallace E. Oates, 261–73. Lexington, Mass.: D.C. Heath, 1977.

Carliner, Geoffrey. "Wages, Earnings and Hours of First, Second, and Third Generation American Males." *Economic Inquiry* 18 (1980): 87–102.

———. "Wage Differentials by Language Group and the Market for Language Skills in Canada." *Journal of Human Resources*, 16 (1981): 384–99.

Chiswick, Barry R. "Speaking, Reading and Earnings." *Journal of Labor Economics*, 9 (1991): 149–70.

———, and Paul W. Miller. "Earnings in Canada: The Roles of Immigrant Generation, French Ethnicity and Language." *Research in Population Economics*, 6 (1988): 183–224.

Grenier, Gilles. "Language as Human Capital: Theoretical Framework and Application to Spanish-Speaking Americans." Ph.D. diss., Princeton University, 1982.

———. "The Effects of Language Characteristics on the Wages of Hispanic-American Males." *Journal of Human Resources*, 19 (1984): 35–52.

———. "Bilinguisme, transferts linguistiques et revenus du travail au Québec: quelques éléments d'interaction." In *Economie et langue*, edited by F. Vaillancourt, 243–88. Québec: Conseil de la langue française, 1985.

———. "Earnings by Language Group in Quebec in 1980 and Emigration from Quebec between 1976 and 1981." *Canadian Journal of Economics*, 20 (1987): 774–91.

———. "Participation au marché du travail, revenus et langues au Québec: le cas des femmes mariées." *L'Actualité économique*, 64 (1988): 5–22.

———, and Guy Lacroix. "Les revenus et la langue: le cas de la capitale nationale." *L'Actualité économique*, 62 (1986): 365–84.

Gwartney, James D., and James E. Long. "The Relative Earnings of Blacks and Other Minorities." *Industrial and Labor Relations Review*, 31 (1978): 336–46.

Hocevar, Toussaint. "Equilibria in Linguistic Minority Markets." *Kyklos*, 28 (1975): 337–57.

Kossoudji, Sherrie A. "English Language Ability and the Labor Market Opportunities of Hispanic and East Asian Immigrant Men." *Journal of Labor Economics*, 6 (1988): 205–28.

Lachapelle, Réjean. "Minorités et langues officielles minoritaires: un demi-siècle d'évolution." Social and Demographic Studies Division, Statistics Canada, Ottawa, 1988.

Lacroix, Robert, and François Vaillancourt. *Les disparités de revenus au sein de la main-d'oeuvre hautement qualifiée au Québec*. Québec: Conseil de la langue française, 1980.

———. *Les revenus et la langue au Québec (1970–1978)*. Québec: Conseil de la langue française, 1981.

Marschak, Jacob. "Economics of Language." *Behavioral Science*, 10 (1965): 135–40.

McManus, Walter. "Labor Market Costs of Language Disparities: An Interpretation of Hispanic Earnings Differences." *American Economic Review*, 75 (1985): 818–27.

———. "Labor Market Effects of Language Enclaves: Hispanic Men in the United States." *Journal of Human Resources*, 25 (1990): 228–52.

———, William Gould, and Finis Welch. "Earnings of Hispanic Men: The Role of English Language Proficiency." *Journal of Labor Economics*, 2 (1983): 101–30.

Reimers, Cordelia R. "Labor Market Discrimination against Hispanic and Black Men." *Review of Economics and Statistics*, 65 (1983): 570–79.

————. "The Wage Structure of Hispanic Men: Implications for Policy." *Social Science Quarterly*, 65 (1984): 401–16.

Rivera-Batiz, Francisco L. "English Language Proficiency and the Economic Progress of Immigrants." *Economic Letters*, 34 (1990): 295–300.

Robinson, Chris. "Language Choice: The Distribution of Language Skills and Earnings in a Dual-Language Economy." *Research in Labor Economics*, 9 (1988): 53–90.

Shapiro, Daniel, and Morton Stelcner. "Male-Female Earnings Differentials and the Role of Language in Canada, Ontario and Quebec, 1970." *Canadian Journal of Economics*, 14 (1981): 341–48.

————. "Language Legislation and Male-Female Earnings Differentials in Quebec." *Canadian Public Policy*, 8 (1982): 106–13.

————. "Earnings Disparities among Linguistic Groups in Quebec, 1970–1980." *Canadian Public Policy*, 13 (1987): 97–104.

Tainer, Evelina M. "English Language Proficiency and the Determination of Earnings among Foreign-Born Men." *Journal of Human Resources*, 23 (1988): 108–22.

Vaillancourt, François. *Differences in Earnings by Language Groups in Quebec, 1970: An Economic Analysis*. Quebec: International Center for Research on Bilingualism, 1980.

————. *Langues and disparités de statut économique au Québec, 1970 et 1980*. Québec: Conseil de la langue française, 1988.

————. "Language and Public Policy in Canada and the United States," chapter 6 in this volume.

Veltman, Calvin, Jac-André Boulet, and Charles Castonguay. "The Economic Context of Bilingualism and Language Transfer in the Montreal Metropolitan Area." *Canadian Journal of Economics*, 12 (1979): 468–79.

10
Some Evidence of the Effects of Admissions Criteria on Immigrant Assimilation

Harriet Orcutt Duleep and Mark C. Regets

The cornerstone of U.S. immigration policy is family reunification. Under current law stemming from the Immigration and Nationality Act of 1965, spouses, minor children, and parents of U.S. citizens are admitted without regard to numerical limitations (see figure 10–1). Of the numerically restricted visas, 80 percent are reserved for the adult children and siblings of American citizens (as well as their spouses and children) and for the spouses and children of legal, permanent resident aliens. Only 20 percent of the 270,000 numerically restricted visas are allocated to applicants on the basis of their occupational skills. The occupational skills classification includes two components: first, the admission of workers, skilled and unskilled, in occupations for which labor is scarce in the United States; and second, the admission of professionals, scientists, and artists of exceptional ability.

The preponderance of immigration on the basis of kinship has raised serious concerns among policy makers and academicians about the prospective productivity of our current and future immigrants. In particular, researchers and policy makers have questioned whether the emphasis on family reunification in the American immigration system has contributed to a decline in the productivity of immigrants entering the U.S. labor market.

Using the predicted wage differential to study the productivity immediately after immigration of immigrants who migrated before and after the Immigration and Nationality Act of 1965, George Borjas concluded that "the quality of immigrants admitted to the United States has been increasing over time when the immigrants originate in Western Europe and has been declining over time when the immigrants originate in the less developed countries. . . . For example, the most recent immigrant wave from the United Kingdom has an earn-

FIGURE 10–1
U.S. Immigration Policy

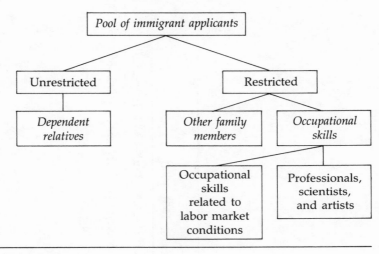

SOURCE: Authors.

ings potential that is about 13 percent higher than the wave that arrived in 1955, while the most recent immigrants from India have 28 percent lower earnings than the earlier cohort."[1] Since the share of U.S. immigrants from Western Europe has fallen dramatically over time whereas the share of immigrants from Asian and Hispanic countries has risen dramatically (see table 10–1), Borjas's analysis suggests there has been a decline in the quality of immigrants admitted to the United States.[2]

Legislation has been debated in Congress that would shift America's immigration policy toward a skills-based selection system and partially away from the current system of family reunification. According to the original legislation put forth by Senators Edward Kennedy and Alan Simpson, prospective immigrants would receive points based on such factors as age, education level, job skills, and knowledge of English.

The envisioned system closely resembles the immigration system in place in Canada since 1962.[3] Like the American system, the Canadian system is divided into two major components: numerically unrestricted and restricted immigration (see figure 10–2). As in the American system, certain relatives, such as the spouses of citizens, are admitted without numerical restriction. Where the Canadian system radically departs from the American system, however, is in its selec-

TABLE 10-1

U.S. IMMIGRATION BY DECADE, 1851–1980

	1851–1860	1861–1870	1871–1880	1881–1890	1891–1900	1901–1910	1911–1920
Total immigration	2,598,214	2,314,824	2,812,191	5,246,613	3,687,564	8,795,386	6,735,811
Total as a percentage of U.S. population	8.26	5.81	5.61	8.33	4.85	9.56	5.43
Immigration by area of origin, as % of total immigration							
Northwestern Europe	89.11	84.53	69.20	68.08	41.66	19.47	14.57
Southern and Eastern Europe	0.42	1.04	6.44	17.82	50.85	68.76	55.02
Asia[a]	1.60	2.80	4.42	1.33	2.03	3.68	4.31
Hispanic Origin[b]	n.a.	n.a.	n.a.	n.a.	n.a.	0.1	4.1

	1921–1930	1931–1940	1941–1950	1951–1960	1961–1970	1971–1980
Total immigration	4,107,209	528,431	1,035,039	2,515,479	3,321,677	4,493,314
Total as a percentage of U.S. population	3.35	0.40	0.69	1.40	1.63	1.98
Immigration by area of origin, as % of total immigration						
Northwestern Europe	28.68	32.17	39.91	31.28	14.57	5.12
Southern and Eastern Europe	26.32	25.71	11.19	13.99	12.35	8.23
Asia[a]	2.73	3.04	6.76	5.97	12.88	35.35
Hispanic Origin[b]	12.6	6.8	10.1	20.5	32.2	30.0

n.a. = not applicable.

a. Asia includes China, Japan (after 1860), India, Turkey, and other Asia. Beginning with 1952, Asia includes the Philippines, which until then was recorded elsewhere. Beginning with 1957, China includes Taiwan.

b. "Hispanic Origin" includes persons from Central America, South America, and Mexico from 1851–1950, after which time Cuban immigrants are added to the original three categories.

Sources: All data for 1971–1980 for all groups except "Hispanic Origin" come from the 1980 Statistical Yearbook of the Immigration and Naturalization Service, table 2, p. 4. Included in "Hispanic Origin" from 1951–1960 and 1961–1970 are figures for Cubans found in the 1960 and 1970 statistical yearbooks of the INS, respectively. All data used to compute immigration by area for the years 1851–1970 for all groups except "Hispanic Origin" come from the 1975 Annual Report: Immigration and Naturalization Service, table 13.

FIGURE 10–2
Canadian Immigration Policy

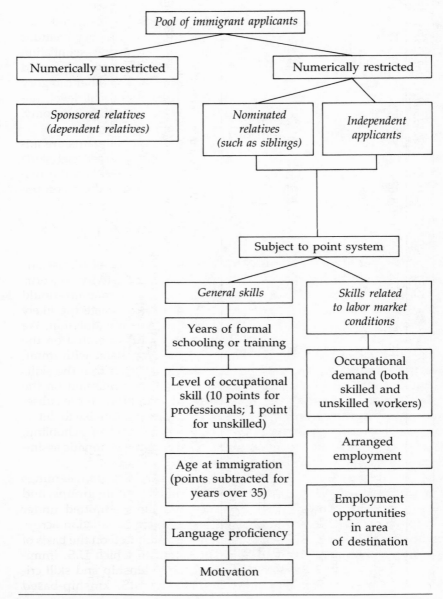

SOURCE: Authors.

414

tion criteria for numerically restricted immigrants. Admission decisions are based on a point system that primarily reflects productivity characteristics; only 5 points out of 100 may be awarded on the basis of kinship.

Productivity characteristics for the numerically restricted visa applicants in Canada fall into two categories. One category includes levels of characteristics believed to promote the economic assimilation of immigrants in general. These include age, years of schooling, and level of language proficiency in English or French. The other category encompasses immigrant characteristics, regardless of skill level, tailored to prevailing demand conditions of the Canadian economy, such as particular occupational backgrounds in high demand.

Thus in both the United States and Canada immigrants are admitted on the basis of kinship, skill levels, and occupational skills linked to labor market conditions. The difference between the two countries' policies lies in the weights given to each of these components.

Summary of Chapter

The purpose of this chapter is to shed light on the effect of admissions criteria on the assimilation of immigrants. As productivity concerns lie at the heart of the current debate on what type of immigrant should be admitted to the United States, we attempt to simulate the likely earnings growth of immigrants based on their type of admission. We would like to know, for instance, how immigrants admitted on the basis of kinship fare in the labor market in comparison with immigrants admitted on the basis of skill characteristics. Within the skills classification, we would like to know what effect admission on the basis of specific occupational skills in high demand has on the subsequent earnings profiles of immigrants. Finally, we would like to determine what effect general skill levels—such as level of schooling, language proficiency, and age at entry—have on the economic assimilation of immigrants.

To analyze the effect of admissions criteria on immigrant earnings we utilize variations across groups, across cohorts within groups, and across countries in the percentage of immigrants admitted under specified criteria. Within the United States, there is variation across groups in the extent to which immigrants are admitted on the basis of kinship versus occupational skills. The extent to which U.S. immigrant groups have been admitted according to kinship and skill criteria has also varied over time. Finally, the U.S. kinship-based admissions policy versus the Canadian skills-based policy provides another source of variation.

These variations, which may shed light on the effect of admissions criteria on immigrant earnings profiles, form the basis of three analyses pursued in this chapter. In the following section, we observe how the earnings profiles of immigrant groups in the United States vary as the percentage admitted on the basis of occupational skills, as opposed to kinship, varies. In the subsequent section, we analyze how variations in admissions criteria across intertemporal cohorts within U.S. immigrant groups affect earnings profiles, and in the final section, we compare the earnings profiles of U.S. and Canadian immigrants originating from the same country.

We focus on immigrants from Asian countries in comparison with those from the United Kingdom and Europe, thereby permitting comparisons between groups whose country-of-origin skills may be quite different from those of the United States and Canada with groups whose skills are likely to be more similar. The importance of obtaining more information on the assimilation of Asian immigrants in the United States and Canadian labor markets is underscored by other salient facts. Asian immigration in both Canada and the United States has grown rapidly, Asians currently contribute more to U.S. legal immigration than any other group, and in the United States Asian immigrants are admitted primarily under the kinship provision of immigration law.

The analyses presented in this chapter are limited to working-age men (25 to 65 years of age) who were at least 20 years old when they migrated and who have positive earnings.[4] Adult migrants compose the appropriate study group for analyzing the effect of admissions criteria on labor market outcomes.[5] We also limit the analysis to immigrants who migrated to the United States or Canada after 1964. Our data sources for this study are the public use samples from the U.S. 1980 Census of Population and the Canadian 1981 Census of Population, as well as records from the U.S. Immigration and Naturalization Service (INS).[6]

Earnings Variations across U.S. Detailed Groups

As shown in figure 10–1, immigrants in the United States are admitted on the basis of either occupational skills or kinship. We would expect that the criteria under which immigrants are admitted would affect their subsequent earnings in the United States. In particular, we would expect that if we control for years of schooling, immigrants admitted on the basis of family would initially earn substantially less than those admitted on the basis of occupational skills, as the latter already have skills that should facilitate procuring employment in the U.S. economy. We would also expect, reflecting greater investment in U.S.-specific skills, family-admitted immigrants to have higher earnings growth than immigrants admitted on the basis of occupational skills.

Family-admitted immigrants may have a greater incentive to invest in U.S.-specific skills than have immigrants admitted on the basis of occupational skills, as the latter already have skills relevant to U.S. employment opportunities. Families may also facilitate investment. For instance, the labor force participation of immigrant wives across groups appears to be positively related to the extent to which immigrant men invest in U.S.-specific skills.[7] Immigrants in groups characterized by high family admissions are also more likely to remain permanently in the United States than are immigrants in groups with higher admissions on the basis of occupational skills. Thus the expected time horizon in which investments in U.S.-specific skills may pay off is likely to be longer for family-admitted immigrants.[8] All of these factors would be expected to contribute to greater investment in U.S.-specific skills by family-admitted immigrants and to result in high earnings growth.

The extent to which immigrants are admitted through occupational skills as opposed to kinship varies across groups. In general, most immigrants from Asian countries enter the United States on the basis of family ties. For instance, in 1980 fewer than 3 percent of all Korean immigrants and fewer than 1 percent of Filipino immigrants were admitted through the occupational skills provision. In contrast, close to 40 percent of immigrants from the United Kingdom were admitted in 1980 on the basis of occupational skills. Other European countries tend to fall in between the Asian countries and the United Kingdom in their admissions patterns.

The contrast in admissions patterns might be even greater if the comparison were limited to working-age men. For instance, among numerically restricted immigrants (who may more accurately reflect the working population than unrestricted immigrants), 60 percent from the United Kingdom were admitted in 1980 on the basis of occupational skills, as compared with fewer than 2 percent from the Philippines and fewer than 5 percent from Korea.

In contrast to other Asian countries, the admissions pattern of Japan resembles that of the United Kingdom. In 1980, 61 percent of the numerically restricted immigrants from Japan and 32 percent of all Japanese immigrants (restricted and unrestricted) were admitted to the United States on the basis of occupational skills.

TABLE 10–2

RELATIVE EARNINGS OF U.S. IMMIGRANTS, EVALUATED AT U.S.
NATIVE-BORN MEAN LEVEL OF SCHOOLING

	Chinese	Japanese	Filipino	Korean	Indian	European	British
Earnings ratio at							
One year	.43	1.01	.59	.54	.49	1.07	1.23
Ten years	.75	1.07	.89	.93	.92	.99	.99
Average earnings growth during first ten years	.09	.03	.07	.08	.09	.02	.006

SOURCE: Author.

Based on their high family admissions, we would predict that Asian immigrants, with the exception of the Japanese, would initially earn substantially less than American-born whites, but that their earnings would grow rapidly with time in the United States. To examine how the various immigrant groups fare in the U.S. economy, we estimated group-specific regressions in which the natural logarithm of earnings was regressed on the following explanatory variables: level of schooling (a three-part spline), age, age squared, age × education, years since migration, education × years since migration, marital status, metropolitan status, and region of residence. The estimated coefficients of this model are presented in appendix 10–A1.

Using the estimated coefficients from the group-specific earnings regressions we simulated the earnings growth of each immigrant group. To provide a benchmark by which the earnings of each immigrant group could be compared we also simulated the earnings growth of American-born non-Hispanic white men. Each simulation begins at age twenty-eight, which for immigrants we also held constant as the age at migration. For each subsequent year of the simulation, age, age squared, years since migration, years since migration squared, age × education, and years since migration × education are all appropriately incremented and multiplied by their estimated coefficients from the group-specific regressions.

Table 10–2 shows the ratio of immigrant to native-born white earnings evaluated at one and at ten years after migration, as well as the average earnings growth of immigrants during the first ten years in the United States. In all of these simulations, years of schooling, marital status, metropolitan status, and region of residence are held constant at the mean values of American-born white men. Thus we can compare what immigrant and American-born men would earn if they possessed the same educational level.[9]

The simulations show remarkable similarities and differences among immigrant groups in their earnings profiles. As predicted, all Asian groups, with the exception of the Japanese, are characterized by initial earnings that are very low relative to native-born whites of the same age and education, but they have a high earnings growth. (After ten years in the United States, Filipino, Korean, and Indian immigrants are predicted to earn about 90 percent of native-born white earnings, adjusting for schooling levels.) By contrast, Japanese, European, and British immigrants are characterized by high initial earnings and low earnings growth.[10]

The similarities in the earnings profiles of the Koreans, Indians, Filipinos, and Chinese are particularly surprising given the enormous variation among these groups in English-language proficiency. Of immigrants entering the United States between 1975 and 1980, 69 percent of Asian Indian men and 51 percent of Filipino men (twenty-five to sixty-five years of age) reported speaking only English or speaking it very well. Indeed, the representation of proficient English speakers among recent Indian and Filipino immigrants far surpasses that of non-British European immigrants, of whom only 36 percent of the 1975–1980 cohort reported high levels of English proficiency. The percentage of proficient English speakers among the other Asian groups, whose countries lack the English-language history of India and the Philippines, is much lower. Of those entering the United States between 1975 and 1980, only 24 percent of the Chinese, 25 percent of the Japanese, and 15 percent of the Koreans reported speaking English very well.

Intertemporal Variations in Admissions

Our analysis of immigrant earnings patterns reveals that Asian immigrants, with the exception of the Japanese, initially earn substantially less than immigrants from Europe and the United Kingdom, but that their earnings grow rapidly. After ten years they approach the earnings of American-born whites with equivalent levels of schooling. These findings appear to be consistent with the hypothesis that immigrants admitted on the basis of family will initially earn less than those admitted on the basis of occupational skills, but they will also experience higher earnings growth.

Alternatively, the lower initial earnings and the subsequent high earnings growth of immigrant groups characterized by high family admissions may have less to do with the criteria under which immigrants are admitted and more to do with country-of-origin conditions. In particular, persons in countries where employment and earnings opportunities are as good as those in the United States would come to the United States only if they did not have to invest in U.S.-specific skills. Immigrants from these countries either would have skills that are transferable to the United States or would have job opportunities in the United States that utilized their country-of-origin skills. Since countries like Japan and the United Kingdom, characterized by relatively high immigrant admissions on the basis of occupational skills, are also high-income countries, it is impossible to distinguish between the two hypotheses without further information. In this regard, intertemporal variations in immigrant admissions may help in determining the importance of admissions criteria versus country-of-origin conditions on the earnings profiles of immigrants.

Our findings are also subject to the potential biases of a cross-sectional analysis. As pointed out by Borjas, earnings patterns based on cross-section data may be contaminated by intertemporal cohort differences in quality: a decline in the quality of immigrants, possibly due to increasing admissions on the basis of kinship, could contribute to a perceived but spurious earnings growth.[11]

The issue of declining cohort quality may be particularly relevant to our study. Because of discriminatory immigration policies, Asian immigration in the United States effectively ceased from 1924 to 1965. Although the immigration reform of 1965 giving preferential treatment to family members and skilled immigrants applied to immigrants from all countries, the virtual cessation of Asian immigration for thirty years meant that new Asian immigrants were more likely to be admitted under the provision granting preference to immigrants with certain occupational skills than as family members. For instance, more than 60 percent of Indian immigrants admitted between 1965 and 1970 were admitted on the basis of occupational skills. As the population base of foreign-born Asian Americans grew, admission on the basis of kinship also grew, eventually resulting in the high family admissions that characterize most Asian immigration today.

The opposite pattern holds for European immigrants. Admission on the basis of kinship has fallen over time, and admission on the basis of skills has risen. For instance, in contrast to the 40 percent of British immigrants admitted via occupational skills in 1980, fewer than 4 percent were admitted on the basis of occupational skills between 1965 and 1970.

These observations suggest that the high earnings growth we observe for Asian groups who are currently admitted primarily on the basis of family may be due to the low earnings associated with recent kinship-admitted immigrants and to the high earnings associated with previous skills-admitted immigrants. The low earnings growth we observe for European and British immigrants may reflect the opposite admissions pattern. Thus the cross-sectional analysis may overstate the earnings growth of current Asian immigrants.

In order to isolate immigrant assimilation from changes in quality across immigrant cohorts, researchers have used 1970 and 1980 census data to measure earnings growth *within* cohorts.[12] Yet the earnings growth of an earlier cohort is not necessarily representative of a current cohort. This caveat seems particularly pertinent given intertemporal changes in the importance of kinship versus skills admissions of various groups. To further test our results, we pursue another strategy that takes advantage of intertemporal variations in the admissions of immigrant groups.

If we believe that the quality of immigrants is a missing variable in our cross-sectional estimations, then a reasonable approach would be to include information on this missing variable in our estimating equation. Since admission on the basis of kinship has been considered a determinant of quality, the inclusion in our estimating equation of whether an immigrant was admitted on the basis of occupational skills or kinship might control for quality differences among immigrants.

What we would like to estimate is

$$Y_i = \alpha + X'\beta_1 + \gamma Z + (\beta_2 + \Theta Z)\, YSM + \epsilon_i$$

where Y_i denotes the earnings of immigrant i; X is a vector of variables measuring education, experience, and region of residence and β_1 the corresponding coefficients; YSM measures years since migration; and Z is a categorical variable that equals one when an immigrant is admitted on the basis of occupational skills and zero when an immigrant is admitted on the basis of kinship.

In accordance with our earlier hypotheses, we would expect γ to be positive, reflecting the higher transferability of skills of immigrants admitted under the occupational skills provision, and for Θ to be negative, reflecting the lower earnings growth among immigrants admitted on the basis of occupational skills relative to immigrants admitted on the basis of kinship.

Unfortunately, information on the criteria by which individual immigrants are admitted that could be matched to our earnings data is not available. As a proxy for this variable, we use the percentage of each immigrant cohort in each group admitted on the basis of occupational skills, which is available from the annual records of the INS.[13] These data were matched to individual census records according to the country of origin and year of immigration of immigrants.

421

TABLE 10-3

SELECTED COEFFICIENTS FROM POOLED EARNINGS REGRESSION
(*t*-statistics in parentheses)

	Without Country-Specific Variables		With Country-Specific Variables	
Intercept	5.7942	(55.42)	5.2561	(22.89)
Percent admitted on basis of occupational skills	2.1098	(8.15)	2.5845	(9.58)
Years since migration[a]	.0553	(12.79)	.0600	(13.53)
Years since migration × percent admitted on basis of occupational skills	−.1235	(−5.92)	−.1599	(−7.37)

a. The coefficient on years since migration is not directly comparable to the average earnings growth shown in table 10-2. The latter refers to the first ten years after migration only, whereas the coefficient presented in this table relates to the entire fifteen-year period captured by the post-1964 immigrant cohorts. For immigrant groups experiencing high-earnings growth, the rate of change tends to decline with years in the United States.
SOURCE: Author.

To incorporate intergroup and intercohort variations in admissions criteria into our estimations, our estimating equation became

$$Y_i = \alpha + G_j X' \beta_1 + \gamma P_{jk} + (\beta_2 + \Theta P_{jk})\ YSM + \epsilon_i$$

where G_j is a categorical variable denoting group j, and P_{jk} is the percent of immigrants in group j and cohort k who were admitted on the basis of occupational skills. This approach permits estimating separate returns to education and experience for each immigrant group, but uses the intergroup, intercohort variations in admissions criteria to estimate γ and Θ. We limited this analysis to countries for which we had annual country-specific information on admission criteria for the years 1965 through 1980. All Asian countries as well as the United Kingdom were included in our data set.[14]

The estimated coefficients on percent admitted on the basis of occupational skills and on the interaction term between this variable and years since migration (*YSM*) are shown in table 10-3. As hypothesized, these coefficients indicate that as the percent admitted on the basis of kinship increases, the initial earnings of immigrants falls—the estimated coefficient is positive on Percent Admitted on Basis of Occupational Skills. But their expected earnings growth increases—the estimated coefficient is negative on Years Since Migration × Percent Admitted on Basis of Occupational Skills. For instance, if all immigrants are admitted on the basis of family, their earnings are projected to grow about 5 and one-half percent each year. If 5 percent are admitted under the occupational preference, their earnings are projected to grow at a rate of 4.9 percent per year. And if 40 percent are admitted on the basis of skills, as is true of current immigrants from the United Kingdom, their earnings are projected to grow at six tenths of a percent per year. To the extent that these estimates reflect differences in earnings patterns by entry program, those admitted on the basis of skills earn substantially more initially, but other immigrants, admitted predominantely on kinship, are projected to catch up within sixteen to seventeen years.

Our information on percent admitted by occupational skills is restricted to three cohorts per country.[15] Given the small number of observations on our variable of interest, it may be that our findings indicating the importance of admissions criteria on earnings growth are due to the effects of coincidental, unobserved, country-specific characteristics. To help control for such effects, we reestimated the model including a categorical variable for each country. These results are shown in the second column of table 10–3. Comparing these results with the results from our previous estimation reveals that the effect of admissions criteria on immigrant earnings increases when country-specific effects are taken into account.

Taken together, our analyses using intertemporal variations in admissions suggests that admissions criteria affect the earnings profiles of Asian immigrants. These results further suggest that cross-sectional earnings analyses may understate the earnings growth of Asian immigrant groups who are currently admitted primarily on the basis of kinship.

U.S.-Canadian Comparisons

As discussed in the introduction, the current Canadian admissions policy, adopted in 1962, is based on a point system that reflects productivity characteristics. The characteristics by which (numerically restricted) visa applicants are judged fall into two categories. One category includes levels of general skill-related variables — education, language proficiency in English or French, and age. For instance, a point is subtracted from an applicant's score card for each year she or he has attained more than thirty-five years of age; points are added for language proficiency and years of formal schooling or training (figure 10–2). The other category includes immigrant characteristics, regardless of skill level, tailored to current conditions of the Canadian labor market.

The U.S. admissions policy, in contrast with the Canadian policy, places a greater emphasis on family reunification in determining who shall enter. With regard to productivity characteristics, the United States does admit immigrants on the basis of occupational skills linked to current labor market conditions. With the exception of the third preference category, however, which admits professionals, scientists, and artists of exceptional ability, immigrants are not selected on the basis of general productivity characteristics, as is the case in Canada.

Given the differences in immigrant admissions policies between Canada and the United States, we would expect to see differences in the characteristics and economic assimilation of Canadian and American immigrants. Since the Canadian policy gives points for the level of general productivity characteristics possessed by visa applicants, we would expect higher levels of schooling, younger ages at migration, and higher language proficiency among immigrants in Canada than in the United States. Furthermore, we would expect differences in levels of schooling, age at migration, and language proficiency to manifest themselves in the earnings profiles of Canadian and American immigrants.

Ideally, we would like to compare the characteristics and earnings profiles of Canadian and American immigrants who originate from the same country. We would, for instance, like to compare Korean immigrants in the U.S. with Korean immigrants in Canada. Unfortunately, the Canadian census public use sample does not provide country-of-origin information for Asian immigrants. We were able to identify Canadian immigrants from Asia only as ethnic Chinese born in Asia or as non-Chinese, Asian-born persons of non-European ethnicity. Our comparison groups for the United States and Canada were thus limited to four groups: Chinese, non-Chinese Asian, British, and non-British Europeans.

Table 10–4 shows the average age, education, and percentage of language proficient American and Canadian immigrants by group and year of immigration for all years in which the Canadian reform policy has been in place. Since the Canadian census provides more detailed year-of-immigration data than does the U.S. census, the Canadian classifications have been aggregated to conform as closely as possible to the U.S. year-of-immigration categories.

The average age of immigrants within year-of-immigration cohorts gives information on the average age of immigration: the older the average age of an immigrant cohort, the older the average age of immigration for these immigrants. Comparing the average ages of American and Canadian immigrants, we see that for all groups, the average age of Canadian immigrants is consistently younger for immigrants who immigrated between 1965 and 1975. It thus appears that

424

TABLE 10–4

AVERAGE AGE, EDUCATION, AND PERCENT LANGUAGE-PROFICIENT
AMERICAN AND CANADIAN IMMIGRANTS, BY GROUP AND YEAR OF
IMMIGRATION, 1960–1980

	1975–80	1970–74[a]	1965–69[b]	1960–64[c]
Chinese				
Age				
U.S.	36.83	39.31	43.20	46.42
Canada	38.19	36.62	39.00	38.07
Schooling				
U.S.	13.01	13.76	14.16	14.34
Canada	12.16	14.23	14.60	13.93
Language-proficient				
U.S.	60.08	71.94	73.99	74.28
Canada	73.38	89.70	94.04	90.74
Non-Chinese Asian				
Age				
U.S.	36.32	37.97	41.23	43.77
Canada	35.75	36.00	40.41	44.25
Schooling				
U.S.	13.95	15.73	16.06	16.44
Canada	13.39	14.03	14.72	14.74
Language-proficient				
U.S.	75.16	92.44	96.31	97.18
Canada	94.36	99.29	99.29	100.00
European				
Age				
U.S.	34.48	42.83	45.43	48.03
Canada	35.35	37.75	39.89	41.43
Schooling				
U.S.	12.63	10.56	10.32	11.49
Canada	12.46	10.75	11.26	10.39
Language-proficient				
U.S.	65.71	63.16	75.29	85.52
Canada	87.07	89.63	91.34	92.80
British				
Age				
U.S.	33.42	38.50	45.39	48.50
Canada	36.05	37.11	40.43	43.45

(Table continues)

TABLE 10–4 (continued)

	1975–80	1970–74[a]	1965–69[b]	1960–64[c]
Schooling				
U.S.	15.37	14.83	14.22	13.50
Canada	14.17	13.92	14.05	13.92
Language-proficient				
U.S.	100.00	100.00	100.00	100.00
Canada	100.00	100.00	100.00	100.00

a. For Canada, 1971–74.
b. For Canada, 1966–70.
c. For Canada, 1961–65.
SOURCE: Author.

the Canadian immigration system has achieved one of its objectives: the selection of younger immigrants.[16]

The way in which educational attainment is measured differs between the U.S. and Canadian censuses. Information on schooling level is collected in the U.S. census by means of a question that asks the highest grade or year of schooling attended, without distinguishing between university and nonuniversity vocational education. The Canadian census asks separate questions to determine years of academic and vocational schooling.

To create a comparable education variable, we added together years of university, nonuniversity, and elementary or secondary schooling reported on the Canadian census. We feel that this variable may upwardly bias Canadian schooling levels in comparison with American levels, because years of education in the U.S. census may not always count vocational training. Yet despite what may be an upward bias in the Canadian schooling levels, the average schooling levels reported in table 10–4 show no clear-cut educational advantage for Canadian immigrants over their U.S. counterparts.

With respect to language proficiency, the U.S. measure is more precise than the Canadian measure. To make the two measures roughly comparable, we aggregated the more detailed U.S. categories and defined "proficient in English" to mean "speaks only English," "speaks English very well," or "speaks English well." The Canadian measure is defined as the ability to conduct a conversation in either English or French. Recognizing the inexact comparability of these measures, language proficiency appears higher among all immigrant groups in Canada regardless of the year of immigration.

From these comparisons, it appears that Canadian immigration policy has succeeded in reducing age at immigration and in increasing language proficiency among the immigrant pool. Yet it appears to have had little effect, relative to the United States, on the educational levels of immigrants.

Previous research has found a deleterious effect of migration at older ages and beneficial effects of greater language proficiency and schooling on immigrant earnings. We therefore predicted that the younger ages at migration and higher language proficiency of Canadian immigrants would result in their earning at a higher level relative to U.S. immigrants coming from the same country.

To determine what effect the Canadian skills-based policy versus the U.S. kinship-based policy has on immigrant earnings, we estimated immigrant earnings profiles. The explanatory variables in our regressions included years of schooling, age, age squared, age × education, years since migration, education × years since migration, proficiency in dominant language, marital status, metropolitan status, and region of residence. U.S. and Canadian earnings estimations for each group are reported in appendix 10–B. As undoubtedly there are differences in the American and Canadian economies that affect earnings levels, we compare the earnings of Canadian and American immigrants with the earnings of native-born, non-Hispanic whites in Canada and in the United States, respectively.[17]

Using the estimated coefficients from the group-specific earnings regressions, we simulated the earnings growth of each immigrant group and the native born of each country. For each immigrant group we did four simulations. The base simulation used each group's mean value of age at migration, education, and language proficiency.[18] Three subsequent simulations assume a common age at immigration, a common age at immigration combined with U.S. native-born values of education, and a common age at immigration combined with U.S. native-born values for both education and language proficiency. This allows us to examine the effects of differing values of these skill characteristics on U.S.-Canadian differences. These simulations, evaluated at one and ten years since migration, are shown in tables 10–5 and 10–6.

Evaluating each group at its own mean characteristics, table 10–5 reveals striking similarities between U.S. and Canadian immigrants. Canadian and U.S. immigrants who originated in the same area have very similar earnings levels relative to native-born whites of their respective adopted countries. With the arguable exception of European immigrants,[19] the growth rates of earnings for each group are also very similar between the United States and Canada. While Canada's immigrants are younger and more language-fluent, this does not appear to translate into a consistent advantage in earnings relative to native-born workers of the same age.

Eliminating the age difference between the U.S. and Canadian

427

TABLE 10-5

Relative Earnings of U.S. and Canadian Immigrants, Evaluated at Immigrant Means of Skill Levels

	Canadian Chinese	U.S. Chinese	Canadian Other Asian	U.S. Other Asian	Canadian European	U.S. European	Canadian British	U.S. British
At own group means								
Earnings ratio at								
One year	.47	.41	.53	.65	.82	.90	1.13	1.22
Ten years	.73	.74	.90	1.02	1.03	.83	1.25	1.23
Annual earnings growth rate[a]	.066	.080	.075	.067	.045	.010	.032	.023
Holding age at entry constant[b]								
Earnings ratio at								
One year	.48	.42	.54	.65	.84	1.02	1.14	1.25
Ten years	.74	.76	.92	1.04	1.04	.86	1.26	1.10
Annual earnings growth rate	.068	.088	.078	.076	.046	.011	.035	.007

NOTE: In all U.S.-Canadian comparisons, region and metropolitan status are held constant at Canadian native-born mean levels for Canadian immigrants and at U.S. native-born mean levels for U.S. immigrants. Marital status is held constant at U.S. native-born mean levels throughout.

a. The slope is the average slope for the first ten years after migration.
b. In this simulation and all simulations that follow, age at entry is set equal to twenty-eight.
SOURCE: Author.

TABLE 10–6: Relative Earnings of U.S. and Canadian Immigrants, Evaluated at U.S. Native-born Means of Skill Levels

	Canadian Chinese	U.S. Chinese	Canadian Other Asian	U.S. Other Asian	Canadian European	U.S. European	Canadian British	U.S. British
Holding education constant[a]								
Earnings ratio at								
One year	.42	.39	.51	.58	.76	1.00	1.04	1.23
Ten years	.62	.69	.81	.89	.95	.92	1.13	.99
Annual earnings growth rate[b]	.064	.086	.072	.070	.047	.020	.034	.006
Holding language ability constant[c]								
Earnings ratio at								
One year	.45	.42	.51	.60	.77	1.07	1.04	1.23
Ten years	.66	.76	.81	.91	.97	.99	1.13	.99
Annual earnings growth rate	.064	.086	.072	.070	.047	.021	.034	.006

NOTE: In all U.S.-Canadian comparisons, region and metropolitan status are held constant at Canadian native-born mean levels for Canadian immigrants and at U.S. native-born mean levels for U.S. immigrants. Marital status is held constant at U.S. native-born mean levels throughout.

a. Level of schooling is held constant at U.S. native-born mean levels.
b. The average earnings growth rate for the first ten years after migration only.
c. Level of education and language proficiency are held constant at U.S. native-born levels.
SOURCE: Author.

429

simulations (second simulation, table 10–5) does not appreciably affect the U.S.-Canadian comparison. This may in part be due to the importance of age at migration on the estimation of the effects of other human-capital variables.

Differences in the educational attainment of Canadian and American immigrants could hide other outcomes of the Canadian skills-based policy. Given high levels of language proficiency among Canadian immigrants, we would expect that, when controlling for differences in education, the relative earnings of Asian and European immigrants would be higher in Canada than in the United States.

In the next set of simulations, shown at the top of table 10–6, all education variables are held constant at the American-born mean values. Our expectations concerning the effect of higher language proficiency on the relative earnings of Canadian immigrants are not borne out. Although Chinese immigrants to the United States initially earn less relative to the Chinese immigrants to Canada, after ten years the relative earnings of the U.S. Chinese immigrants surpass the earnings of their Canadian counterparts. The other Asian immigrant groups in the United States also continue to do better than the Canadian "other Asian" group.

In the final simulations, all skill variables—age at migration, education, and language proficiency—are held at the same values for each group. The results of this simulation are shown in the bottom half of table 10–6.

Holding these variables constant, we find that the U.S. immigrant advantage for Asian groups widens at the ten-year mark. Conceivably, the higher earnings of U.S. Asian immigrants may reflect greater investment, which may in turn be facilitated by the presence of immigrant families and communities.

Conclusions

Admission on the basis of kinship and point systems based upon occupational demand and skills are often considered to represent opposing immigration philosophies. Typically, admission on the basis of kinship has been justified solely on humanitarian grounds. Yet families may facilitate investment in U.S.-specific skills that then augment the earnings growth of immigrants who begin their new economic lives with abysmally low earnings. Beyond the family, the existence of close-knit communities—the development of which would be aided by the admission of immigrants on the basis of kinship—could facilitate human capital investment and other types of investment by immigrants. For instance, immigrant communities have been hypothesized to promote immigrant entrepreneurial activities.[20]

In assessing different immigration policy alternatives, analysts should probably give more attention to economic ramifications of family-based admissions. In our analysis of cross-sectional and intertemporal variations in U.S. admissions criteria we found higher earnings growth among immigrant cohorts with high family admissions.

Comparing the characteristics of Canadian and American immigrants, we found that the Canadian skills-based immigration policy is apparently successful in selecting immigrants who are younger and more language proficient. Canadian policy does not appear to have a consistent effect on the educational levels of immigrants.

Other research suggests that migrating at older ages has a detrimental effect on the earnings of immigrants, perhaps because it is more difficult to adjust to a foreign culture and learn a new language at older ages, or because the return from doing so is smaller.[21] Research has also documented the positive effect within immigrant groups of proficiency in the adopted country's language.[22]

Yet although U.S. immigrants from Asia appear to have a language and age-at-migration disadvantage when compared with their Canadian counterparts, their earnings profiles are quite similar to those of Canadian immigrants originating in the same areas of the world. One possible explanation is that families and close-knit communities fostered by the U.S. family-based admissions policy may help U.S. immigrants to succeed in the labor market despite skill dissimilarities. This may explain why the Canadian skills-based policy has apparently had little effect on the earnings of Asian immigrants.

APPENDIX 10–A1
Regression on L_N (Earnings) for U.S. Immigrant Groups

	Chinese	Filipino	Indian	European
Intercept	6.2202	7.7138	5.5940	9.9722
	(0.3320)	(0.3309)	(0.4069)	(1.2251)
Age	0.0930	0.0607	0.1516	−0.0054
	(0.0135)	(0.0120)	(0.0165)	(0.0466)
Age squared	−0.0012	−0.0009	−0.0018	−0.0001
	(0.0001)	(0.0001)	(0.0002)	(0.0005)
Age × education	0.0004	0.0008	0.0001	0.0019
	(0.0003)	(0.0003)	(0.0004)	(0.0011)
Yrs. educ. to 11	−0.0245	−0.0199	−0.0178	−0.1020
	(0.0147)	(0.0188)	(0.0193)	(0.0589)
Completed 12th year	0.0682	−0.1400	0.0755	0.1567
	(0.0522)	(0.0513)	(0.0674)	(0.1652)
Yrs. educ. after 12	0.0405	0.0295	0.0764	−0.0382
	(0.0115)	(0.0135)	(0.0152)	(0.0502)
Married	0.2244	0.2191	0.2158	0.0371
	(0.0348)	(0.0306)	(0.0354)	(0.1338)
North-Central	0.0606	0.1342	0.0570	−0.0532
	(0.0443)	(0.0415)	(0.0310)	(0.1281)
South	0.0776	−0.0778	0.0106	0.1722
	(0.0415)	(0.0449)	(0.0321)	(0.1666)
West, not California	0.0293	0.0407	−0.0427	−0.1731
	(0.0618)	(0.0579)	(0.0732)	(0.3090)
California	0.1430	−0.0814	0.0332	0.3302
	(0.0310)	(0.0336)	(0.0370)	(0.1641)
Hawaii	0.3838	−0.0843	−0.0537	0.7884
	(0.0970)	(0.0500)	(0.3460)	(0.7243)
Metro	0.1980	−0.1906	−0.0844	−0.0951
	(0.0786)	(0.0522)	(0.0614)	(0.2790)
Yrs. since migration × education	0.0035	0.0031	0.0012	0.0042
	(0.0006)	(0.0007)	(0.0009)	(0.0025)
Yrs. since migration	0.0865	0.0720	0.1032	−0.0312
	(0.0168)	(0.0160)	(0.0182)	(0.0694)
Yrs. since migration squared	−0.0051	−0.0043	−0.0044	−0.0006
	(0.0010)	(0.0008)	(0.0009)	(0.0038)
R–squared	.2643	.2692	.2287	.2233
Observations	4555	4479	4316	221

APPENDIX 10–A1 (continued)

	Japanese	Korean	British
Intercept	6.5524	6.0398	6.7106
	(0.8354)	(0.5547)	(7.5376)
Age	0.1762	0.1319	0.2983
	(0.0336)	(0.0214)	(0.1865)
Age squared	−0.0023	−0.0017	−0.0025
	(0.0004)	(0.0002)	(0.0015)
Age ×	0.0027	0.0009	−0.0047
education	(0.0010)	(0.0007)	(0.0088)
Yrs. educ.	−0.1560	−0.0273	−0.3011
to 11	(0.0457)	(0.0310)	(0.5544)
Completed	0.0485	−0.2114	—
12th year	(0.1617)	(0.0971)	—
Yrs. educ.	−0.1040	−0.0205	0.1306
after 12	(0.0372)	(0.0267)	(0.2710)
Married	0.4332	0.2653	0.3499
	(0.0577)	(0.0594)	(0.4048)
North-Central	−0.2269	0.0367	0.1337
	(0.0757)	(0.0555)	(0.4212)
South	−0.2984	−0.0684	0.3882
	(0.0809)	(0.0556)	(0.4868)
West, not	−0.2657	−0.0868	0.0279
California	(0.1013)	(0.0725)	(0.5100)
California	−0.2701	−0.0280	−0.6719
	(0.0571)	(0.0465)	(0.4765)
Hawaii	−0.5727	−0.2371	—
	(0.1073)	(0.1161)	—
Metro	0.4603	0.1065	1.1250
	(0.1709)	(0.1093)	(0.7043)
Yrs. since	0.0032	0.0051	0.0237
migration ×	(0.0020)	(0.0017)	(0.0205)
education			
Yrs. since	−0.0666	0.0671	−0.3604
migration	(0.0446)	(0.0278)	(0.3966)
Yrs. since	0.0006	−0.0060	−0.0013
migration	(0.0023)	(0.0016)	(0.0151)
squared			
R–squared	.2258	.1867	.3771
Observations	1351	2563	46

NOTE: Standard errors in parentheses.
SOURCE: Authors.

APPENDIX 10–A2
REGRESSION ON L_N (EARNINGS)
FOR U.S.-CANADIAN COMPATIBLE GROUPS

U.S. Groups	Native Non-Hispanic White	Chinese	Asian Non-Chinese	British	Other European
Intercept	6.4752	6.1362	6.4636	6.7106	9.7360
	(0.1575)	(0.3298)	(0.2019)	(7.5376)	(1.2257)
Age	0.0966	0.0954	0.1152	0.2983	−0.0008
	(0.0051)	(0.0135)	(0.0080)	(0.1865)	(0.0464)
Age squared	−0.0011	−0.0012	−0.0015	−0.0025	−0.0001
	(0.0000)	(0.0001)	(0.0001)	(0.0015)	(0.0005)
Age× education	0.0007	0.0005	0.0007	−0.0047	0.0015
	(0.0002)	(0.0003)	(0.0002)	(0.0088)	(0.0011)
Yrs. educ. to 11	0.0298	−0.0322	−0.0322	−0.3011	−0.0965
	(0.0103)	(0.0146)	(0.0106)	(0.5544)	(0.0586)
Completed 12th year	0.0991	−0.0100	−0.0045	—	0.1604
	(0.0220)	(0.0527)	(0.0344)	—	(0.1644)
Yrs. educ. after 12	0.0272	0.0276	0.0317	0.1306	−0.0284
	(0.0071)	(0.0115)	(0.0080)	(0.2710)	(0.0502)
Married	0.3808	0.2288	0.2400	0.3499	0.0339
	(0.0144)	(0.0345)	(0.0194)	(0.4048)	(0.1331)
North-Central	0.0315	0.0623	0.0054	0.1337	−0.0260

	(1)	(2)	(3)	(4)	(5)
	(0.0159)	(0.0440)	(0.0220)	(0.4212)	(0.1283)
South	-0.0475 (0.0156)	0.0652 (0.0413)	-0.0657 (0.0220)	0.3882 (0.4868)	0.1226 (0.1680)
West, not California	-0.0299 (0.0221)	0.0406 (0.0614)	-0.0353 (0.0330)	0.0279 (0.5100)	-0.2225 (0.3086)
California	0.0223 (0.0220)	0.1435 (0.0308)	-0.0880 (0.0191)	-0.6719 (0.4765)	0.2933 (0.1645)
Hawaii	-0.0953 (0.1267)	0.3781 (0.0964)	-0.1108 (0.0384)	—	0.7832 (0.7204)
Metro	0.1576 (0.0141)	0.2047 (0.0781)	-0.0307 (0.0352)	1.1250 (0.7043)	-0.0860 (0.2776)
Yrs. since migration × education	—	0.0034 (0.0006)	0.0025 (0.0004)	0.0237 (0.0252)	0.0042 (0.0025)
Yrs. since migration	—	0.0787 (0.0167)	0.0554 (0.0106)	-0.3604 (0.3966)	-0.0361 (0.0691)
Yrs. since migration squared	—	-0.0048 (0.0010)	-0.0034 (0.0006)	-0.0013 (0.0151)	-0.0007 (0.0038)
Language proficiency	—	0.2773 (0.0344)	0.2007 (0.0220)	—	0.2278 (0.1273)
R-squared	.1567	.2747	.2295	.3771	.2353
Observations	18576	4555	14402	46	221

(Table continues)

APPENDIX 10–A2 (continued)

Canadian Group	Native European	Chinese	Asian Non-Chinese	British	Other European
Intercept	6.7590	6.5140	7.2695	7.1909	7.5540
	(0.2893)	(0.8413)	(0.7195)	(0.7089)	(0.5314)
Age	0.0795	0.0868	0.0734	0.0672	0.0754
	(0.0094)	(0.0306)	(0.0262)	(0.0209)	(0.0206)
Age squared	−0.0009	−0.0009	−0.0011	−0.0011	−0.0009
	(0.0001)	(0.0003)	(0.0003)	(0.0002)	(0.0002)
Age× education	0.0007	−0.0009	0.0009	0.0017	0.0000
	(0.0003)	(0.0008)	(0.0007)	(0.0008)	(0.0006)
Yrs. educ. to 11	0.0456	0.0299	0.0076	0.0445	−0.0285
	(0.0188)	(0.0520)	(0.0461)	(0.0500)	(0.0291)
Completed 12th year	0.1501	−0.1023	−0.1311	−0.0052	0.0603
	(0.0315)	(0.1176)	(0.0889)	(0.0730)	(0.0673)
Yrs. educ. after 12	0.0034	0.0316	−0.0338	−0.0244	0.0487
	(0.0131)	(0.0353)	(0.0299)	(0.0308)	(0.0251)
Married	0.3764	0.3296	0.0547	0.2776	0.2741
	(0.0247)	(0.0747)	(0.0661)	(0.0502)	(0.0540)
Quebec	0.1075	−0.5061	−0.1294	0.0944	−0.0131
	(0.0390)	(0.1939)	(0.1097)	(0.1252)	(0.1055)
Maritime	−0.0189	−0.0610	−0.0934	0.0854	0.3848
	(0.0458)	(0.2696)	(0.1937)	(0.1319)	(0.1791)

Ontario	0.1387	−0.1102	0.0277	−0.0508	0.0531
	(0.0385)	(0.1561)	(0.0977)	(0.0884)	(0.0950)
British Columbia	0.2319	0.0111	0.1434	−0.1150	0.1093
	(0.0455)	(0.1582)	(0.1052)	(0.0931)	(0.1038)
Alberta	0.2254	0.0030	0.1357	0.0210	0.1671
	(0.0470)	(0.1672)	(0.1104)	(0.0991)	(0.1087)
Metro	0.1091	0.1292	0.0225	0.0885	−0.0008
	(0.0205)	(0.0944)	(0.0644)	(0.0395)	(0.0464)
Yrs. since migration	—	−0.0633	−0.0308	0.0031	0.0181
	—	(0.0418)	(0.0327)	(0.0283)	(0.0307)
Yrs. since mig. squared	—	0.0013	0.0019	−0.0001	−0.0016
	—	(0.0025)	(0.0019)	(0.0017)	(0.0018)
Yrs. since migration × education	—	0.0082	0.0058	0.0010	0.0027
	—	(0.0014)	(0.0010)	(0.0007)	(0.0008)
Language proficiency	—	0.4627	0.0831	—	0.1833
	—	(0.1014)	(0.1906)	—	(0.0837)
R-squared	.1522	.2185	.1652	.1292	.1522
Observations	5449	1027	1614	4439	5184

NOTE: Standard errors in parentheses
SOURCE: Authors.

APPENDIX 10–A3
LIST OF VARIABLES

AGE	An individual's age at the time of the survey.
AGESQ	An individual's age.
AGEXED	Age multiplied by years of education.
EDLT12	Part of a spline variable—years of education < 12.
ED12	Part of a spline variable—completion of twelfth year of education.
EDGT12	Part of a spline variable—years of education > 12.
MARRIED	Married, spouse present.
METRO	Residence in a metropolitan area.
LANG	Ability to speak English for the United States data or the ability to speak English or French for the Canadian data.
YSM	Years since migration to the host country.
YSMSQ	YSM squared.
YSMXED	YSM multiplied by years of education.

SOURCE: Authors.

Bibliography

Bloom, David E., and Morley Gunderson. "An Analysis of the Earnings of Canadian Immigrants." Working paper no. 3035, National Bureau of Economic Research, July 1989.

Bonacich, Edna, and John Modell. *The Economic Basis of Ethnic Solidarity: Small Business in the Japanese-American Community.* Berkeley, Calif.: Univ. of California Press, 1980.

Borjas, George. "Assimilation, Changes in Cohort Quality, and the Earnings of Immigrants." *Journal of Labor Economics* 3 (October 1985): 389–463.

———. "The Earnings of Male Hispanic Immigrants in the United States," *Industrial and Labor Relations Review,* 35 (April 1982): 343–53.

———. "Self-Selection and Immigrants." *American Economic Review,* vol. 77, 1987, pp. 531–53.

Chiswick, Barry. *An Analysis of the Economic Progress and Impact of Immigrants.* Report submitted to U.S. Department of Labor, Employment and Training Administration, N.T.I.S. No. PB80-200454. Washington, D.C.: National Technical Information Service, 1980.

———. "The Economic Progress of Immigrants: Some Apparently Universal Patterns." In William Fellner, ed., *Contemporary Economic Problems, 1979.* Washington, D.C.: American Enterprise Institute, 1979, pp. 359–99.

———. "The Effect of Americanization on the Earnings of Foreign-Born Men." *Journal of Political Economy* (October 1978): 897–922.

————. *The Employment of Immigrants in the United States.* Washington, D.C.: American Enterprise Institute, 1982.

————, and Paul W. Miller, "Language in the Labor Market: The Immigrant Experience in Canada and the United States," chapter 7 in this volume.

Duleep, Harriet Orcutt. *The Economic Status of Americans of Asian Descent: An Exploratory Investigation.* Washington, D.C.: U.S. Commission on Civil Rights, Government Printing Office, 1988.

————, and Seth Sanders. "The Role of Women in the Economic Assimilation of Asian Immigrant Families." Working paper presented at the Annual Meeting of the American Economic Association, 1988.

Erikson, Charlotte. *Invisible Immigrants: The Adaptation of English and Scottish Immigrants in Nineteenth Century America.* Miami: University of Miami Press, 1972.

Jasso, Guillermina, and Mark R. Rosenzweig. "Family Reunification and the Immigration Multiplier: U.S. Immigration Law, Origin-County Conditions, and the Reproduction of Immigrants." *Demography* (August 1986): 291–311.

Kim, Kwang Chung, Won Moo Hurh, and Marilyn Fernandez. "Intra-Group Differences in Business Participation: Three Asian Immigrant Groups." *International Migration Review* (Spring 1989): 73–95.

Kossoudji, Sherrie A. "English Language Ability and the Labor Market Opportunities of Immigrant Men." *Journal of Labor Economics* 6 (1988): 205–28.

————. "Immigrant Worker Assimilation: Is It a Labor Market Phenomenon?" *Journal of Human Resources* (Summer 1989): 494–527.

Light, Ivan. *Ethnic Enterprises in America: Business and Welfare among Chinese, Japanese, and Blacks.* Berkeley, Calif.: University of California Press, 1972.

McManus, Walter, William Gould, and Finis Welch. "Earnings of Hispanic Men: The Role of English Language Proficiency." *Journal of Labor Economics* (April 1983).

Parai, Louis. "Canada's Immigration Policy, 1962–74." *Immigration and Migration Review* 9 (1975): 469–72.

Piore, Michael J. *Birds of Passage: Migrant Labor and Industrial Societies.* Cambridge: Cambridge University Press, 1979.

Portes, Alejandro, and Robert L. Bach. *Latin Journey: Cuban and Mexican Immigrants in the United States.* Berkley, Calif.: University of California Press, 1985.

Tanier, Evelina M., "English Language Proficiency and the Determination of Earnings among Foreign-Born Men." *The Journal of Human Resources* (Winter 1988).

Waldinger, Roger. "Structural Opportunity or Ethnic Advantage? Immigrant Business Development in New York." *International Migration Review* (Spring 1989): 48–72.

Commentary on Part Four

Christopher Robinson

The most useful feature of chapter 10 is its Canadian-U.S. comparison, which provides a natural experiment closely related to the U.S. immigration debate. The similarity of the two countries' economies and labor markets make it possible to hold as constant many "confounding factors."

A major advantage of the authors' data was their ability to compare individuals migrating from the same location and at the same time to the two destinations, Canada and the United States. This minimizes the problems of immigrant variation—by country of origin and by cohort—that occur in assessing the effects of the two destination countries' procedures for choosing immigrants. To attribute differences to the two countries' different ways of choosing immigrants, however, it is also necessary to assume that the same type of immigrant applies in equal proportions to each country for possible admission—that is, the applicant pool must also be the same. Otherwise selection by the immigration authorities and selection by the applicants themselves cannot be disentangled. A surprising feature of the comparison is the lack of difference between education levels of immigrants under the two systems. In effect this leaves only age at immigration and language skills as potential differences between those admitted under the U.S. and under the Canadian systems. Would a new U.S. policy therefore have any affect on the average education level of immigrants?

As a background for interpreting the comparisons it would be useful to know the fraction who are admitted on the "non family" system. If this were only 10 percent of the samples used we would not expect to see much difference between the Canadian and U.S. averages. As education is the same in the earnings simulations and age at migration is held the same in many cases, language ability is the only factor left to have any effect—and other studies have shown that this is often temporary. In tables 10–5 and 10–6 it would be useful to have a description of the calculation performed and to examine sensitivity to the specification of the age and age-since-immigration variables. For example, are the data obtained by setting $YSM = 1$ and age = average age for people with $YSM = 1$, and by then advancing both variables by nine years? The lack of interaction between age and YSM limits the effects those variables can have. An extra year since migration could affect earnings differently at different ages.

An earlier version of chapter 10 indicated that there are many zero earners among immigrants, who should not be ignored. In this version attention is restricted to positive earners, but the labor supply issues are still important and worthy of study. How long do immigrants actually take to enter the market? This is especially important for the language issue. The main effect of poor language skills may be to delay the effect of labor market entry, or to make it more intermittent when it occurs. This delay effect is not picked up in earnings regressions. Similarly, the age at immigration may have important effects on the speed of entry into the labor market that also will not be picked up by earnings.

Concerning the earnings experience of immigrants, the authors implicitly assume that it is better to have higher-earning immigrants. But is this necessarily the case? From a world point of view, would total output be more increased by moving the highest or the lowest earners to the United States? Suppose that high earners would be equally productive in their origin country or in the United States, whereas low earners would be more productive in the United States. The total world gain in output would then not necessarily go up if U.S. policy were changed to take more high earners.

Is there necessarily a gain even to the existing U.S. population from assembling a collection of rich people here? There may be complementarities that would make the existing U.S. population better off; but it is not obvious that their net contribution to the United States would differ much from that of more moderate earners who "improve" themselves in the United States. After all, immigrants are consumers, too. The call on welfare or unemployment resources merits some consideration, but beyond a certain level of earnings, what effect does an increase in the "quality" of immigrants have on these costs to the host country?

These issues should caution us against focusing solely on earnings for the immigration question. Nevertheless, it is important to understand the effects of immigration policies on the earnings potential of the average immigrants, and chapter 10 usefully addresses them.

The differences in language skills were noted by Duleep and Reget as one of the measurable differences between Canadian and U.S. immigration. The chapter by Monica Boyd attempts to assess the effects of language skills on earnings of immigrant females. She goes further than Duleep and Regets in examining the means by which language differences operate. A strong, though not unexpected, finding is the high correlation between education and language skills. This raises the possibility that other, possibly unmeasured traits are similarly correlated with language skills, making it difficult to isolate the separate effects.

The approach in chapter 8 is based on models of earnings determination that include language skills and education and that incorporate a successively longer list of other variables. Boyd finds that language effects are reduced as the other variables are included. In the Canadian case they have no effect when all other variables—including occupation and industry—are included. The interpretation of those results depends on one's view of the language-skills-determination process and its interaction with earnings. When language effects are wiped out by the inclusion of occupation and industry dummy variables, Boyd concludes, language skills probably affect the occupation or industry in which the immigrant can obtain employment. This is a crucial point, and it is worth further investigation. It would be useful to specify and estimate a full structural model of the relation between language skill and earnings. The alternative hypotheses could then be tested—do language deficiencies operate primarily by restricting occupational and industry choice?

An issue arises here, as in chapter 10, from the focus on earnings. The cross-tabulation tables show a gross, positive relation between language skills and labor force participation, and this holds up when other variables such as education are held constant. Does labor force participation encourage language skills, or vice versa? Are they simultaneously determined? Again, the specification and estimation of a structural model would be useful. In an expected-lifetime-earnings sense, the language effects via participation may be more important than the language effects on earnings given employment.

A related selection issue is also present. Past studies have shown that estimated effects of such factors as education do not appear to be substantially biased by restricting the analysis to the nonrandom sample of working women. It is not clear that this would hold for the language issue, however. For example, those women who make it into the sample—that is, who gain employment despite language handicaps—may be there precisely because they have other non-measured characteristics that make employment likely and earnings high. In that case the handicap caused by poor language skills would be underestimated, as the women in the sample would not be representative of women in general with poor language skills. A structural analysis of the type mentioned earlier may also help sort out these issues.

On a related point, chapter 8 concludes with some discussion of government programs for language training, and it emphasizes the differential access of men and women for a variety of these programs. Some caution is needed, however, in advocating an extension of these programs, because the evidence as presented is insufficient to demonstrate that such expenditures justify the cost. Program evaluation is a complicated business and has spawned a huge literature. I wonder if any good studies have evaluated language training programs? This might be worth investigating before expanding these programs.

Finally, the contribution of the chapter is important because it helps to redress the balance of research on immigrants that focuses on males, at least for studies of earnings. The generally high and increasing participation rates of immigrant women make it increasingly important to examine the effects of immigration and related policies on women as well as men.

The Grenier and Bloom chapter begins with a valuable summary of research on language as it relates to earnings in the U.S. and Canadian labor markets. These results show some variation, especially between Canada and the United States, but also within Canada and over time. The authors' framework for an explanation is a simple demand-supply model that is assumed to operate at a local labor market level. Does the model explain the variation? Is it useful? Chapter 9 provides some evidence that constructing an economic model may contribute to our understanding of these issues, but not enough evidence to persuade noneconomists to take such models seriously.

The logical structure of the model itself shows some weaknesses. The specification of the supply of labor has people choosing to supply to the French or the English market (in the Canadian case), depending on the relative wages in the two markets. People are endowed with a mother tongue but may acquire a second language and work in that language if it pays to do so. This is perfectly sensible from an economist's point of view. When it comes to the specification of the demand for labor, however, there appears to be an inconsistency. According to the Grenier-Bloom specification, consumers consume only French products if their mother tongue is French. This seems inconsistent; the French-mother-tongue person who learns English and works in the English-language labor market in response to a wage difference at the same time can surely consume the products of this English-language market if they are cheaper than comparable French ones.

There is also a specification of an exogenous component of demand relating to multinationals that makes little economic sense. While a multinational firm may wish to have some English speakers on staff, presumably the ratio of French to English will depend on how expensive they are on relative wage rates, like the rest of the demand.

A useful feature of the model is a typology of cases that relates movements in quantities (the amounts of labor) to movements in prices (the wage rates for different types of labor). One of the chapter's major strengths is its attempt to link the actual relationships between these quantities of employment and wages across different language markets rather than focusing only on the different relative wage outcomes. Unfortunately there is also a major omission here of an important issue for a model that includes both the number of people speaking the languages and the respective wage rates—that is, what are the conditions for an equilibrium in which more than one language can survive within a single country? This is of crucial importance for Canada right now, and it may become increasingly so for the United States with the rise in demand for Spanish-language services and the movements for declaring the United States English-only. If Spanish does get a foothold in some areas in an official sense, would the United States become bilingual? What are the dynamics of language coexistence?

The discussion of the relation between equilibrium wage on employment outcomes could benefit from a more explicit characterization of the effects in terms of the marginal as well as average worker in a given language, where marginal refers to those without preference between working in the two sectors. If the costs of acquiring the alternative language were high at the margin, the wage rate difference would have to be high. And conversely the observation of a zero differential implies that costs at the margin are zero. Some assumption about the distribution of these costs within each population is implicit in much of the discussion in this section; why is it not explicit?

The results for changes over time in earnings differentials in Quebec reinforce results of other studies. The point in chapter 9, however, is to interpret this pattern in the light of essentially no change outside Quebec. The authors argue that there was an exogenous increase in demand for French in Quebec—and the evidence offered is the absence of change outside. But there are other possible explanations, such as that of an out migration of Anglos from Quebec. In the 1970 census the Quebec Anglos were different from non-Quebec Anglos in their higher education and earnings. (Note that this was for current residents, not those born in Quebec.) After various legislation was passed in Quebec, some of these individuals migrated out, and presumably others who would otherwise have migrated in did not, and so the differential disappeared in Quebec. This out-migration would have little effect on English-language wages in the larger English-language market outside Quebec.

The exogenous demand increase that the authors point to has to do with various laws requiring French use (or more French use) in business. From a theoretical point of view this can have two effects, however: (a) for a given output French is substituted for English; but also, (b) costs presumably rise, as the legislation was imposed on cost-minimizing firms that have to change their behavior. In equilibrium, therefore, there may also be output effects that could reduce the demand for French labor. Substitution could also occur away from labor altogether to other factors of production.

Generally, however, a model of the language-labor markets is useful in allowing us to consider simultaneously a rich variety of patterns that have been documented in the substantial literature on language issues.

Peter Skerry

In their analysis of the economic position of linguistic minorities in the United States and Canada, David Bloom and Gilles Grenier report that while the earnings gap between English and French speakers in Canada has declined since 1970, the gap between English and Spanish speakers in the United States has remained high. Indeed, even after controlling for intervening variables, Bloom and Grenier found a slight deterioration in the relative economic position of Spanish speakers in the United States during the 1970s.

Bloom and Grenier trace the improved economic position of French speakers in Canada to increased demand for their labor, which the authors acknowledge flows from political factors excluded from their analysis. Although they do not elaborate, Bloom and Grenier are obviously referring to the assertion of Quebeçois nationalism since the 1960s.

For Spanish speakers in the United States, by contrast, Bloom and Grenier note an increase not in labor demand but in supply. Yet while their analysis of the Canadian case at least acknowledges the effects of political factors, their analysis of Spanish speakers does not. Indeed, the authors regard the increased supply of Spanish-speaking labor as a given—with no apparent political causes. This is extremely misleading.

Examining these developments exclusively in terms of a labor supply–demand model, Bloom and Grenier fail to relate their analysis group that is hardly in danger of losing its identity or of assimilating. Within the context of a polity where ethnic identities are relatively strong and overarching national identity relatively weak, group mobilization has been vigorous. Given relatively low fertility and immigration among French speakers, the creation and sustenance of demand by political means for French-speaking labor and services has led to increased returns to that labor. Political mobilization of French-speaking Canadians has therefore led to economic advancement of the group.

Merely to state the case in this way underscores immediately the different situation of Spanish speakers in the United States. First, Hispanics here are simply not as cohesive a group as French-speaking Canadians. For some time Hispanics have been assimilating socially and economically and gradually losing their separate identity.[1] This is not to deny that barriers to assimilation have existed, or that Hispanics themselves have formed movements to resist assimilation. Indeed, the assertion of bilingual and bicultural rights by some Hispanics speaks to just such sentiments. Yet such efforts to foster a demand for Spanish-speaking labor analagous to what we see in Canada have been ineffective in the United States. And in light of our stronger national identity and aversion to assertive group identities, this is hardly surprising.

Nevertheless, Hispanics have been mobilizing politically. And while their full political potential has yet to be realized, they have made enormous gains. Indeed, their political advance has been greatly abetted by the sheer increase in their numbers in recent decades. Much of this increase is driven by immigration, illegal as well as legal. This demographic factor by itself is of course another significant difference between French Canadians and U.S. Hispanics.

Throughout the 1980s the implicit, unarticulated position of virtually all Hispanic leaders has been to resist all efforts to control or restrict immigration. Of course, Hispanic opposition to such efforts has been explicitly premised on civil rights grounds—that policies restricting immigration would lead to infringements on the civil rights of all Hispanics, including Hispanic citizens. But Hispanic leaders also realize that their own visibility and power depend fundamentally on continued growth in their numbers.

Yet as Bloom and Grenier demonstrate, this increase in the numbers of Hispanics has increased the supply of Spanish-speaking labor relative to demand—with the result that returns to it have been stagnant. Thus political mobilization of Hispanics here in the United States has not led to economic advancement. This contrast with the situation of French Canadians is simply never examined by Bloom and Grenier.

446

Despite this, it is important to recognize that the political calculus has not always been thus for Hispanics and their leaders. Indeed, until the late 1960s or early 1970s, the position of Hispanic and particularly Mexican-American leaders was to limit, however ambivalently, immigration of their countrymen. It was thought that newcomers invariably stigmatized and undercut the position of those who had already settled here and were struggling to assimilate.

All this changed in the late 1960s and early 1970s, when Hispanic leaders realized that their power did not depend exclusively—or even primarily—on the socioeconomic well-being of their group, or even on its voting strength. Rather, as our present affirmative-action regime came into being, Hispanic leaders realized that their power lay in their status as an aggrieved minority group who, like blacks, deserved special help and benefits commensurate with their numbers. Now that they are defined as a minority group in our post–civil rights political culture, Hispanic leaders look to continued immigration to augment their numbers. Increased numbers translate into more attention and visibility for leaders and more affirmative-action jobs and legislative seats carved out under the Voting Rights Act.

Harriet Duleep and Mark Regets's chapter poses basic questions to those advocating that the United States adopt a more skills-oriented, less family-oriented immigration policy. Their finding that prevailing U.S. admissions criteria result in admitting male immigrants as educated as those admitted under Canada's skills-oriented point system suggests that we need to examine carefully the on-the-ground operation of the Canadian program. Michael Malloy, a Canadian immigration, official, has emphasized that as it is implemented by immigration officers in the field, his country's policy is more discretionary than would otherwise appear.

Another Duleep-Regets finding worth noting is the similarity in earnings profiles between English-speaking Indian and non-English-speaking Korean male immigrants in the United States. Not only should this sound a cautionary note about the importance of language in any point system; more generally, it raises a warning about our ability to identify the skills that are critical to immigrant success in America. Similarly, we need to consider that skills criteria once established would not be easily changed. Indeed, our ability to learn from mistakes may be limited by the political forces set in motion by any new admissions criteria. If reform is guided by the image of a technocratically smooth, fine-tuned immigration policy relying on rational skills criteria, we will be disappointed.

Of course, the more fundamental challenge posed by Duleep and Regets to a skills-oriented immigration policy is their finding that, despite differences in admissions criteria, Asian immigrants to the

447

United States enjoyed earnings patterns similar to their counterparts' in Canada. Duleep and Regets point out that our longstanding family-oriented admissions criteria have much more than a humanitarian basis. Indeed, the authors argue that family and community ties promote long-term investment by immigrants and thus result in their economic adjustment and advancement.

An objection can be raised that Duleep and Regets look at Asians, among whom family values are highly consonant with individual achievement. What would Duleep and Regets conclude if they looked at Hispanic immigrants, for whom strong family values are much more in tension with individual achievement? One legacy of the Reagan social agenda has been to look upon strong family values as an unqualified good. Yet as such observers as Thomas Sowell and Edward Banfield have pointed out, these values can inhibit individual mobility and achievement. That is no definitive argument against family-oriented admissions criteria—merely a cautionary note.

Duleep and Regets offer here an economic analogue to a well-established sociological rationale for a family-oriented immigration policy. Earlier in this century sociologists at the University of Chicago conducted research on immigrant communities and found—contrary to dominant views against "hyphenated Americans" and in favor of aggressive Americanization campaigns—that the primary-group ties of family and village that immigrants brought to the United States from the Old World actually helped them adapt to their new environment. Indeed, the Chicago school argued that it was paradoxically the intense group life of urban villages in the United States that helped immigrants become individuals in America.

Such noneconomic rationales, whatever their merits, should serve as a reminder that immigration policy ought not be exclusively concerned with narrowly construed, technocratic goals.

Duleep and Regets examine data pertaining exclusively to immigrant men. Monica Boyd's chapter reminds us that women are also immigrants, and they face unique problems. For example, Boyd documents that immigrant women in Canada and the United States are much more likely than immigrant men not to speak the languages of their host countries. She then demonstrates that inability to speak the host language results, not surprisingly, in lower earnings for immigrant women.

I have no quarrel with Boyd's findings, but I wish to comment on her policy recommendations. At the end of chapter 8 she argues not only for more language training programs for immigrant women but for such programs to be combined with literacy instruction and skill upgrading. Yet Boyd never offers a justification for such efforts. She does reveal an unfortunate tendency with regard to immigrants today in the United States and, judging from her chapter, in Canada as well.

Other things being equal, of course it seems like a worthy policy objective for immigrant women to be fluent in the language of their host country, as well as literate and trained. Yet are other things equal? In the United States at present it is difficult to justify such programs, especially training efforts, for immigrants when many citizens feel deprived of such help.

First, if language deficiencies reduce their earnings power, one must ask why immigrant women do not themselves undertake to learn their adopted country's language. Perhaps some do, though such endeavors are likely to be slow going. Undoubtedly many women do not pursue such efforts in part, as Boyd suggests, because such help is not readily available—hence her call for more such programs.

At this point Boyd acknowledges what she calls the "laissez-faire" social-welfare tradition of both Canada and the United States, but then she seems to regard this tradition as an inconvenient datum or unfortunate vestige of an earlier era. She goes on to extol the programmatic efforts directed at immigrants by European societies with very different, social-democratic traditions.

To be sure, it is not enough to argue against Boyd's policy recommendations by merely asserting that they do not fit into the political traditions of our two countries. But her recommendations, which self-consciously fly in the face of those traditions, require much more justification than merely pointing to European social democracy as self-evidently superior to our system.

Although Boyd does not explictly or forcefully articulate such a justification, I believe we can discern in her remarks the basis for it. At the end of her chapter she alludes to the economic and social consequences of female immigrants' not knowing the host language. She specifically mentions the isolation and dependence of such women on linguistic brokers.

We all appreciate what Boyd is saying. Economic and social independence for all individuals, perhaps especially for women, is an evolving value in both Canada and the United States. But what she fails to consider is the importance of such values to women—particularly poorly educated women from the third world—immigrating to North America. It is surely reasonable to assume that such women come here with more traditional roles and expectations in mind. And while we might well assert that adaptation to their new home would be promoted by a change in their views, we should acknowledge that assertion. For if we assume, as Boyd seems to, that the only obstacle to to the possible effects of political variables exogenous to their economic model. Because political dynamics differ in Canada and the United States, the Bloom-Grenier analysis is particularly disappointing to anyone interested in comparing immigration and labor-market policies in these two countries. Moreover, because of the fundamentally different political-economic interaction factors between French speakers in Canada and Spanish speakers in the United States, Bloom and Grenier simply ignore important differences in the situations of the two groups. I address my remarks to this topic.

In Canada, of course, French speakers constitute a cohesive overcome is our own "laissez-faire" tradition, then we are deceiving ourselves, and our efforts will result in wasted resources, frustration, and disappointment. I am reminded of Malloy's observation that in his years as a Canadian immigration official he learned that administrators see things one way, immigrants another.

But there is an even more important consideration. It may well be that the value of individual self-sufficiency that Boyd would impress on immigrant women works against the successful adaptation of immigrants. At the least, one man's "dependency" is another's tie of mutual obligation. The family- and community-oriented rationales articulated by Duleep and Regets for assimilating immigrants may well result in group gains that come at the expense of individuals within the group—particularly wives and mothers. One suspects, for example, that the wage gains of Asian immigrant males found by Duleep and Regets would not be mirrored by their female counterparts. It may then be that the self-sufficiency for immigrant women sought by Boyd would come at the expense of their families' successful adaptation to their new homes. Or it may simply be that immigrant women have values different from our own that we cannot easily change. In either case, I discern in Boyd's recommendations a readiness to alter immigrant values that reflects the preferences of constituencies in the host societies more than they reflect the preferences or interests of immigrant women themselves. Ironically, in the name of eliminating dependency Boyd may be advocating programs that would create new dependencies on—and new clients for—social welfare providers.

We have come a long way since the aggressive Americanization campaigns directed at immigrants at the turn of the century. Boyd's policy prescriptions remind me that the tolerance toward immigrant values and cultures that we have learned in recent decades ought not now to be abandoned in favor of some apparently enlightened perspective that is in fact not shared by immigrants.

Notes

Chapter 1: Introduction, *Barry R. Chiswick*

1. According to biblical tradition (Gen. 11:1–9) at one time all people spoke the same language and worked together in Babel to build a tower to reach Heaven. To thwart the potential success of this project, God dispersed them across the world and imposed different languages. Hence, the text recognizes the increase in transaction costs from a multiplicity of languages.

2. A somewhat comparable situation would be created in the United States were Puerto Rico to become a state.

3. Major constitutional changes in Canada in the 1990s may also sharply alter the relationships among the provinces and, as a consequence, with the United States.

4. For two excellent studies, one historical and the other contemporary, of migration between the United States and Canada, see Marcus Lee Hansen, *The Mingling of the Canadian and American Peoples* (New Haven: Yale University Press, 1940), and the U.S. Bureau of the Census, *Migration between the United States and Canada* (Washington, D.C.: U.S. Government Printing Office, 1990), Current Population Reports, Series P23, no. 161.

Chapter 2: Immigration Policy since 1945, *Reimers and Troper*

1. For Canada, see Irving Abella and Harold Troper, *None Is Too Many: Canada and the Jews of Europe 1933–1948* (New York: Random House, 1983); for the United States, see David S. Wyman, *The Abandonment of the Jews: America and the Holocaust, 1941–1945* (New York: Pantheon, 1984).

2. Abella and Troper, *None Is Too Many,* pp. 190–279; Lubomyr Luciuk, "Searching for Place: Ukrainian Refugee Migration to Canada After World War II," unpublished Ph.D. dissertation, University of Alberta, 1984.

3. Canadian Institute of Public Opinion, public opinion news service release, October 30, 1946.

4. Canadian *House of Commons Debates,* May 1, 1947, pp. 2644–47.

5. Anthony H. Richmond, *Post-War Immigrants in Canada* (Toronto: University of Toronto Press, 1967), p. 9.

6. William Paterson, *Planned Migration: The Social Determinants of the Dutch-Canadian Movement* (Berkeley: University of California Press, 1955).

7. Luciuk, "Searching for Place"; Abella and Troper, *None Is Too Many,* pp. 238–79; Milda Danys, *DP: Lithuanian Immigration to Canada After the Second*

World War (Toronto: Multicultural History Society of Ontario, 1986); Karl Aun, *The Political Refugees: A History of the Estonians in Canada* (Toronto: McClelland & Stewart, 1985), pp. 20–8.

8. For a discussion of the 1952 Act and its application, see Freda Hawkins, *Canada and Immigration: Public Policy and Public Concern* (Montreal: McGill-Queen's University Press, 1972), pp. 101–10.

9. Reginald Whitaker, *Double Standard: The Secret History of Canadian Immigration* (Toronto: Lester and Orpen Dennys, 1987). For a discussion of the issue of Nazi war criminals in Canada, see David Matas and Susan Charendoff, *Justice Delayed: Nazi War Criminals in Canada* (Toronto: Summerhill Press, 1987), and Harold Troper and Morton Weinfeld, *Old Wounds: Jews, Ukrainians and the Hunt for Nazi War Criminals in Canada* (Chapel Hill: University of North Carolina Press, 1989).

10. Hawkins, *Canada and Immigration*, p. 99.

11. N. F. Dreiziger, *Struggle and Hope: The Hungarian Canadian Experience* (Toronto: McClelland and Stewart, 1982); Gerald Dirks, *Canada's Refugee Policy* (Montreal: McGill-Queen's University Press, 1977), pp. 190–213.

12. For a discussion of the repeal of Chinese Exclusion Act, see Fred Riggs, *Pressures on Congress: A Study of the Repeal of the Chinese Exclusion Act* (New York: King's Crown Press, 1950).

13. David M. Reimers, *Still the Golden Door: The Third World Comes to America* (New York: Columbia University Press, 1985), pp. 15–16, and Robert Divine, *American Immigration Policy* (New Haven: Yale University Press, 1957), pp. 152–53.

14. *Congressional Record*, October 10, 1945, pp. 9529–30.

15. Roger Daniels, *Asian America: Chinese and Japanese in America Since 1950* (Seattle: University of Washington Press, 1988), p. 306, and Reimers, *Still the Golden Door*, pp. 21–22 and 27.

16. An excellent and thorough study of the Displaced Persons Act is Leonard Dinnerstein, *America and the Survivors of the Holocaust* (New York: Columbia University Press, 1982).

17. Ibid., chapters 7 and 9.

18. Reimers, *Still the Golden Door*, p. 23.

19. U.S. Congress, Senate Committee on the Judiciary, *The Immigration and Naturalization Systems of the United States*, Senate Report 1515, 81st Congress, 2nd session, pp. 454–56. A comprehensive account of the McCarran-Walter Act is Marius Dimmitt, "The Enactment of the McCarran-Walter Act of 1952," unpublished Ph.D. dissertation, University of Kansas, 1971. A sympathetic view is Divine, *American Immigration Policy*.

20. Report of the President's Commission on Immigration and Naturalization, *Whom Shall We Welcome?*, 1953, p. 177.

21. Dimmitt, "McCarran-Walter Act," pp. 233–37. For a somewhat favorable treatment of the McCarran-Walter Act, see Divine, *American Immigration Policy*, pp. 164–91.

22. U.S. Congress, Subcommittees of the Committees on the Judiciary, *Revision of Immigration, Naturalization, and Nationality Laws*, Hearings, 82nd

Congress, 1st session, p. 74. See also Bill Hosokawa, *Nisei: The Quiet Americans* (New York: William Morrow and Co., 1969), pp. 450–55, and Daniels, *Asian America*, pp. 305–06.

23. Reimers, *Still the Golden Door*, pp. 26–27, 64.

24. Gil Loescher and John Scanlan, *Calculated Kindness: Refugees and America's Half-Open Door, 1945–Present* (New York: The Free Press, 1986), pp. 49–60.

25. Daniels, *Asian America*, pp. 283–84, 296–300. Congress in 1988 voted to compensate Japanese Americans who were interned during World War II. The first checks were sent out in 1990.

26. For the civil rights movement, see Harvard Sitkoff, *The Black Struggle for Equality, 1954–1980* (New York: Hill and Wang, 1981).

27. For public opinion after 1945, see Rita Simon, *Public Opinion and the Immigrant: Print Media Coverage, 1880–1980* (Lexington: Lexington Books, 1985). Public opinion polls over the years have indicated sympathy for refugees and the tradition of immigration in American history, but considerable ambivalence about increasing the actual numbers of immigrants.

28. A general account of the 1965 act is William Stern, "H.R. 2580: The Immigration and Nationality Amendments of 1965—A Case Study," unpublished Ph.D. dissertation, New York University, 1974. See also Reimers, *Still the Golden Door*, chapter 3.

29. *Congressional Record*, August 25, 1965, p. 21812.

30. Reimers, *Still the Golden Door*, pp. 73–74.

31. Ibid., pp. 77–80. Abba Schwartz, who played a key role in formulating the administration proposal, believed it was not necessary to accept this ceiling. See his account in Abba Schwartz, *The Open Society* (New York: Morrow, 1968).

32. Immigration and Naturalization Service (INS), *Statistical Yearbook*, 1987, p. xxi. In 1986 the figure was 223,468 and in 1987, 218,575.

33. An excellent discussion of the Cuban refugees is Felix Roberto Masud-Piolot, *With Open Arms: Cuban Migration to the United States* (Totowa, N.J.: Rowman & Littlefield, 1988).

34. Ibid., pp. 45–54, 58–59.

35. Ibid., p. 60.

36. Reimers, *Still the Golden Door*, p. 124.

37. L.W. St. John-Jones, "Canadian Immigration Trends and Policies in the 1960's," *International Migration* (1973), p. 141; Hawkins, *Canada and Immigration*, pp. 379–82; Vic Satzewich, "Racism and Canadian Immigration Policy: The Government's View of Caribbean Migration, 1962–1966," *Canadian Ethnic Studies* (1989), pp. 67–97; D. Stasiulis, "Racism and the Canadian State," *Explorations in Canadian Ethnic Studies* (1985), pp. 13–32.

38. Canadian *House of Commons Debates*, October 8, 1971, pp. 8545–8546; report of the Royal Commission on Bilingualism and Biculturalism, Book IV, *The Cultural Contribution of the Other Ethnic Groups* (Ottawa, 1969).

39. John Porter, "Dilemmas and Contradictions of a Multi-ethnic Society," *Transactions of the Royal Society of Canada* (1972), pp. 193–205; Manoly Lupul, "Multiculturalism and Canada's White Ethnics," *Canadian Ethnic Studies*

(1983), pp. 99–107; Raymond Breton, "From a Different Perspective: French Canada and the Issue of Immigration and Multiculturalism," *TESL Talk*, vol. 10, no. 3 (1979), pp. 45–56.

40. Sudhas Ramcharan, *Racism: Non-whites in Canada* (Toronto: Butterworths, 1982), pp. 15–16.

41. Statistics Canada, *Immigrants in Canada: Selected Highlights* (Ottawa: Statistics Canada, 1990), p. 28.

42. Dirks, *Canada's Refugee Policy*, pp. 233–42.

43. "Immigration," *International Canada* (April 1974), p. 28.

44. W. Carroll, "The Response of the Canadian Academic Community to the Chilean Crisis," *Bulletin of the Canadian Association of University Teachers* (October 1974), p. 1.

45. Dirks, *Canada's Refugee Policy*, p. 248, and Whitaker, *Double Standard*, pp. 254–61.

46. For a discussion of the Canadian boat people rescue effort, see Howard Adelman, *Canada and the Indochinese Refugees* (Regina: L.A. Weigl Educational Associates, 1982); Howard Adelman, ed., *The Indochinese Refugee Movement: The Canadian Experience* (Toronto: Operation Lifeline, 1980); Canada Employment and Immigration Commission, *Indochinese Refugees: The Canadian Response, 1970–1980* (Ottawa: Employment and Immigration Canada, 1980).

47. For the 1989 rules and their application, see *New York Times*, February 4, 1990. In 1988 the minister of employment and immigration estimated that Canada had a backlog of 85,000 claims for refugee status. Release from the minister of employment and immigration, December 28, 1988.

48. U.S. Congress, House Subcommittee No. 1 of the Committee on the Judiciary, *Western Hemisphere Immigration*, Hearings, 93rd Congress, 1st session, p. 105.

49. For a discussion of the first wave of Southeast Asian refugees, see Gail Kelly, *From Vietnam to America: A Chronicle of the Vietnamese Immigration to the United States* (Boulder, Colo.: Westview Press, 1977).

50. For the Southeast Asian refugee crisis, see Barry Wain, *The Refused: The Agony of the Indochina Refugee* (New York: Simon and Schuster, 1981).

51. Edward Kennedy, "Refugee Act of 1980," in Barry Stein and Silvano Tomasi, eds., *Refugees Today; International Migration Review* (Spring–Summer, 1981).

52. Reimers, *Still the Golden Door*, pp. 192–93.

53. For the anti-Communist bias of refugee police, see Loescher and Scanlan, *Calculated Kindness*.

54. Ibid., pp. 172–79 and Reimers, *Still the Golden Door*, pp. 184–89.

55. Masud-Piolot, *With Open Arms*, chapter 6.

56. In addition to Zolberg, see Elizabeth G. Ferris, *The Central American Refugees* (New York: Praeger, 1987); Loescher and Scanlan, *Calculated Kindness*; Ann Crittenden, *Sanctuary: A Story of American Conscience and the Law in Collision* (New York: Weidenfeld & Nicholson, 1988).

57. For this period, see Julian Samora, *Los Mojados: The Wetback Story* (Notre Dame: University of Notre Dame Press, 1983).

58. An excellent account of Operation Wetback is Juan Garcia, *Operation*

Wetback: The Mass Deportation of Mexican Undocumented Workers in 1954 (West-port, Conn.: Greenwood Press, 1980).

59. INS, *Annual Report*, 1955, pp. 14–15.

60. Garcia, *Operation Wetback*, pp. 224–25.

61. The best account of the bracero program is Richard Craig, *The Bracero Program: Interest Groups and Foreign Policy* (Austin: University of Texas Press, 1971).

62. Reimers, *Still the Golden Door*, pp. 233–34.

63. The literature on illegal immigration is vast. For a summary of the view that it has negative effects on American workers, see Vernon Briggs, Jr., *Immigration Policy and the American Labor Force* (Baltimore: Johns Hopkins Press, 1984), pp. 128–84.

64. Ibid., pp. 236–40. An excellent summary of the early bills is Harris N. Miller, "The Right Thing to Do: A History of Simpson-Mazzoli," in Nathan Glazer, ed., *Clamor at the Gates: The New American Immigration* (San Francisco: Institute for Contemporary Studies, 1985).

65. U.S. Congress, House Report 99–100, conference report, *Immigration Reform and Control Act of 1986*, 99th Congress, 2nd session.

66. *New York Times*, March 1, 1989, and *Congressional Record*, October 21, 1988, pp. 17149–51. These were called "Berman visas," after Representative Howard Berman of California, who sponsored them. The *Irish Echo* claimed that many Irish applicants might win these visas, but when the draw was made they won few slots. Several thousand of the visas went to persons from Bangladesh.

67. For a summary of the controversy over IRCA, see *New York Times*, June 18, 1989, and October 9, 1989.

68. *Washington Post*, April 28, 1981.

69. Los Angeles, after the English-language referendum passed, an-nounced an expansion and not contraction of its bilingual educational pro-grams and said it faced a shortage of bilingual staff. See *New York Times*, May 10, 1988 and December 15, 1988.

70. Ibid., February 8, 1990.

71. *Bergen (County) Record*, October 2, 1987, November 8, 1987; *New York Times*, September 17, 1984, February 15, 1987, and July 10, 1988.

72. For the provisions see U.S. Congress, Senate Subcommittee Report 100–290, Immigration Act of 1988, 100th Congress, 2nd session.

73. See, for example, the statement of Norman Lee Kee of U.S. Asia Institute, in U.S. Congress, House Subcommittee on Immigration, Refugees, and International Law, of the Committee on the Judiciary, *Legal Immigration*, Hearings, 99th Congress, 2nd session, pp. 78–79. For the fifth preference in particular, see U.S. Congress, Senate Subcommittee Report 100–34, *Legal Immigration to the United States: A Demographic Analysis of the Fifth Preference Visa Admissions*, 100th Congress, 1st session. For summaries of the controversy see "Giving Immigration Points to the Skilled and Educated," *Insight* (September 5, 1988); Scott McConnell, "The New Battle Over Immigration," *Fortune* (May 9, 1988), pp. 89–102; and Constance Holden, "Debate Warming Up on Legal Migration Policy," *Science* (July 15, 1988), pp. 288–90.

74. *New York Times,* February 14, 1988. For the bill, see U.S. Senate, Sub-committee Report 100–290, *Immigration Act of 1989,* 100th Congress, 2nd session.

75. The English language provisions were eventually dropped, but there is no doubt that Ireland and West European nations would benefit from the proposal, a fact that both the *Irish Echo* and the *Irish Voice* were well aware of.

76. The Report of the Canadian Immigration and Population Study was issued in four volumes: *Immigration Policy Perspectives* (Ottawa: Manpower and Immigration, 1974); *The Immigration Program* (Ottawa: Manpower and Immigration, 1974); *Immigration and Population Statistics* (Ottawa: Manpower and Immigration, 1974); and *Three Years in Canada* (Ottawa: Manpower and Immigration, 1974). All four volumes were also published simultaneously in French.

77. *Immigration Policy Perspectives,* p. 20; for scholarly discussion of the Green Paper, see *Canadian Ethnic Studies,* special issue: *The Green Paper on Immigration* (1975).

78. Anthony Richmond, "Recent Developments in Immigration to Canada and Australia: A Comparative Analysis," *International Journal of Comparative Sociology* (1976), p. 188; Employment and Immigration Canada, *Profiles of Canadian Immigration* (Ottawa: Employment and Immigration, 1982), p. 20.

79. Statistics Canada, *Immigrants in Canada,* p. 28.

80. Ibid.

81. Margaret Cannon, *China Tide: The Revealing Story of the Hong Kong Exodus to Canada* (Toronto: Harper & Collins, 1989); John DeMont and Tom Fennell, *Hong Kong Money: How Chinese Families and Fortunes Are Changing Canada* (Toronto: Key Porter Books, 1989).

82. See, for example, Morton Weinfeld, "Immigration and Canada's Population Future: A Nation-Building Vision," working papers on social behavior, sociology (Montreal: McGill University, 1988); T. John Samuel, "Immigration, Visible Minorities, and the Labor Force in Canada: Vision 2,000," unpublished paper presented at the Canadian Population Society annual meeting in Windsor, Ontario, June 5–7, 1988; and Chris Taylor, *Demography and Immigration in Canada: Challenge and Opportunity* (Ottawa: Employment and Immigration Canada, 1987).

Chapter 3: RESPONSE TO CRISIS, *Aristide R. Zolberg*

1. On the subject more generally, see Michael Marrus, *The Unwanted: European Refugees in the Twentieth Century* (New York: Oxford University Press, 1985), pp. 296–345; Jacques Vernant, *The Refugee in the Post-War World* (London: Allen and Unwin, 1953); Louise W. Holborn, *Refugees: A Problem of Our Time: The Work of the United Nations High Commissioner for Refugees, 1951–1972* (Metuchen, N.J.: The Scarecrow Press, 1975); and Leon Gordenker, *Refugees in International Politics* (New York: Columbia University Press, 1987).

2. Opposing extension of the IRO, the Truman administration refused to sign the 1951 Convention and successfully insisted that the United Nations High Commissioner for Refugees (UNHCR) be given no resettlement and

virtually no relief responsibilities. While withholding all financial support from the UNHCR until 1955, the United States poured millions into the regional agencies: United Nations Relief and Work Agency for Palestinians, and United Nations Korean Relief Agency for Koreans driven from their homes during the war.

3. Unless otherwise indicated, the information that follows is drawn from Gil Loescher and John A. Scanlan, *Calculated Kindness: Refugees and America's Half-Open Door, 1945 to the Present* (New York: Free Press, 1986).

4. Citation from Senator Alexander Wiley (R-Wis.), Ibid., p. 23.

5. National Security Council, "Psychological Value of Escapees from the Soviet Orbit," Security Memorandum, March 26, 1953 (typewritten, 4 pp.).

6. Richard F. Fagen, R. A. Brody, and T. J. O'Leary, *Cubans in Exile: Disaffection and the Revolution* (Stanford: Stanford University Press, 1968), p. 102.

7. Scanlan and Loescher, "U.S. Foreign Policy, 1959–80: Impact on Refugee Flow from Cuba," in Gilbert Loescher and John A. Scanlan, eds., *The Global Refugee Problem: U.S. and World Response* (Philadelphia: American Academy of Political and Social Science, May 1983), p. 125. The wave included many professionals and skilled workers, and it was largely white.

8. Alan Dowty, *Closed Borders: The Contemporary Assault on Freedom of Movement* (New Haven, Conn.: Yale University Press, 1987), pp. 196–204.

9. Arnold H. Leibowitz, "The Refugee Act of 1980: Problems and Congressional Concerns," in Loescher and Scanlan, *Global Refugee Problem*, p. 165; Deborah Anker, "The Development of U.S. Refugee Legislation," in Lydio A. Tomasi, ed., *In Defense of the Alien*, vol. VI (New York: Center for Migration Studies, 1984), p. 160.

10. U.S. Department of State, *Country Reports on the World Refugee Situation*, 1981, p. 9.

11. The distinction between the two hemispheres had been eliminated in 1976, making for a total of 17,400 entries a year reserved for refugees worldwide.

12. Anker, "U.S. Refugee Legislation," pp. 161–62.

13. Dennis Gallagher, Susan Forbes, and Patricia Weiss Fagen, *Of Special Humanitarian Concern: U.S. Refugee Admissions Since Passage of the Refugee Act* (Washington, D.C.: Refugee Policy Group, September 1985).

14. Arthur C. Helton, "Political Asylum under the 1980 Refugee Act: An Unfulfilled Promise," in Tomasi, *In Defense of the Alien*, p. 201.

15. Helsinki Watch, *Detained, Denied, Deported: Asylum Seekers in the United States* (New York: U.S. Helsinki Watch Committee, June 1989), pp. 75–76.

16. For details, see chapter 2. The present account is based on Irving Abella and Harold Troper, *None is Too Many: Canada and the Jews of Europe, 1933–1948* (Toronto: Random House, 1982); Gerald E. Dirks, *Canada's Refugee Policy: Indifference or Opportunism?* (Montreal: McGill-Queen's University Press, 1977); and Reg Whitaker, *Double Standard: The Secret History of Canadian Immigration* (Toronto: Lester and Orpen Dennys, 1987).

17. Freda Hawkins, *Critical Years in Immigration: Canada and Australia Compared* (Kingston: McGill-Queen's University Press), p. 167.

18. Ibid., pp. 46–47.

19. Ibid., pp. 174–75; James C. Hathway, "Selective Concern: An Overview of Refugee Law in Canada," *McGill Law Journal*, vol. 33, no. 4 (September 1988), pp. 676–715.

20. Ibid., pp. 700–02. Albeit not spelled out as such, the program is provided for indirectly by Section 115(2) of the 1976 act, which grants the Governor-in-Council (that is, the Federal Cabinet) the authority to exempt any persons from the general requirements of the act, and to facilitate the admission of persons for reasons of public policy or because of the existence of compassionate or humanitarian considerations.

21. Gerald E. Dirks, "A Policy Within a Policy: The Identification and Admission of Refugees to Canada," *Canadian Journal of Political Science*, vol. 17, no. 2 (June 1984), pp. 288–91.

22. Hawkins, *Critical Years*, p. 184.

23. This section is based on Aristide R. Zolberg, Astri Suhrke, and Sergio Aguayo, *Escape from Violence: Conflict and the Refugee Crisis in the Developing World* (New York: Oxford University Press, 1989); the coauthors are not responsible for the present analysis, however. The research was made possible by grants from the Ford and Rockefeller Foundations.

24. United States Committee for Refugees, *World Refugee Survey* (Washington, D.C.: 1990.

25. See Aristide Zolberg, Astri Suhrke, and Sergio Aguayo, "International Factors in the Formation of Refugee Movements," *International Migration Review*, vol. 20, no. 74 (Summer 1986), pp. 51–69.

26. The term was coined by Michael Teitelbaum in "Political Asylum in Theory and Practice," *The Public Interest* (1984), 74–86.

27. See Susan Forbes Martin, "Development and Politically Generated Migration," *Commission for the Study of International Migration and Cooperative Economic Development*, working paper no. 5 (Washington, D.C.: July 1989).

28. Norman L. and Naomi Flink Zucker, *The Guarded Gate: The Reality of American Refugee Policy* (San Diego: Harcourt, Brace, Jovanovich, 1987), pp. 58–71; Loescher and Scanlan, *Calculated Kindness*, pp. 180–87.

29. Zucker and Zucker, *The Guarded Gate*, p. 58.

30. U.S. Committee on Refugees, *Despite a Generous Spirit: Denying Asylum in the United States* (Washington, D.C.: American Council for Nationalities Service, December 1986), pp. 14–26; Helsinki Watch, *Detained, Denied, Deported*, p. 50; Lawyers Committee on Human Rights, *Refugee Refoulement: The Forced Return of Haitians under the U.S.-Haitian Interdiction Agreement* (New York: February 1990).

31. Lawyers Committee on Human Rights, *Refugee Refoulement*, p. 33. After a vessel is stopped, it is boarded by a Coast Guard party to establish whether it is bound for the United States with undocumented Haitians. The passengers and crew are then transferred to the Coast Guard cutter for questioning. Reports suggest the interviews are usually perfunctory and take place when the interviewees are in bad physical and mental state, mostly on a group rather than on an individual basis, and with no assurance of privacy. Until 1986 the interview took place in the presence of a Haitian naval officer in

uniform. After the transfer, the Haitians are interviewed by an INS officer and interpreter to establish whether they may have a legitimate claim for asylum. If they have, they are to be brought to the United States for a hearing. Under the agreement, the Coast Guard is to return the vessel and its passengers to the country from which it came; but in fact the largely home-made vessels are almost always destroyed, as hazardous to health and navigation. It has also been suggested that destruction is being used by U.S. authorities as a deterrent to immigration. The LCHR has also questioned the president's authority to interdict, because Section 1185 of the INA was designed to give him powers to prevent the infiltration of enemy agents, not asylum seekers. It has pointed out that these doubts seem to be shared by the executive branch, which in 1981 initiated legislation to provide power to interdict vessels on the high seas specifically for preventing illegal immigration.

32. Ibid., pp. 5, 75.

33. Sergio Aguayo and Patricia Weiss Fagen, *Central Americans in Mexico and the United States* (Washington, D.C.: Center for Immigration Policy and Refugee Assistance, Georgetown University, 1987).

34. For a good overview, see United States Committee for Refugees, *Despite a Generous Spirit*.

35. Helsinki Watch, *Detained, Denied, Deported*, pp. 20, 71. For example, in an advisory opinion issued in the spring of 1988 in the case of a Salvadorean woman who is one of the leaders of COMADRES, the BHRHA stated among other things that evidence of torture was indecisive, and that claims of torture should be discounted because the Frente Farabundo Marti para lâ liberacion Nacional has instructed detained activists to allege torture. They further said that COMADRES was linked to guerrillas, and that "there is no evidence that peaceful activity of a leftist character would cause" the applicant "to be at risk in El Salvador at the hands of rightist inclined assassins."

36. Helsinki Watch, *Detained, Denied, Deported*, p. 27.

37. U.S. Committee for Refugees, *Refugees at our Border: The U.S. Response to Asylum Seekers* (Washington, D.C.: September 1989), p. 14.

38. Helsinki Watch, *Detained, Denied, Deported*, p. 33.

39. Ibid., pp. 36–37. Immigration judges would have been eliminated as well, and "defensive" proceedings would have become nonadversarial, thereby depriving applicants of the opportunity to present their cases in an open hearing, with the aid of counsel. The following April the INS proposed to replace the district directors with asylum officers trained in international law and international affairs. Moreover, these officers would have access to nongovernmental sources of information on which to base their judgments. Another significant innovation was that asylum applicants need not establish the likelihood of persecution directed at them individually, but could make their case by demonstrating a pattern of persecution against a group with which they were clearly identified. Although it found the proposals more acceptable, the refugee advocacy community objected that they still failed to give asylum seekers the benefit of the doubt, as set forth in the UNHCR guidelines, and failed to overcome the structural flaw embedded in the present system.

40. Helsinki Watch, *Detained, Denied, Deported*, p. 35.

41. UCSR, *Refugees at Our Border*, p. 11.

42. Unless otherwise indicated, the following account is based on various issues of *Refugee Reports* and *Interpreter Releases*.

43. Most of them were students, including an estimated 32,000 on J-1 visas, 8,000 on F-1, and 200 on M-1 (*Interpreter Releases*, July 31, 1989). J-visas require the students to return to their home country for two years upon expiration before being permitted to adjust their status to permanent resident. Questioned about Deferred Enforced Departure (DED), the acting general counsel for INS said there was no distinction in practical effect with Extended Voluntary Departure, and explained the agency preferred DED for semantic reasons, and because of the continuing controversy over EVD.

44. U.S. Congress, *Senate Report 101-241*, 101st Congress, 2nd session, 1989.

45. Aguayo and Fagen, *Central Americans*, p. 5. There are reports, however, that the authorities have informally collaborated with the INS in the gathering of intelligence concerning the "underground railway" organized by the Sanctuary movement, which was used in the arrest and prosecution of some of its leaders, and in returning Salvadorans apprehended in the United States to their country of origin via Mexico City. This approach was initiated by the INS in 1986 in response to mounting opposition to its deportation policy (Ibid., p. 59; personal communication from S. Aguayo, March 13, 1990.

46. "The way asylum applications were being filed had the appearance of a feeding frenzy. At the time there was no control over frivolous applications, and the system clearly was open to abuse. . . . The Central Americans themselves often had no idea that they were applying for asylum." (USCR, *Refugees at Our Borders*, p. 3). By the same token a number of genuine refugees probably filed bad applications.

47. Elements of the plan included: an increase in the number of adjudicators and support staff, to reduce processing time to a single day; increased Border Patrol activity, to reduce the flow; the systematic issuance of deportation warrants (Order to Show Cause); detention of the aliens in enlarged INS or other federal facilities; prompt hearings before immigration judges; speedy deportation. The plan was in fact outlined on February 16, with a concomitant public relations campaign. The plan also included a nonpublic component, however: the use of asylum applicants as a source of intelligence on home country conditions, to be gathered by a team of specialists located in Harlingen. No thought was expressed in the memo about possible repercussions of this for the asylum seekers (USCR, *Refugees at Our Borders*, p. 6).

48. Committee for U.S. Action on Asylum Concerns, *Second National Conference Report*, February 1990.

49. *Network News*, January–February 1990; *New York Times*, January 28, 1990.

50. This section is based on reports in the *New York Times*, various issues, 1990–1991; and *Refugee Reports*, various issues, 1990–91.

51. Analyses of the law are provided in Joyce C. Vialet and Larry M. Eig,

"Immigration Act of 1990 (P.L. 101-649)," *CRS Report for Congress* (Washington: Congressional Research Service, the Library of Congress, December 14, 1990); Bureau of International Labor Affairs, U.S. Department of Labor, *The Immigration Act of 1990* (December, 1990); Gary E. Rubin and Judith Golub, *The Immigration Act of 1990: An American Jewish Committee Analysis* (New York: American Jewish Committee, 1990).

52. *Refugee Reports,* July 20, 1990, p. 11; the *New York Times,* July 24, 1990.

53. Dirks, *Canada's Refugee Policy,* p. 299.

54. Whitaker, *Double Standard,* p. 295.

55. Hathaway, "Selective Concern," pp. 701–02.

56. As Hawkins has suggested, "the undocumented migrant and the claimant for refugee status are in very similar situations and can often be, at different times, the same person. An undocumented migrant can sometimes achieve entry via refugee status, while the claimant for refugee status who is turned down often becomes one of the army of undocumented migrants" (*Critical Years,* p. 195). In November 1982 the minister of immigration's advisory council estimated there were 200,000 illegal aliens in Canada, and proposed a six-year probationary program together with an aggressive approach to enforcement. The usually evenhanded Freda Hawkins characterizes the report as "alarmist and unhelpful, . . . based on very inadequate research, reflecting the fact that no single member of the Council at that time had any real knowledge or expertise in the field of immigration" and that they accepted uncritically inflated estimates of the number of illegal immigrants in the United States (Ibid., p. 206). Unacceptable to the Liberal government, the report was followed by another that lowered the estimate to 50,000, consisting mainly of overstayers from the United States, Jamaica, Guyana, and Portugal.

57. *La Monde* (Paris), January 6, 1987.

58. See W. Gunther Plaut, *Refugee Determination in Canada* (Ottawa: Ministry of Supply and Services Canada, 1985).

59. *New York Times,* November 23, 1986.

60. *The Economist,* January 7, 1989, p. 35; Hawkins, *Critical Years,* pp. 175, 190.

61. Whitaker, *Double Standard,* p. 296.

62. Hawkins, *Critical Years,* p. 192; Hathaway, "Selective Concern."

63. The state of public opinion at this time is difficult to evaluate. At the end of 1988, *The Economist* judged Canadians to be "now just about the most tolerant people on earth," but it suggested, "People are angry about the way their liberal arrangements for political refugees are being exploited by economic refugees." The analysis went on to point out that "the anger is ostensibly about queue-jumping, but the racist undertones are inescapable. They suggest that the country is nearing the limits of the number of difficult-to-assimilate people it is prepared to welcome. This leaves Canada with the unhappy choice of keeping immigration at its current inadequate level or of getting more easy-to-assimilate people in a larger total number of immigrants. The second course is the right one, though it would cause Canada embarrassment at home and abroad." (October 8, 1988, *Canada Survey,* p. 2.)

64. Whitaker, *Double Standard,* p. 298.

65. Ibid., p. 297.

66. *Refugee Reports,* January 27, 1989, p. 12.

67. James C. Hathaway, "Postscript—Selective Concern: An Overview of Refugee Law in Canada," *McGill Law Journal,* vol. 34 (1989), p. 354.

68. *New York Times,* December 31, 1988, p. 5. Leading countries of origin for the backlog were Trinidad and Tobago, Sri Lanka, Iran, El Salvador, Portugal, Ghana, India, Nicaragua, Lebanon, and Guatemala. They include people whose examinations were still pending, and those arriving from countries on the B-1 list between May 1986 and February 1987. The review process starts with an interview in which some may be granted permanent resident status on family grounds. Following this there is a "credible basis" hearing before a two-person panel (that is, the first stage in the new process). Then there is a "Humanitarian/Compassionate Review." Beyond this there is a limited appeal process on questions of law and capricious findings of fact.

69. *Refugee Reports,* January 27, 1989, pp. 10–13.

70. *Toronto Globe and Mail,* January 24, 1989; USCR, *World Refugee Survey: 1989 in Review,* p. 84.

71. IRB News Release, December 21, 1989.

72. Ibid., November 22, 1989, pp. 4, 6.

73. Helsinki Watch, *Detained, Denied, Deported,* pp. 39–40, 82–83; Anthony H. Richard, "Recent Developments in Canadian Immigration" (unpublished paper, York University, North York, Ontario, November 1989), p. 5.

74. Aristide Zolberg, "International Migration in Political Perspective," in Mary Kritz, Charles Keely, and Selvano Tomasi, eds., *Global Trends in Migration* (New York: Center for Migration Studies, 1981), p. 17; Jagdish N. Bhagwati, "Incentives and Disincentives: International Migration," *Weltwirtschaftliches Archiv,* vol. 120 (1984), p. 684.

75. Helsinki Watch, *Detained, Denied, Deported,* p. 82.

76. According to newspaper accounts, in the course of a visit to Washington, D.C., in 1987, Prime Minister Shamir reportedly asked President Reagan to deny refugee status to the Soviet Jews so they would go to Israel; a year later the Israeli Cabinet reportedly decided to effectively force most Soviet Jews to go to Israel first by requiring them to pick up their visas in Romania, from where they would be flown directly to Israel. Secretary of State Shultz, however—possibly concerned with the impact of a change of policy on the Middle East—insisted they must be given a choice. As it was, the policy was not put into effect.

77. Helsinki Watch, *Detained, Denied, Deported,* p. 39.

78. Refugee Policy Group, *Emigration, Immigration and Changing East-West Relations* (Washington, D.C.: November 1989), p. 7.

79. Subsequent congressional hearings focused extensively on the new procedures. The new U.S. Coordinator for Refugee Affairs, Jewel S. Lafontant, argued it was better to rule on applications in Moscow, because then Soviet citizens would not have to give up their homes; she indicated, however, that the INS would continue to review applications already filed in Vienna and Rome until the 30,000-applicant backlog was cleared up. An additional reason was surely the embarrassing situation in Italy, where the

number of Soviet Jews who were denied refugee status reached some 5,000, more than the number of refuseniks still in the Soviet Union. Subsequently the attorney general instructed the INS to reconsider these unsuccessful applications (*New York Times*, September 24, 1989).

80. With projections of the immigration rising to as many as 100,000 in 1990 and possibly 250,000 the following year, the Israelis solicited loan guarantees from the United States to finance the construction of housing for Soviet emigrés, but this action provoked objections over their possible location in occupied territories. Concurrently the Jewish Agency launched a $2 billion drive to raise private funds, mostly in the United States.

81. Astri Suhrke and Aristide R. Zolberg, "Beyond the Refugee Crisis: Disengagement and Durable Solutions for the Developing World," *Migration: A European Journal of International Migration and Ethnic Relations*, vol. 5 (1989), pp. 69–119.

82. See for example R. J. Vincent, "Political and Economic Refugees: Problems of Migration, Asylum and Re-Settlement," Ditchley conference report no. D89-11. In June 1990 members of the European Community signed an agreement that imposes additional restrictions on the asylum process.

83. This does not preclude the possibility that some of the conflicts in the region will generate internationally displaced persons who will qualify as refugees under the Convention, or as victims of violence deserving temporary protection.

CHAPTER 4: CHANGING DEMOGRAPHIC CHARACTERISTICS IN CANADA, *Teresa A. Sullivan*

The 1981 and 1971 census data on which this chapter is based were obtained through the assistance of the Embassy of Canada to the United States. François Vaillancourt, of the University of Montreal, graciously provided comparative data from the 1986 census. Funding came from the William H. Donner Foundation. Starling Pullum assisted in the computer programming, and Debra Haden and Winona Schroeder provided clerical assistance. My greatest debts, however, are to the two research assistants who diligently toiled on this paper, graduate assistant Audrey Singer and undergraduate assistant George A. Harper, Jr.

1. See Monica Boyd, "Immigration Policies and Trends: A Comparison of Canada and the United States," *Demography*, vol. 13 (February 1976), pp. 83–104.

2. See Frank D. Bean, Georges Vernez, and Charles B. Keely, *Opening and Closing the Doors: Evaluating Immigration Reform and Control* (Santa Monica, Calif.: Rand Corporation and the Urban Institute, 1989); and Pastora Cafferty, S.J., Barry R. Chiswick, Andrew M. Greeley, and Teresa A. Sullivan, *The Dilemma of American Immigration: Beyond the Golden Door* (New Brunswick, N.J.: Transaction Press, 1983).

3. See Robert F. Harney, " 'So Great a Heritage as Ours': Immigration and the Survival of the Canadian Policy," *Daedalus*, vol. 117 (Fall 1988), pp. 51–97.

4. Daniel Kubat, "Asian Immigrants to Canada," in James T. Fawcett and Benjamin V. Cariño, eds., *Pacific Bridges: The New Immigration from Asia and the*

Pacific Islands (Staten Island, N.Y.: Center for Migration Studies, 1987), p. 237.

5. Monica Boyd and Chris Taylor, "Canada: International Migration Policies, Trends, and Issues," in Charles Nam, William Serow, David Sly, and Bob Weller, eds., *International Handbook on International Migration* (New York: Greenwood Press, in press).

6. Canada, Health and Welfare Canada, *Charting Canada's Future: A Report of the Demographic Review* (Ottawa: Ministry of Supply and Services Canada, 1989), p. 44.

7. Barry R. Chiswick, "Immigration Policy, Source Countries, and Immigrant Skills: Australia, Canada, and the United States," Working paper no. 45, Center for the Study of the Economy and the State, University of Chicago.

8. Boyd and Taylor, "Canada: Policies, Trends, Issues."

9. United Nations, *World Population Trends and Policies: 1987 Monitoring Report*, Population Studies no. 103 (New York: United Nations, 1988), pp. 227–29.

10. Ibid., p. 230.

11. United Nations, *World Population Chart* (New York: United Nations, 1988).

12. K. G. Basavarajappa and Ravi B. P. Verma, "Asian Immigrants in Canada: Some Findings from the 1981 Census," *International Migration*, vol. 23 (March 1985), pp. 97–121; Don Devoretz and Dennis Maki, "The Immigration of Third World Professionals to Canada: 1968–1973," *World Development*, vol. 11 (January 1983), pp. 55–64; Kubat, "Asian Immigrants."

13. The data for 1986 are limited to the population aged fifteen and over, which may be taken as a proxy to the working-age population.

14. Jean-Pierre Gosselin, "Une Immigration de la Onzieme Heure: Les Latino-Americains," *Recherches Sociographiques*, vol. 25 (September–December 1984), pp. 393–420.

15. Calculated from United Nations, *Demographic Yearbook, 1983* (New York: United Nations, 1983), pp. 760–61.

16. United Nations, *Demographic Yearbook, 1987* (New York: United Nations, 1989), p. 173.

17. See Eric Larson and Teresa A. Sullivan, "Conventional Numbers in Immigration Research: The Case of the Missing Dominicans," *International Migration Review*, vol. 21 (Winter 1987), pp. 1474–96.

18. Canada, Minister of Employment and Immigration, "Minister Announces 1987 Immigration Levels," Press release 86–36, October 30, 1986.

19. Calculated from United Nations, *Demographic Yearbook, 1983*, pp. 760–61.

20. Barry R. Chiswick and Paul W. Miller, "Earnings in Canada: The Roles of Immigrant Generation, French Ethnicity, and Language," *Research in Population Economics*, vol. 6 (1988), pp. 183–228.

21. Canada, "Minister Announces 1987 Immigration Levels."

22. Ibid., p. 3.

23. I am indebted for this observation to George A. Harper, Jr., whose honors B.A. thesis at the University of Texas at Austin on the adjustment of Middle Eastern immigrants to the United States showed large differences by within-nationality ethnic and language groups.

NOTES TO PAGES 138–150

24. Calculated from United Nations, *Demographic Yearbook, 1972* (New York: United Nations, 1973), p. 484.

25. United Nations, *Demographic Yearbook, 1983*, p. 321.

26. United States, Department of Commerce, Bureau of the Census, *Statistical Abstract of the United States, 1989* 109th ed. (Washington, D.C.: U.S. Government Printing Office, 1989), p. 817.

27. Some parts of Asia, such as Hong Kong, have low fertility and send many immigrants to Canada. Others such as India generally have high fertility, but the immigrants are likely to be so selected for education and language ability that their fertility may have already converged to the low levels of native-born Canadians.

28. Canada, Employment and Immigration Canada, "Business Immigrants," WH-5-095 (Ottawa: the Ministry, 1985).

29. Canada, Employment and Immigration Canada, "Family Reunification," WH-5-096 (Ottawa: the Ministry, 1986).

30. Canada, Employment and Immigration Canada, "Annual Report to Parliament on Future Immigration Levels," WH-5-097 (Ottawa: the Ministry, 1986), p. 2.

CHAPTER 5: WAGE RATES OF IMMIGRANT AND NATIVE MEN, *Nakamura and Nakamura*

We are grateful for the helpful comments of Robert Goldfarb, Harriet Duleep, and Barry Chiswick, as well as others.

1. This issue is discussed in George J. Borjas, "Self-Selection and the Earnings of Immigrants," *American Economic Review* (1987), pp. 531–53; and Guillermina Jasso and Mark R. Rosenzweig, "Self-Selection and the Earnings of Immigrants: Comment," *American Economic Review* (1990), pp. 298–308. For a simplified discussion of the econometric problems caused by self-selection see Alice Nakamura and Masao Nakamura, "Selection Bias: More Than a Female Phenomenon," in B. Raj, ed., *Advances in Econometrics and Modelling* (The Netherlands: Kluwer Academic Publishers, 1989), pp. 143–58.

2. See, for example, George J. Borjas, "The Earnings of Male Hispanic Immigrants in the United States," *Industrial and Labor Relations Review* (April 1982), pp. 343–53; George J. Borjas, "Assimilation, Changes in Cohort Quality, and the Earnings of Immigrants," *Journal of Labor Economics* (October 1985), pp. 463–89; Geoffrey Carliner, "Wages, Earnings, and Hours of First, Second, and Third Generation American Males," *Economic Inquiry* (January 1980), pp. 87–102; Barry R. Chiswick, "The Effect of Americanization on Earnings of Foreign-born Men," *Journal of Political Economy* (October 1978), pp. 897–921; Barry R. Chiswick, "The Impact of Immigration on the Level and Distribution of Economic Well-Being," in Barry R. Chiswick, ed., *The Gateway: U.S. Immigration Issues and Policies* (Washington, D.C.: American Enterprise Institute, 1982), pp. 119–58; Barry R. Chiswick, "Is the New Immigration Less Skilled Than the Old?" *Journal of Labor Economics* (April 1986), pp. 168–92; Carmel U. Chiswick, "The Impact of Immigration on the Human Capital of Natives," *Journal of Labor Economics* (October 1989), pp. 464–86; and Guillermina Jasso and Mark R. Rosenzweig, "Family Reunification and the Immigration Multi-

plier: U.S. Immigration Law, Origin-Country Conditions, and the Reproduction of Immigrants," *Demography* (August 1986), pp. 291–311.

3. Examples include Alice Nakamura and Masao Nakamura, "A Comparison of the Labor Force Behavior of Married Women in the United States and Canada, with Special Attention to the Impact of Income Taxes," *Econometrica* (1981), pp. 451–89; and Alice Nakamura and Masao Nakamura, *The Second Paycheck: A Socioeconomic Analysis of Earnings* (Orlando, Fla.: Academic Press, 1985), as well as the studies of female labor supply cited in these two references.

4. Sherrie A. Kossoudji, "Immigrant Worker Assimilation: Is It a Labor Market Phenomenmon?" *Journal of Human Resources* (Summer 1989), pp. 494–527.

5. Census Metropolitan Area versus all other places of residence for Canada; Central SMSA versus all other places of residence for the United States.

6. Ann P. Bartel, "Where Do the New U.S. Immigrants Live?" *Journal of Labor Economics* (October 1989).

7. See, for example, Barbara Bergmann, "Occupational Segregation, Wages and Profits When Employers Discriminate by Race or Sex," *Eastern Economic Journal* (1974), pp. 103–10; Stephen Cole, "Sex Discrimination and Admission to Medical School, 1919–1984," *American Journal of Sociology* (1986), pp. 549–67; Richard A. Easterlin, *Birth and Fortune: The Impact of Numbers on Personal Welfare* (New York: Basic Books, 1980); Richard B. Freeman, "The Effects of Demographic Factors on Age-Earnings Profiles," *Journal of Human Resources* (1979), pp. 284–318; Alice Nakamura and Masao Nakamura, "Effects of Excess Supply on the Wage Rates of Young Women," in R. T. Michael, H. I. Hartmann, and B. O'Farrell, eds., *Pay Equity: Empirical Inquiries* (Washington, D.C.: National Academy Press, 1989), pp. 70–90; Finis Welch, "Effects of Cohort Size on Earnings: The Baby Boom Babies' Financial Bust," *Journal of Political Economy* (1979), pp. 565–97.

8. Kossoudji, "Immigrant Worker Assimilation", pp. 494–527.

COMMENTARY ON PART TWO, *Robert S. Goldfarb*

1. In constructing these comments I have benefited from conversations with Bryan Boulier, Ashfaq Ishaq, David Pritchett, and Larry Promisel.

2. One can imagine all sorts of descriptive studies about immigrant populations that would be of no conceivable interest to most students of population policy. It is hard to imagine, for example, much interest in a study that showed whether a larger percentage of immigrants than natives lived in residences with red shutters, or had a higher incidence of spinach pasta consumption. My conclusion is that Sullivan chose to focus on those aspects of heterogeneity she views as particularly relevant. Even if red shutter data had been available, I feel confident in asserting that she would not have included it.

3. Ministry of Health and Welfare, Canada, *Charting Canada's Future* (Ottawa, Canada: Minister of Supply and Services, 1989), pp. i, 9.

4. In his well-known work *The General Theory of Population*, the demographer Alfred Sauvy devotes several chapters to the notion of an optimum population. In discussing the attractiveness of the notion of an economic optimum, he indicates that "it is a fact that among Western populations welfare does play such an important part that in many minds it becomes the essential aim. Men tend to prefer greater wealth combined with smaller numbers. On the scale of the individual family this ideal almost always predominates. It is therefore useful to see what this wish can and does lead to" in terms of an aggregate optimum. See Alfred Sauvy, *The General Theory of Population*, trans. C. Campos (New York: Basic Books, 1969; originally published in French, 1966), p. 40.

5. In a discussion about the United States some years ago I argued that objectives related to aggregate economic output and the native-born population's economic welfare were, "at least in principle, capable of suggesting a meaningfully derived numerical limit on . . . immigration" (p. 423). "Unfortunately, although economic analysis suggests a way of approaching the problem of setting immigration quotas if the goals are economic, it is not currently possible to present a specific simple, but dependable, numerical estimate of these optimal immigration quotas" (p. 428). The empirical problem was (and, I think, still is) that very particular kinds of empirical estimates of the production structure of the economy are required, and dependable forms of such estimates were simply not available. See Robert Goldfarb, "Occupational Preferences in the U.S. Immigration Law: An Economic Analysis," in Barry Chiswick, ed., *The Gateway: U.S. Immigration Issues and Policies* (Washington, D.C.: American Enterprise Institute, 1982), pp. 412–48.

6. A dynamic formulation of Alternative I's optimal population idea might result in an optimal population level that was changing over time (for example, because the capital stock was growing). This would imply a rate of change of population to keep the country at its optimum. This kind of change in population to keep at or near the optimum is not part of the rate-of-change variant of Alternative II; rather, it is a fancy version of Alternative I. Alternative II is unrelated to optimum population notions.

7. Julian Simon has been an advocate of the benefits of population growth. See, for example, his article in Chiswick, ed., *The Gateway*. An interesting quotation bearing on this idea appeared on the back cover of the June 1990 *Journal of Political Economy* under the heading, "The Principles of Immigration Policy." The quotation (which I have only reproduced a part of) is from Thomas Mortimer, *Lectures on the Elements of Commerce, Politics, and Finances* (London: Strahan, 1801), pp. 70–71.

> (I)f a scarcity of labouring hands from these and other causes, principally from destructive wars, should be universally complained of, we shall be obliged to have recourse to partial naturalization. . . . A partial naturalization is not liable to those objections, that are brought against a general naturalization, which might, in the end, enable foreigners to extirpate the native flock; to change the constitution, and . . . to become masters and possessors of the whole. . . . And under no other circumstances but those of a plague, or devasta-

tions by fire, inundations, or the sword, should we admit of a general naturalization. . . . But a partial naturalization, by occasional introductions of ingenious and industrious artists and manufacturers, who bring with them new inventions and improvements, as well as an addition to useful population, is a great political benefit to every commercial nation; and it is always understood that such naturalizations are subject to wise regulations and limitations adapted to the commercial circumstances of any state that receives foreigners into her bosom, as native children.

8. Goldfarb (in "Occupational Preferences," pp. 432–41) argues that the United States did exactly this in response to a perceived physician shortage in the 1960s. See also the quotation in the previous footnote for a much older claim that on the one hand indicates how particular classes of migrants can contribute to national economic goals, while on the other hand it reveals some of the goals behind preventing large-scale immigrations.

9. Ministry of Health and Welfare, *Charting Canada's Future*, p. 2.

10. See Barry Chiswick, "The Impact of Immigration on the Level and Distribution of Economic Well-Being," in Chiswick, ed., *The Gateway*, pp. 289–313, quoted pp. 289–90.

11. Such a "failure" might of course be viewed as an economically rational policy choice in a world where enforcement costs associated with keeping out every potential immigrant were prohibitively expensive.

12. I am incapable of hazarding a guess about different Canadian views on which noneconomic goals Canadian immigration policy *should* have. A thoughtful friend has indicated his view, however, of which goals U.S. immigration policy should have in a way that nicely illustrates the possible interaction between noneconomic goals and economic cost constraints. He suggests that U.S. immigration policy should be formulated as follows: "It is consistent with the best features of our heritage as a nation that we admit as many immigrants as possible, subject only to acceptable limits on adverse economic effects."

13. The Nakamuras' rationales for each of the two variables has considerable intellectual appeal. The idea that it may be important to control for the labor market conditions that the immigrant faces upon arrival seems particularly attractive. As is often the case in economics, however, there are potential difficulties with the particular variables used. As Barry Chiswick has pointed out, well-informed immigrants may choose to migrate only when unemployment conditions are favorable. To the extent that this happens, the unemployment variable may be a proxy for the economic sophistication of immigrants, rather than being what the Nakamuras intend—an exogenous indicator of the strength of labor demand for the immigrant's services. The Nakamuras' wage variable raises complex questions about the extent to which cost-of-living versus other sources of variation are being measured. Moreover, one could wonder to what extent economically well-informed migrants *choose* to go to high-wage locations.

14. In discussion of this robustness-of-results issue, the Nakamuras have indicated that a careful comparison of their findings with a previous work, by

George Borjas, that did not include the unemployment and average wage variables showed virtually identical results for shared variables. A second and particularly telling comparison can be made with the Chiswick-Miller chapter in this volume. That chapter includes some innovative variables different from those the Nakamuras use: for example, a minority group concentration measure and controls for the country of marriage. Moreover, the Chiswick-Miller chapter uses a more complex statistical framework that models the degree of language fluency of an immigrant as something that the immigrant himself can decide upon. The statistical result is that, instead of estimating an earnings equation in isolation, Chiswick-Miller estimate both an earnings equation and a language fluency equation. Because of this joint estimation, the earnings-equation results reflect the possible interactions with the immigrant's decision about how much fluency to acquire. Despite these considerable differences in variables included and statistical method, the earnings-equation results for shared variables in the two studies appear to be quite similar, at least in terms of which variables show up as important and of the direction of effects of these variables. Not only does this verdict about the similarity of the earnings results represent my impression after comparing the studies, but this same verdict was reached by a coauthor of each of the studies.

15. In general, there might be systematic differences between the immigrant pools being attracted to the United States and Canada and systematic differences in the environment for the immigrants once they arrive. Under the first category ("pool differences"), there are differences in legal rules and other institutions affecting how immigrants may be chosen. In addition, one might expect divergences in immigrant pools depending on differentially attractive characteristics of the two countries; these might include, for example, tax and income transfer systems and languages in use. These latter factors (taxes, languages in use) also represent environmental differences— that is, once an immigrant arrives in one of the two countries, his economic opportunities and therefore his earnings may be affected by these features of the economic environment. In addition, there may be large differences between the sociocultural settings for immigrants in the two countries. A personal experience made me particularly aware of the possibility of such differences. As a graduate student in the 1960s, I had the opportunity to teach a summer school course at a university in a small city in Ontario. An overwhelming bit of culture shock occurred when people came up to me and introduced themselves as (for instance) fifth-generation Italians. This was quite an unexpected mode of presentation to someone raised in a culture with a "melting pot" mentality! This is only an anecdote, so I cannot know whether it typifies a general sociological difference between U.S. and Canadian settings. But if such sociocultural differences do in fact exist, would one expect these differences to translate into differences in how immigrant earnings are generated?

16. Another innovation that I found interesting and provocative was the inclusion of an average geographical wage rate to control for differences in location. I would have liked to be able to examine the results for this variable,

since it has multiple possible interpretations. The authors have indicated that they did not include results because the inclusion of this variable did not affect the general regression results, and the variable itself was not a central focus of this study.

CHAPTER 6: LANGUAGE AND PUBLIC POLICY, *François Vaillancourt*

The author thanks François Grin, Walter McManus, André Raynauld, and the participants at the March 1990 workshop on this topic for comments on a preliminary version of this study; the Donner Foundation and the American Enterprise Institute for supporting this project; and the library staff of the Equal Employment Opportunity Commission, Andrea Vincent of the National Clearing House for Bilingual Education, and Kathryn S. Brikner of U.S. English for helping him better understand the language policy of the United States.

1. Abigail M. Thernstrom, "Bilingual Miseducation," *Commentary* (February 1990), pp. 44–48.

2. Ibid. Gary Imhoff, "The Position of U.S. English on Bilingual Education," *Annals of the American Academy of Political and Social Sciences* (March 1990), pp. 48–61.

3. Arthur Larson and Lex K. Larson, *Employment Discriminations: Volume 3, Race, Religion and National Origin* (June 1989), Cumulative Supplement, Matthew Bender.

4. Alfred J. Sutherland, "National Origin Discrimination Based on Accent or Manner of Speaking," Personal Management Series, Prentice Hall, 1987.

5. Jonathan Lemco, "Official Language Legislation in the United States and Canada: A Route to National Disharmony," in M. Lubin, ed., *Public Policy in Canada and the United States*, mimeo, Greenwood Press, 1990, p. 4.

6. François Vaillancourt, "The Economics of Language and Language Planning," *Language Problems and Language Planning* (Summer 1983), pp. 162–78.

7. David E. Bloom and Gilles Grenier, "The Earnings of Linguistic Minorities: French in Canada and Spanish in the United States," chapter 9 in this volume.

8. Ibid.

9. Robert Lacroix and François Vaillancourt, "Les revenus et la langue au Québec (1970–1978)," Conseil de la langue française, Québec, 1981.

10. François Vaillancourt, "Langue et statut économique au Québec en 1985 et l'évolution depuis 1980," mimeo, Conseil de la langue française, Québec, 1990.

11. Jacques Maurais and Philippe Plamondon, "Le visage français du Québec—Enquête sur l'affichage," Notes et documents, no. 54, Conseil de la langue française, Québec, 1986.

12. Bloom and Grenier, "Earnings Position of Linguistic Minorities," tables 9–3 and 9–5.

13. Lacroix and Vaillancourt, "Les revenus et la langue au Québec," Québec, 1981.

14. François Vaillancourt, "La Charte de la langue française: un essai d'analyse," *Canadian Public Policy/Analyse de Politique* (Summer 1978), pp. 284–308.

15. Institut Gamma, *Prospective de la langue française au Québec*, Document no. 25, Conseil de la langue française, Québec, 1986.

16. Albert Breton, "The Economic of Nationalism," *Journal of Political Economy* (August 1964), pp. 376–86.

17. François Vaillancourt, *Langue et disparités de statut economique au Québec, 1970–1980*, Conseil de la langue française, Québec, 1988.

18. François Vaillancourt, "Demolinguistic Trends and Canadian Institutions: An Economic Perspective," in *Demolinguistic Trends and the Evolution of Canadian Institutions*, Canadian Issues, Association for Canadian Studies, 1989.

19. Laura F. Carazos, *Annual Evaluation Report, Fiscal Year 1988*, Department of Education.

20. William J. Bennett, *The Condition of Bilingual Education in the Nation, 1988*, Department of Education, 1988.

21. Albert Breton and Peter Mieszkowski, "L'investissement linguistique et la francisation du Québec," in François Vaillancourt, ed., *Economie et langue* (Quebec: Conseil de la langue française, 1985), pp. 83–100.

22. Breton, "The Economics of Nationalism."

23. François Vaillancourt, "Pour un nouveau pacte linguistique," *L'Actualité Economique*, vol. 63, 1988b, pp. 486–88.

24. Yvan Allaire and Roger Miller, *L'enterprise canadienne et la loi sur la francisation du milieu de travail* (Montréal: Institut C. D. Howe, 1980).

25. Centre de linguistique de l'enterprise, "Mémoire sur la charte de la langue française" (Montréal: 1983), mimeo, p. 66.

26. Allaire and Miller, *L'enterprise canadienne*.

27. Centre de linguistique de l'enterprise, "Mémoire sur la charte."

CHAPTER 7: LANGUAGE IN THE IMMIGRANT LABOR MARKET, *Chiswick and Miller*

We are grateful to participants in workshops at Queen's University and the University of Illinois at Chicago for helpful comments, as well as to Chris Robinson, Houston Stokes, and our colleagues on the project. We appreciate the financial support for this project provided by grants from the William H. Donner Foundation, the Sloan Foundation, and the Embassy of Canada, Washington, D.C.

1. The biblical account of the tower of Babel is instructive (Genesis, chapter xi, v. 1–9). According to tradition all people spoke the same language and gathered at Babel to work together to construct a tower to reach heaven. Offended by this, the Lord inflicted on the people a diversity of languages, thereby increasing transaction costs and halting the progress of the tower.

2. The language questions contained in the census questionnaires are reproduced in Appendix 7–A.

3. Calvin Veltman, *Language Shift in the United States* (Berlin: Mouton Publishers, 1983); Calvin Veltman, "Modelling the Language Process of Hispanic Immigrants," *International Migration Review*, vol. 22 (1988) pp. 545–62;

Barry R. Chiswick, "Speaking, Reading, and Earnings among Low-skilled Immigrants," *Journal of Labor Economics*, vol. 9 (April 1991), pp. 149–70.

4. The coauthors of this chapter, for example, disagree on the spelling of labor or labour.

5. Veltman, "Modelling the Language Process."

6. Chiswick, "Speaking, Reading, and Earnings."

7. John DeVries and Frank E. Vallee, *Language Use in Canada* (Ottawa: Statistics Canada, 1980).

8. Chiswick, "Speaking, Reading, and Earnings," pp. 149–70.

9. Veltman, *Language Shift*.

10. Perhaps the classic example is the myth, perhaps not too far from reality, that Jewish immigrant parents in Israel learned Hebrew from their children.

11. The equations were also estimated using a logit model. The signs and significance of the estimates were broadly similar for the two methods of estimation.

Diagnostic testing using the Breusch-Pagan test suggested that the residuals were not homoskedastic; T. S. Breusch and A. R. Pagan, "A Simple Test for Heteroskedasticity and Random Coeffcient Variation," *Econometrica*, vol. 47, 1979, pp. 437–41. All t values for the linear probability model have been calculated using White's heteroskedasticity-consistent covariance matrix estimator; Halbert White, "A Heteroskedasticity-Consistent Covariance Matrix Estimator and a Direct Test for Heteroskedasticity," *Econometrica*, vol. 48 (1980), pp. 817–38.

12. Tests were conducted to determine whether the relationship between English-language fluency and educational attainment was nonlinear. We did not attain any gain in economic insights from attempting to capture this nonlinearity through the use of complex functional forms for education (for example, higher order polynomials, linear splines, or a large number of dummy variables). Accordingly, a simple linear education variable is used.

13. Equations were also estimated with a second-degree polynomial in age. The squared term was not significant at conventional levels, however.

14. Veltman, "Modelling the Language Process."

15. For older cohorts of immigrants (pre-1945), there is a negative partial effect of duration of residence on language skills. Most pre-1945 immigrants in these data arrived during the 1930s, and a disproportionate number were young-adult refugees who may not have been self-selected for acquiring U.S.-specific skills and may have anticipated returning to Europe after the fall of fascism.

16. Veltman, *Language Shift*.

17. Those not fluent in English may have access to a much smaller marriage market and may be less likely to marry. This reverse causation argument would be more compelling for numerically small groups. Yet the same effect appears among a very large group, Mexican immigrants.

18. There is some degree of endogeneity in the veteran status variable, although this would be less intense during the period of conscription.

19. Gilles Grenier and François Vaillancourt, "An Economic Perspective on

NOTES TO PAGES 239–246

Learning a Second Languages," *Journal of Multilingual Development*, vol. 4 (1983), pp. 471–83.

20. The children variables record the presence in the household of children younger than eighteen years of age at the time of the census enumeration. Ideally we would like to use information on the number and ages of all children ever in the household in the United States, and not simply those currently living at home.

21. Barry R. Chiswick, "Soviet Jews in the United States: A Preliminary Analysis of Their Linguistic and Economic Adjustment," *International Migration Review* (forthcoming).

22. Spanish is spoken in the home by 10 percent or more of the population in California, Texas, Arizona, and New Mexico. For further information on home language usage in the various states, see table 7–B3.

23. Chiswick, "Speaking, Reading, and Earnings."

24. Barry R. Chiswick, "The Effect of Americanization on the Earnings of Foreign-born Men," *Journal of Political Economy*, vol. 85 (1978) pp. 897–921.

25. Among immigrants from Mexico, the Anglicization process continues for about the same period as reported for the table 7–1 results. This suggests that the differences in conclusions drawn from table 7–1 and from Veltman, "Modelling the Language Process," derive mainly from the different methodologies employed. The table 7–3 finding is similar to that reported by Grenier and Vaillancourt, "An Economic Perspective," also on the basis of a multivariate analysis.

26. The minority-language coefficient is −0.014 in table 7–1. In table 7–3 the within-birthplace region estimates of the minority-language coefficients are within two standard errors of that estimate for Other Asia, Mexico, Other America, and Africa. While this is not a valid statistical test because the coefficients are not estimated independently, it does strengthen the point that the table 7–1 minority-language effect is more than merely a proxy for country of origin.

27. The census reports all Chinese dialects as one category, a practice followed here. Although they share a common written language, the differences in the spoken language among the Chinese dialects is so great that it is as if they were different languages. The minority-language variable is positive and significant for those from South Asia, but fewer than 2 percent of this sample (twenty cases) are not fluent in English.

28. It is, however, positive and significant for the small sample of immigrants from Africa. The reasons for this unexpected result are as yet unclear. The small sample of Africans is heterogenous: 33 percent are white North Africans, 19 percent are white South Africans, 38 percent are black, and 10 percent are other Africans.

29. When only those who report that they cannot speak English at all are considered as lacking in English fluency, the fluency rate increases to 94 percent in the U.S. census data.

30. There are nine factors in the selection procedure, and the maximum points they carry are: education (twelve points), special vocational preparation (fifteen), experience (eight), occupation (ten), arranged employment

(ten), demographic factors (ten), age (ten), knowledge of official languages (fifteen), and personal suitability (ten). Thus, of the 100 points in the assessment procedure, fifteen are allocated to knowledge (speaking, reading, and writing) of the official languages. The threshold number of points varies by category of immigrant. It is seventy for independent workers, fifty-five for assisted relatives, and twenty-five for entrepreneurs. Further details can be obtained from the *Immigration Manual: Selection and Control, section 4.08,* Employment and Immigration Canada.

31. Direct information on the language skills of children is available in the family file, and it is possible that this would provide the opportunity to ascertain more definitely whether there is a relationship between the use of the dominant language in the home by children and adult dominant language. When a variable for children's dominant language use within the home was included in the estimating equation, it was highly significant. This suggests that adults' dominant-language fluency is higher in families where children speak the dominant language. In view of the statistical insignificance of the children variables, however, the direction of causation here is very problematic, and little weight can be attached to this result.

32. There is, of course, possible endogeneity; those not fluent in the dominant language may be less successful in the marriage market for dominant-language speakers. As was found in the United States, however, premigration marriage has an adverse impact on fluency larger than the impact of postmigration marriage among those country groups with the largest ethnic marriage market in the destination (that is, among those most likely to find in the destination a spouse who also speaks the same nondominant language).

33. This positive effect arises even though schooling and language fluency are alternative sources for points in the immigrant rationing system.

34. When the equation was reestimated using a logit model, this anomaly disappeared.

35. DeVries and Vallee, *Language Use in Canada.*

36. This compares with the impact of -0.010 ($t = 4.14$) attributed to this variable on the basis of analysis of the Household-Family File. Using more detailed information in the construction of this variable, therefore, appears to be associated with a stronger estimated impact.

37. As was noted previously, if only those who reported that they spoke English "not at all" are considered as lacking English-language fluency, the U.S. fluency rate is 95 percent.

38. The Heckman technique is developed in James J. Heckman, "Sample Selection Bias as a Specification Error," *Econometrica,* vol. 47 (1979), pp. 153–62.

These methods have recently been investigated in some depth in the union wages effects literature; see, for example, the analyses in John T. Addison and Pedro Portugal, "The Endogeneity of Union Status and the Application of the Hausman Test," *Journal of Labor Research,* vol. 10 (1989) pp. 437–41; Chris Robinson, "The Joint Determination of Union Status and Union Wage Effects: Some Tests of Alternative Models," *Journal of Political Economy,* vol. 97 (1989) pp. 639–67; and Chris Robinson, "Union Endogeneity and Self-Selection,"

Journal of Labor Economics, vol. 7 (1989) pp. 106–12. Both methods are used in this chapter.

A simultaneous equations system in which earnings and languages are both endogenous cannot be estimated because of the absence of instruments that enter an equation for earnings but not for language. While weeks worked might seem to be one such variable, it largely standardizes annual earnings for the amount of time worked. The citizen and race variables are also inappropriate, as citizenship may be determined endogenously with language skills, and the race variable is highly collinear with the country of birth variables.

39. J. A. Hausman, "Specification Tests in Econometrics," *Econometrica*, vol. 46 (1978), pp. 1251–71.

40. Chiswick, "The Effect of Americanization"; and Barry R. Chiswick and Paul W. Miller, "Earnings in Canada: The Roles of Immigrant Generation, French Ethnicity, and Language," *Research in Population Economics*, vol. 6 (1988) pp. 183–224.

41. Price V. Fishback and Joseph V. Terza, "Are Estimates of Sex Discrimination by Employers Robust? The Use of Never Marrieds," *Economic Inquiry*, vol. 27 (1980) pp. 271–85.

42. Recall also that duration of residence is an important determinant of language proficiency.

43. Michael G. Abbott and Charles M. Beach, "Immigrant Earnings Differentials and Cohort Effects in Canada," Institute for Economic Research, Queen's University, discussion paper no. 705 (1987); Chiswick, "Speaking, Reading, and Earnings"; Chiswick and Miller, "Earnings in Canada."

One study (Walter M. McManus, William Gould, and Finis Welch, "Earnings of Hispanic Men: The Role of English-Language Proficiency," *Journal of Labor Economics*, vol. 1 (1983), pp. 101–30), reports that including language in the earnings function eliminates the Hispanic–non-Hispanic earnings differential. It has been shown, however, that this result is a consequence of a specification error in the equation for predicting English-language fluency (see Chiswick, "Speaking, Reading, and Earnings").

44. See the analysis in Chris Robinson, "Language Choice: The Distribution of Language Skills in Earnings in a Dual-Language Economy," *Research in Labor Economics*, vol. 9 (1988), pp. 53–90.

This result is consistent with the union wage effects literature where, according to Robinson, there is "substantial evidence of a consistent rise in the union differential relative to OLS estimates when the endogeneity of union status is addressed by the instrumental variables or inverse Mills ratio method." Robinson, "Joint Determination of Union Status," p. 659.

45. The selectivity correction factors are computed for logit estimates of the language attainment model developed in the second section. The method applied is outlined in Lung-Fei Lee, "Generalized Econometric Models with Selectivity," *Econometrica*, vol. 51 (1983) pp. 507–12.

46. Robinson, "Joint Determination of Union Status."

47. This finding concerning the assumption of exogeneity of the language-fluency variable is supported by results of an alternative test based on

Hausman "Specification Tests," as outlined in Addison and Portugal, "Edogeneity of Union Status." For this procedure, the compared value of the test statistic was 17.687, which exceeds the critical F value at the 5 percent level of significance.

48. Chiswick and Miller, "Earnings in Canada," pp. 183–224, and Ronald Meng, "The Earnings of Canadian Immigrants and Native-born Males," *Applied Economics*, vol. 19 (1987), pp. 1107–19.

49. Differences between the table 7–9 results and those presented in Chiswick and Miller, "Earnings in Canada," are due to different treatment in the analyses of workers with nonpositive incomes. In Chiswick and Miller these individuals were purged from the sample, and the results obtained are consistent with the Canadian literature. In the present analysis, this small group of workers (2 percent of the sample) are assigned $100 in earnings. The results are very similar to those reported in the U.S. literature where the same procedure is used.

50. Chiswick and Miller, "Earnings in Canada."

51. See Chiswick and Miller, "Earnings in Canada," where it is shown that this is largely a post-1971 phenomenon.

52. Abbott and Beach, "Immigrant Earnings Differentials"; Chiswick and Miller, "Earnings in Canada."

53. The estimates for the Addison and Portugal test differ from the instrumental variables estimates discussed previously in that a logit model is used to predict dominant-language fluency in preference to the linear probability model, and interaction terms with dominant-language proficiency are included in the estimating equation.

CHAPTER 8: GENDER ISSUES IN IMMIGRATION, *Monica Boyd*

1. Caroline Brettell and Rita J. Simon, "Immigrant Women: An Introduction," in Rita James Simon and Caroline Brettell, eds. *International Migration: The Female Experience* (Totowa, N.J.: Rowman and Allanheld, 1986), pp. 3–20; Roy S. Bryce-Laporte, "Introductions: The New Immigration: The Female Majority," in Delores M. Mortimer and Roy S. Bryce-Laporte, eds., *Female Immigrants to the United States: Caribbean, Latin American and African Experiences*, Research Institution on Immigration and Ethnic Studies Occasional Papers, no. 2. (Washington, D.C., Smithsonian Institution, 1981); Mirjana Morokvasic "Women in Migration: Beyond the Reductionist Outlook," in Annie Phizacklea, ed., *One-Way Ticket: Migration and Female Labour* (London: Routledge and Kegan Paul, 1983), pp. 13–32; Mirjana Morokvasic, "Birds of Passage Are Also Women . . .," *International Migration Review*, Vol. 28 (Winter 1984), pp. 886–907.

2. See Monica Boyd, "The Status of Migrant Women in Canada," *Canadian Review of Sociology and Anthropology*, vol. 12 (November 1975), pp. 406–16; Boyd, "Occupations of Female Immigrants and North American Immigration Statistics," *International Migration Review*, vol. 10 (1976), pp. 73–80; Boyd, "Migrant Women in Canada," in Rita James Simon and Caroline Brettell, eds., *International Migration: The Female Experience*, (Totowa, N.J.: Rowman and

Allanheld, 1986), pp. 45–61; Nancy Foner, "Introduction: New Immigrants and Changing Patterns in New York City," in Nancy Foner, ed., *New Immigrants in New York* (New York: Columbia University Press, 1987), pp. 1–34; Marion F. Houston, Roger G. Kramer, and Joan Mackin Barrett, "Female Predominance in Immigration to the United States since 1930: A First Look," *International Migration Review,* vol. 18 (Winter 1984), pp. 908–63; "Women in Migration," *International Migration Review,* vol. 18 (Winter 1984), pp. 881–1382; Roger Kramer, "United States Government Policy in Relation to Women from Ethnic Minority Groups," Report submitted to the Monitoring Panel on Migrant Women, Organization for Economic Co-operation and Development, Directorate for Social Affairs, Manpower and Education (Washington, D.C.: U.S. Department of Labor, 1987); Delores M. Mortimer and Roy S. Bryce-Laporte, eds., *Female Immigrants to the United States: Caribbean, Latin American and African Experiences,* Research Institution on Immigration and Ethnic Studies Occasional Papers, no. 2. (Washington, D.C.: Smithsonian Institution, 1981); U.S. Department of Labor, Bureau of International Labor Affairs, *The Effects of Immigration on the U.S. Economy and Labor Market* (Washington, D.C.: DOL, 1989); Rita James Simon and Caroline Brettell, eds., *International Migration: The Female Experience* (Totowa, N.J.: Rowman and Allanheld, 1986), pp. 1–310.

3. Lloyd Axworthy, "Multiculturalism: The Immigrant Woman in Canada: A Right to Recognition," in Canada, Secretary of State, Multi-culturalism Directorate, *The Immigrant Women in Canada. Part 1. Report of the Proceedings of the Conference* (Ottawa: Minister of Supply and Services Canada, Ci96-15/1981-1, 1981), p. 26.

4. See M. D. R. Evans, "Immigrant Entrepreneurship: Effects of Ethnic Market Size and Isolated Labor Pool," *American Sociological Review,* vol. 54 (December 1989), pp. 950–62.

5. See Thomas R. Bailey, *Immigrant and Native Workers* (Boulder, Colo.: Westview Press, 1987); Boyd, "Migrant Women in Canada"; Adriana Marshall "New Immigrants in New York's Economy," in Nancy Foner, ed., *New Immigrants in New York* (New York: Columbia University Press, 1987), pp. 79–101; Patricia Pessar, "The Dominicans: Women in the Household and the Garment Industry," in Nancy Foner, ed., *New Immigrants in New York* (New York: Columbia University Press, 1987), pp. 103–29; and Saskia Sassen, *The Mobility of Labor and Capital* (Cambridge, Eng.: Cambridge University Press, 1988).

6. Everett Lee, "A Theory of Migration," *Demography,* vol. 25, no. 1 (1966), pp. 47–57.

7. Before 1933, data by sex for Canada are available only for the adult population. The numerical dominance of males that appears in table 8–1 for the United States also is found in the flows of adults to Canada during the early part of the twentieth century. This is shown in table 5 in Monica Boyd, *Migrant Women in Canada: Profiles and Policies, March 1987,* Immigration Research Working Paper, no. 2 (Ottawa, Employment and Immigration Canada, Policy Analysis Directorate, Immigration Policy Branch, 1989).

8. The lowest sex ratio in Canada occurs in 1951–1955, when 788 females immigrated for every 1,000 males. This reflects a period when labor recruit-

ment was substantial and when male workers sent for their families after establishing themselves. Discussion of this period appears in Monica Boyd, "Immigration Policies and Trends: A Comparison of Canada and the United States," *Demography*, vol. 13 (February 1976), pp. 82–102; Freda Hawkins, *Canada and Immigration: Public Policy and Public Concern* (Montreal: McGill and Queen's University Press, 1972); Freda Hawkins, *Critical Years in Immigration: Canada and Australia Compared* (Montreal: McGill and Queen's University Press, 1989); and Louis Parai, *Immigration and Emigration of Professional and Skilled Manpower*, Economic Council of Canada Special Study, no. 1 (Ottawa, 1965). Interpretations for the changing sex ratios for the United States appear in Houston, Kramer, and Barrett, "Female Predominance in Immigration to the United States since 1930," and in the U.S. Department of Labor, Bureau of International Labor Affairs, *The Effects of Immigration on the U.S. Economy and Labor Market* (Washington, D.C.: Department of Labor, 1989).

9. In Canada, females are principal applicants only in the family class, under which many of them are applying to join husbands or adult children after the expiration of the original visa issued to immediate family members of husbands or adult children. This visa normally is in effect for one year. If close relatives do not enter under this visa within the period, they must apply for admission as a principal applicant in an appropriate category (such as a member of the immediate family, applying in the family class).

10. For the United States, the pattern is most evident in the two preference classes that admit immigrants on the basis of economic criteria (the third and sixth preferences) and in the second preference class, which admits spouses and unmarried sons and daughters of permanent resident aliens. The slightly lower percentage of females compared with males who are spouses in the immediate relative category reflects the large numbers of older women who enter as parents of U.S. citizens rather than as spouses (25.6 percent and 25.3 in 1972–1979 and 1980–1987, respectively, versus 16.4 and 14.9 for males).

11. Using flow data for country comparisons is difficult because of different practices in the classification of data. Immigration statistics produced by the U.S. Immigration and Naturalization Service provide age and sex data for country of last residence. Canadian immigration statistics, which are collected and published by Employment and Immigration, Canada, provide data by country of birth. In addition, in both Canadian and U.S. publications, temporal changes in data type and data format confound attempts to produce meaningful time series.

Census data present a snapshot of the foreign-born stock taken at one point in time. The liabilities and benefits of using census stock data are well documented. See Ellen Kraly, "Sources of Data for the Study of U.S. Immigration," in Stephen R. Couch and Roy S. Bryce-Laporte, eds., *Quantitative Data and Immigration Research*, Research Institution on Immigration and Ethnic Studies, Research Note, no. 2 (Washington, D.C., Smithsonian Institution, 1979); Ellen Kraly, "U.S. Immigration Policy and the Immigrant Populations of New York," in Nancy Foner, ed., *New Immigrants in New York* (New York: Columbia Press, 1987), pp. 35–78; and Daniel Levine, Kenneth Hill, and Robert Warren, eds., *Immigration Statistics: A Story of Neglect* (Washington,

D.C.: National Academy Press, 1985). Omitted are persons who emigrated or died. Persons who are in the country may or may not be included in the census enumerations. At the same time, census data provide detailed information about the characteristics of immigrants. When released in the form of public use samples, census data permit customized and highly focused analyses. This chapter uses the most recent public use census data available, notably from the 1980 U.S. census and the 1986 Canadian census of population. The latter was preferred over the existing public use sample from the 1981 Canadian census for two reasons. First, third world birthplace groups are aggregated into Asian, Africa, and South-Central America in the 1981 census. The 1986 Public Use Sample Tape (PUST) provides information on more birthplace regions (see tables 8–5 and 8–6). Second, Canadian data for 1986 may indicate what are likely trends for the United States (see tables 8–5 and 8–6 and related discussion).

12. The similarity of the figures should be taken as approximate, as they are based on a 1986 Canadian census compared with a 1980 U.S. census. Analysis of the 1981 Canadian census data probably would modify the Canadian percentages somewhat, although it is doubtful that general conclusions on Canadian-U.S. similarities and differences would change.

13. Replies probably underestimate the inability to converse in English or French. The 1986 census question asks whether the enumerated person knows English or French well enough to carry on a conversation. The census guide indicates that the purpose of this question is to tap the ability to carry on a conversation of some length. If the guidebook was not consulted, some answers might indicate an ability to speak English or French when in fact the designated person was unable to undertake a sustained conversation on various topics. Several researchers note the tendency of survey respondents to inflate their language skills. See Edite Noivo, *Migrations and Reaction to Displacement: The Portuguese in Canada* (M.A. thesis, Carleton University, 1984), and Calvin Veltman, "Testing the Effects of Language as Measured by the Canadian Census" (Paper presented at the meeting of the Association International de Linguistique Applique, Brussels, 1984). In her research on the Portuguese in Montreal, Noivo observed that individuals who replied in the affirmative to her questions about the ability to speak English or French were in fact unable to sustain telephone conversations in the specified language (conversation with the author, March 21, 1984, Carleton University, Ottawa, Canada).

14. Comparisons with the native-born also could be made as part of a more exhaustive analysis into what is variously called the double-negative effect or doubly disadvantaged status. According to this argument, migrant women are the recipients of two negative statuses, female and foreign-born. Reflecting this combination, immigrant women often are found at the bottom of distributions in many socioeconomic indicators compared with the distributions observed for native-born women or for foreign-born men. See Monica Boyd, "At a Disadvantage: Occupational Attainments of Canadian Immigrant Women," *International Migration Review,* vol. 18 (Winter 1984), pp. 1091–1119; Brettell and Simon, "Immigrant Women."

15. Monica Boyd, "Immigration and Income Security Policies in Canada: Implications for Elderly Immigrant Women," *Population Research and Policy Review*, vol. 8 (January 1989), pp. 5-24; Boyd, "Immigration and Living Arrangements: Elderly Women in Canada," *International Migration Review*, vol. 25 (Spring 1991), pp. 4-27.

16. These Canadian data on children present do not refer to one's own children. Rather, 1986 census data indicate the presence of children for the households in which an individual resides.

17. Experts consider persons with less than ninth grade education to be functionally illiterate.

18. See table 4 in Monica Boyd, "Gender, Visible Minority and Immigrant Earnings Inequality: Reassessing an Employment Equity Premise," in Vic Satzewich, ed., *Deconstructing a Nation: Immigration, Multiculturalism and Racism in the 90s Canada* (Toronto: Garamond Press, 1992).

19. In response to these difficulties, European countries such as Germany and Sweden now provide programs targeted at immigrant women that combine literacy and language instruction.

20. Edna Acosta-Belen and Barbara R. Sjostrom, eds., *The Hispanic Experience in the United States* (Westport, Conn.: Praeger Publishers, 1988), pp. 1-261; Frank D. Bean, Jurgen Schmandt, and Sidney Weintraub, eds., *Mexican and Central American Population and U.S. Immigration Policy* (Austin: University of Texas at Austin, Center for Mexican-American Studies, 1989); Frank D. Bean and Marta Tienda, *The Hispanic Population of the United States* (New York: Russell Sage Foundation, 1987), pp. 1-455; and Elizabeth Bogen, *Immigration in New York* (Westport, Conn.: Praeger Publishers, 1987), pp. 1-268.

21. Bean and Tienda, *Hispanic Population of the United States*.

22. For additional discussion of the relationship between language and labor force participation, see Patricia Robinson, "Language Retention among Canadian Indians," *American Sociological Review*, vol. 50 (August 1985), pp. 515-29.

23. Janet Badets, "Canada's Immigrant Population," *Canadian Social Trends*, no. 14 (Autumn 1989); Boyd, "Migrant Women in Canada"; Pessar, "The Dominicans: Women in the Household and the Garment Industry"; Shirley Seward, "Immigrant Women in the Clothing Industry," in Shiva S. Hali, Frank Trovato, and Leo Driedger, eds., *Ethnic Demography: Canadian Immigrant, Racial and Cultural Variations* (Ottawa: Carleton University Press, 1990), pp. 343-62.

24. The industrial sectors are adaptations of the classifcation developed in Browning and Singelmann and used extensively in discussions of the service economy. See Harley L. Browning and Joachim Singlemann, "The Emergence of a Service Society: Demographic and Sociological Aspects of the Sectoral Transformation of the Labor Force in the U.S.A.," Report prepared for the Manpower Administration, U.S. Department of Labor (Washington, D.C.: U.S. Department of Commerce, National Technical Information Service, 1985). My coding of the U.S. data departs in several ways from the original Browning and Singelmann classification. The industry representing postal services is classified as a distributive industry rather than included in govern-

mental industries (as is done in the Canadian industry codes). Social services and public administration industries are not combined into one sector but are kept as two sectors. And retail industries are kept as a separate sector of employment.

25. Hourly wages are not presented for two reasons. First, the codebook for the United States Public Use Microdata Samples (PUMS) explicitly warns against using hourly wage rates, cautioning that pay rate estimates that include hours worked may be unreliable. Second, in Canada, hours-worked data refers to hours worked in the reference week preceding the census taken in June 1986. Hours worked in the reference week may or may not be equivalent to the hours worked per week by a respondent in the preceding year. As well, the earnings data in table 8–14 are for the foreign-born in Canada who immigrated before 1984 for two reasons. First, Statistics Canada assigned a zero value to the 1985 earnings of migrants who arrived in 1986. Earnings for persons arriving in 1985 also are affected to the extent that not all migrants arrived on January 1, 1985, and had full-year earnings in Canada. Since the Canadian PUST combines 1984 and 1985 as one period of immigration, all income analyses in this essay's analysis are based on Canadian immigrants arriving by 1983. The data from the United States PUM are evenly more aggregated, with migrants entering between 1975 and 1980 representing one category. Given this level of aggregation, no sample restrictions were invoked for the U.S. sample (tables 8–15 and 8–16) since deletion of the 1975–1980 group would result in a considerable loss of information.

26. Bailey, *Immigrant and Native Workers;* Marshall "New Immigrants in New York's Economy"; and Sassen, *Mobility of Labor and Capital.*

27. The low R-square for language should not be overinterpreted. Zero order correlations and Rs based on dummy variables are weighted by the proportion of cases falling into categories coded zero or one. For further discussion, see John Myles, "The Use of Nominal Categories in Regression Analysis," *Canadian Review of Sociology and Anthropology,* vol. 15 (February 1978), pp. 97–101.

28. Models 2–4 constrain the effect of other control variables so as to be the same for women who know the host language and those who do not. These sociodemographic variables are fairly standard control variables in models of female earnings determination, consisting of controls for age distributions, region of residence, size of place, marital status and country or region of birth. The number of children present was not included in these regressions because in the 1986 Census of Canada the variable was not created from a question on the number of live births for a woman. Instead the variable refers to the number of children, one's own or otherwise, in a household. In addition to these sociodemographic variables, models also were constructed to include weeks worked, full-time/part-time status, industry, and occupation. These analyses did not change the general conclusions reached with data presented in table 8–17. The models in table 8–17 constrain the effects of sociodemographic variables so as to be the same for the language groups. Models also were constructed separately for each group, but the estimates changed in magnitude only minimally.

29. As discussed in the text, the U.S. PUM provides a more refined measure of English-speaking ability than a simple yes-no categorization. Regression models using more detailed categories of language skill were constructed from the U.S. data base. These models indicate a 6 percent loss in earnings and a 40 percent loss in earnings for women whose home language is not English but who speak it well or women who speak it poorly or not at all compared with the incomes of women whose home language is English or who speak English very well (respectively operationalized as columns 4 and as columns 4 and 6 versus columns 2 and 3 in table 8–15).

30. Bean and Tienda, *Hispanic Population of the United States;* Anthony H. Richmond, "The Income of Caribbean Immigrants in Canada," in Shiva Hali, Frank Trovato, and Leo Driedger, eds., *Ethnic Demography: Canadian Immigrant, Racial and Cultural Variations* (Ottawa: Carleton University Press), pp. 363–79.

31. According to the result of the increment to R-square test, which is equivalent to the Chow test, model 4 is an improvement compared with model 3 in both Canada and the United States.

32. These dummy codes and interaction terms can be rewritten to depict the earnings determination regression equation specific to each language group. Column 8, table 8–17, for example, can be rewritten as two equations: $Y = 7.923 + .051$ (education) and as $Y = 8.117 + .018$ (education) for women who can converse in English and for those who cannot. The difference between these two equations corresponds to .181 and to $-.032$ (education), observed in column 8, table 8–17.

33. Walter McManus, William Gould, and Finis Welch, "Earnings of Hispanic Men: The Role of English Language Proficiency," *Journal of Labor Economics,* vol. 1 (April 1983), pp. 101–130; Walter S. McManus, "Labor Market Assimilation of Immigrants: The Importance of Language Skills," *Contemporary Policy Issues,* vol. 3, pt. 1 (Spring 1985), pp. 77–89; and Walter S. McManus, "Labor Market Costs of Language Disparity: An Interpretation of Hispanic Earnings Differences," *American Economics Review,* vol. 75 (September 1985), pp. 818–27. See also the exhaustive analysis by Chiswick and Miller in this volume (chapter 7, table 7–10, columns 4 through 7; table 7–11, columns 4 through 7).

34. A description of the debate in the United States can be found in Dick Kirschten, "Come in! Keep Out!" *National Journal* (May 19, 1990), pp. 1206–1211.

35. James S. Duesenberry, "Comment" [on 'An Economic Analysis of Fertility' by Gary Becker], in National Bureau of Economic Research, *Demographic and Economic Change in Developed Countries* (Princeton: Princeton University Press), p. 233.

36. These disciplinary differences are evident in Conrad P. Waligorski, *The Political Theory of Conservative Economics* (Lawrence: University Press of Kansas, 1990), and in Mildred A. Schwartz, *The Environment for Policy Making in Canada and the United States* (Montreal: C. D. Howe Institute, 1981).

37. Waligorski, *Political Theory of Conservative Economics,* p. 18 and chap. 2. See also Thomas J. Courchene, *Social Policy in the 1990s: Agenda for Reform,*

Policy Study, no. 3, (Scarborough, Ontario, C. D. Howe Institute, Prentice Hall Canada, 1987), p. xviii.

38. Seymour Martin Lipset, *Continental Divide* (New York: Routledge Kegan Paul, 1989); Lars Osberg, "Distributional Issues and the Future of the Welfare State," in K. Newton, T. Schweitzer, and J. P. Voyer, eds., *Perspective 2000: Proceedings of a Conference Sponsored by the Economic Council of Canada December, 1988* (Ottawa: Supply and Services), pp. 159–80.

39. Gosta Esping-Anderson, "The Three Political Economies of the Welfare State," *Canadian Review of Sociology and Anthropology*, vol. 26 (February 1989), 10–36.

40. See Kramer, "U.S. Policy in Relation to Women from Ethnic Minority Groups," p. 48.

41. Bean and Tienda, *Hispanic Population of the United States*; Pastora San Juan Cafferty, "Language and Social Assimilation," in Pastora San Juan Cafferty and William C. McCready, eds., *Hispanics in the United States* (New Brunswick, N.J.: Transaction Books, 1985), pp. 33–48; Neil Fligstein and Roberto M. Fernandez, "Hispanics and Education," in Pastora San Juan Cafferty and William C. McCready, eds., *Hispanics in the United States*, pp. 113–46.

42. For reviews on this debate, see Cafferty, "Language and Social Assimilation," and B. Cazden Courtney and Catherine Snow, eds., "English Plus: Issues in Bilingual Education" *Annals of the American Academy of Political and Social Science*, vol. 508 (March 1990), pp. 9–184.

43. See Bogen, *Immigration in New York*, p. 125; Kramer, "U.S. Policy in Relation to Women from Ethnic Minority Groups," pp. 51–53; and Silvia Pedraza-Bailey, *Political and Economic Migrants in America: Cubans and Mexicans* (Austin: University of Texas Press, 1985) pp. 44–46.

44. Boyd, "Migrant Women in Canada"; Boyd, *Migrant Women in Canada: Profiles and Policies*; B. Burnaby, M. Holt, N. Steltzer, and N. Collins, *The Settlement Language Training Program: An Assessment* (Ottawa: Employment and Immigration Canada, Immigration Group, Policy and Program Development Branch, Research Division, 1987); Alma Estable, "Immigrant Women in Canada—Current Issues," Background paper (Ottawa: Canadian Advisory Council on the Status of Women, 1986); Wenona Giles, "Language Rights Are Human Rights: Discrimination against Immigrant Women in Canadian Language Training Policies," *Resources for Feminist Research*, vol. 17 (1989), pp. 129–32; Roxanna Ng and Judith Ramirez, *Immigrant Housewives in Canada* (Toronto: Women's Centre Press, 1981); Milagros Paredes, "Immigrant Women and Second Language Education," *Resources for Feminist Research/documentation sur la recherche féministe*, vol. 16 (March 1987), pp. 23–27; Shirley Seward and Kathryn McDade, *Immigrant Women in Canada: A Policy Perspective*, Background paper (Ottawa: Canadian Advisory Council on the Status of Women, 1988); and K. Seydegart and G. Spears, *Beyond Dialogue: Immigrant Women in Canada, 1985–1990* (Ottawa: Secretary of State, Multiculturalism, 1985).

45. A third program, the language instruction program funded through the secretary of state, ceased to be funded in the 1989 federal budget. For further discussion of this program, see Monica Boyd, "Immigrant Women: Language, Socioeconomic Inequalities and Policy Issues," in Shiva Hali,

Frank Trovato, and Leo Driedger, eds., *Ethnic Demography: Canadian Immigrant, Racial and Cultural Variations* (Ottawa: Carleton University Press, 1990), pp. 275–96.

46. Kramer, "U.S. Policy in Relation to Women from Ethnic Minority Groups."

47. See Boyd, *Migrant Women in Canada: Profiles and Policies*; Giles, "Language Rights Are Human Rights"; and Paredes, "Immigrant Women and Second Language Education."

48. See Susan Huelsebusch Buchanan, "Profiles of Haitian Migrant Women," in Delores M. Mortimer and Roy S. Bryce-Laporte, eds., *Female Immigrants to the United States: Caribbean, Latin American and African Experiences*, Research Institution on Immigration and Ethnic Studies, Occasional Papers, no. 2 (Washington, D.C., Smithsonian Institution, 1981); and Ng and Ramirez, *Immigrant Housewives in Canada*.

CHAPTER 9: EARNINGS OF THE FRENCH AND SPANISH MINORITIES,
Bloom and Grenier

The authors thank Melissa Binder, Barry Chiswick, David Gray, Chris Robinson, and Peter Skerry for their comments. This research was supported by the Donner, Russell Sage, and Sloan Foundations.

1. Jacob Marschak, "Economics of Language," *Behavioral Science*, vol. 10 (1965), pp. 135–40; Toussaint Hocevar, "Equilibria in Linguistic Minority Markets," *Kyklos*, vol. 28 (1975), pp. 337–57; Albert Breton and Peter Mieszkowski, "The Economics of Bilingualism," in Wallace E. Oates, ed. *The Political Economy of Fiscal Federalism* (Lexington, Mass.: D.C. Heath, 1977), pp. 261–73; François Vaillancourt, *Differences in Earnings by Language Groups in Quebec, 1970: An Economic Analysis* (Quebec: International Centre for Research on Bilingualism, 1985); Gilles Grenier, "Language as Human Capital: Theoretical Framework and Application to Spanish-Speaking Americans" (Ph.D. diss., Princeton University, 1982); Chris Robinson, "Language Choice: The Distribution of Language Skills and Earnings in a Dual-Language Economy," *Research in Labor Economics*, vol. 9 (1988), pp. 53–90.

2. In 1971 and before, the question on ethnicity referred to paternal ancestry, and only one ethnic origin was allowed per person; since 1981, the reference to paternal ancestry has been dropped, and it is possible for the same person to have multiple ethnic origins.

3. Although the definitions remained the same over time, there have been some slight changes in the way some responses are coded. In 1971, for instance, a person who reported English or French as mother tongue was assumed by Statistics Canada to speak that language, even if also reporting an inability to do so. In 1981 and 1986 the possibility that individuals might "forget" their mother tongue was allowed. The responses were adjusted in this study to the 1971 definition. In 1971 and 1981 Statistics Canada also allowed a person to have only one mother tongue, even though a few people reported more than one. In 1986, multiple mother tongues were permitted. To make the data comparable to previous censuses, each individual was allocated only one mother tongue in this study. In some cases (those who were of

English and French mother tongues and bilingual) this was done randomly.

This procedure can be justified on the basis of calculations made by Réjean Lachapelle, "Minorities et langues officielles minoritaires: un demi siecle d'évolution" (Ottawa, Statistics Canada, 1988). Lachapelle showed that respondents who indicated both English and French as mother tongues were represented in about equal numbers in each mother tongue group in the 1981 census. Statistics Canada has an imputation procedure to allocate non-responses or inconsistent responses that includes a set of criteria for the mother tongue question in the 1981 census. Unfortunately we do not have enough information to replicate this procedure for the 1986 census. Given this situation, a random allocation seems to be the best solution. Although the proportion of such cases is small for the entire country, it is not negligible in comparison to the number of people who declare themselves of French mother tongue in the regions where the French speaking minority is small.

4. In addition, records from the 1970 census that report mother tongue do not report the year of immigration. Two nonoverlapping public use data sets were produced from the 1970 U.S. census, each with a different set of questions.

5. The 1980 census categorized English-speaking ability into four levels: very well, well, not well, and not at all. A similar question was asked in the 1976 Survey of Income and Education. This latter survey also includes a variety of questions about language use and ability.

6. This test could not be performed using either of the U.S. censuses since none of the available public use samples for either census contain information on both Spanish ethnic origin and mother tongue.

7. Further research is needed to determine whether these variables are capturing a true language effect, a true ethnicity effect, or both a language and an ethnicity effect. To this end we estimated wage equations that included *both* Spanish ethnic origin and Spanish mother tongue as independent variables. In most cases neither of these two variables was statistically significant, which partly reflects the facts that the two variables are highly correlated. Thus our data are not informative about the meaning of the language and ethnicity coefficients. Longitudinal data would appear to provide a better approach for addressing this issue.

8. The category "Central and South American" was included in 1970 but not in 1980. Some people who came from the central and south regions of the United States apparently reported themselves in that category even though they were not of Spanish origin. In 1980, people of Spanish origin from Central and South America had to report themselves in the category "other Spanish."

9. In the 1970 census, information on state and metropolitan area was not available simultaneously on the same public use tape. The state public use tape that we used, however, had information on whether a person lived in a metropolitan area without specifying the name of the metropolitan area. Given this constraint, and since the largest metropolitan areas in New York state and Florida (New York City and Miami) have large Spanish-origin populations, all the metropolitan areas in those two states were defined as

high Spanish-origin population regions. For the sake of consistency, the same definition was used for the 1980 census, even though information on specific metropolitan areas was available.

10. Earnings are defined in this study as wages and salaries only. Individuals who reported self-employment income are excluded.

11. This outward shift in the demand for French language skills can be related to language policies that were implemented in Quebec since 1969 (see Vaillancourt, "Language and Public Policy in Canada and the United States," chapter 6 in this volume).

CHAPTER 10: ADMISSIONS CRITERIA AND IMMIGRANT ASSIMILATION, *Duleep and Regets*

We would like to thank Masao Nakamura for help with using the Canadian census data and James Joslin of the U.S. Immigration and Naturalization Service. Comments by Barry Chiswick, Guy Orcutt, Chris Robinson, and Peter Skerry are gratefully acknowledged. The views expressed in this chapter are those of the authors and should not be attributed to the U.S. Commission on Civil Rights. This work was done outside of the authors' work for the commission.

1. George Borjas, "Self-Selection and Immigrants," *American Economic Review,* vol. 77 (1987), pp. 550, 544.

2. George Borjas, "Assimilation, Changes in Cohort Quality, and the Earnings of Immigrants," *Journal of Labor Economics,* vol. 3 (October 1985), and Borjas, "Self-Selection and Immigrants."

3. Louis Parai, "Canada's Immigration Policy, 1962–1974," *Immigration and Migration Review,* vol. 9 (1975), pp. 469–72.

4. We also estimated earnings equations, using a tobit model, that included zero earners, while correcting for the truncation bias that this causes. The results for all U.S. and Canadian groups were similar to those reported in this chapter.

5. Furthermore, the work of Kossoudji (Sherrie A. Kossoudji, "Immigrant Worker Assimilation: Is It a Labor Market Phenomenon?" *Journal of Human Resources* [Summer 1989]) suggests that much of the assimilation effect found in the pathbreaking work of Chiswick (Barry R. Chiswick, "The Effect of Americanization on the Earnings of Foreign-born Men," *Journal of Political Economy* [October 1978]) is due to inclusion in the study population of immigrants who migrated as children, and reflects pre-labor market assimilation as opposed to labor market assimilation by immigrants. In a comparison with estimations that included all immigrants, however, including those who immigrated before age twenty, we found that the exclusion of those who immigrated as children did not greatly affect the results.

6. We used the 5 percent "A" Public Use Sample from the 1980 U.S. Census of Population and the "individual file" from the 1981 Census of Canada Public Use Sample. In the U.S. data we subsampled whites so that the resulting sample is a 1 percent sample of the U.S. white population. This resulted in a small sample size for immigrant groups of European origin. No subsampling was done for any of the Asian groups.

7. Harriet Orcutt Duleep and Seth Sanders, "The Role of Women in the Economic Assimilation of Asian Immigrant Families," working paper presented at the Annual Meeting of the American Economic Association, 1988.

8. The connection between permanence and investment in U.S. specific skills has been discussed and explored in a variety of contexts. Refer to Charlotte Erikson, *Invisible Immigrants: The Adaptation of English and Scottish Immigrants in Nineteenth Century America* (Miami: University of Miami Press, 1972); Michael J. Piore, *Birds of Passage: Migrant Labor and Industrial Societies* (Cambridge: Cambridge University Press, 1979); George Borjas, "The Earnings of Male Hispanic Immigrants in the United States," *Industrial and Labor Relations Review,* vol. 35 (April 1982), pp. 343–53; Alejandro Portes and Robert L. Bach, *Latin Journey: Cuban and Mexican Immigrants in the United States* (Berkeley: University of California Press, 1985); Harriet Orcutt Duleep, *The Economic Status of Americans of Asian Descent: An Exploratory Investigation* (Washington, D.C.: U.S. Commission on Civil Rights, Government Printing Office, 1988, chapter 8); and Roger Waldinger, "Structural Opportunity or Ethnic Advantage? Immigrant Business Development in New York," *International Migration Review* (Spring 1989), pp. 48–72.

9. To the extent immigrants invest in schooling, holding schooling constant with years since migration is inappropriate. Controlling for age, years since migration, and level of schooling, we found that Chinese men twenty-five years of age and older were about twice as likely to be in school as men in the other immigrant groups considered here. Taking schooling growth into account in our simulations would have a larger earnings effect on the Chinese than is true of the other immigrant groups.

10. The dichotomy between the earnings pattern of Japanese immigrants and other Asian immigrants is explored in Duleep, *Americans of Asian Descent.*

11. Borjas, "Assimilation, Changes and the Earnings of Immigrants."

12. David E. Bloom and Morley Gunderson, "An Analysis of the Earnings of Canadian Immigrants," working paper no. 3035, National Bureau of Economic Research (July 1989); Borjas, "Self-Selection and Immigrants," pp. 531–553, and "Assimilation, Changes in Cohort Quality, and the Earnings of Immigrants."

13. One minus the percentage admitted on the basis of occupational skills is the percentage of immigrants admitted through the kinship provisions or as refugees. Our variable, percent admitted on the basis of occupational skills, includes both the third and the sixth occupational preference categories. Based on the 1979 INS annual report, the occupational breakdown of the combined occupational preference beneficiaries is as follows: 67 percent, professional, technical, and managerial; 4 percent, sales and kindred workers; 8 percent, crafts; 3 percent, operatives; 1.7 percent, laborers; 9.5 percent, service workers; and 6.5 percent, private household workers. The third preference category is almost exclusively made up of professional workers: 95.5 percent report professional, technical, and kindred occupations. The occupational distribution of sixth preference beneficiaries is more diversified but is still dominated by professional and managerial workers: 52 percent, professional and managerial; 5.1 percent, sales and clerical; 12 percent, crafts; 4.7

percent, operatives; 2.4 percent, laborers; 13.6 percent, service workers; and 9.3 percent, private household workers.

14. Admissions criteria information for Western Hemisphere countries (Canada, Central America, and South America) is not available for years prior to 1975. Information on individual European countries other than the United Kingdom is available. In the future we hope to expand this analysis to include all European countries.

15. The U.S. census data only provide year-since-migration information from 1965 to 1980 in five-year categories. Thus to match the INS information to the census data annual INS data on percent admitted by occupational skills had to be averaged over five-year intervals.

16. That Canadian average ages are not always younger for immigrants in the 1960–1964 and 1975–1980 cohorts may reflect the fact that the Canadian skills-oriented policy was not in effect before 1962, and that reforms were again instituted in 1978 that increased the family-admissions orientation of the policy.

17. The benchmark group in Canada is that of Canadian-born males of European (including British) descent.

18. To adjust for possible price-level variations among areas of the United States and Canada, metropolitan status and region of residence are held constant for all simulations at the native-born distributions for Canada and the United States. We also held marital status at the native-born mean values of native-born, U.S., non-Hispanic whites (which differs from Canadian native-borns by 0.001).

19. European immigrants to both the United States and to Canada during this period included substantial numbers of political refugees. An obvious area for further work is the analysis of more detailed groups of European immigrants.

20. Edna Bonacich and John Modell, *The Economic Basis of Ethnic Solidarity: Small Business in the Japanese-American Community* (Berkeley, Calif.: Univ. of California Press, 1980); Kwang Chung Kim, Won Moo Hurh, and Marilyn Fernandez, "Intra-Group Differences in Business Participation: Three Asian Immigrant Groups," *International Migration Review* (Spring 1989), pp. 73–95; Ivan Light, *Ethnic Enterprises in America: Business and Welfare Among Chinese, Japanese, and Blacks* (Berkeley, Calif.: Univ. of California Press, 1972); Roger Waldinger, "Structural Opportunity or Ethnic Advantage? Immigrant Business Development in New York," *International Migration Review* (Spring 1989), pp. 48–72.

21. Barry R. Chiswick and Paul W. Miller, "Language in the Labor Market: The Immigrant Experience in Canada and the United States," chapter 7 of this volume; Duleep, *Americans of Asian Descent*, p. 85.

22. See, for example, Evelina M. Tanier, "English Language Proficiency and the Determination of Earnings among Foreign-born Men," *The Journal of Human Resources* (Winter 1988); Sherrie A. Kossoudji, "English Language Ability and the Labor Market Opportunities of Immigrant Men," *Journal of Labor Economics*, vol. 6 (1988), pp. 205–28; Walter McManus, William Gould,

and Finis Welch, "Earnings of Hispanic Men: The Role of English Language Proficiency," *Journal of Labor Economics* (April 1983).

COMMENTARY ON PART FOUR, *Peter Skerry*

1. Hispanics, of course, are a diverse group, and assimilation is a complex, multidimensional process. The assimilation to which I refer is nevertheless true of Cuban Americans and Mexican Americans. Puerto Ricans have experienced more substantial barriers to integration into the mainstream.

A Note on the Book

This book was edited by Cheryl Weissman and Ann Petty,
staff editors of the AEI Press.
The figures were drawn by Hördur Karlsson.
The text was set in Palatino, a typeface designed by
the twentieth-century Swiss designer Hermann Zapf.
Coghill Book Typesetting Co., of Richmond, Virginia,
set the type, and Edwards Brothers Incorporated,
of Ann Arbor, Michigan, printed and bound the book,
using permanent acid-free paper.

THE AEI PRESS is the publisher for the American Enterprise Institute for Public Policy Research, 1150 17th Street, N.W., Washington, D.C. 20036; *Christopher C. DeMuth*, publisher; *Edward Styles*, director; *Dana Lane*, assistant director; *Ann Petty*, editor; *Cheryl Weissman*, editor; *Susan Moran*, assistant editor (rights and permissions). Books published by the AEI PRESS are distributed by arrangement with the University Press of America, 4720 Boston Way, Lanham, Md. 20706.